EYEWITNESS TRAVEL

AUSTRIA

Main Contributors **Teresa Czerniewicz-Umer,
Joanna Egert-Romanowska and Janina Kumaniecka**

D0050492

Produced by Wydawnictwo Wiedza i Życie S.A., Warsaw

Art Editor Paweł Pasternak
Consultant Małgorzata Omilanowska
Cartographers Magdalena Polak, Olaf Rodowald, Dariusz Romanowski
Photographers Wojciech and Katarzyna Mędrzakowie
Illustrators Michał Burkiewicz, Paweł Marczak, Bohdan Wróblewski
DTP Designer Paweł Pasternak
Editors Teresa Czerniewicz-Umer, Joanna Egert-Romanowska
Designers Elżbieta Dudzińska, Ewa Roguska, Piotr Kiedrowski

Contributors
Janina Kumianiecka, Ewa Dan, Marianna Dudek, Konrad Gruda, Małgorzata Omilanowska,
Marek Pernal, Jakub Sito, Barbara Sudnik-Wójcikowska, Roman Taborski, Zuzanna Umer

Dorling Kindersley Limited

Editor Sylvia Goulding / Silva Editions Ltd.
Translator Magda Hannay
DTP Designers Jason Little, Conrad Van Dyk
Production Controller Bethan Blase

Printed and bound in China

First American Edition, 2003
15 16 17 18 10 9 8 7 6 5 4 3 2 1

Published in the United States by:
DK Publishing, 345 Hudson Street,
New York, New York 10014

Reprinted with revisions 2006, 2008, 2010, 2012, 2014, 2016

Copyright © 2003, 2016 Dorling Kindersley Limited, London

ISBN 978-1-46543-960-4

ISSN 1542-1554

Floors are referred to throughout in accordance with
European usage; ie the "first floor" is the floor above ground level.

MIX
Paper from
responsible sources
FSC™ C018179
www.fsc.org

**The information in this
Dorling Kindersley Travel Guide is checked regularly.**
Every effort has been made to ensure that this book is as up-to-date as possible at
the time of going to press. Some details, however, such as telephone numbers,
opening hours, prices, gallery hanging arrangements and travel information are
liable to change. The publishers cannot accept responsibility for any consequences
arising from the use of this book, nor for any material on third party websites, and
cannot guarantee that any website address in this book will be a suitable source of
travel information. We value the views and suggestions of our readers very highly.
Please write to: Publisher, DK Eyewitness Travel Guides, Dorling Kindersley, 80
Strand, London, WC2R 0RL, Great Britain, or email: travelguides@dk.com.

Front cover main image: Alpine roses near Ehrwald, Tyrol

◀ Beautiful Alpine mountain view, Tyrol

Contents

How to Use this Guide 6

Detail of the façade of a pharmacy in
Obernberg, Upper Austria

Introducing
Austria

Discovering Austria 10

Putting Austria on
the Map 16

A Portrait of
Austria 18

Austria Through
the Year 36

The History of
Austria 40

12th-century Burg Clam in Upper Austria,
seen from the Danube

Hollabrunn

Krems

Linz

Wels

Melk   St Pölten   Vienna

LOWER AUSTRIA
AND BURGENLAND

Steyr

UPPER
AUSTRIA

Eisenstadt

Wiener Neustadt

Oberpullendorf

Leoben

Tamsweg

STYRIA

Graz

St Veit an
der Glan

Gamlitz

Villach   Klagenfurt

0 kilometres   50

0 miles   50

EYEWITNESS TRAVEL

AUSTRIA

Vienna

Grundlsee and Totes Gebirge (Dead Mountains), Styria

Travellers' Needs

Survival Guide

Stained-glass window of a church in Bürserlberg, Vorarlberg

Memorial on a tombstone in the church in Maria Saal, Carinthia

Austria Region by Region

Mariazell Basilica
(see pp 188–9)

HOW TO USE THIS GUIDE

This guide will help you to get the most out of a visit to Austria. The first section, *Introducing Austria,* locates the country geographically, and provides an invaluable historical and cultural context. Subsequent sections describe the main sights and attractions of the capital,

Vienna, and the different regions. Information on shopping, entertainment, accommodation, restaurants and sports can be found in the *Travellers' Needs* section, while the *Survival Guide* provides many useful tips on everything you need to know during a visit to Austria.

Vienna

This section is divided into three parts: Inner City, North of Mariahilfer Strasse and South of the Ring. Sights outside the centre are described in the *Further Afield* section. All sights are numbered and plotted on the area map. Detailed information for each sight is given in numerical order.

Sights at a Glance lists the sights in an area by category: Historic Streets and Buildings, Museums and Galleries, Churches, Parks and Gardens.

2 Practical Information All the sights of Vienna are described individually. The practical information includes addresses, telephone numbers, opening hours, admission charges, transport links and disabled access. The key to the symbols used is on the back flap.

Pages referring to Vienna are marked with a red thumb tab.

A locator map shows where you are in relation to other areas of the city.

1 Area Map For easy reference the sights are numbered and located on the area map as well as on the map of Vienna, on pp121–5.

A suggested route for sightseeing is indicated with a dotted red line.

3 Street-by-Street Map This gives a bird's-eye view of each sightseeing area described in the section.

STYRIA

Austria's second-largest province, in the country's southeast, Styria has a population of 1.2 million. It is dominated by forests, meadows and vineyards covering some three-quarters of its total area of 16,387 sq km (6,327 sq miles). It is also an area of iron ore extraction and processing, and Erzberg (Iron Ore Mountain), glittering in every hue of red and brown, is a major tourist attraction.

Austria Region by Region

In this guide Austria is divided into six regions, each of which is explored in a separate section. The most interesting cities, towns, villages and sights are shown on each Regional Map.

1 Introduction The landscape, history and character of each region are described, showing how the area has changed through the ages, and the sights on offer for the visitor today.

2 Regional Map The regional maps show the main roads and the topography. All the important sights are numbered and details on how to get there are given.

Boxes highlight interesting aspects connected with a sight.

Colour coding on each page makes it easy to find a region; the colours are explained on the inside front cover.

3 Detailed Information Major towns, villages and other tourist sights are listed in order and numbered as on the Regional Maps. Each entry contains detailed information on the main places of interest.

The Visitors' Checklist for each of the main sights provides practical information to help you plan your visit.

4 Austria's Major Sights At least two pages are devoted to each major sight. Historic buildings are dissected to reveal their interiors. For interesting towns or town centres, street maps are provided, with the main sights marked and described.

INTRODUCING AUSTRIA

DISCOVERING AUSTRIA

The following tours have been designed to take in as many of the country's highlights as possible, while keeping long-distance travel manageable. The first tour outlined here is a 2-day tour of Austria's fascinating capital, Vienna, a city packed with monuments, family attractions and cultural diversions. This itinerary can be followed individually or combined to form a week-long tour, with any of the regional itineraries that follow. Next, there are four 7-day tours, covering the forests and vineyards of Eastern Austria, the historic treasures and sub-Alpine hills of Southern Austria, the lakes-and-mountains wonderland of Salzburg and the Salzkammergut and the stunning highland scenery of the Austrian Alps. Choose and combine tours or dip in and out and be inspired.

0 kilometres 50

0 miles 50

Wolfgangsee, the Salzkammergut
With an impressive backdrop of sandcastle-shaped mountains, this 15-km (9-mile) long lake, with its emerald green waters, is one of the most charming lakes in the Salzkammergut region.

A Week in the Austrian Alps

- Spend a day getting to grips with **Innsbruck**, the historic capital of the Austrian Tyrol.

- Feast on the scenic beauty of **Seefeld**, an idyllic village set amid cow-grazed pastures.

- Venture into the most dramatic of Austria's Alpine valleys, the **Ötztal**.

- Explore the Arlberg pass region, home to the chic mountain resorts of **St Anton** and **Lech**.

- Spend a day hiking in the hills around **Kitzbühel**, surrounded by some of Tyrol's most spectacular peaks.

- Stroll through the meadows and barns of **Pinzgau** before visiting the foaming **Krimmler Wasserfälle**.

- Take a ride on a steam train and marvel at the all-year glaciers in **Zillertal**.

Kufstein

Kitzbühel

Seefeld

Lech

Arlberg Pass

St Anton

Inn

Ötztal

Innsbruck

Pinzgau

Zillertal

Krimmler Wasserfäll

Sölden

Obergurgl

Melk Abbey, Eastern Austria
Perched spectacularly on a rocky outcrop, overlooking the Danube, the magnificent Baroque Melk Abbey is one of the country's most rewarding to visit.

◀ Watercolour of the area around the Neo-Gothic town hall, Neues Rathaus

A Week in Salzburg and the Salzkammergut

- Admire the splendid Baroque architecture and pay tribute to the city's most famous inhabitant, Mozart, in the lovely city of **Salzburg**.

- Tour the stately home of **Schloss Hellbrunn** before heading for the ice caves at **Werfen**.

- Marvel at the Gothic art and beautiful lakes-and-mountains landscapes around **Wolfgangsee**.

- Spend a day discovering the enchanting, historic town of **Hallstatt**.

- Venture into the world of Emperor Franz Josef I by visiting his favourite spa resort, **Bad Ischl**.

- Visit the pretty lakeside communities of the **Traunsee**.

- Explore Salzkammergut's quieter corners around **Bad Aussee**.

A Week in Eastern Austria

- Spend a couple of days exploring **Vienna**, Austria's compelling capital.

- Head south towards the **Neusiedler See**, a reed-fringed habitat for rare birds.

- Explore the provincial capital **St Pölten** and the sumptuously decorated abbey at **Melk**.

- Follow the Danube riverbank through the historic towns of **Wachau**.

- Enjoy a lazy tour of the low hills and scramble through the dense woods of **Waldviertel**.

- Stroll through the leafy pathways of the **Vienna Woods (Wienerwald)**.

A Week in Southern Austria

- See the rich collections of antiquities and contemporary art in museum-filled **Graz**.

- Head to the hills east of Graz to **Riegersburg**, one of Styria's greatest castles.

- Follow the Mur river to **Murau**, a historic town nestled in the shadow of the Niedere Tauern mountains.

- Explore the valleys of northern Carinthia, home to medieval **Friesach** and the fine Romanesque cathedral at **Gurk**.

- Visit the dramatic fortress of **Hochosterwitz**; end the day in the Carinthian capital of **Klagenfurt**.

- Take to the road or the water to tour **Wörthersee**, Austria's glitziest summer-holiday lake.

- Continue the Carinthian lake tour and discover the charming **Millstätter See**.

Key

— Eastern Austria

— Salzburg and the Salzkammergut

— Southern Austria

— Austrian Alps

Two Days in Vienna

Exploring Vienna's cobbled streets, lavish churches and grand architecture is a fascinating journey through centuries of history.

- **Arriving** Vienna's Schwechat Airport is located 19 km (12 miles) southeast of the city centre. The CAT (City Airport Train) takes around 20 minutes to reach the city centre.

- **Moving on** Vienna has a smooth and reliable public transport system and it is possible to explore a great deal of the city in a short period of time.

Day 1

Begin your exploration of Vienna's Innere Stadt or "Inner City" with a visit to the Gothic cathedral **Stephansdom** (p62). Its spire dominates the busy square of Stephansplatz. The **Mozarthaus Vienna** (p61), where Mozart composed the *Marriage of Figaro*, is just a few steps away. Next, head to the south of Stephansplatz, where the pedestrianized Kärntnerstrasse sweeps past several boutiques and cafés. Afterwards, venture to the western end of the Innere Stadt to see the **Hofburg** (pp68–9), a vast complex of palaces and offices that was once the symbolic heart of the Habsburg Empire. Visit the **Reichskanzleitrakt** (the former apartments of Franz Josef, p73) and the **Schatzkammer** (treasury, p73) for a taste of former imperial splendour. Opposite the

Striking façade of the Spanish Riding School in Vienna

Hofburg is the famous **Spanish Riding School** (p71), where white Lipizzaner horses peer inquisitively at passers-by from their street-side stables. In the evening, head west across Vienna's monument-lined Ringstrasse to the **Kunsthistorisches Museum** (pp88–91), one of the world's leading collections of antique treasures and old masters.

Day 2

Start by exploring the cluster of sights that are within easy walking distance of the Innere Stadt. Just west of the Ringstrasse is the vibrant **MuseumsQuartier** (p86), home to the Leopold Museum, the modern art gallery MUMOK and a growing number of cafés and theatres. Take a short eastward stroll from here to Karlsplatz, site of the late-Baroque masterpiece, the **Karlskirche** (pp98–9). Continue on to the **Belvedere** (pp102–103) to explore its beautiful gardens and art museum. Next, board the U4 metro line from Karlsplatz station to **Schönbrunn** (pp114–15), another

former imperial residence packed with breathtaking interiors. End the day by taking the metro once again to **Prater** (p108), north of the Danube. This park is a huge expanse of lawns and trees. It is an ideal spot for a stroll or a bicycle ride. Look out for the Prater's iconic Riesenrad (Ferris wheel), which attracts visitors until late in the evening.

A Week in Eastern Austria

- **Airports** Arrive at Vienna's Swechat Airport, which is the best entry point to access Eastern Austria.

- **Transport** There are good rail connections between Vienna and Eastern Austria's main towns. A car is essential for exploring areas such as the Neusiedler See, the Waldviertel and Vienna Woods.

Day 1 & 2
See the city itinerary.

Day 3: Eisenstadt and the Neusiedler See

Head southeast from Vienna to explore the town of **Eisenstadt** (pp158–9). Visit the Baroque chateau, **Schloss Esterházy** (p158). Next, pay a visit to **Haydn-Haus** (p159), now a museum dedicated to composer Josef Haydn. From here it is a short distance to the **Neusiedler See** (pp156–7), ringed by fishing villages and grassy plains. The town of **Rust** (p156), with its seasonally nesting storks, is the most picturesque of the lakeside settlements. Round the day off with a drive around the northern end of the lake to the reedbeds and marshes of the eastern shore, a landscape best enjoyed in the **Seewinkel National Park** (p157).

Day 4: St Pölten and Melk

Visit **St Pölten** (pp136–7), a lively market town with a well-preserved Baroque centre. Reserve most of the day for the stunning abbey at **Melk** (pp146–7), located 30 km (19 miles) west. The abbey contains a host of artworks, a historic library and a dizzyingly decorated Baroque church.

The giant Riesenrad or Ferris wheel at Prater

For practical information on travelling around Austria, *see pp354–9*

Day 5: The Wachau

Stretching between Melk and Vienna is the Wachau, where a stretch of the Danube loops its way between vineyard-covered hills. Enjoy an excellent day-long tour here. Moving on, admire the ruins of the medieval castle at **Dürnstein** *(p142)*. Stop off at the delightful town of **Krems** *(p142)* and finally, tour the **Egon-Schiele-Museum** *(p138)* at Tulln.

Day 6: The Waldviertel Tour

North of the Wachau is the **Waldviertel** *(pp144–5)*, a rustic region of low hills and forests that stretches to the Czech border. Take a clockwise circuit of the area through the lovely old towns of **Zwettl** *(p144)* and **Gmünd** *(p144)* and past the impressively turreted **Schloss Rosenburg** *(p145)*.

Day 7: The Vienna Woods

To the southeast of Vienna are the forested hills known as **Vienna Woods** *(p141)*, which are perfect for walking or cycling. Stop at the Seegrotte underground lake at Hinterbrühl before ending the day at a *Heuriger* wine bar in **Gumpoldskirchen** *(p141)*.

A Week in Southern Austria

- **Airports** Arrive at Graz Thalerhof and depart from Klagenfurt.
- **Transport** Train transport from Vienna to Graz is swift, comfortable and scenic, taking you over the 965 m (3,166 ft) Semmering Pass. Trains are a good way to explore the main towns of the region, although a car is needed to reach the smaller towns.

Day 1: Graz

Full of fine architecture and parks, the Styrian capital of **Graz** *(pp164–7)* is one of Austria's most elegant cities. Explore a clutch of outstanding art museums here and take time out to see the weaponry collections of the **Landeszeughaus** *(pp168–9)*. Consider a half-day trip to the Austrian Open-Air Museum at **Stübing** *(pp170–71)*, which provides fascinating insights into rural life.

Pretty view of the Wörthersee, Austria's warmest lake

Day 2: Riegersburg and Bad Blumau

Head through the rolling countryside east of Graz to **Castle Riegersburg** *(p174)*, an imposing hilltop fortress with an absorbing museum. Continue on to the spa resort, **Bad Blumau** *(p174)* to see the wacky buildings designed by Friedensreich Hundertwasser.

Day 3: Bruck an der Mur to Murau

Head to the north of Graz and spend the morning in the historic market towns of **Bruck an der Mur** *(p172)* and **Leoben** *(p187)*. Next, follow the Mur valley west past the foothills of the Niedere Tauern. Take a side-trip to the historic silver-mining village of **Oberwölz** *(p179)* before arriving at **Murau** *(p179)*, the prettiest of Styria's well-preserved medieval towns.

Day 4: Friesach and Gurk

Venture out to the green hills of northern Carinthia with a stop

Rooftops of Graz's Old Town, a UNESCO World Heritage Site

off in the perfectly preserved medieval town of **Friesach** *(p278)*, before heading up the Gurk valley to admire the **cathedral** *(p273)*, which is a masterpiece of Alpine Romanesque architecture.

Day 5: Hochosterwitz and Klagenfurt

Spend half a day seeing the famously dramatic medieval castle of **Hochosterwitz** *(p272)*, before moving on to explore the Renaissance squares of the Carinthian capital, **Klagenfurt** *(pp274–7)*. Packed with good hotels and restaurants, Klagenfurt is the ideal base for the last few days of this tour.

Day 6: The Wörthersee

Experience Riviera chic, Carinthian style, with a trip round the **Wörthersee** *(pp280–81)*, stopping off at the lake resort, Pörtschach. End the day in swanky bustling **Velden** *(p280)*, with its casino and glitzy café-bars.

Day 7: Villach and the Millstätter See

Wander through the well-preserved historical centre of **Villach** *(p278)* before taking a scenic drive round the **Millstätter See** *(p278)*. If it's too cold for a dip in the lake, then head to Schloss Porcia in nearby **Spittal an der Drau** *(p278)*. Explore the excellent local museum here.

To extend your trip…

Just north of Spittal an der Drau, the turreted medieval town of **Gmünd** *(p279)* is the site of a Porsche Car Museum.

A Week in Salzburg and the Salzkammergut

- **Airports** Arrive at Salzburg's W.A. Mozart Airport, which has good connections with other European cities.

- **Transport** Salzburg is only 2 and a half hours from Vienna by train. Little of the Salzkammergut region is covered by the Austrian rail network, although there is a good public bus service based in the regional centre, Salzburg.

Bad Ischl, a popular health resort in the Salzkammergut region

Day 1: Salzburg
Spend the day exploring one of the most stunning Baroque towns in Europe, **Salzburg** (pp218–19), which features churches and palaces framed by distant snowy Alps. Wander through the lovely Old Town before stepping into the cathedral or **Dom** (p224) or the **Kollegienkirche** (p223) to get a taste of 18th-century architecture at its best. Devote an hour each to the **Mozarts Geburtshaus** (p223), the house where he was born, and the art collections of the **Residenzgalerie** (p223), before strolling up to **Hohensalzburg** (pp226–7), the hilltop fortress that overlooks the town centre. In the afternoon, relax among the flower-and rose-beds of the famous **gardens** (p219) at Schloss Mirabell.

Day 2: Schloss Hellbrunn and Werfen
No visit to Salzburg is complete without a trip to **Schloss Hellbrun** (p228). Explore the 17th-century retreat, built by Archbishop Marcus Sitticus, which is located 4 km (2 miles) south of the town. Its beautifully preserved interiors are surrounded by pleasure gardens. Consider extending your trip to **Werfen** (p229), 40 km (25 miles) south of Salzburg, where you can see the Eisriesenwelt show caves that contain spectacular ice formations. If time allows, break your journey in **Hallein** (p228), midway between Werfen and Salzburg, to visit its museum devoted to Celtic archaeology.

Day 3: Around the Wolfgangsee
Travel to one of the most picturesque lakes in the Salzkammergut region, the Wolfgangsee, fringed by the pretty villages of Strobl, St Gilgen and **St Wolfgang** (p209). The last is famous for its pilgrimage church, home to a stunning Gothic altarpiece by Michael Pacher. Allow time for a cup of coffee and cake at **Weisses Rössl** (p209), the historic resort hotel that inspired a famous operetta in the 1920s.

> **To extend your trip…**
> North of the Wolfgangsee is the **Attersee** (p211), a magnet for boating and sailing enthusiasts. Detour westwards to the **Mondsee** (p210). The lake's main settlement (also called Mondsee) is home to a historic Benedictine Abbey.

Splendid interiors of the Dom, the first cathedral church in Salzburg

Day 4: Hallstatt
Reserve an entire day for **Hallstatt** (p212), arguably the most breathtaking of the Salzkammergut settlements. With Bronze Age artifacts in the local museum, a historic graveyard, and a salt mine high above town, there's a great deal to see. Next, visit the spectacular **Dachstein Caves** (Dachsteinhöhlen) (p213), high above the southern end of the Hallstätter See.

Day 5: Bad Ischl
Situated mid-way between Wolfgangsee and the Traunsee, the historic spa town of **Bad Ischl** (p209) oozes with Habsburg tradition. Take a tour of Emperor Franz Josef's summer retreat, the **Kaiservilla** (p209), and follow it up with a trip to one of the town's traditional patisseries for coffee and delicious cake.

Day 6: The Traunsee
Surrounded by craggy peaks, the Traunsee represents the Salzkammergut at its most picturesque. Tour the delightful historic towns of **Traunkirchen** (p208), Altmünster and **Gmunden** (p208), each of which serves as a bathing resort in summer.

Day 7: Bad Aussee and the nearby lakes
Head to the historic salt-mining town of **Bad Aussee** (p184), the jumping-off point for two of the Salzkammergut's lesser-known lakes, **Altausseer See** (p184) and Grundlsee. Enjoy the charming views from these lakes, which are surrounded by a green meadow and forest.

For practical information on travelling around Austria, *see pp354–9*

A Week in the Austrian Alps

- **Airports** Arrive and depart from Innsbruck Kranebitten Airport.
- **Transport** Innsbruck, Kitzbühel and the Arlberg are all connected to Austria's train network. You will need to rely on a private car or public bus to explore Austria's Alpine valleys.

Day 1: Innsbruck

Begin a day in Tyrol's vibrant capital with a stroll around the compact medieval centre, pausing to admire its many highly decorative façades – of which the Renaissance-era **Goldenes Dachl** *(p244)* is the most celebrated. Get a taste of Innsbruck's imperial heritage with a visit to the **Hofkirche** *(pp246–7)*, where a monument to Maximilian I presides over a flamboyant collection of statues. Stroll along the elegant boulevard of Maria-Theresien-Strasse with its famous views of the Alps, or take the cable car to **Bergisel** *(p247)*. The hill is popular for easy walking trails and extensive mountain panoramas. Next, visit **Schloss Ambras** *(p245)*, the Renaissance chateau filled with the artistic treasures and curiosities collected by Archduke Ferdinand II.

Day 2: Seefeld

Spend a day in the pretty mountain village of **Seefeld** *(pp256–7)* northwest of Innsbruck. Take a leisurely hike over the Alpine meadows and enjoy the awe-inspiring views. Return to Innsbruck for an evening in one of its folksy restaurants.

Day 3: The Ötztal

Head west from Innsbruck to Imst before turning south into the **Ötztal** *(p256)*, one of Austria's longest, deepest and most majestic Alpine valleys. Head to the village of Obergurgl, at the head of the valley, which is surrounded by high peaks. Return to the hiking and skiing resort of **Sölden** *(p256)* in the middle of the valley, which offers plenty in the way of refreshment and accommodation.

Day 4: The Arlberg and Vorarlberg

Continue west by road or rail over the **Arlberg Pass** *(pp260–61)*, the stark mountain barrier that divides the Tyrol from Austria's westernmost province, Vorarlberg. If you are travelling by car, opt to take a detour to the world-famous mountain resorts of **St Anton** *(p261)* and **Lech** *(p258)*, busy with skiers and après-ski life in winter, and blissfully fresh and invigorating during the summer hiking season.

Day 5: Kitzbühel and Kufstein

Head to the main mountain resort of eastern Tyrol, **Kitzbühel** *(p251)*, a pretty medieval town, and once the undisputed winter sports capital of the country. Spend the entire day outdoors hiking in the local mountains. There are several cable cars taking tourists up onto the high Alpine meadows: ride the Hahnenkammbahn for a superb panorama of the surrounding Alps, or take the Hornbahn to reach the Alpine Flower Garden. Afterwards, take a side-trip to **Kufstein** *(p251)* in the shadow of the Kaisergebirge, site of a historic fortress and an absorbing regional museum.

Day 6: The Pinzgau

Begin the morning south of Kitzbühel in the green pastures of Pinzgau. Follow the rustic road east towards the spectacular foaming waters of the **Krimmler Wasserfälle** *(p237)*, then head west towards the lakeside centre of **Zell am See** *(p236)*, the starting point for the breathtaking mountain road over the Grossglockner Pass.

Day 7: The Zillertal

Before heading back to Innsbruck, be sure to explore at least part of the **Zillertal** *(pp252–3)*, a picture-postcard valley of pretty villages squeezed between the lofty Alps. Don't forget to take time out for a trip on the Zillertal's famous narrow-gauge railway, or take a side-trip up the Tux valley to enjoy year-round skiing on the Hintertux glacier.

Winter sport resort Golling and the Wilder Kaiser mountains, Tyrol

Putting Austria on the Map

Located in the southeastern part of Central Europe, Austria covers an area of 83,858 sq km (32,378 sq miles), and spans five major geological formations: the Eastern Alps, the Alpine and Carpathian Foreland, the Pannonian Basin, the Vienna Valley and the Czech Massif. Its longest river is the Danube, which flows from west to east. Landlocked, Austria borders Germany, the Czech Republic, Slovakia, Hungary, Slovenia, Italy, Switzerland and Liechtenstein. It has over 8.5 million inhabitants, 1.8 million of whom live in Vienna.

Key

National border
Motorway
Major road
Railway
Minor road

0 kilometres   50

0 miles   50

A PORTRAIT OF AUSTRIA

Magnificent mountains span two-thirds of present-day Austria, gathering in a massif at the centre of the country. The breathtaking scenery of Alpine peaks, lakes and enchanting valleys, together with excellent year-round facilities for a variety of sports, attracts many visitors. Innumerable cultural events and fascinating historical sights make every visit unforgettable.

Austria grew at a crossroads, when the main routes between northern Europe and Italy, and from western to eastern Europe, met at Vienna. The Habsburg kings and emperors, who ruled the country for almost seven centuries, pursued expansion via matrimonial alliances rather than sending troops into battle. Although not entirely without bloodshed, they managed to incorporate several provinces into Central Austria through a series of arranged marriages, beginning with the duchy of Tyrol, followed by the powerful Czech kingdom, the equally strong Hungary and a sizeable chunk of Italy. Austrian culture, while traditionally linked with that of Germany, also absorbed many Roman, Slav and Hungarian influences, thus creating its own unique combinations. As well as producing many outstanding artists and composers, such as Mozart, it also offered foreign artists the opportunity to further their talents.

Present-day Austria is a federal state, consisting of nine provinces (Bundesländer). The head of state is the president, elected for a term of six years; the most important political figure is the head of the federal government, or Chancellor (as in Germany). Austria's legislative power rests with a two-chamber parliament. Parliamentary elections are held every four years, when votes are cast for the candidates put up by the political parties. The present Austrian parliament includes representatives of six political parties: the Social Democratic Party of Austria (SPÖ), the Austrian People's Party (ÖVP), the far right Freedom Party of Austria (FPÖ), the Greens (die Grünen), Team Stronach (FRANK) and the New Austria and Liberal Forum (NEOS).

For modern-day Austrians, the might of their former empire is only a distant memory, yet their country continues to

View over the Hohe Tauern mountain range, from Heiligenblut in Carinthia

◀ Riding a motorcycle on the high Grossglockner Alpine road, Austrian Alps

Europabrücke, connecting northern and southern Europe

play an important role in international politics. Since 1955, when the Austrian State Treaty was signed and the country found itself at the centre between two worlds – Western capitalism and Soviet communism – it has often acted as an intermediary. Vienna has served as the venue for important summits, and is home to many UN agencies and international organizations, including the United Nations Industrial Development Organization (UNIDO), the International Atomic Energy Agency (IAEA) and the Organization of Petroleum Exporting Countries (OPEC) Central Office. A member of the European Union, Austria does not belong to NATO. The 1955 Treaty pledges neutrality for all time, and despite external and internal pressures, Austria retains this.

At the heart of Europe

Roads once trodden by foreign armies are today packed with sun-seeking tourists from the north. Travelling through Vienna and the Semmering Pass, they cross the Alps at the Brenner Pass, where the huge Europabrücke (European Bridge), a vast viaduct, connects northern Europe with the warm south. The heavy transit traffic constitutes a major problem for Austria, where great emphasis is placed on protecting the natural environment. Protest action by local ecology groups stopped the building of a nuclear power station in Zwentendorf and later prevented the destruction of the unique flora around Hainburg, the intended site for a hydroelectric power plant. The ecology movement gave rise to the Green Federation, which is winning ever more seats in Parliament. It is perhaps thanks to its activities that Austria remains a natural paradise for its many visitors.

Tourism

The country has much to offer: winter sports on snow-covered slopes, or year-round on the glaciers, and beautiful mountains and lakes in summer all attract large numbers of visitors. The impressive infrastructure offers superb conditions for rest and recreation. Nearly every resort boasts funicular railways and cable cars, chair and drag lifts, magnificent pistes and toboggan runs, outdoor and indoor swimming pools, well maintained river banks and lakes. There are plenty of places for eating, and overnight accommodation ranges from small pensions and private homes to luxury hotels, all guaranteeing a very pleasant visit.

The regional authorities take care to ensure that entertainments are not limited to large resorts, and organize sports events and art exhibitions, theatre and music festivals, as well as festivities

Guests enjoying a dip in the thermal pool at a hotel in Lutzmannsburg

Skiing at Mooserwirt, Tyrol, in winter

devoted to individual towns, streets or even squares. Visitors may enjoy the traditional religious festivities, and the Giant Chocolate Festival in Bludenz and the Dumpling Festival in St Johann will prove memorable. Many restaurants organize special weeks when regional cooking or local game dishes feature on the menu. Although events are often local, Austria is also a venue for acclaimed international festivals, such as the famous music and theatre festivals in Salzburg and Bregenz, the Wiener Festwochen and the Viennale.

A traditional horse-drawn carriage

every German speaker will find it easy to communicate with every Austrian. While the Vienna Burgtheater is regarded as one of the foremost German-language theatres in the world, many Austrians speak a pronounced local dialect. When travelling, the visitor needs to remember that many things have different names here than in Germany. A bread roll, for instance, is called a *Semmel* instead of a *Brötchen*, a tomato is a *Paradeiser* and not a *Tomate*, and the hospital is the *Spital*, rather than a *Krankenhaus*.

Austria is traditionally a Roman Catholic country, although only 60 per cent of its inhabitants today belong to the Roman Catholic church.

Language and Religion

Modern Austria is virtually a one-nation state, but there are some Slovenians in Carinthia, Croatians in Burgenland, and Czech and Hungarian minorities in Vienna. Austria became a haven for refugees fleeing from the former Yugoslavia in the 1990s, as well as for people from other regions of the Balkan peninsula, and for Turks coming in search of work. Around 95 per cent of the country's population speaks German, although not

A typical Alpine pension in Kartitsch, East Tyrol

The annual church festival in Villach in Carinthia, a weekend of folk music and parades

Culture

Austrian culture has reached acclaim and importance far beyond its borders. *The Good Soldier Schweik*, by the Czech writer Jaroslav Hašek, is a bawdy satire about the Habsburg monarchy. The Austrian film directors Ernst Lubitsch, Billy Wilder and Fred Zinneman played an important role in the creation of Hollywood shortly before and immediately after World War II. Today, the best-known Austrian is probably Arnold Schwarzenegger, star of action movies, former governor of California and, by marriage, a member of the Kennedy clan. His fame is unmatched even by winter sports champions, who are so popular in Austria. Another prominent Austrian actor is Klaus-Maria Brandauer, who played Mephistopheles in Isztvan Szabo's film of the same name. The late Romy Schneider, revered star of French cinema, was also Austrian and won fame as the unhappy Empress Elisabeth, in the Austrian film *Sissi*.

Austria has also produced many Nobel Prize winners. Perhaps the most famous among them is Konrad Lorenz, a researcher into animal and human behaviour, who was awarded the Nobel Prize for Medicine in 1973. The work of Sigmund Freud, the Viennese psychiatrist who became the founding father of psychoanalysis, has heavily influenced modern psychology, as well as other domains of science and culture.

Traditions

Austria is one of the most modern and efficiently run countries in Europe. However, while admiring the stunning landscapes or strolling along the streets of the impeccably tidy towns and villages, visitors may get the impression that time has stood still here, feeling immersed in the past, a bygone age of

View of the impressive Millenium Tower and Brigittenauer Bridge across the Danube

The traditional parade of Tyrolean hunters in Götzens

the Habsburg empire when the benevolent Franz Joseph I was the guardian of stability and justice, and his unhappy wife Sissi fulfilled the public craving for romance.

The Austrians are very fond of their traditions. The most popular newspaper is the arch-conservative tabloid *Neue Kronen Zeitung*, which has offices in almost every federal province, while the highly respectable Viennese daily *Die Presse* represents the solid opinions of the Austrian centre. *Der Standard* is the leading liberal newspaper.

In Austria, as perhaps nowhere else in Europe, the *Tracht*, or traditional folk costume, is accepted as formal wear. The costumes, made of high-quality wool and natural linen, can be worn anywhere, even to an elegant ball at the Viennese Opera. An entire branch of the textile industry is devoted to their design and manufacture. Men wear green loden jackets and *Lederhosen* (leather breeches), the women *Dirndl* dresses.

Another Austrian speciality is the *Heurige*. These are wine taverns serving the year's new-vintage wines. Mostly found in and around Vienna, these taverns were

Child in folk costume

originally attached to vineyards whose owners had a licence to sell beverages but not food. Secretly, though, they also offered home-produced meats, especially when a pig had been slaughtered. Today, they serve grilled pork knuckles – delicious, but very filling – as well as roast hams, grilled ribs and other specialities. As of old, the wine is brought to the tables by waiters who also take payment; the food is available from self-service buffet counters. The *Heurige* are characterized by a uniquely sociable ambience, with all the guests joining in the merriment. Many a dedicated beer-drinker has become a devotee of young wine at a *Heuriger* evening.

One of the many wine taverns *(Heurige)* around Vienna

The Formation of the Alps

About 70 million years ago, during the Cretaceous period, the African plate and the Adriatic microplate both began to move north. The Alpine range was thrown up when the latter collided with the European plate. The Tethys Sea that lay between them was almost entirely obliterated, and sediment deposited at its bottom over millions of years was carried far to the north, and tossed as vast nappes over the rigid block of indigenous rocks of the Central Alps. The formation of the present Alps ended in the Miocene period, some two million years ago, and subsequent erosion gave them their final shape.

The Krimmler Falls in the Hohe Tauern National Park are the highest waterfalls in the Alps and the fifth highest in the world, dropping almost 400 m (1,312 ft).

The Northern Limestone Alps are formed of soft carbonate rock. The mountains, such as the Dachstein Group (2,995 m/9,826 ft), have characteristically steep slopes, yet their summits are rounded domes rather than sharp peaks.

Northern Limestone Alps

European Plate

Mantle, between crust and core

Downward flow of magma (molten rock)

The central part of the Austrian Alps consists of hard crystalline rock (gneiss, shale). The oldest and the hardest among them form the steep fells of the Hohe Tauern.

The Alps possess the right conditions for the formation of glaciers. Largest in the Eastern Alps is the Pasterze; together with 40 others it forms a thick mantle on the Grossglockner massif, covering 40 sq km (15 sq miles).

The end of the Ice Age marked the beginning of a new type of erosion. The Northern Limestone Alps have Europe's largest cave systems and underground streams, typical features in limestone regions.

Mountain Scenery

The current shape of the Alps was created during the Ice Age (between 600,000 and 10,000 years ago). It is characterized by distinctive post-glacial cirques, suspended valleys, moraines, thaw lakes and vast U-shaped valleys filled with material carried down the mountains.

The Austrian Alps

The Austrian Alps are part of the European section of the Alpide belt, which rose between 70 million and two million years ago. In geological terms they form an entity known as the Eastern Alps. They occupy an area about 500 km (310 miles) long and 150 km (95 miles) wide. One of Europe's most fascinating regions, the Austrian Alps enchant visitors with their beautiful high peaks and the unique idyllic atmosphere in the mountain villages and small towns that nestle in vast, cultivated valleys. The most valuable ecological areas have been made into National Parks, including the Hohe Tauern – the largest in the Alps and one of the largest in Europe, featuring Austria's highest mountain range with some 266 peaks of over 3,000 m (9,800 ft) in height. In summer, the Alps are a magnificent area to explore on foot or bike, while in winter they provide an excellent base for winter sports.

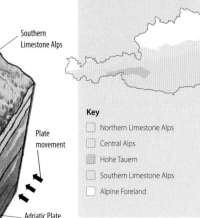

Central Alps

Southern Limestone Alps

Plate movement

Adriatic Plate

Mantle

Key

	Northern Limestone Alps
	Central Alps
	Hohe Tauern
	Southern Limestone Alps
	Alpine Foreland

The majority of Alpine lakes have been created by retreating glaciers. Some of the most beautiful can be found in the Salzkammergut region, in the Northern Limestone Alps.

The Landscape of Austria

Austria has a highly diverse landscape because of its location at the junction of four regions. The north of the country is part of the Central European natural region, originally dominated by deciduous and mixed forests, while the southern part belongs to the Alpine region. The southeast lies in the Illyrian region, which benefits from a Mediterranean climate, resulting in a rich flora and fauna including edible chestnuts and rare species of lizards and snakes. The northeastern part of the country belongs to the Pontian-Pannonian region, with surviving species of steppe flora and characteristic fauna including the suslik (a ground squirrel), hamster and great bustard.

The Alpine belt stretches from the zone of the mountain pine up to the ice and snow fields. At altitudes of 2,500–3,200 m (8,200–10,500 ft), snow is present all year (this snow-line is called the "nival belt").

The transition zone between forests and Alpine grassland is covered in scrub (dwarf mountain pine, rhododendron and alder). Here, the growing season lasts only 70–100 days.

Alpine high mountain grasslands and low meadows include a wide variety of species and plant communities. Mountain arnica (in the foreground) avoids limestone soils; it is a highly regarded medicinal plant.

In gulleys and hollows, in valleys and along the banks of the streams, Austrian flora is at its most magnificent.

Traditional grazing in the forest belt has preserved the natural fauna and flora of the Alpine meadows and pastures.

Mountainscapes

Climate and flora change with altitude, as is typical of mountain environments. The lower regions are covered with mixed forests (including beech). The upper parts have coniferous trees (Arolla pine, spruce and larch) up to about 1,800 m (5,900 ft) – above which are brush thickets and colourful Alpine meadows.

Humid, cool valleys are the perfect habitat to encourage the growth of herbaceous plants.

Lakes situated at higher altitudes are poor in nutrients and hence their surrounding flora and fauna are extremely sparse.

Upper forest region, mainly spruce

Austrian Fauna

Austrian fauna is typical of Central Europe. Along with invertebrates (primarily insects: beetles and butterflies), it features a rich avifauna, small numbers of amphibians (newts, salamanders, fire-bellied toads and frogs) and reptiles (Aesculapian snake, grass snake, lizards), and mammals, including rodents, marten, fox, weasel and hoofed animals. Mountain animals – insects, rodents (marmots) and deer (red deer, chamois) – are particularly fascinating.

The marmot, a rodent, burrows deep into mountain meadows and Alpine pastures. When disturbed, it emits a high-pitched whistle.

Chamois are ideally adapted for moving over steep rocks.

Red deer (above) live in the deciduous and mixed forests in the high mountains. They have a fawn-coloured coat. The male sheds its antlers in spring.

The Alpine ibex (right, a female) came close to extinction towards the end of the 20th century, but is now being successfully reintroduced.

Austrian Flora

Some 60 per cent of Austria's territory is mountainous, which determines the country's key flora. Forests occupy as much as 39 per cent of the country's entire area, occurring mainly in the Alps and in the Czech Massif. Many areas of special environmental interest enjoy some form of legal protection as nature reserves, nature monuments and national parks. One of the first was the Hohe Tauern National Park.

The Arolla pine (Pinus cembra), along with the larch, forms large tree populations in the upper forest regions.

Swiss Rock Jasmin (Andro-sace helvetica) and its rounded clusters are typical on limestone soil.

Bitterwort (Gentiana lutea) is common in meadows, clusters of herbaceous plants and forest verges. Bitterwort liqueur has long been used in folk medicine.

The Music of Austria

Austria was – and remains to this day – a world-renowned centre for music. Musical life in present-day Austria has typically been closely linked with that of Germany, as well as the Habsburg Empire. Composers belonging to the old Viennese school contributed to the emergence of the Viennese Classical style, with Joseph Haydn, Wolfgang Amadeus Mozart and the German composer, Ludwig van Beethoven, its main proponents. Their work guided 19th-century composers such as Franz Schubert, Johann Strauss, Anton Bruckner, Hugo Wolf and Gustav Mahler.

Franz Schubert, one of the earliest exponents of the Romantic style, is best-known for his *Lieder*, or songs. He also composed piano music, chamber music and symphonies.

Wolfgang Amadeus Mozart

Arnold Schönberg, together with his students, Alban Berg and Anton Webern, developed the Viennese dodecaphonic school after 1918. His best-known work is the sextet *Verklärte Nacht*.

Mozart's sister, Maria Anna, known as Nannerl

Joseph Haydn, one of the Viennese Classicists, was a court composer to Count Esterházy. In 1790, he moved to Vienna. His works include over 100 symphonies, 83 string quartets, 52 piano sonatas, 14 masses and many other compositions.

Wolfgang Amadeus Mozart

A child prodigy, Mozart had the gift of perfect pitch and an unrivalled memory. He achieved musical perfection with his symphonies, operas (The Marriage of Figaro, Don Giovanni, The Magic Flute), and his masses including the unfinished Requiem, *which is shrouded in mystery.*

Timeline:

1715–77 Georg Christoph Wagenseil	**1756–91** Wolfgang Amadeus Mozart	**1824–96** Anton Bruckner	**1860–1911** Gustav Mahler
		1819–95 Franz von Suppé	**1825–99** Johann Strauss (son)
	1739–99 Karl Ditters von Dittersdorf	**1791–1857** Carl Czerny	**1804–49** Johann Strauss (father)	**1852–95** Josef Schrammel
	1732–1809 Joseph Haydn			**1860–1903** Hugo Wolf
		1797–1828 Franz Schubert	**1801–43** Joseph Lanner	

1700 1725 1750 1775 1800 1825 1850

Wolfgang Amadeus Mozart

Joseph Haydn

Johann Strauss (son) has been proclaimed the king of the waltz, thanks to his compositions including *The Blue Danube* and *Tales from the Vienna Woods*.

Foreign Musicians in Austria

Vienna, an important cultural centre on the European map, has always attracted musicians and composers from other countries. The Renaissance brought Flemish artists, and the Baroque period attracted Italians. Vienna was home to Christoph Gluck, Ludwig van Beethoven, Johannes Brahms and others. The main exponent of the New Viennese operetta was the Hungarian, Franz Lehár.

Johannes Brahms (1833–97), German composer, outstanding creator of traditional symphonies, piano and chamber music, was unsympathetic towards progressive trends.

Portrait of Anna Maria, Mozart's mother

Leopold, Mozart's father

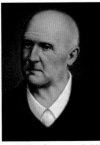

Anton Bruckner is probably best known for his nine symphonies but he also wrote church music, in particular choral works.

Ludwig van Beethoven (1770–1827), German composer and one of the Viennese Classicists, battled from 1798 with his progressive deafness. His best-known work is perhaps the *Ninth Symphony*, with the Ode to Joy in its finale.

Gustav Mahler started his career as a conductor and only in later years devoted himself to composing music. His most important work is the cycle of ten monumental symphonies.

	1900–1991 Ernst Křenek	1935 b. Kurt Schwertsik	1941 b. Dieter Kaufmann	1971 b. Michael F. P. Huber	2009 Haydn Year
1874–1951 Arnold Schönberg	1926 b. Friedrich Cerha		1956 b. Herbert Willi	2006 Mozart Year	
1875	**1900**	**1925**	**1950**	**1975**	**2000** **2025**
1874–1949 Edmund Eysler	1883–1945 Anton von Webern		1960 b. Karlheinz Essl		1998 Arnold Schönberg Center opened in Vienna
1885–1935 Alban Berg	*Edmund Eysler*		1943 b. H. K. (Heinz Karl) Gruber	1971 b. Bernhard Gál	

The Architecture of Austria

Since the Middle Ages, Austria has been at the forefront in the development of architecture. Particularly typical of the Austrian architectural landscape are the vast abbeys built in medieval times and modernized during the late Baroque period, as well as the multi-storey town palaces and large country residences built for the aristocracy in the 17th and 18th centuries. The late 1800s and early 1900s marked the birth of modern town architecture, with public buildings such as theatres, banks and government offices. These and other buildings displayed typical Habsburg-era features – monumentality and a distinctly ornamental character.

Cupolas crowned with openwork lanterns, inspired by Renaissance domes in Italy.

Pediment with an early-Renaissance statue of Christ blessing the people.

Windows with grab-frames, typical of the early Baroque period.

Statues of saints by Michael Bernhard Mandl

Heiligenkreuz Abbey *(see p140)* was built in the 12th to 13th centuries, but only the Romanesque church remains from that period. The abbey itself is a magnificent Baroque structure erected in the 17th century. The courtyard has an imposing St Mary's column.

Schwaz church, dating from the 15th century *(see p249)*, with its opulent star vaulting resting on slender columns, and its interior illuminated by vast windows, typifies the lightness of Baroque architecture.

The decorative railings of the famous staircase at Mirabell Palace in Salzburg *(see p219)* are the masterpiece of architect Johann Lukas von Hildebrandt and sculptor Georg Raphael Donner.

The octagonal layout of the top storey of the tower is a typical feature of the Lombardy style.

Statues of Moses and Elijah

The Vienna State Opera House *(see p96)*, conceived by August von Siccardsburg and Eduard van der Nüll, was completed in 1869. Its façade and interior, particularly the auditorium, the foyer and the grand staircase, are examples of the opulence, ornamentation and pomposity typical of 19th-century Austrian architecture.

Oval tower windows serve to amplify the sound of the bells.

Vast clock faces

Melk is one of the most famous Benedictine abbeys and the largest surviving abbey complex in Europe. The spectacular Baroque abbey was designed by Jakob Prandtauer *(see pp146–7)*.

Salzburger Dom

The cathedral, begun in 1614 to a design by Santino Solari and finished in 1657, is one of the earliest twin-towered churches of the modern era found anywhere north of the Alps. It is also the earliest and most magnificent example of the Early Baroque style in the entire Danube region (see p224).

Friedensreich Hundertwasser

Hundertwasser (1928–2000) was a highly successful painter, graphic designer and architect. He was born Friedrich Stowasser, but adopted a new name while studying at the Academy of Fine Arts in Vienna. His decorative style of painting was close to that of abstract artists, with subject matter often associated with the natural environment. His buildings *(see pp108–109)* are distinguished by their highly experimental, extravagant shapes, combining colourful new architectural ideas with the artist's vision of structures that blend with the natural environment. Irregular in shape, they employ a variety of unusual materials, including ceramics.

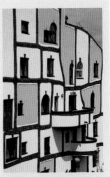

The Bad Blumau resort complex *(see p174)*

Austrian Art

Austrian painting, like the country's literature, cannot be considered in isolation from artistic movements in neighbouring countries. Art in Austria developed in close relationship with German art, but it was also influenced by the Italian, Hungarian and Czech cultures. Over many centuries, the imperial court in Vienna acted as a strong magnet for artists from all over Europe. In the 19th century, the artists of the Viennese Secession produced outstanding works of art. Some of Austria's painters have gained international acclaim, but it is well worth becoming acquainted with its lesser artists, too.

The Entombment, by Albrecht Altdorfer

Medieval

The earliest examples of pictorial art in Austria include illuminations and wall paintings. The late 8th-century *Codex Millenarius (maior)*, kept in Kremsmünster Abbey, is regarded as the oldest illuminated manuscript. The Austrian art of illumination flourished during the 11th and 12th centuries, particularly thanks to the Salzburg monastery scriptoria, which, among other works, produced the famous Admont Bible (c.1130–40).

The oldest wall paintings in Austria, dating from the first half of the 11th century, are found in the Church of St Ulrich in Wieselburg. The Benedictine abbey church in Lambach has original wall paintings of Old Testament scenes, created in the last quarter of the 11th century. Paintings dating from the 12th century can be seen in St John's Chapel in Pürgg, the Benedictine abbey church in Nonnberg and in the castle chapel of Burg Ottenstein, near Zwettl.

From the 14th century, panel painting flourished, particularly in Vienna under Rudolph IV. The 15th century is notable for the works of Jakob Kaschauer and Thomas von Villach. At the turn of the 16th century, Austrian painting was influenced by Italian *Quattrocento* art, especially the works of Michael Pacher and his students. The Danube School, influential in the early 1500s, was represented by Wolf Huber and Albrecht Altdorfer of Regensburg, who painted the altar in the abbey of St Florian, near Linz.

Renaissance

The Renaissance style entered Austrian painting around 1530. Interesting wall paintings, created soon after that date, include the secular decoration of the Knights' Room in Goldegg Castle near St Johann (1536), and the paintings devoted to Reformation themes in Pölling Church, near Wolfsberg. Hans Bocksberger, one of the most outstanding Renaissance artists, decorated Freisaal Castle and the castle chapel in Burg Strechau.

Until the 16th century, Austrian painting was strongly influenced by Italian artists such as Giulio Licinio, Teodoro Ghisi and Martino Rota, who worked at the court in Graz, and Donato Arsenio Mascagni in Salzburg. Local artists, such as Anton Blumenthal, whose paintings adorn the presbytery of Gurk

Cathedral, and Jakob Seisenegger, a portrait-painter, were also influenced by Italian art.

Baroque

In the 17th century, Italian art continued to influence Austrian painting. One of the most important painters of the Baroque period was Pietro de Pomis.

The Austrian victory in the Battle of Vienna in 1683 was a historic event that proved very influential in the development of art. It brought about political and economic stability and with it many new artistic initiatives. The capital, Vienna, began to attract foreign artists, such as Andrea Pozzo, the Italian master of illusionist painting. Vast interior compositions were created to complement the magnificent architectural works by Johann Bernhard Fischer von Erlach and Johann Lukas von Hildebrandt. This particular style of fresco painting flourished thanks to artists such as Johann Michael Rottmayr, Martino Altomonte and, in the following generation, Paul Troger, Daniel Gran and Bartolomeo Altomonte. Great portrait-painters of the 18th-century included Johann Kupetzky, Martin van Meytens and Johann Baptist von Lampi.

The Holy Family with St Joachim and St Anna, by Franz Anton Maulbertsch

A prominent representative of late Baroque painting, Franz Anton Maulbertsch created frescoes as well as numerous works on religious and secular themes. The last great artist of the Baroque era was Martin Johann Schmidt, who produced magnificent wall paintings, for example for Melk Abbey.

Portrait of Hanna Klinkosch, by Hans Makart

19th Century

The most important Neo-Classical painters in Austria were Heinrich Friedrich Füger and Joseph Anton Koch. In 1809, the Brotherhood of St Luke was formed at the Vienna Academy of Fine Arts. Its members, the Nazarenes, mostly German painters, including Julius Schnorr von Carolsfeld, and only a few Austrians, set out to revise religious art.

An important figure during the Biedermeier and Realism periods in Austria was Ferdinand Georg Waldmüller, creator of small-scale genre paintings. The most outstanding academic painter was undoubtedly Hans Makart, who created vast compositions on allegorical or historic themes, as well as brilliant portraits. In the town of Szolnok, in today's Hungary, an artists' colony was established by a group of landscape painters inspired by the French Barbizon School.

Probably the best-known of all Austrian painters was Gustav Klimt, the founding member and main representative of the Vienna Secession. He used gold in his paintings and embellished them with striking "mosaics". The subject matter was often allegorical, infused with a subtle eroticism.

Time of the Rose Blossom, by F. G. Waldmüller

Modern

Expressionism played a major role in early 20th-century Austrian art. The foremost artists associated with this movement included Egon Schiele, Richard Gerstl and Oskar Kokoschka, and, in Upper Austria, Alfred Kubin. An important figure of the 1930s and the period following World War II was Herbert Boeckl. A versatile artist – he also produced wall paintings – Boeckl drew his inspiration from fantasy realism, popular in post-war Vienna. Ernst Fuchs, Anton Lehmden and Wolfgang Hutter were members of the Vienna

School of Fantastic Realism, which was inspired by surrealism. Abstract art was represented by Max Weiler and Josef Mikl. An unusual late 20th-century figure who escapes easy classification was Friedensreich Hundertwasser, who became famous with his architectural project of unusual buildings erected in and around Vienna.

The artists of Viennese Actionism achieved considerable notoriety in the 1960s. "Happenings" organized by the group revolved around the use of the body as a sculptural medium. Their fascination with self-mutilation and sadomasochism culminated in the death of one of the group's members, Rudolf Schwarzkogler.

Gustav Klimt's *Danaë* (1907), one of his famous erotic paintings

Sport in Austria

Austria is one of the most sport-loving nations in Europe, a fact reflected in the great popularity of recreational sports as well as in the country's success in international competitions – relative to its small population, the number of European and world champions, as well as Olympic medallists, in Austria is very high.

Some three million people – members of 27,500 sports clubs – participate in various sports and sports contests. The most popular and widely pursued sport is downhill skiing, followed by soccer, nordic (or cross-country) skiing, tennis, swimming, golf, cycling and windsurfing. New sports, such as snowboarding, are also becoming more popular.

Alpine Skiing

Alpine or downhill skiing has been the number one national sport in Austria for over 100 years. Mathias Zdarsky (1856–1940) wrote the first handbook of skiing in 1897, invented the first ski bindings worthy of mention, and organized, in 1905, the first slalom race.

The Winter Olympics have twice been held in Innsbruck (1964 and 1976), and European and world championships are hosted by other resorts. The best-known venues for downhill skiing contests are Arlberg in Tyrol, St Anton (which hosts the Alpine World Championships), Kitzbühel and St Christoph, with its Ski Academy, the training centre for ski instructors. The international Hahnenkamm races in Kitzbühel are famous the world over. In January, the spectacular World Cup Men's Downhill and Slalom race takes place here; past Austrian champions have included Toni Sailer, Franz Klammer and Hermann Maier.

Austria's eight glacial regions permit year-round skiing. Most popular are the glaciers situated above Kaprun and Stubai.

Up-to-date information on snow cover and the running of some 3,500 ski lifts and cable cars is available from the Alpine Association's website at www.alpenverein.at (in German only).

Nordic Skiing

It is no coincidence that, in 1999, the World Championships in nordic or cross-country skiing events were held in Styria, in the beautiful town of Ramsau. The local glacier, Dachstein, is a popular year-round training ground for cross-country skiers from around the world. Even the national teams of Finland and Norway practise here in summer, polishing up their techniques and developing stamina dressed only in their swimwear – or less: nude cross-country skiing is famously permitted in this resort.

Two of the prestigious Four Hills ski jump tournaments take place in Innsbruck and Bischofshofen. The event, straddling the last week of December and the first week in January, sees the final event in Bischofshofen.

Record-breaking ski jumper, Andreas Goldberg

Tobogganing

Tobogganing is another winter sport at which Austria excels on the international stage; worldwide, only Germany and Italy achieve comparable results. Over the last decades, Austrian competitors have won several medals in this discipline at the Olympic Games, as well as various World Championships and World Cup events in all age categories.

The reason for this great Olympic and international success is the widespread popularity of the sport in Austria. Competitors train in some 310 tobogganing clubs and associations, represented in all provinces, with the exception of Burgenland.

Hermann Maier on his final slalom run in Hinterstoder

Johann Wolfmayr and team in the World Championship in pair driving

Soccer

The days when Austria ranked as one of the world's great soccer nations, in the 1920s and 1930s, are now buried deep in the past, along with the names of its former stars, including Matthias Sindelar, Toni Polster and Hans Krankl. Yet, although the national team did not qualify for the World Cup 2014 in Brazil, soccer remains the second most popular spectator and participation sport in Austria after skiing.

The present star of the national squad is the defender David Alaba, who plays for the German Bundesliga team Bayern Munich and holds records as the youngest player in several competitions. As in other countries, many football players are "bought" in from other countries to play in Austrian football clubs, while the best Austrian players join clubs in other countries. Many play in the German Bundesliga, with just a few going to Italy or Spain.

As the Austrian clubs have little success in international competitions, most of the spectators prefer to watch the matches of the Austrian league. The most famous football stadiums are the Ernst-Happel-Stadion and the Hanappi-Stadion, both in Vienna. The First Division consists of ten soccer teams, including two from Vienna.

Roman Mählich of Sturm Graz, playing against Bayer Leverkusen

Horse Riding

The first sports riding club in Austria, the Campagnereiter-Gesellschaft, founded in 1872, had the Emperor Franz Joseph I, himself a keen rider, as a patron. It consisted mainly of military personnel, and is now considered to be the predecessor of the Bundes-fachverband für Reiten und Fahren (Federal League for Riding and Driving), established as recently as 1962.

Austrian riders have achieved many international successes. One of its legends is the pre-war master of horse dressage, Alois Podhajsky. The greatest character among Austrian riders in the 1980s and 1990s was showjumping champion, Hugo Simon. In the 1980s, Austrian competitors began to achieve considerable success in harness racing, involving one- and two-horse carts.

Rodeos – known as *Westernreiten* (wild west riding) – have been introduced from America, and are very popular across the country.

Canoeing and Mountain Biking

With its many rivers and lakes and its superb mountain scenery, Austria boasts the perfect natural conditions, as well as a well-developed infrastructure, for both these disciplines (though this does not always translate into international medals). The huge popularity of summer mountain sports among Austrians and visitors is nevertheless very noticeable. Mountain canoeing is practised on turbulent mountain streams.

Mountain biking is well-liked throughout Austria: the 2012 World Championship was held in Saalfelden.

Helmut Oblinger competing in the individual slalom in Sydney

AUSTRIA THROUGH THE YEAR

Austria is a conservative country and Austrians value their traditions highly. In many regions the population maintains such ancient customs as the rites of spring and ritual re-enactments of death and resurrection, as well as various festivals associated with the grape harvest. Carnival festivities and parades are also big crowd-pullers, and many festivals are associated with the main religious holidays, such as Easter, Corpus Christi and Christmas.

Labour Day (1 May) is the traditional day for workers' processions. These national festivities, plus scores of regional and local cultural events catering for the arts, fill the Austrian events calendar almost every day of the year. Many festivals enjoy an international reputation, including the Salzburg Festival, the Bregenz Festival and the Vienna Viennale. Information on all events is available from tourist offices or the Internet.

Spring

Spring sees the re-opening of regional museums that were closed for the winter. The Viennese Prater funfair starts up at full steam. Traditionally, Lent is a period of abstinence, but the shops are already full of Easter specialities, their shelves laden with chocolate bunnies, Easter eggs and other sweet delicacies.

March

Palmprozessionen Palm Sunday processions, such as the one in Thaur, in Tyrol, based on ancient traditions, yet highly imaginative.
Frühlingsfestival Vienna. Classical music festival.
Easter carols During Holy Week and the run up to Easter, singers carol through the streets of some towns. The most famous carolers are the Leiden-Christi-Singen in Grossarl (Salzburger Land) and the Antlasssingen in Traunkirchen (Upper Austria).

Osterfestspiele
(Holy Week and Easter) Salzburg. Easter Festival with opera and classical music concerts.

April

Easter On Easter night, mountain slopes are lit with Easter bonfires called **Osterfeuer**. Easter Sunday begins with the traditional chocolate Easter egg hunt, **Eiersuchen**. A pastry in the shape of a lamb (*Osterlamm*) is traditionally given to children at Easter by their godparents.
Donaufestival *(mid-April–mid-May)* Krems. Festival of contemporary theatre and music.

May

Wiener Festwochen *(early May–early June)* Vienna. The biggest arts festival.

Narzissenfest on Altausseer See

Labour Day *(1 May)*. Day of workers' marches and demonstrations; also of numerous shows and sporting events.
Passionsspiele Erl in Tirol. Passion plays organized every six years (the next event is in 2019). Following the May première, the plays are then performed every Saturday and Sunday until early October.
Pfingstfestspiele Salzburg *(Whitsun weekend)* Salzburg. Opera and classical music concerts.
Musikwochen Millstadt *(mid-May–early October)* Millstadt, in Carinthia. International music festival.
Gauderfest *(1st weekend in May)* Zell am Ziller, in Tyrol. Festival of strong beer, with animal fights and wrestling.
Kufenstechen *(Whit Sunday/Monday)* Gailtal, in Carinthia. Jousting tournament.
Internationale Barocktage *(Whit Friday–Monday)* Melk Abbey. Baroque music days.
Narzissenfest *(late May–early June)* on the banks of the Altausseer See in Salzkammergut. Narcissus flower festival, music and processions.

Palm Sunday procession, Thaur

Average daily hours of sunshine

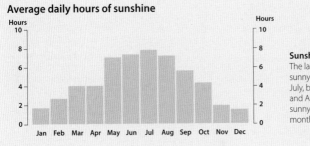

Sunshine Chart
The largest number of sunny days occurs in July, but May, June and August are also sunny. The cloudiest month is December.

Summer

Summer is the height of the tourist season. Theatres close for the summer, but the most important arts festivals, including the Salzburg and Bregenz Festivals, take place during this season. There are also numerous popular entertainment events and traditional village festivals.

Corpus Christi procession in Hallstatt, Salzkammergut

June

Corpus Christi Processions throughout Austria; the best take place in Salzkammergut, Gmunden, Hallstatt and Traunkirchen.
St Pauler Kultursommer (June–mid-August) St Paul's Abbey, in Carinthia. Festival of classical music.
Schubertiade (June, August, September) Schwarzenberg, in Vorarlberg. Festival of Schubert's music.
Styriarte (end June–end August) Graz. Festival of early and contemporary music.
Donauinselfest (late June) Danube Island, Vienna. A three-day pop music event.
Internationale Konzerttage Stift Zwettl (late June–late July) Zwettl, in Lower Austria. Festival of organ music.

July

Oper Klosterneuburg (July) Klosterneuburg, north of Vienna. Throughout the month, a programme of opera performances is held in the courtyard of the palatial Kaiserhof.
Jazzfestival (mid-July) Wiesen, Burgenland. Jazz festival.
Salzburger Festspiele (July–late August) Salzburg. Festival of music, opera and theatre; most important event of the summer.
Bregenzer Festspiele (end July–late Aug) Bregenz. Performances of theatre, opera and music on the stage on Lake Constance.
Rathaus Film Festival (July–August) Vienna. Opera and music films, shown on a big screen in front of the town hall.
Kammermusikfest Lockenhaus Schloss Lockenhaus, in Burgenland. Chamber music.
Samsonumzug (late July) Tamsweg, Salzburger Land. Samson's procession; saints' statues are paraded in town.
Operettenfestival Baden (late July–early September) Baden, near Vienna. Festival of operetta.
Operettenfestspiele Mörbisch, on Neusiedler See, Festival of operetta.

Carinthischer Sommer Ossiach, Villach, in Carinthia. Carinthian summer festival.
Operettenfestival (July–August) Bad Ischl, Salzkammergut. Festival of operetta.
Innsbrucker Festwochen der Alten Musik (July–August) In and around Innsbruck. World-renowned festival of early music and Baroque opera.

August

Jazzfestival Saalfelden. Jazz concerts, performed by several hundred artists.
Piratenschlacht (early August) Oberndorf. Pirates fight it out on the Salzach River.
Chopin Festival (mid-August) Gaming Abbey. Musicians perform in a series of concerts celebrating the work of Chopin.
Assumption of the Virgin Mary (15 August). Colourful processions all over Austria. The most interesting is the **Schiffsprozession** (ship procession) on Wörthersee.
Internationaler Johannes Brahms Wettbewerb Velden and Pörtschach on Wörthersee. An annual international Brahms competition featuring string and piano soloists.

Fire dance during the Salzburg Festival

Average monthly rainfall

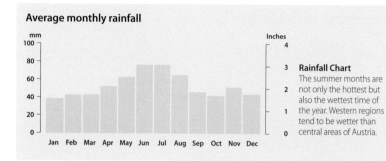

Rainfall Chart
The summer months are not only the hottest but also the wettest time of the year. Western regions tend to be wetter than central areas of Austria.

Autumn

In the towns, autumn marks the start of the theatre and opera season. In the mountains, the sheep and cows are rounded up and brought back down from their summer pastures, accompanied by various festivities. Grape harvest festivals are held in the wine-producing areas, mainly in Lower Austria and Burgenland. The lightly fizzing *Sturm* appears on the tables, quickly followed by new-vintage wines. Numerous music events attract music lovers throughout the country.

September

Ars Electronica *(early September)* Linz. Technology exhibition accompanied by concerts of electronic music.
Haydntage *(early September)* Eisenstadt. Festival of Music by Haydn.
Festlicher Almabtrieb *(mid-September–mid-October)*. Flocks return from the mountains.

Various festivities, and the mountains echo to the sound of cows' bells.
Brucknerfest Linz *(September)* Linz. The Bruckner festival starts with **Klangwolken** (sound clouds), a series of concerts on the banks of the Danube with laser light shows.
Badener Beethoventage *(September–October)* Baden. Festival of Beethoven music.
Internationale Woche der Alten Musik *(early September)* Krieglach, in Styria. International Week of Early Music.
Internationales Brahmsfest *(mid-September)* Mürzzuschlag. International Brahms festival.

October

Winzerumzüge *(mid-October)* Weinviertel and Wachau Valley, Lower Austria; wine-producing regions of Burgenland. Grape harvest festivals.
Niederösterreichischer Weinherbst Lower Austria. The "Wine Autumn" is a time of increased eating and drinking in the old inns of ancient wine-producing villages, often regarded as historic architectural treasures.
Steirischer Herbst Graz. The Styrian Autumn is an avant-garde arts festival, one of the most prestigious events of the season, taking place over four weeks. Festival-goers are mainly young people, and the events include theatre and opera productions,

performance arts, films, music concerts, talks and art exhibitions.
National Day *(26 October)*. Celebration of the Declaration of Neutrality in 1955.
Viennale *(late October)* Vienna. Two-week International Film Festival.
Wien Modern *(end October–end November)* Vienna. Contemporary Music Festival, initiated by Claudio Abbado.

Krampus Devil and St Nicholas at a St Nicholas party

November

Salzburger Jazz-Herbst *(early November)* Salzburg. Ten days of traditional jazz concerts and films.
St Martin's Day *(11 November)*. This is the day when all Austria feasts on *Martinigans* – roast St Martin's goose.
Voice Mania *(November–December)* Vienna. A capella festival in unusual venues.
Weihnachtsmärkte *(late November–December)*. Start of the Christmas market season. On offer: tree decorations, gifts, food and drink; best in Vienna, Salzburg, Klagenfurt, Spittal an der Drau and Villach.

Start of Bruckner Festival, Linz

Average monthly temperature

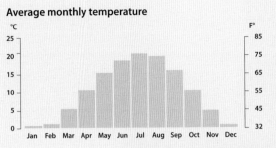

Winter

Winter begins with the pre-Christmas shopping rush. Christmas figures and decorations adorn every shop window. The main shopping streets in the towns and villages sparkle with lights. As soon as Christmas is over, fresh festivities get under way: New Year's Eve marks the beginning of the Carnival season, celebrated in Austria with numerous balls.

The famous Vienna Opera Ball held in February

December

St Nicholas parties *(early December)* Tyrol. The most interesting of these include **Klaubaufgehen**, a masquerade in Matrei, and **Nikolospiel** in Bad Mitterndorf. In Thaur (Tyrol), people traditionally display cribs in their homes.

Adventsingen Advent concerts held in Salzburg.

Steyrer Kripperl, one of the last stick-puppet theatres, performs nativity plays using the various crib displays. The crib display in Bad Ischl is also worth seeing. Nativity plays are staged throughout the country.

St Stephen's Day (Stephanitag) *(26 December)*. Colourful festival in the Lavanttal Valley (**Stefaniritt**) in Carinthia.

January

New Year's Day *(1 January)*. Austria welcomes the New Year with champagne and fireworks; people dance in the streets and squares, regardless of the weather.

Neujahrskonzert *(1 January)*. Traditional New Year's concert of the Vienna Philharmonic Orchestra transmitted throughout the world from the Golden Hall of the Wiener Musikverein.

Epiphany *(6 January)*. *Dreikönigssingen* (singing for the Three Kings) – Austria bursts into song on the Day of the Three Magi.

Perchtenlauf Carnival procession to mark the start of the party season. It rotates between four towns in Pongau: St Johann, Altenmarkt, Bischofshofen and Bad Gastein.

Salzburger Mozartwoche *(late January)* Salzburg. Mozart Week.

Resonanzen. A festival of early music held at Vienna's Konzerthaus.

February

February is the main Carnival season.

Masquerades and magnificent balls are held throughout the country.

Opernball *(last Thursday of Carnival)* Vienna Opera Ball.

Villacher Fasching *(end of Carnival)* Villach.

Maschkerertanz *(end of Carnival)* Steinfeld, Carinthia. Colourful festivities mark the end of the Carnival season.

Public Holidays

Neujahr New Year (1 Jan)

Dreikönigsfest Epiphany (6 Jan)

Ostern Easter

Tag der Arbeit Labour Day (1 May)

Fronleichnam Corpus Christi

Pfingsten Pentecost

Mariä Himmelfahrt Assumption of the Virgin Mary (15 Aug)

Nationalfeiertag (26 Oct)

Allerheiligen All Saints (1 Nov)

Mariä Empfängnis (8 Dec) Immaculate Conception

Weihnachten/Stephanitag Christmas (25/26 Dec)

Christmas decorations in Kohlmarkt, Vienna

THE HISTORY OF AUSTRIA

During the Middle Ages, Austria was only one of several small duchies within the Holy Roman Empire, but during 600 years of Habsburg rule it rose to the ranks of a world power and was a determining factor in Europe's fate. The Austro-Hungarian Empire ended with World War I. Since the end of World War II, Austria has been a central element in European democracy.

Prehistory and Early Middle Ages

The geographic nature of Austria's territory, opening up towards the Bohemian-Moravian Valley and the Hungarian Plains, meant that, from the 7th century BC, this area was regularly raided and populated by belligerent Scythians, Celts and Germanic tribes. At the end of the 1st century BC, the land south of the Danube was occupied by the Romans, who in the middle of the 1st century AD, during the reign of the Emperor Claudius, founded the Province of Noricum here, with its main centres in Carnuntum (near Hainburg) and Vindobona (Vienna).

The influence of the dominant Roman culture and civilization over the entire region began to wane in the 2nd century AD, during a period of increased German raids. In AD 180, Emperor Marcus Aurelius died in Vindobona, in the war against the Marcomanni and Quadi tribes.

From the 4th century onwards, during the Great Migration of Nations, the territories of present-day Austria saw successive waves of invading Huns, Goths and Avars. Later arrivals included Slav and Bavarian settlers. The Bavarian tribal state, established and consolidated during the 7th and 8th centuries, was crushed in 787 when Charlemagne deposed his vassal Tassilo III, the last Prince of Bavaria, and annexed his territories. In 803, Charlemagne also defeated the Avars and established a margravate (territory) on the banks of the Danube, between the Enns River and the Vienna Woods, which became the nucleus of the Austrian state. Its existence was cut short by Magyars, who raided it in the early 10th century.

Babenberg Austria

Following the defeat of the Magyars in 995, on the banks of the Lech River near Augsburg, the German King Otto I restored the margravate; his successor, Otto II, handed it as a fief to Leopold I of the Babenberg dynasty (976–94). The centre of the margravate was Melk, on the Danube river. Having defeated the Magyars, Leopold extended the frontiers of his province up to the Vienna Woods. In 1156, Henry II Jasomirgott was given the title of Duke, and Austria became a hereditary fief of the Empire. Vienna began to assume its role as capital city.

170 Raid by the Germanic tribes of Marcomanni and Quadi

493 Raid by Theodoric, King of the Ostrogoths

739 Founding of the bishopric of Salzburg

The "Ostarrichi Urkunde" document of 996

803 Charlemagne founds the eastern margravate

AD 1 — 500 — 650 — 800 — 950 — 1100

AD 4th–7th century The Great Migration of Nations. Raids by Huns, Goths, Avars, Slavs and Bavarians

45 Foundation of the Roman province, Noricum

787 Charlemagne deposes the last independent Bavarian prince, Tassilo III

976 Leopold I Babenberg becomes the first Margrave of the margravate

Tassilo's chalice of 777

◀ Emperor Franz Joseph I, who ruled 1848–1916

Bohemian Austria

In 1246, the Babenberg line died out and Austria fell into the hands of the Bohemian kings, Vaclav I and Ottokar II. The latter, having annexed Carinthia and Carniola (1269), became the most powerful duke in the Empire. He had his eyes on the German crown, but in the 1273 election a more modest feudal lord rose to the German throne, the landgrave (count) of Upper Alsace, Rudolf von Habsburg (1273–91). He defeated his opponent, Ottokar II, in 1278, took the Austrian territories and handed them to his sons as hereditary fiefs. From then on, for the next 640 years, the fate of Austria became tied to that of the Habsburg dynasty.

Death of Frederick II Babenberg

The double seated Carinthian ducal throne, joined by pieces of Roman stone, Maria Saal

The Habsburg Rise to Power

Rudolf I and his successors pursued a very successful policy of acquiring new territories. During the 14th century, in addition to Austria, Styria, Carinthia and Carniola, the Habsburgs gained control of Tyrol (1363) and Trieste (1382). An important contribution to the strengthening of the dynasty was made by Rudolf IV, called the Founder (1358–65), who founded Vienna University and laid the foundation stone for St Stephen's Cathedral, the church that to this day remains one of the symbols of the Austrian capital. Rudolf signed a treaty with the Emperor Charles IV – Bohemian king of the Luxemburg dynasty – stating that in the event of one of the dynasties (Habsburgs or Luxemburgs) dying out, the other would reign over both territories. This situation arose in 1438, when, following the death of Emperor Sigismund of Luxemburg, both the imperial crown of Germany and the throne of Hungary and Bohemia passed to the Austrian Duke Albrecht II of Habsburg, and on his death to his cousin Frederick III (1440–93), who was regarded as the last emperor of the Middle Ages. His motto was written as the five vowels – AEIOU – which were variously interpreted, for example as "Austriae Est Imperare Orbi Universo" (The Entire World is Austria's Empire).

The Empire of Charles V

This maxim appeared close to becoming true during the reign of Maximilian I (1486–1519), who by his marriage to Maria of

1156 Thanks to privileges granted by Frederick Barbarossa, Austria is elevated to the status of a Duchy of the Reich. Margrave Henry II Jasomirgott becomes its first duke

1358 Rudolph IV, the Founder, ascends to the throne

1251 Austria ruled by Ottokar II

| 1100 | 1150 | 1200 | 1250 | 1300 | 1350 |

1246 End of the Babenberg line. Vienna occupied by the Bohemian King Vaclav I

Fragment of a medieval altar from Verdun, 1185

1278 Rudolf von Habsburg defeats Ottokar II in the Battle of Dürnkrut. Austria becomes a hereditary fief of the Habsburgs

Gothic altar in Zwettl Abbey

he represented the younger line of Habsburgs, taking control of Austria, Styria, Carniola, Carinthia and Tyrol and the Jagiellon inheritance, Bohemia, Moravia, Silesia and western Hungary.

Reformation and Turkish Threat

During the Reformation, the state, now with a population of seven million, became the scene of fierce religious conflicts. Ferdinand and his successor, Maximilian II (1564–76), pursued a policy of tolerance towards the Protestants, but Rudolf II (1576–1612), brought up in the staunchly Catholic Spanish court, declared himself in favour of the Counter-Reformation. The growing religious conflict led to the Thirty-Years' War (1618–48), which ravaged large areas (51 castles, 23 towns and 313 villages in Austrian-ruled countries alone).

Burgundy in 1477 gained control of Alsace, Lorraine and the Netherlands, one of the richest countries in Europe. He also entered into a treaty with the Jagiellons – thus reviving his claims to the Bohemian and Hungarian crowns – and, by arranging the betrothal of his son Philip to the Spanish Infanta Joan, extended Habsburg rule over the Iberian Peninsula and the South American dominions. In 1519, Maximilian's successor, his grandson Charles V (1519–56), heir to the Spanish and Austrian territories, succeeded to the throne of an empire over which, it could be said, "the sun never set".

Panel inscribed "AEIOU", Frederick III's motto

Following the abdication of King Charles in 1556, the imperial crown passed to his brother Ferdinand (1556–64);

Even greater destruction was caused by the wars fought during the 16th and 17th centuries against the Turks, who twice tried to conquer Vienna (1529, 1683). The crushing defeat suffered by the Sultan's army during the second siege of Vienna allowed the Habsburgs to take control of the whole of Hungary, Transylvania and Croatia.

Turkish banner, captured in 1683

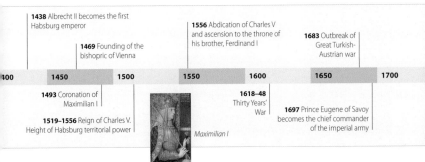

1438 Albrecht II becomes the first Habsburg emperor

1469 Founding of the bishopric of Vienna

1493 Coronation of Maximilian I

1519–1556 Reign of Charles V. Height of Habsburg territorial power

1556 Abdication of Charles V and ascension to the throne of his brother, Ferdinand I

1618–48 Thirty Years' War

1683 Outbreak of Great Turkish-Austrian war

1697 Prince Eugene of Savoy becomes the chief commander of the imperial army

| 400 | 1450 | 1500 | 1550 | 1600 | 1650 | 1700 |

Maximilian I

The First Habsburg Monarchy

The Habsburgs rose to the ranks of the most influential German feudal families during the first half of the 1300s, and in the following centuries they became the rulers of one of Europe's most powerful countries. This advancement was due mainly to their far-sighted dynastic policy and expedient marriages. Strategic matches brought under their control territories far beyond their native Austria and Styria, to include Tyrol, Flanders, the Netherlands, Bohemia, Hungary and the possessions of the Spanish crown in both Europe and South America. The Habsburgs' marriage policy was later summed up in the motto "Let others fight wars, you, lucky Austria, get married".

Austria of Rudolf I
Austria in 1278

Sauce Boat of Rudolf II
The sauce boat from the famous collection of objets d'art from the Mannerist period, collected by Rudolf II, can be seen in Vienna's Kunsthistorisches Museum (*see pp88–91*).

Regalia of Rudolf II
The intricate sceptre, orb and crown became the insignia of the Austrian Empire.

Maximilian I

Ferdinand I, grandson of Maximilian I, ruled Bohemia, Austria and Hungary.

Relief of the Siege of Vienna in 1683
The 70,000-strong Christian army, led by the Polish King Jan III Sobieski, broke through the ring around Vienna and forced the 110–115,000 Turkish troops of the Grand Vizier Kara Mustapha to flee.

Rudolf II
During his reign, Rudolf II attracted scholars such as Kepler, as well as famous sorcerers, alchemists and seers to the imperial court.

Philip I, son of Maximilian I, gained control of Spain as the result of his marriage to Joanna the Mad.

Mary of Burgundy,
wife of Maximilian I

Rudolf I
The first Habsburg king of Germany, having defeated Bohemian King Ottokar II in 1276, seized Austria, Carinthia and Styria.

Karl V, grandson of Maximilian I, inherited Spain from his mother.

Where to see Gothic Austria

The most interesting early-Gothic remains to be found in Austria, dating back to the 13th–14th centuries, are the cloisters of the Cistercian abbeys in Heiligenkreuz *(see p140)* in the Wienerwald, as well as Lilienfeld and Zwettl, both in Lower Austria. Among the best examples of Gothic architecture are the impressive Stephansdom (St Stephen's Cathedral) in Vienna, the Franciscan church in Salzburg *(see p224)*, and the four-nave parish church in Schwaz *(see pp248–9)*, in Tyrol. The most famous late-Gothic (1481) winged altar, an outstanding work by the Tyrolean artist Michael Pacher, is found in St Wolfgang *(see p209)*, in the Salzkammergut. Many churches feature original Gothic sculptures.

Stephansdom (St Stephen's Cathedral) in Vienna *(see pp62–3)* is Austria's best-known Gothic building.

Family of Maximilian I
This painting by Bernhard Strigel (c.1520) depicts Maximilian I with his family, a dynasty that turned Austria into a powerful empire.

Rudolf IV the Founder
Rudolf IV died very young (only 26 years old) and was buried in St Stephen's Cathedral – the church he had founded in Vienna.

Goldenes Dachl The "Golden Roof" in Innsbruck *(see p242)* is an attractive example of secular Gothic architecture.

The Struggle for Spanish and Austrian Succession

The expiration of the Spanish line of Habsburgs led to the Spanish War of Succession (1701–14), which brought further territorial gains for Austria, including Belgium, Milan, Naples and Sardinia. Soon the problem of succession also arose in Austria, where Emperor Charles VI (1711–40) had died without a male heir. The so-called Pragmatic Sanction, established by Charles in 1713, stipulated that the Habsburg Austrian territories remain an integral, indivisible whole, with female members of the house also eligible for succession. The Emperor's only daughter, Maria Theresa (1740– 80), however, was forced to defend her rights by fighting Prussia, France, Spain and a number of German states in the War of Austrian Succession (1740–48), during which she lost Silesia to Prussia. In 1772 and 1775, Austria participated in the first and third Partitions of Poland, annexing that country's southern territories.

Enlightened Absolutism

Maria Theresa and her son Joseph II (1780–90) embarked on an extensive course of reforms, in the spirit of enlightened absolutism. They curtailed the rights of the Church, abolished serfdom, created a new administrative structure of the state and declared German the official language for all institutions. Their aim was to obliterate the differences between the individual countries of the Empire, to unify the multi-ethnic state and to centralize power.

Revolution and Restoration

Apotheosis of Eugene of Saxony

During the revolutionary changes that took place in Europe at the turn of the 18th century, the Habsburgs joined the anti-French coalition forces. Initially they suffered major territorial losses (Belgium, Lombardy, southern Poland). Franz II, Maria Theresa's grandson, relinquished his title of Holy Roman Emperor and in 1806 declared himself Emperor Franz I of Austria. Following the defeat of Napoleon and the Congress of Vienna where proceedings were dominated by the Austrian Foreign Minister, Klemens Metternich, the Habsburg Empire became once again a European superpower. Metternich, who from 1821 held the office of Chancellor,

Emperor Franz I of Austria and Maria Theresa surrounded by their children

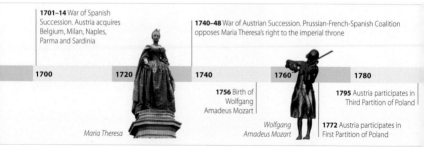

1701–14 War of Spanish Succession. Austria acquires Belgium, Milan, Naples, Parma and Sardinia

1740–48 War of Austrian Succession. Prussian-French-Spanish Coalition opposes Maria Theresa's right to the imperial throne

| 1700 | 1720 | 1740 | 1760 | 1780 |

1756 Birth of Wolfgang Amadeus Mozart

1795 Austria participates in Third Partition of Poland

1772 Austria participates in First Partition of Poland

Maria Theresa

Wolfgang Amadeus Mozart

The Congress of Vienna in 1815

and in fact ruled Austria, became the main exponent of absolutism and the policy of ethnic oppression; hence his nickname, "Europe's coachman".

The 1848 Revolution

In 1848–9, a wave of revolutions swept across Europe and the Austrian Empire. Uprisings against absolute government broke out in Vienna, Milan, Venice, Budapest, Cracow and Prague; the Hungarian revolution was suppressed only with the help of the Russian army. Emperor Ferdinand I saw himself forced to grant several concessions, including giving Austria a constitution (1848). Badly affected by the revolutionary events, the Emperor abdicated in 1848 and the Austrian throne passed to his 18-year-old nephew, Franz Joseph I (1848–1916), who quickly reintroduced absolute rule, thus inviting increased resistance, particularly in the Hungarian part of the empire.

The Austro-Hungarian Empire

Defeat suffered in the wars with Sardinia and France (1859), and with Prussia and Italy (1866), testified to the weakening position of Austria, particularly when confronted with the growing power of the unifying Germany. Defeat in the international arena also brought about changes in internal policy. In 1867, the emperor signed a treaty with Hungary and transformed the Austro-Hungarian Empire into a state consisting of two parts, united under one common ruler as well as a common army, finances and foreign policy. The adopted model of government eased the tensions in Austro-Hungarian relations, but did not contribute to the solution of other conflicts, including those with the Czechs, who revolted afresh, led by nationalist feelings.

Internationally, the Empire's attention was focused on the Balkans where, with Russian approval, it occupied Bosnia and Herzegovina (1878). Key to Vienna's political strategy was the political-military treaty signed in 1882 with Germany and Italy, the Triple Alliance.

In the late 1800s, Vienna developed as a centre of fashion and became the birthplace of the avant-garde Viennese Secession style.

Buildings on fire in Vienna during the Austrian Revolution of 1848

1806 Franz II relinquishes title of Holy Roman Emperor

1815 Congress of Vienna

Johann Strauss (son)

1848 Revolution in Vienna

1867 Austria becomes Austro-Hungarian state

1898 Assassination of Empress Elisabeth, by an Italian anarchist

1820   1840   1860   1880   1900

1825 Birth of Johann Strauss (son)

1848 Ferdinand I abdicates and Franz Joseph I ascends the throne

1889 Death of the Crown Prince, Archduke Rudolf

1805 Napoleon defeats the Austrian and Russian armies in the Battle of Austerlitz

1866 Defeated by Prussia, Austria loses its status as the main German power

The Monarchy of Franz I

At the turn of the 19th century, Austria had to face social and political changes brought about by the French Revolution. Franz II ascended the Austrian throne as Holy Roman Emperor in 1792, and Austria entered a 22-year-period of war with France. Franz II declared his opposition to all reformist ideas and, in response to Napoleon's self-coronation, he established the Austrian Empire in 1804. As Emperor Franz I, and with his all-powerful chancellor Klemens Metternich, his main concern in the field of domestic policy, was the preservation of the monarch's absolute power.

After the Vienna Congress
Austria in 1815

The coffin contains the body of Franz I, which was later laid in a sarcophagus in the crypt of the Capuchin Church in Vienna.

Franz I crosses the Vosges Mountains
Following Napoleon's defeat at Waterloo in 1815, Franz I marched into France at the head of troops belonging to the coalition's occupying forces.

An officer in
Austrian uniform

The Imperial crown of Austria –
once the crown of Emperor Rudolf II.
Alongside lie other regalia.

Emblem of the Empire
In 1836 Austria's national emblem combined Lorraine's two-headed eagle, with imperial crown, sword, sceptre and a shield with the Habsburg family crest.

Radetzky Statue
Johann Radetzky was one of the most outstanding commanders in Austrian history. After the victory over Italy in the Battle of Custozza (1848), the 82-year old became famous as the mainstay of the Habsburg monarchy.

Technological Progress
The first railway line on the European continent was built in Austria, in 1832. It linked Linz with České Budejovice.

Where to see Biedermeier style in Austria

The Biedermeier style of furniture, interior design and painting, popular during the early 19th century, reflected the virtues and aspirations of the middle classes. Draped curtains, patterned carpets, bureaus and glazed cabinets became standard features. Domestic architecture flourished. Typical interiors can be seen in Vienna, in the Geymüllerschlössel, which is part of the Museum of Applied Arts (MAK – *see p64*), and the Dreimäderlhaus. Works of prominent artists such as Ferdinand Waldmüller, Josef Danhauser and Moritz Daffinger can be found in the Belvedere *(see p102)*, the Wien Museum Karlsplatz *(see p101)*, and in the Schlossmuseum in Linz *(see p194)*, among others.

An officer in Hungarian uniform

Biedermeier-style furniture was highly valued by the prosperous middle classes, particularly in the first half of the 19th century.

Funeral Ceremony Of Franz I
When Napoleon declared himself Emperor of France in 1804, Franz II countered by proclaiming himself Franz I, Emperor of Austria. He was the last ruler of the Holy Roman Empire of the German Nation. He died in 1835.

Franz I in his Coronation Robes
In 1804, Franz I took on the newly created role of Emperor of Austria and King of Hungary. Two months later, he added the title King of Bohemia.

The Dreimäderlhaus, at No. 10 Schreyvogelgasse, is one of the most beautiful examples of Viennese Biedermeier.

Depiction of the sensational murder of Archduke Franz Ferdinand and his wife, Sophie

World War I

In 1908, Austro-Hungary decided on a formal annexation of Bosnia-Herzegovina, leading to increased tensions with Russia, which had begun to strengthen its position in the Balkans, and with Serbia, which pursued its own expansionist aims. On 28 June 1914, in Sarajevo, the Serbian student Gavrilo Princip shot dead the heir to the Austrian throne, Franz Ferdinand. His assassination resulted in the outbreak of World War I. Germany, Austria's old ally from the Triple Alliance, declared itself on the side of Austria (Italy remained neutral for a while), while the Entente countries – Russia, France and England – sided with Serbia. The war exposed the weakness of the Habsburg monarchy and brought about its collapse. Charles I, Austria's last emperor, was exiled to Madeira in 1921.

The First Republic

On 12 November 1918, the Provisional National Assembly proclaimed the birth of the Austro-German Republic. Its first elected chancellor was the socialist Karl Renner. The peace treaty, signed in St-Germain-en-Laye (1919), imposed war compensations on Austria and forbade unification with Germany. During the 1920s, Austria's economic situation steadily worsened, giving rise to radical sentiments. The worsening internal problems were exploited by nationalist circles calling for Austria to join with Germany. Chancellor Engelbert Dollfuss, elected to office in 1932, tried to counteract such dangers by introducing "strong-arm government", repressing the Social-Democratic opposition and dissolving Communist and Nazi parties. These steps led to bloody riots in Vienna and Linz, in February 1934. In July of that year, the Nazis unsuccessfully attempted a coup, and murdered Dollfuss in the process. The new chancellor, Kurt Schuschnigg, under pressure from Adolf Hitler, agreed in February 1937 to admit Nazi politicians into his government, but resigned in the face of demands for Austria to be incorporated into Germany. His successor, the Nazi activist Arthur

Townspeople give the Nazi salute as German troops march into Austria during the annexation

1908 Annexation of Bosnia and Herzegovina

1914 Assassination of Archduke Franz Ferdinand, in Sarajevo. Outbreak of WWI

1938 Anschluss – Austria's integration into the Third Reich

1934 Workers riot in Vienna and Linz; bloody suppression by the police

1943 Moscow Conference

1900	1910	1920	1930	1940	1950

1916 Death of Franz Joseph I. Emperor Charles I ascends the throne

Archduke Franz Ferdinand's jacket

1918 End of WWI. Collapse of Austro-Hungary. Creation of the Republic of Austria

1934 Nazi coup failed. Engelbert Dollfuss killed

Engelbert Dollfuss

1955 Treaty of State restoring full sovereignty to Austria. Parliament declares Austria to be neutral for all time

Soldiers of the occupying forces salute each other in Vienna, 1951

Seyss-Inquart, proclaimed Austria's integration into the Third Reich *(Anschluss)* on 13 March 1938, which met with the approval of the majority of the Austrian population. German troops marched into the country. In 1938, some 200,000 Jews lived in Vienna, yet after the Holocaust only 7,000 remained.

World War II and the Second Republic

Following the *Anschluss*, Austria became a part of Greater Germany until the end of World War II. Opposition against the Nazi administration was negligible. Before the end of the war, at the Moscow Conference in 1943, the Allied forces decided to restore an independent Austrian state. In April 1945, Karl Renner formed the first provisional government of the restored Second Republic, and in December he was elected president. In July 1945, Austria was divided into four occupation zones by the Allied powers.

The first parliamentary elections, in November 1945, were won by the Christian-Democratic Party (ÖVP), with the Socialist Party (SPÖ) coming second. Both parties were to control the political life of the country for the next 50 years. De-Nazification continued until 1948. In 1955 the Austrian State Treaty was signed, restoring Austria to full sovereignty. Foreign troops were withdrawn from its territory and Parliament proclaimed permanent neutrality. In December 1955 Austria became a member of the United Nations, and in 1995 joined the European Union.

In the 1990s, the nationalist and anti-immigration Austrian Freedom Party (FPÖ) gained in popularity. It formed a coalition government with the Austrian People's Party ÖVP in 2000, arousing fears of a resurgence of Nazi activity in Austria. However, the coalition soon collapsed, and in 2002 the nationalist vote plummeted to around 10 per cent. In 2007, a coalition government was formed between the Socialist Party (SPÖ) and the Austrian People's Party ÖVP.

Simon Wiesenthal and Ariel Musicant, Austrian investigators into Nazi crimes, at the Jewish memorial

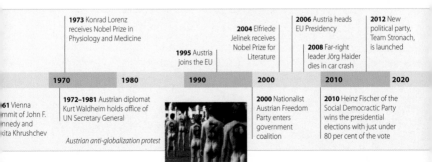

1973 Konrad Lorenz receives Nobel Prize in Physiology and Medicine

1995 Austria joins the EU

2004 Elfriede Jelinek receives Nobel Prize for Literature

2006 Austria heads EU Presidency

2008 Far-right leader Jörg Haider dies in car crash

2012 New political party, Team Stronach, is launched

| 1970 | 1980 | 1990 | 2000 | 2010 | 2020 |

61 Vienna mmit of John F. nnedy and kita Khrushchev

1972–1981 Austrian diplomat Kurt Waldheim holds office of UN Secretary General

Austrian anti-globalization protest

2000 Nationalist Austrian Freedom Party enters government coalition

2010 Heinz Fischer of the Social Democractic Party wins the presidential elections with just under 80 per cent of the vote

VIENNA AREA BY AREA

Introducing Vienna

Central Vienna includes the Inner
City demarcated by the Ringstrasse
(often shortened to Ring) and Franz-
Josefs-Kai, plus the area between Ring
and Gürtel. Gürtel is Vienna's second
ring road, running almost parallel
with the Ring. In this guide, central
Vienna is divided into three districts,
in line with its administrative
sectors. The most interesting
sights outside the centre are
also featured.

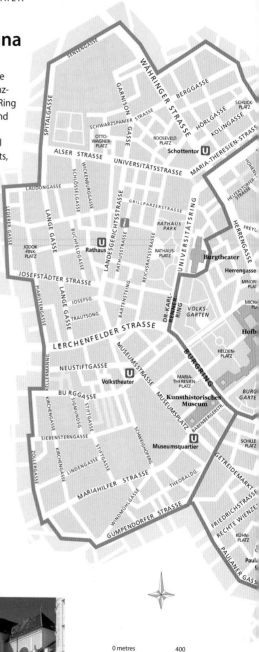

Majolikahaus Façade
The façade of Majolikahaus,
at No. 40 Linke Wienzeile,
was designed in 1899 by Otto
Wagner, one of the foremost
representatives of Viennese
Secession style.

| 0 metres | 400 |
| 0 yards | 400 |

Freyung
Freyung Square is dominated by the
Austria Fountain; in the background is
the Schottenkirche, the church of
Vienna's Benedictine monks.

◀ Aerial view of the city of Vienna from the bell tower of Stephansdom

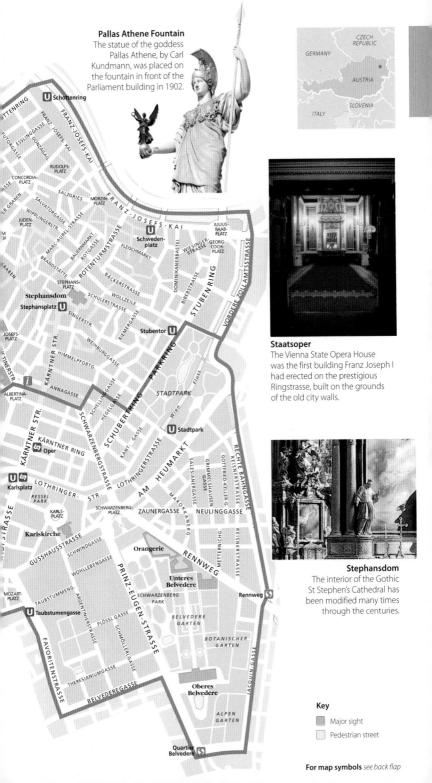

Pallas Athene Fountain
The statue of the goddess
Pallas Athene, by Carl
Kundmann, was placed on
the fountain in front of the
Parliament building in 1902.

Staatsoper
The Vienna State Opera House
was the first building Franz Joseph I
had erected on the prestigious
Ringstrasse, built on the grounds
of the old city walls.

Stephansdom
The interior of the Gothic
St Stephen's Cathedral has
been modified many times
through the centuries.

Key

Major sight

Pedestrian street

For map symbols *see back flap*

INNER CITY

Vienna's old town, the Innere Stadt or "inner city", developed in the area enclosed on one side by the present-day Danube canal, and on the other three sides by fortifications. In the 19th century, these were replaced by the town's elegant artery – the Ringstrasse. The Ring encircles many splendid historic remains, bearing witness to Vienna's turbulent history from Roman times until the present day, while numerous museum collections convey Austria's rich heritage. It is also one of Vienna's liveliest areas, where the smartest cafés and restaurants and most expensive shops await the visitor, and where bars and clubs stay open until the early hours.

Sights at a Glance

Streets and Squares
2 Graben
8 Dr-Ignaz-Seipel-Platz
12 Schwedenplatz
14 Jewish Quarter
17 Hoher Markt
19 Schulhof
20 Am Hof
21 Freyung
22 Herrengasse
23 Minoritenplatz
24 Michaelerplatz
26 Heldenplatz
29 Josefsplatz
34 Kärntner Strasse

Historic Buildings
5 Mozarthaus Vienna
11 Urania

16 Altes Rathaus
18 Böhmische Hofkanzlei
27 *Alte Burg pp72–3*
28 *Spanish Riding School p71*
33 Winterpalais des Prinzen Eugen

Churches
1 Peterskirche
3 *Stephansdom pp62–3*
6 Deutschordenskirche St Elisabeth
7 Franziskanerkirche
9 Dominikanerkirche

13 Ruprechtskirche
15 Maria am Gestade
30 Augustinerkirche
32 Kapuzinerkirche, Kaisergruft

Museums
4 Dom- und Diözesanmuseum
10 Österreichisches Museum für Angewandte Kunst
31 Albertina

Parks and Gardens
25 Volksgarten

See Street Finder, maps 2 & 3

```
0 metres    250
0 yards     250
```

◀ Spectacular frescoes adorning the dome and altar of Peterskirche

Street-by-Street: Around Stephansdom

The origins of this district date back to the 13th century, but much of it was changed in the 17th and 18th centuries, when many churches and public buildings were refashioned in the spirit of the increasingly powerful Habsburg monarchy. Narrow, medieval alleys adjoin monumental Baroque structures and bourgeois town houses, whose ground floors are often occupied by shops, cafés and restaurants. In the evenings, when the churches and museums close for the night, the area is still lively with people.

❹ ★ Dom-und Diözesanmuseum
This crucifix, containing the relics of St Andrew, is one of the many treasures of medieval sacred art kept in the Cathedral Museum.

Haas & Haas Tea Shop
and Restaurant offers the best selection of teas and coffees in Vienna, as well as delicious snacks. The tea house is set in a courtyard filled with lush greenery.

❸ ★ Stephansdom
St Stephen's Cathedral has a Baroque main altar, the work of Tobias Pock, showing the martyrdom of its patron saint.

❻ Deutschordenskirche St Elisabeth
This church belonged to the Teutonic Order which, after having been relegated from Eastern Prussia by Napoleon, moved its headquarters to Vienna.

Along Blutgasse and neighbouring streets the tenement houses feature lovely, green courtyards.

❺ Mozarthaus Vienna
Wolfgang Amadeus Mozart lived in this house from 1784–7, and composed *The Marriage of Figaro* here.

For hotels and restaurants in this area see pp292–3 and pp310–12

Schönlaterngasse is a popular street, which owes its name to the wrought-iron lantern, a copy of which can be seen at No. 6. Robert Schumann lived at No. 7. Also noteworthy are the Basiliskenhaus and the Baroque chapel of St Bernard *(see left)*.

Locator Map
See Street Finder, maps 2 & 3

❽ Dr-Ignaz-Seipel-Platz
This square, one of the most beautiful in Vienna, has an ornate Baroque Jesuit church on one side. Shown here is a detail from its pulpit.

The Academy of Science is based in the assembly hall of the former university.

0 metres   50

0 yards   50

Key

— Suggested route

Bäckerstrasse, once the home of Vienna's bakers, is now more popular for its nightlife. The house at No. 12 has a magnificent Renaissance façade, and the one at No. 7 is famous for its arcaded courtyard and stables.

❶ Peterskirche

Petersplatz 6. **Map** 2 B4. **Tel** 53 36
443. Ⓤ Stephansplatz. 🚊 1A, 2A,
3A. **Open** 7am–8pm Mon–Fri,
9am–9pm Sat, Sun.

St Peter's church, one of
Vienna's oldest, was, according
to legend, founded in 792 by
Charlemagne, as commemo-
rated in a marble relief on the
church's façade, *The Placing of
the Cross by Charlemagne*, by
Rudolf Weyr (1906).

The site was occupied by a
Roman basilica as early as the
12th century. The present
Baroque church was built in
the 18th century to designs
by Gabriele Montani. It received
its final form from Johann Lukas
von Hildebrandt, who also
gave the church its magnificent
green patina-covered dome,
which towers over the whole
district. The frescoes inside the
dome, depicting the Assumption
of the Virgin Mary, were created
by Johann Michael Rottmayr.

The Chapel of St Michael, the
first on the right, holds a glass
coffin containing the relics of
St Benedict.

The striking patina-covered copper
dome of Peterskirche

❷ Graben

Map 2 B4, C4. Ⓤ Stephansplatz.
🚊 1A, 2A, 3A. Jewish Museum:
Tel 53 50 431. **Open** 10am–6pm
Sun–Fri. 🅿 📷 🖳 jmw.at

This fully pedestrianized street,
running through a bustling part
of the city centre, is one of the
most fashionable shopping areas

The Baroque plague column in Graben

in Vienna, full to bursting with
lively restaurants and cafés. There
are two identical fountains in
the square, St Joseph Fountain
on the northwestern side and
St Leopold Fountain on the
southeastern side.

In the centre of the square
stands the Baroque Pestsäule
(Plague Column), also known
as the Dreifaltigkeitssäule
(Trinity Column), which the
Emperor Leopold I had erected
after the end of the 1679
plague that decimated the
town. It depicts the Holy Trinity,
with a statue of the praying
emperor at the top. A carved
group, entitled *Faith Conquers
the Plague*, adorns the southern
side of the column. A short
distance from here, towards
Stephansplatz, stands a modest
statue of St John
of Nepomuk, which
is a favourite spot
with buskers.

The modern Haas
Haus on Graben, at
Stephansplatz, was
built in 1985–90 on
the site of older
buildings destroyed
during a bombing raid.
Made from glass and
aluminium, it is the
most controversial
building at the heart
of the city. Its windows
beautifully reflect the
cathedral towers. The
top floor houses a
café-restaurant,
offering great views.

One of the original Baroque
structures is the Bartolotti
Palace, at the corner of
Dorotheergasse. Next to
it is a popular Trzesniewski
Sandwich Buffet. Further
along Dorotheergasse, at
No.11, is the **Jewish Museum**
(Jüdisches Museum Wien),
which moved into the
former Eskeles Palace from
the old synagogue. The
museum chronicles the
history of Jews in Vienna.

Otto Wagner, an
outstanding architect of
the Viennese Secession,
had his studio at Graben
No.10; in the 1980s, the
house belonged to
the eccentric Austrian artist
Friedensreich Hundertwasser.

❸ Stephansdom

See pp62–3.

❹ Dom-und Diözesanmuseum

Stephansplatz 6. **Map** 2 C4.
Tel 51 552-35 60. Ⓤ Stephansplatz.
🚊 1A, 2A, 3A. **Open** 10am–6pm
Tue–Sat. 🅿 🖳 dommuseum.at

The cathedral museum contains
a large collection of sacral paintings and sculptures, as well as
fascinating examples of folk art.
Many pieces were donated to
the cathedral by Duke Rudolf IV.
Star exhibits include the famous
portrait of the duke (c.1360),
and the *Erlacher Madonna*,
a life-size statue of the
Madonna and Child, a
Gothic masterpiece
(c.1330) from Lower
Austria. The Cathedral
Museum also holds sacral
vessels and reliquaries
from St Stephen's Cathedral,
valuable masterpieces of
the Gothic, Baroque and
Romantic eras, and the
Otto Mauer collec-
tion of 20th-century
Austrian art.

The museum
has been undergoing
renovations. It is
expected to reopen
in 2016.

Gothic Madonna and Child,
Cathedral Museum

❺ Mozarthaus Vienna

Domgasse 5. **Map** 2 C4.
Tel 51 21 791. Ⓤ Stephansplatz.
🚌 3A. **Open** 10am–7pm daily. 🅿
🆆 mozarthausvienna.at

Domgasse 5 is the most famous of Mozart's various homes in Vienna. He lived here with his family in 1784–7, and composed many of his masterpieces here, including *The Marriage of Figaro*. Restored for the anniversary year of 2006, the Mozarthaus Vienna has exhibitions on two upper floors as well as the Mozarts' first-floor flat.

❻ Deutschordenskirche St Elisabeth

Singerstrasse 7. **Map** 2 C4.
Tel 51 21 065. Ⓤ Stephansplatz.
🚌 1A, 2A, 3A. Church: **Open** 7am–7pm daily. Treasury: **Open** 10am–noon Tue, Thu, Sat, 3–5pm Wed, Fri. 🅿

The knights of the Teutonic Order arrived in Vienna in the 13th century. They established their quarters near the Stephansdom, but only the tower still stands today. In the 15th century, they built the present Gothic **church** of St Elizabeth. Its Baroque façade, added between 1725 and 1735, hides the original Gothic features.

In 1807, when Napoleon abolished the Order of Teutonic Knights in Eastern Prussia, the knights moved their headquarters to Vienna and brought the Order Treasury here. The four rooms of the **Treasury** hold collections of objects associated with the history of the Order: insignia of the Grand Masters, coins, medals, seals, sacral vessels and tableware, as well as masterpieces of European art collected by the knights.

The walls of the church are hung with the coats of arms of the Teutonic knights. The beautiful winged altar (1520) is made from elaborate carved and painted panels depicting scenes from the Passion, surrounded by intricate tracery.

Within the complex of buildings belonging to the Order is the apartment where Mozart first lived in Vienna, later occupied by Johannes Brahms (1863–5).

❼ Franziskanerkirche

Franziskanerplatz 4. **Map** 2 C4.
Tel 51 24 578. Ⓤ Stephansplatz.
Open 6:30am–noon, 2–5:30pm Mon–Sat, 7am–5:30pm Sun.

In the 14th century, the Franciscans took over this church, originally built by wealthy citizens as a "house of the soul" for prostitutes wishing to reform. The present church, designed in the South German Renaissance style by Bonaventura Daum, was built in 1601–11. Its façade is topped by a scrolled gable with obelisks and carvings. The interior was decorated by Austrian and Italian masters of the Baroque, including Andrea Pozzo and Johann Georg Schmidt. An axe has been stuck in the wooden statue of the Madonna and Child above the tabernacle, known as *Madonna and Axe*, ever since an attack during the religious wars. The Moses Fountain in front of the church dates from 1798.

A charming 18th-century wall fountain, Academy of Science

❽ Dr-Ignaz-Seipel-Platz

Map 3 D4. Ⓤ Stephansplatz, Schwedenplatz. 🚌 3A.

Dr Ignaz Seipel, a conservative politician, was twice Chancellor of Austria in the 1920s. The square bearing his name is one of the most attractive in Vienna. At its centre (at No. 2) stands a Rococo structure designed by Jean Nicolas Jadot de Ville-Issey, originally intended as an auditorium for the Old University. Since 1857 it has served as the headquarters of the Österreichische Akademie der Wissenschaften (Austrian Academy of Sciences). The frescoes on the ceiling of the Rococo assembly hall, painted by Gregorio Guglielmi, show an allegory of the four academic faculties. Damaged by fire in 1961, they have been meticulously restored.

Opposite the Academy of Sciences stands the impressive High Baroque Jesuitenkirche. The Jesuits took over the university in the 1620s and, from 1703–5, rebuilt the church next to it, with a new façade and interior, the works of the Italian painter Andrea Pozzo.

The impressive winged altarpiece in Deutschordenskirche

❾ Stephansdom

Situated in the centre of Vienna, the cathedral, dedicated to the first Christian martyr, St Stephen, is the very soul of the city. Although built on this site some 800 years ago, the present building is mainly late-Gothic in style – the only fragments remaining of the original 13th-century Romanesque church are the Giants' Doorway and the Towers of the Heathens. Largely destroyed during World War II, the cathedral was restored to its former glory by the efforts of the entire nation. In a vault beneath its main altar are urns containing the internal organs of some of the Habsburgs – other body parts were kept elsewhere in Vienna.

★ Giants' Doorway
This masterpiece of late-Romanesque art, with its richly carved portal and the twin Towers of the Heathens, stands on the site of an earlier heathen shrine.

Entrance to the catacombs

★ Cathedral's Pulpit
The pulpit in the main nave is decorated with portraits of the Four Fathers of the Church. The sculptor himself looks on from a "window" below, under the stairs.

KEY

① **The North Tower** houses the Pummerin Bell.

② **The Bronze Sphere** is crowned with a twin-headed eagle – the Habsburg emblem.

③ **Viewing platform**, at 72 m (236 ft)

④ **The mosaic roof** is covered with almost 250,000 glazed tiles.

⑤ **Lifts** to the bell

⑥ **Singer Gate** was at one time the entrance for male visitors. The superb sculptures depict scenes from the life of St Paul and Duke Rudolf IV the Founder.

Main entrance

VISITORS' CHECKLIST

Practical Information
Stephansplatz 1.
Map 2 C4.
Tel 51 552-3526.
Open 6am–10pm Mon–Sat,
7am–10pm Sun.
in English:10:30am Mon–Sat;
in German: 3pm daily.
stephanskirche.at

Transport
Stephansplatz.
1A, 2A, 3A.

★ **Steffl or South Spire**
This 137 m (450 ft) high Gothic spire, built in the 15th century, is the symbol of the cathedral and of Vienna.

The majestic Baroque façade of Dominikanerkirche

❾ Dominikanerkirche

Postgasse 4. **Map** 3 D4.
Tel 51 29 174. Stubentor, Schwedenplatz, Stephansplatz. 2.
3A, 74A. **Open** 7am–7pm Mon–Sat, 7:30am–9pm Sun.

The Dominican monks came to Vienna in 1226, at the invitation of Duke Leopold VI. They built and consecrated their first church and convent here in the second half of the 13th century. The church that stands now, built between 1631 and 1674, was designed by Cypriano Biasino and Antonio Canevale.

The church has a richly ornamented interior, with a ring of chapels surrounding the nave, with early-Baroque frescoes on the ceiling and a painting by Franz Geyling inside the dome. The second chapel on the right, St Vincent Chapel, has swirling Rococo grilles and candelabra, and a very beautiful gilt organ above the west door, set within a mid-18th century decorative enclosure.

Niches in the majestic façade contain statues of Dominican saints. The two statues in the corner recesses commemorate two great scientists and medieval religious figures, St Albert the Great and St Thomas Aquinas.

Worth seeing are the frescoes by Tencalla and Rauchmüller, and the high altar (1839–40) by Karl Rösner, with a painting by Leopold Kupelwieser.

Wiener Neustädter Altar
Commissioned in 1447 by the Emperor Friedrich III, this elaborately carved altarpiece is situated to the left of the main altar.

❿ Österreichisches Museum für Angewandte Kunst

Stubenring 5. **Map** 3 D4. **Tel** 712 80 00. 🚋 2. 🚌 1A, 74A. **Ⓤ** Stubentor, Landstrasse. Ⓢ Landstrasse. **Open** 10am–10pm Tue, 10am–6pm Wed–Sun. 🅿 Admission free Tue. **Ⓦ** mak.at

The Austrian Museum of Applied Arts (MAK), founded in 1864, the first of its kind in Europe, exercised a strong influence on the development of the applied arts for some time. It houses the archives and collections of the Wiener Werkstätte – workshops famous for their promotion of good design.

The building was designed by one of the Ring architects, Heinrich von Ferstel, in Florentine Renaissance style. A new wing was added in 1909, and in 1994 the Arenbergpark flak tower became an annexe of the museum. Each room is unique, designed by a different artist, thus creating a fine setting for the items on display.

The eclectic permanent collection includes glass, pottery, porcelain, jewellery, metalwork, furniture, textiles, Eastern carpets and decorative items from the Far East. Separate rooms are devoted to the Secession period.

Biedermeier-style sofa, MAK

⓫ Urania

Uraniastrasse 1. **Map** 3 E3. 🚋 1, 2, N. **Ⓤ** Schwedenplatz. Planetarium: **Tel** 89 174 150 000. **Open** Term time: 9am–8pm, 2–8pm Sat, Sun; school holidays: 9am–4pm Mon–Fri, 2–8pm Sat, Sun. **Ⓦ** urania-sternwarte.at

On the south side of Julius-Raab-Platz, on the banks of the Danube Canal, stands a round building with a distinctive dome that is visible from afar. Urania, named after the Greek muse, was built in 1910 to designs by Max Fabian. It is home to Vienna's oldest educational establishment that is not a school. Inside the building are lecture halls and a theatre for visiting theatre performances as well as a resident puppet theatre; it is also home to a cinema and a **planetarium**. Every year, Urania holds a symposium devoted to the outstanding Austrian writer and Nobel prize winner, Elias Canetti.

⓬ Schwedenplatz

Map 3 D3. **Ⓤ** Schwedenplatz.

Schwedenplatz, the Swedish Square, is one of Vienna's busiest spots. Here, on the banks of the Danube Canal, under Schwedenbrücke, is a landing stage with riverboats inviting visitors on to a variety of pleasure cruises.

Eissalon am Schwedenplatz, another attraction, awaits at No. 17 (near Franz Josefs-Kai): it is reputed to sell the best ice cream in Vienna.

In Laurenzberg, on one side of Schwedenplatz, remains of the old town wall can be seen, with a metal ring that was used to tie up horses and an old sign with traffic regulations. At Fleischmarkt 11, steep, narrow steps lead down to the wine bar of Griechenbeisl, which claims to be the oldest restaurant in the city. Visitors are welcomed by a board showing the *Lieber Augustin*; from the entrance hall you can see down to a small, illuminated cellar where his statue is on display. The story of Augustin, a piper, goes back to the times of the Great Plague in Vienna. In a drunken stupor, he slumped into the gutter. When undertakers mistook him for dead and threw him into a plague pit, he woke up and terrified them by singing: *O du lieber Augustin*… (Oh, dear Augustin). Miraculously, he survived, and today, tourists wishing to return to Vienna throw a coin into the cellar.

Striking ivy-clad façade of Ruprechtskirche, Vienna's oldest church

⓭ Ruprechtskirche

Ruprechtsplatz. **Map** 2 C3. **Tel** 53 56 003. **Ⓤ** Schwedenplatz. 🚌 1A, 2A, 3A. 🚋 1, 2, N. 🕒 9pm–midnight Fri (German), 5pm Sat (German), 11am Sun (Arabic). **Ⓦ** ruprechtskirche.at

The church of St Ruprecht, rising on an escarpment overlooking Ruprechtsplatz, is Vienna's oldest church. At one time, an arm of the Danube flowed nearby with a landing stage for salt transported from Salzburg. According to legend, the church was founded in 740 by disciples of the Salzburg bishop, St Ruprecht, patron saint of salt merchants. The Romanesque nave and three lower floors of the tower date from the 11th century. In the choir is a 12th-century stained-glass window, Vienna's oldest, depicting the Crucifixion and the Virgin Mary on the throne.

⓮ Jewish Quarter

Map 2 C2, 3. **Ⓤ** Schwedenplatz, Herrengasse. 🚌 1A, 2A, 3A. Jewish Museum: Palais Eskeles, Dorotheergasse 11. **Tel** 535 04 31. **Ⓤ** Stephansplatz. **Open** 10am–6pm Sun–Fri. 🅿 Museum Judenplatz: Misrachi-Haus, Judenplatz 8. **Ⓤ** Schwedenplatz, Herrengasse. **Open** 10am–6pm Sun–Thu, 10am–2pm Fri. 🅿

A tangle of narrow streets west of Rotenturmstrasse makes up the earliest Jewish quarter in Vienna. Today, the Jewish quarter is a busy area of discothèques, bars and kosher restaurants, but during the Middle Ages, Judenplatz was the site of the Jewish ghetto, with a synagogue, the remains of which can be seen under the square. There was also a Jewish hospital, rabbi's house, bathhouse and school.

Stadttempel, Vienna's only synagogue to have survived World War II, is hidden behind a façade on Seitenstettengasse. It is now guarded by armed police, a precaution taken following a terrorist attack in 1983.

In 1895, the world's first **Jewish Museum** was founded here. It was closed down by the Nazis, but a new museum opened in 1993 in Palais Eskeles in Dorotheergasse (see p60).

In 2000, the **Museum Judenplatz**, devoted to medieval Jewish life, opened in Misrachi House. A modern monument by Rachel Whiteread at the centre of the square commemorates the victims of the Holocaust.

The Gothic interior of the church Maria am Gestade

⓯ Maria am Gestade

Salvatorgasse 12. **Map** 2 C3. **Tel** 533 95 94. Ⓤ Schwedenplatz, Stephansplatz. 🚋 1A, 3A. **Open** 7am–6pm daily.

The church of St Mary's on the Riverbank was once flooded by the waters of an old Danube canal, but today it rises on a steep escarpment, its lofty, 56-m (180-ft) high Gothic steeple dominating the town. The stone helmet at the top of the steeple is a masterpiece of Viennese Gothic art.

First mentioned in the 12th century, the present building dates from the late 1300s, and is one of Vienna's oldest churches. It was used as an arsenal during Napoleon's occupation of the city in 1809, but later restored.

Inside, the stained-glass panes behind the main altar are mostly original medieval features. The pillars are adorned with six Gothic statues, plus some from the 17th and 19th centuries. To the left of the main altar is a chapel with a Renaissance stone altar, adorned with colourful painted carvings. The church also holds the tomb of Clemens Maria Hofbauer, the city's patron saint.

⓰ Altes Rathaus

Wipplingerstrasse 8. **Map** 2 B3. Ⓤ Schwedenplatz, Stephansplatz. 🚋 1, 2. 🚌 1A, 3A. Archives and Museum of the Austrian Resistance: **Tel** 228 9469 319. **Open** 9am–5pm Mon–Wed, 9am–7pm Thu. 📷 by appointment.

Vienna's oldest town hall probably first stood at neighbouring Tuchlaubenstrasse. The building at Wipplingerstrasse was once owned by the rich and influential brothers Otto and Haimo von Neuhaus, who headed a burghers' rebellion against the Habsburgs. In 1309, Prince Friedrich the Fair confiscated the building and

Ironwork at the entrance to Altes Rathaus, Wipplingerstrasse

gave it to the town. It served as the town's main administrative centre until 1883.

The entrance of Altes Rathaus is festooned with beautiful Baroque ironwork. In the courtyard stands the Andromeda Fountain (1741), the last work of the sculptor Georg Raphael Donner. A door leads from the courtyard to Salvatorkapelle (St Saviour's chapel), the former Neuhaus family chapel, which has a Renaissance portal (1520–30), facing Salvatorgasse, a rare example in Vienna of the Italian Renaissance style.

Today, the Old Town Hall houses the **Archives and Museum of the Austrian Resistance**, devoted to the memory of those who risked their lives by opposing National Socialism in Austria, in the years 1934–45.

Vienna's Jews – Past and Present

A Jewish merchant community thrived in Vienna from the 12th century, with the original Jewish quarter centred around Judenplatz. During the 1421 persecutions many Jews were murdered, while others were forced to convert to the Christian faith or to leave the town. The 1781 Edict of Tolerance, issued by Joseph II, lifted legal constraints on Jews, and the centre of Jewish life gradually moved to the opposite bank of the Danube Canal, around the Prater. In 1938, some 200,000 Jews lived in Vienna, contributing to its cultural and intellectual life. After the Nazi genocide, only 7,000 remained. Now Eastern European immigrants are again adding to their total number.

The lavish interior of Stadttempel

Anker Clock in Hoher Markt, with cut-out historical figures

ⓗ Hoher Markt

Map 2 C3. Ⓤ Stephansplatz, Schwedenplatz. ⓦ 1A, 3A.

Hoher Markt is the oldest square in Vienna. After World War II, the foundations of the Roman military camp of Vindobona, where Emperor Marcus Aurelius died in AD 180, were discovered under the square. The ruins are now a popular tourist attraction.

In medieval times, fish and cloth markets as well as executions were held in the square. Since the early 18th century, it has been a venue for town court trials.

The Ankeruhr (Anker Clock), above the way to Bauernmarkt, is a copper and bronze sculptural clock designed in 1911 by Franz von Matsch. It features 12 historical figures who contributed to Vienna's development and reputation. Every hour one of these emerges, and at noon the entire set parades past. The procession is headed by Marcus Aurelius, followed by Rudolf IV, and closes with the composer Joseph Haydn.

In the centre of the square stands the remarkable Baroque Josephsbrunnen (Joseph's fountain) or Vermählungsbrunnen (nuptial fountain), commissioned by Leopold I and designed by Johann Bernhard Fischer von Erlach, depicting Joseph and Mary's betrothal by the high priest.

ⓘ Böhmische Hofkanzlei

Judenplatz 11. **Map** 2 B3. **Tel** 53 122. Ⓤ Stephansplatz. ⓦ 1A, 3A. **Open** 8am–3:30pm Mon–Fri. ⓦ **vfgh.gv.at**

The Habsburg rulers were also kings of Bohemia, which was initially governed from Prague; in 1627, however, Emperor Ferdinand II transferred the administration to Vienna. In 1714, the Bohemian Court Chancery moved into this grand palace, designed by Johann Bernhard Fischer von Erlach, and henceforth the Austrian emperors ruled Bohemia from here.

The vast original Baroque portals, with sculptures added later by Lorenzo Mattielli, create a harmonious exterior, which is subtle yet powerful. Also noteworthy are the beautiful carved and elegantly curved window frames.

ⓙ Schulhof

Map 2 B3. Ⓤ Stephansplatz, Herrengasse. ⓦ 1A, 2A, 3A. Clock Museum: **Tel** 53 32 265. **Open** 10am–6pm Tue–Sun. **Closed** 1 Jan, 1 May, 25 Dec. 🅿

Schulhof is a small alley connecting the imperial Am Hof square with the elegant, Baroque residential area of Kurrentgasse. The building at No. 2, the former Obizzi Palace (1690), now houses

Entrance to the unique Clock Museum in Schulhof

a fascinating **Clock Museum**, which has more than 3,000 exhibits. The museum provides its visitors with a comprehensive account of the history of chronometry through the ages and of clock technology from the 15th century to the present day. The Biedermeier and Belle Epoque periods are particularly well presented. A major highlight is the interesting 18th-century astronomical clock by the Augustinian friar David a Sancto Cajetano.

At every full hour the three floors of the museum resound to the striking, chiming and playing of numerous clocks. All are carefully maintained to keep the correct time. This is something of a startling experience, although quite enchanting.

A short distance from here, at No. 10 Kurrentgasse, is the bakery Grimm, one of the most famous in Vienna.

ⓚ Am Hof

Map 2 B3. Ⓤ Stephansplatz, Herrengasse. ⓦ 1A, 2A, 3A.

The name of the square (meaning "by the Court") refers to the medieval princes' residence nearby. It later housed the mint, and then the royal military chancery. Today it is a bank.

The main architectural gem of present-day Am Hof is the church of the Nine Angel Choirs, built in the late 14th century by the Carmelite Friars and rebuilt after the fire of 1607. It was adorned with a Baroque façade crowned with a triangular pediment featuring Our Lady, the queen of the nine angel choirs. The dissolution of the Holy Roman Empire was proclaimed from the church's terrace on 6 August 1806.

There are a number of other interesting houses in the square. The building at No. 10 with a magnificent façade incorporating sculptures by Lorenzo Mattielli, is the former citizens' armoury, today housing the headquarters of the city's fire services. No. 14 is the

Statue on top of No. 10 Am Hof, the former citizens' armoury

Collalto Palace, where, in 1762, the six-year-old Mozart gave his first performance.

In front of the church stands the Mariensäule (Column of Our Lady), a monument commissioned by Ferdinand III to commemorate the end of the threat of the Swedish invasion, at the conclusion of the Thirty Years' War.

㉑ Freyung

Map 2 B3. Ⓤ Herrengasse, Schottentor. 🚌 1A, 2A. 🚋 1, 71, D.

The square derives its name from the right of sanctuary (frey is an old word for "free") granted to any fugitive seeking refuge in the Schottenkirche (Scottish church), now at No. 6. The priory church was founded by Irish Benedictine friars, who came to Vienna in 1177. Although much altered, the church has

Ferstel's fountain in the passage linking Freyung with Herrengasse

a Neo-Classical façade and a magnificent Baroque interior, which still bears features of its former Romanesque decor. Above the tabernacle stands the 13th-century statue of Our Lady, the oldest Romanesque sculpture in Vienna.

The adjacent abbey buildings house a picture gallery with an interesting collection of medieval art.

Other interesting buildings in Freyung include the Baroque Harrach Palace at No. 3, designed by Domenico Martinelli (1690) and, at No. 4, the Kinsky Palace, designed by Johann Lukas von Hildebrandt, who became the court architect in 1700.

Nearby is one of the few remaining, largely unaltered Renaissance buildings, the Porcia Palace of 1546, one of the oldest in Vienna.

At the centre of the square, in a glass-roofed, hexagonal atrium, stands the Austria Fountain. Erected in 1846, it shows an allegorical figure of Austria surrounded by four mermaids representing the major rivers (Danube, Elbe, Po, Vistula) in the Habsburg Empire at the time.

㉒ Herrengasse

Map 2 A3, B4. Ⓤ Herrengasse. 🚌 1A, 2A.

Herrengasse was once one of the smartest addresses in Vienna, where the nobility had their palaces. Nowadays, most buildings are occupied by government offices.

Herrengasse's name, meaning gentlemen's alleyway, dates from the 16th century, when the Landhaus at No. 13 was the seat of the Provincial Government of Lower Austria, the province surrounding Vienna. It fulfilled this function until 1986, when the small town of St Pölten became the new capital of the province. Some very old parts of the Landhaus still remain; the chapel is believed to have been built by Anton Pilgram, one of the architects of Stephansdom. The present building was

rebuilt in 1837–48, under the supervision of Ludwig Pichl. In the courtyard, a tablet from 1571 warns visitors not to carry weapons or fight here. The injunction was famously ignored when the 1848 Revolution was ignited on this very spot. In 1918 the Republic was proclaimed from the Landhaus.

Liechtenstein Palace, seen from Minoritenplatz

㉓ Minoritenplatz

Map 2 B4. Ⓤ Herrengasse. 🚌 1A, 2A. 🚋 1, 71, D.

The dominant feature of the square is Minoritenkirche. Built originally by Minor Friars in 1224, the present structure is a Franciscan church from the 14th century. It was rebuilt during the Baroque period, and restored to its original Gothic form in the 19th century. The church retains a fine west portal (1340). The tower acquired its unusual pyramid shape during the Turkish siege of Vienna in 1529, when a shell sliced the top off the steeple. Inside the church is a mosaic copy of Leonardo da Vinci's *Last Supper*.

Between Minoritenplatz and Bankgasse is the town palace of the Liechtenstein family.

On the west side of the square, at No. 3, is the former palace of the Dietrichstein family. This palace, an early work in 1755 by Franz Hillebrand, now houses the Austrian Chancellor's Office and the Foreign Office. Its rooms have witnessed many historic events.

Street-by-Street: The Hofburg Complex

The Hofburg Complex, the former Emperor's residence, is a permanent reminder of the glory of the Habsburg Empire, with its majestic palace – particularly impressive when seen from Heldenplatz – and the harmony of the squares and palaces in Augustinerstrasse. This part of Vienna is one of the capital's most fashionable and lively areas, both during the daytime and at night, when the former palace rooms serve as theatre and concert halls.

㉔ Michaelerplatz
The Michaelertrakt, on the site of the former court theatre on the south side of the square, was commissioned by Franz Joseph as a passageway and built to designs by Ferdinand Kirschner.

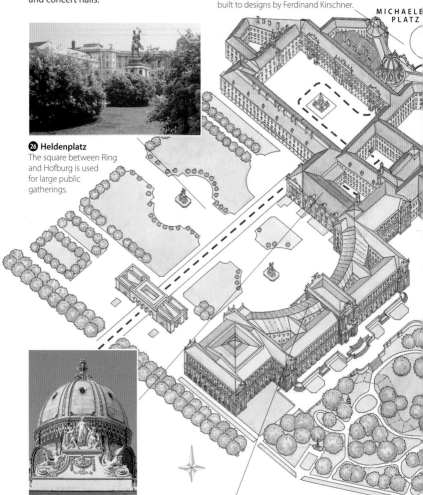

MICHAELE
PLATZ

㉖ Heldenplatz
The square between Ring and Hofburg is used for large public gatherings.

㉗ ★ Alte Burg
The old palace was the official Habsburg residence from the 13th century.

Neue Burg, the last wing of Hofburg, was built just before the outbreak of World War I, during the final days of the monarchy.

Kohlmarkt has some of the smartest shops in town, including some designed by the renowned architect Hans Hollein.

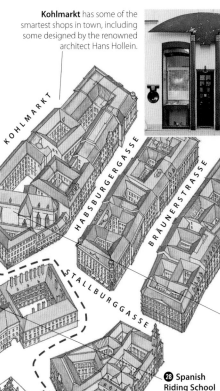

K O H L M A R K T

H A B S B U R G E R G A S S E

B R Ä U N E R S T R A S S E

S T A L L B U R G G A S S E

A U G U S T I N E R S T R A S S E

Locator Map
See Street Finder, map 2

INNER CITY

SOUTH OF THE RING

Inside Michaelerkirche the Rococo main altar and the 14th-century Renaissance frescoes are spectacular.

㉘ Spanish Riding School
The Riding School, where shows of the graceful, white Lipizzaner horses take place, is one of Vienna's star attractions.

```
0 metres        30
0 yards         30
```

Key
━ Suggested route

㉚ Augustinerkirche
The church's Loreto chapel contains silver urns preserving the hearts of the Habsburg family.

㉛ ★ Albertina
The palace, built in 1781, now houses one of the finest collections of graphic art in Europe.

㉙ ★ Josefsplatz
This beautiful square was named after Emperor Joseph II, whose statue stands at its centre.

Stucco angels in Michaelerkirche, Michaelerplatz

❷ Michaelerplatz

Map 2 B4. Ⓤ Herrengasse. 🚌 2A, 3A.

Michaelerplatz faces the grand main entrance into the imperial residence, the Michaelertor (St Michael's Doorway), which leads to the Hofburg's inner courtyard. On both sides of the doorway are 19th-century wall fountains, designed by Rudolf Weyr, which represent the empire's land and sea power.

Michaelerkirche (St Michael's Church) was once the parish church of the court. Its oldest parts date from the 13th century. According to legend, the church was built in 1221 by Leopold VI of Babenberg. Its present form dates from 1792, when it was given a Neo-Classical façade, while still preserving its Baroque portal. The interior features one of the most beautiful Rococo altars in Vienna. Above the altar is a stucco relief depicting the expulsion of the rebel angels from heaven and the Archangel Gabriel at the head of the heavenly host.

In the 17th and 18th centuries, affluent parishioners were buried under the church. Their well-preserved corpses, clothed in their burial finery, are displayed in the crypt, in open coffins.

The remains of a Roman encampment, as well as some medieval foundations, were discovered underneath the square in 1990.

❷ Volksgarten

Dr-Karl-Renner-Ring. **Map** 2 A4.
Ⓤ Herrengasse. 🚋 1, 2, 71, D. 🚌 2A.
Open Apr–Oct: 6am–10pm daily;
Nov–Mar: 7:30am–5:30pm daily.

Volksgarten (the People's Garden) was created in 1820, when Napoleon had the city walls destroyed. The sophisticated, formal plantations created in the French style, particularly the splendid rose gardens, became a place of relaxation for fashionable society.

People met at one of two Classicist structures by Peter von Nobile, Theseustempel (the Temple of Theseus) or Cortisches Kaffeehaus, remains of which are visible in today's Garden Café. Canova's statue of Theseus was meant for the temple, but today it graces the Kunsthistorisches Museum (see pp88–91). Instead, a statue of an athlete (1921) by Josef Müllner stands in front of the temple. There is also a monument devoted to the writer Franz Grillparzer and a fountain memorial dedicated to Empress Elisabeth.

❷ Heldenplatz

Map 2 A4, A5. Ⓤ Volkstheater, Herrengasse. 🚋 1, 2, 71, D. 🚌 1A, 2A, 46, 49, 57A. Neue Burg museums:
Tel 52 524-5202. **Open** 10am–6pm Wed–Sun. 🅿 🖼

During Vienna's grand 19th-century reconstruction, Heldenplatz was planned as the centre of a majestic imperial forum that was to adjoin the old Hofburg complex, surrounded by new buildings housing the emperor's art collection. Neue Burg (New Castle) was completed in 1913, but by then the monarchy was dying out.

The vast, undeveloped Heroes' Square, the largest public space in Vienna, remained. It was here, in March 1938, that Adolf Hitler announced Austria's incorporation into the German Reich.

The entrance to the square is via Ballhausplatz or Burgtor (Palace Gate), built in 1824 to commemorate the victory of the coalition against Napoleon in the Battle of Nations, at Leipzig (1813). Later, it served as the Monument to the Unknown Soldier. The two equestrian statues in the square, by Anton Dominik von Fernkorn, are of Archduke Charles and Prince Eugene of Saxony.

The latter stands in front of Neue Burg, which now houses a number of museums including the Ephesos Museum, named after the archaeological site in Turkey which yielded the finds on display here; a collection of early musical instruments, some owned by famous musicians; and one of the most impressive arms collections in Europe.

The equestrian statue of Prince Eugene of Saxony, Heldenplatz

❷ Alte Burg

See pp72–3.

❷❽ Spanish Riding School

The Spanish Riding School was founded in 1572. Initially, its circus-style training of horses served a practical purpose, but today performances are staged purely for entertainment, and have become one of the city's top attractions. Shows are held in the building known as the Winterreitschule (Winter Riding School), constructed between 1729 and 1735 by Joseph E. Fischer von Erlach. The Hofburg fire, in 1992, destroyed some of the stables and almost put an end to the school's activities.

VISITORS' CHECKLIST

Practical Information
Michaelerplatz 1. **Map** 2 B4.
Tel 53 39 031. **Open** 9am–4pm
daily. Shows: Jan–Jun, Aug–Dec:
10am– noon Tue–Sat. 🖭 🖰 2pm,
3pm & 4pm daily. 🆆 **srs.at**

Transport
Ⓤ Herrengasse, Stephansplatz.
🚌 1A, 2A.

Black bicorn hat with gold braid stripe

Coffee-coloured jacket with rows of brass buttons

Long boots covering the knees

Pale leather gloves

Interior of the Winter Riding School
The opulent interior is lined with 46 columns and adorned with stucco ornaments, chandeliers and a coffered ceiling.

Buckskin jodhpurs

Rider in Typical Uniform
The riders of the Winter Riding School wear historical uniforms, which are complemented by elegant saddles with embroidered cloth.

The Horses' Steps
The steps made by the horses are part of a carefully orchestrated ballet. The riders perform on the specially trained white Lipizzaner stallions, a breed originally produced by crossing Spanish, Arab and Berber horses.

The Levade
The horse stands on its hind legs, hocks almost touching the ground.

The Capriole
The horse leaps into the air with a simultaneous kick of the hind legs.

The Piaffe
The horse trots on the spot, often between two pillars.

The Croupade
The horse leaps into the air with hind legs and forelegs bent under its belly.

⑰ Alte Burg

The Imperial Palace is a vast complex. Its construction was started by the Babenbergs, but the Neue Burg (New Castle) was not completed until 1913. Apart from housing several museums, including in the royal apartments a museum dedicated to Empress Elisabeth, the Alte Burg is today also a conference centre. Different architectural styles are represented in individual parts of the complex: the Gothic Schweizerhof, the Renaissance Stallburg courtyard and the Baroque Josefsplatz.

In der Burg
This large inner courtyard, called "inside the fortress", has a large statue of Franz I, built by Pompeo Marchesi, in 1842–46.

The Silberkammer
The Silver Chamber displays stunning silver, gold and porcelain tableware, and vessels used at official receptions, such as this 1821 goblet.

Amalienburg
In the 19th century, this Renaissance palace, built for Rudolf II in 1575, was the home of Empress Elisabeth. Shown above is her dressing room with gymnastic equipment.

KEY

① **The Leopoldinischer Trakt**, dating from 1660–70 and built by Leopold I, today houses the offices of the President of Austria.

② **Michaelertor**, leading to Hofburg

③ **The Spanish Riding School** stages its world-famous horse riding performances at the Winterreitschule (Winter Riding School).

④ **Stallburg**, a Renaissance palace, houses the stables.

⑤ **Redoutensäle**, the former ballrooms.

★ **Schweizertor**
The 16th-century Baroque Swiss Gate leads to the oldest parts of the castle, originally a four-tower stronghold.

★ **Reichskanzleitrakt**
Franz Joseph's apartments in the Imperial Chancery Wing, built in 1726–30, are open to visitors. This portrait of Empress Elisabeth (1865) hangs in the Sisi Museum.

VISITORS' CHECKLIST

Practical Information
Michaelerplatz 1. **Map** 2 B4.
Tel 533 75 70.
Imperial Apartments: **Tel** 533 75 70.
Open 9am–5:30pm daily (until 6pm Jul & Aug). **W** hofburg-wien.at
Treasury: **Tel** 525 24. **Open** 9am–5:30pm Wed–Mon.
W kaiserliche-schatzkammer.at

Transport
U Stephansplatz, Herrengasse.
1, 2, 71, D. 1A, 2A, 49, 57A.

★ **Schatzkammer**
The collection of sacred and secular treasures, including this 10th-century crown, is regarded as the most magnificent of its kind in the world.

The Burgkapelle
The Gothic Royal Chapel was completed in 1449. The Wiener Sängerknaben (the Vienna Boys' Choir) sings here on Sundays.

Nationalbibliothek
The showpiece of the Austrian National Library (1722–35) is the opulent Prunksaal, or Hall of Honour, panelled in wood.

The magnificent Prunksaal in the National Library, Josefsplatz

㉙ Josefsplatz

Map 2 B4. Ⓤ Stephansplatz, Herrengasse. 🚌 1A, 2A.

In the centre of Josefsplatz stands an equestrian statue (1807) of Joseph II portrayed as a Roman emperor, by Franz Anton Zauner.

Behind the statue, to the right, is the entrance to the National Library building designed by Johann Bernhard Fischer von Erlach. Its Prunksaal (Hall of Honour) is regarded as the most beautiful library in Europe. Frescoes by the Baroque painter Daniel Gran adorn its vault. The walls of the historic reading room are graced by Johann Bergl's frescoes.

Perhaps the grandest items in the library's rich collection are the cartographic treasures exhibited just behind the Prunksaal.

The Redoutensäle, in the wing adjacent to the library and once the Court Ballrooms, now serve as the head office of the Vienna Congress Centre.

On the opposite side of Josefsplatz are two interesting palaces: at No. 5 is the 18th-century Pallavicini Palace by Johann Ferdinand Hetzendorf von Hohenberg, and at No. 6 the 16th-century Palffy Palace

by Nikolaus Pacassi. They now serve as cultural venues for the city.

㉚ Augustinerkirche

Augustinerstrasse 3. **Map** 2 B5. **Tel** 53 37 099. Ⓤ Stephansplatz, Karlsplatz, Oper. 🚌 2A. **Open** 7am–6pm daily. Mass: 11am Sun & church hols.

The 14th-century Gothic Augustinian church was refurbished in the Baroque style, but some 100 years later was restored again to its original character. Inside is one of the most powerful works by Antonio Canova (1805), the tomb of Maria Christina, Maria Theresa's favourite daughter. It is shaped like a pyramid, approached by a funeral procession. St George's Chapel, on the right, contains a marble cenotaph dedicated to Emperor Leopold II, while further along in the Loreto chapel are silver urns containing the hearts of the Habsburg family, including Leopold II's, as well as the heart of Napoleon's son, the King of Rome, who died when young.

Tomb of Maria Christina in Augustinerkirche

The church was once the Court Chapel and, as such, the scene of many historic

events including the royal wedding of Marie Louise (1812) to Napoleon, and that of Elisabeth of Bavaria (Sisi) to Franz Joseph (1854).

㉛ Albertina

Albertinaplatz 1. **Map** 2 B5. **Tel** 534 830. Ⓤ Stephansplatz, Karlsplatz. 🚋 1, 2, 62, 71, D. 🚌 2A. **Open** 10am–6pm daily, 10am–9pm Wed. 🌐 albertina.at

The Albertina was once the Habsburg palace of Duke Albert of Sachsen-Teschen and his wife Archduchess Maria Christina, the favourite daughter of Maria Theresa.

The beautiful Neo-Classical Historic State Rooms in the palace are among the most valuable examples of Classical architecture. They have been opened up to visitors.

The Albertina houses one of the world's finest collection of prints and drawings, including works by famous artists such as Leonardo da Vinci, Michelangelo, Dürer, Rubens, Manet and Cezanne, as well as by Schiele, Klimt and Picasso. It has a million prints, over 65,000 watercolours and drawings and some 100,000 photographs. It is also home to the Sammlung Batliner, a collection of paintings under the motto "Monet to Picasso".

🟤 Kapuzinerkirche and Kaisergruft

Neuer Markt. **Map** 2 C5. **Tel** 51 26 853.
🚇 Stephansplatz, Karlsplatz. 🚃 2A.
Open 10am–6pm daily. 🚫

The Capuchin church stands at the southwestern corner of Neuer Markt, formerly a cereal and flour market. In 1617, Anna of Tyrol, wife of Emperor Matthias, founded a crypt in its vaults in which the Habsburg family members were laid to rest. Today, the Kaisergruft (imperial crypt) contains the earthly remains of 138 family members. The only Habsburg monarchs not present are Ferdinand II, whose vast tomb-mausoleum is in Graz, and Charles I, the last Austrian emperor who died in exile and is buried on Madeira. The only non-Habsburg buried here is Maria Theresa's governess, Countess Caroline Fuchs.

The double sarcophagus of Maria Theresa and her husband Franz Stephan I, the work of Balthasar Ferdinand Moll, is worth looking at. It bears the statues of the imperial couple and four figures with the crowns of Austria, Hungary, Bohemia and Jerusalem (the Habsburgs were also the titular Kings of Jerusalem).

The most poignant tomb is the crypt of Franz Joseph I, where the long-lived monarch rests, flanked by separate tombs containing the remains of his wife Elisabeth, assassinated by an Italian anarchist, and their only son Crown Prince Rudolf, who committed suicide in 1889.

The last person to be buried in the imperial crypt was Archduke Otto, son of Charles I, the last Emperor of Austria, who was interred in 1989.

It is worth noting that, on their death, the Habsburgs were dismembered; their hearts are kept in silver urns in Augustinerkirche (*see p74*), their entrails are held in the catacombs of Stephansdom (*see pp62–3*), and only what remained is in the Kaisergruft (imperial crypt).

Tomb of Karl VI, by Balthasar Moll

Grand stairway in the Winterpalais des Prinzen Eugen

🟤 Winterpalais des Prinzen Eugen

Himmelpfortgasse 8. **Map** 2 C5.
Tel 51 433. 🚇 Stephansplatz. 🚃 2A.
🚋 2. **Open** 10am–6pm daily.

The palace was commissioned in 1694, by Prince Eugene of Savoy, one of the most brilliant military commanders of his day, who entrusted the task to Johann Bernhard Fischer von Erlach. It was subsequently extended by Johann Lukas von Hildebrandt. Its central part includes the original magnificent staircase, adorned with sculptures by Giovanni Giuliani. The central portal reliefs depict the figure of Aeneas carrying his father out of the burning city of Troy, and the hero Hercules who is slaying a monster.

From 1848 until 2006, the palace was home to the Ministry of Finance. After extensive renovation, the palace today houses the Baroque collection of the Belvedere (*see pp102–3*).

Nearby, at Seilerstätte No. 30, is the Haus der Musik (House of Music). This is a museum dedicated to the Wiener Philharmoniker (Vienna Philharmonic), it also houses a high-tech exhibition on the nature of sound, which allows visitors to see and feel as well as hear music.

🟤 Kärntner Strasse

Map 2 B5, C4, C5. 🚇 Stephansplatz, Karlsplatz. 🚃 1A, 2A, 3A.
🚋 1, 2, 62, 71, D.

Kärntner Strasse was once the main road running south across town to Kärnten (Carinthia), hence its name.

Today, the view down the street is blocked at its Ring end by the silhouette of the opera house, and at the Stock-im-Eisen-Platz end by the modern Haas-Haus, which reflects the spires of the Stephansdom. At Stock-im-Eisen-Platz there is a wooden block into which every passing apprentice ironworker used to drive a nail, in the hope that this would ensure his safe return.

In the mid-section, at No. 37, stands the Malteserkirche (Church of the Knights of Malta). The Maltese Knights came to Vienna in the early 13th century, and the church remains under their jurisdiction to this day. The church walls display the coats of arms of the Grand Masters of the Maltese Order.

Malteserkirche is one of the few older buildings in the street. When Kärntner Strasse was widened during the 19th century, to transform it into the old town's main artery, most of the buildings were demolished.

Today, the pedestrianized street is one of Vienna's most fashionable and expensive shopping streets. Here, you can shop at one of many exclusive boutiques, eat and drink in busy restaurants, bars and outdoor cafés, and listen to street musicians or just watch others stroll by.

Frauenhuber, a café near Kärntner Strasse

NORTH OF MARIAHILFER STRASSE

This district, to the north of Mariahilfer Strasse and along the Ring, includes some of the most magnificent and monumental buildings in Vienna. The semicircular Ring or Ringstrasse, developed during the 1870s and 1880s, is a grand boulevard divided into nine sections, each named after architectural landmarks or prominent politicians from the Habsburg era. Today, it is still Vienna's most prestigious street and is home to several important sights. In this district visitors will find many of the city's cultural institutions, including the biggest concentration of museums in Austria. Mariahilfer Strasse is also a very busy shopping street, with large department stores and many quaint cafés and bars, concentrated especially in the cobbled, pedestrianized streets of the bustling Spittelberg area.

Sights at a Glance

Streets
⓲ Mariahilfer Strasse
⓳ Spittelberg

Historic Buildings
❶ Neues Rathaus
❷ Parlament
❸ Burgtheater pp82–3
❹ Universität
❼ Josephinum
❽ Old AKH – University Campus
⓬ Theater in der Josefstadt
⓭ Palais Trautson
⓮ Volkstheater

Churches
❺ Votivkirche
❾ Dreifaltigkeitskirche
⓫ Maria-Treu-Kirche

Museums and Galleries
❻ Freud-Museum
❿ Museum für Volkskunde
⓯ Naturhistorisches Museum
⓰ Kunsthistorisches Museum pp88–91
⓱ MuseumsQuartier

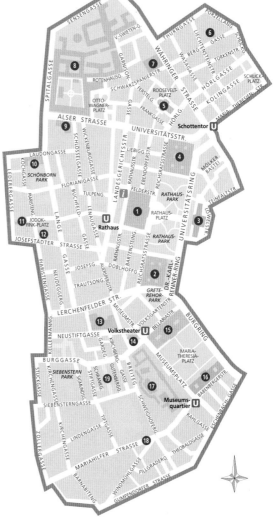

0 metres 300
0 yards 300

See also Street Finder, maps 1, 2 & 4

◀ Impressive Gothic spires of the Votivkirche

Street-by-Street: Around the Town Hall

The most prestigious buildings in Vienna were erected in the second half of the 19th century, in Ringstrasse, at the command of Emperor Franz Joseph I. These include Neues Rathaus (the new town hall, seat of the town administration), the immense Parlament (the seat of Austria's Upper and Lower Houses), the magnificent buildings of the University, and the Burgtheater.

The square in front of the town hall, with its adjacent park, is Vienna's largest open-air arena, serving as a stage for theatre and concert performances, and in the summer for vast film screenings.

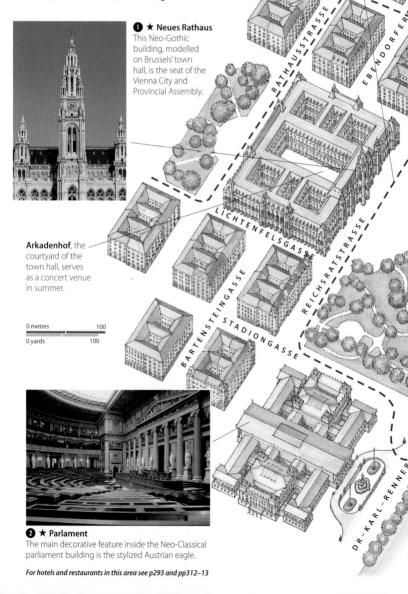

The Town Hall forecourt turns into a vast Christmas market in December, selling gifts and Christmas decorations.

❶ ★ **Neues Rathaus**
This Neo-Gothic building, modelled on Brussels' town hall, is the seat of the Vienna City and Provincial Assembly.

Arkadenhof, the courtyard of the town hall, serves as a concert venue in summer.

| 0 metres | | 100 |
| 0 yards | | 100 |

❷ ★ **Parlament**
The main decorative feature inside the Neo-Classical parliament building is the stylized Austrian eagle.

For hotels and restaurants in this area see p293 and pp312–13

❹ ★ Universität
The University courtyard is surrounded by arcades lined with busts of its professors.

Locator Map
See Street Finder maps 1 & 2

Plaque from the Pasqualati house at Mölker-Bastei No. 8, which, in 1804–8 and again in 1810–15, was the home of Ludwig van Beethoven. It was here that he composed his opera Fidelio, as well as Symphonies 4, 5, 7 and 8. Today, the house is a small museum.

Statue of Liebenberg, the gallant mayor of Vienna during the Turkish siege of the town in 1683.

Café Landtmann, opened in 1873, is the coffee house of the affluent middle classes, and was once Sigmund Freud's favourite haunt.

Key

— Suggested route

❸ ★ Burgtheater
The high attic above the centre of the building is decorated with a frieze depicting a Bacchanalian procession.

Pallas Athena monument in front of the parliament building

the representatives of the 17 peoples of the Empire. The magnificently decorated state apartments and conference rooms can be visited in a guided tour. The lower vestibule contains busts of prominent members of the Austrian National Assembly.

The side wings have four bronze chariot groups, each driven by Nike, the Greek goddess of victory. Another, smaller statue of Nike is held aloft by her fellow goddess, of wisdom, Pallas Athena, whose 5-m (16-ft) statue is the main feature of the monumental fountain in front of the central portico, designed by Carl Kundmann and placed here in 1902. It is flanked by allegorical figures representing Law Enforcement (left) and Legislation (right), as well as figures symbolizing the major rivers of the empire.

❶ Neues Rathaus

Friedrich-Schmidt-Platz 1. **Map** 1 C3.
Tel 52 550. Ⓤ Rathaus. 🚋 1, 71, D.
Open 8am–6pm Mon–Fri. 🎫 1pm
Mon, Wed & Fri. **Closed** during
meetings and public holidays.

The new town hall, built in 1872–83 by Friedrich Schmidt, lies in an attractive park. The symmetrical, triple façade of the Neo-Gothic building faces Ringstrasse. Its central tower, 98 m (321 ft) high, is topped by the statue of a knight-in-armour, one of Vienna's symbols. The main tower is flanked by two smaller towers, 60 m (197 ft) high. The town hall cellar is a restaurant. The whole length of the first floor is taken up by a reception hall. The forecourt is used for many events, including the Christmas fair.

❷ Parlament

Dr-Karl-Renner-Ring 3. **Map** 1 C4.
Tel 40 11 00-25 70. Ⓤ Volkstheater.
🚋 1, 2, 71, D. 🎫 Sep–mid-Jul: 11am,
2pm, 3pm, 4pm Mon–Sat (also 1pm
Fri, noon & 1pm Sat); mid-Jul–Aug:
11am, noon, 1pm, 2pm, 3pm, 4pm
Mon–Sat. 🆆 **parlament.gv.at**

Today's assembly hall of Austria's two-chamber parliament originally served as the location

of the highest legislative body of the Austrian part of the Austro-Hungarian Empire. An imposing Neo-Classical building, the Parlament was completed in 1883 to designs by the Dutch architect, Theophil Hansen.

The entrance is raised above street level. A gently sloping ramp leads to the main portico, which is modelled on a Greek temple. Both the ramp and the attic are adorned with carved marble figures of Greek and Roman historians, scholars and statesmen. The relief depicts the Emperor Franz Joseph I handing the constitution to

❸ Burgtheater

See pp82–3.

❹ Universität

Universitätsring. **Map** 2 A3. **Tel** 42 77 0.
Ⓤ Schottentor. 🚋 1, 37, 38, 40, 41,
42, 43, 44, 71, D. 🚌 1A.

Vienna University is the oldest university in the German-speaking world and the third oldest in Central Europe, after Prague and Cracow. It was founded in 1365, by Rudolf IV, and flourished and grew in the late 15th century. Its present

The main building of Vienna University

home, designed by Heinrich von Ferstel in the style of the Italian Renaissance, was completed in 1883.

The university complex has its buildings arranged around one large and eight smaller courtyards. The courtyard arcades, modelled on the Palazzo Farnese in Rome, are adorned with statues of famous scholars associated with Vienna University, including one of Freud.

Neo-Gothic stone figures from the façade of Votivkirche

❺ Votivkirche

Rooseveltplatz. **Map** 2 A2.
Tel 40 61 192. Ⓤ Schottentor.
🚊 1, 37, 38, 40, 41, 42, 43, 44, 71, D.
Open 7am–6pm daily.

Opposite the spot where a deranged man tried to assassinate Franz Joseph I in 1853, stands this Neo-Gothic church with its two 99-m (325-ft) high, lacy steeples completed 26 years later as a grateful offering for sparing the Emperor's life. The architect was Heinrich von Ferstel.

The most beautiful historic relic in the Votivkirche is its late 15th-century Antwerpian altar, a masterpiece of Flemish woodcarving, representing scenes from Christ's Passion. The main portal sculptures depict the four Evangelists and figures from the Old Testament, along with four patrons of the Empire's regions.

Many of the chapels inside the church are dedicated to the Austrian regiments and to military heroes.

Sigmund Freud's waiting room in the Freud-Museum

❻ Freud-Museum

Berggasse 19. **Map** 2 A1.
Tel 31 91 596. Ⓤ Schottentor.
🚊 37, 38, 40, 41, 42, D. 🚌 40A.
Open 10am–6pm daily.
Ⓦ freud-museum.at

Berggasse No. 19, a typical 20th-century Viennese town house, was the home of Sigmund Freud, the famous doctor and father of psychoanalysis, from 1891–1938. Here he created his most acclaimed works and treated patients before he was forced to flee Austria at the arrival of the Nazis.

The room in which Freud received patients is on the mezzanine floor. In the small, dark lobby hangs Freud's frayed hat; in a corner stands his travel trunk. His walking stick can also be seen here. A cabinet contains some archaeological objects collected by Freud. The world-famous couch, however, is now on display in the Freud museum in London.

A Foundation for the Arts was initiated in 1989 in order to confront a scientific institution with contemporary art.

❼ Josephinum

Währingerstrasse 25. **Map** 1 C2.
Tel 40 160-26 001. Ⓤ Schottentor.
🚊 37, 38, 40, 41, 42. **Open** 10am–6pm Mon–Sat. **Closed** public holidays.

Designed by Isidor Canevale and built in 1783–85, this building once housed the Military Surgical Institute. Life-sized anatomical wax models, commissioned by Joseph II to teach human anatomy to his army surgeons, are now the main attraction of the medical museum based here today.

❽ Old AKH – University Campus

Alser Strasse 4/Spitalgasse 2.
Map 1 A1, B1. Ⓤ Schottentor.
Federal Museum of Pathological Anatomy: Spitalgasse 2. **Tel** 521 77 606. **Open** 10am–6pm Wed, 10am–1pm Sat. **Closed** public holidays. Ⓦ univie.ac.at

Vienna's Old General Hospital (AKH), built in 1784, was donated to the University of Vienna in 1988 and adapted to house the 15 academic faculties of the university.

It was inaugurated in 1998 as university campus. The huge complex consists of several buildings around one vast and 12 smaller courtyards. The Narrenturm (Madman's Tower) of the former lunatic asylum, designed by architect Isidor Canevale, now houses the **Federal Museum for Pathological Anatomy**.

Freud's Theories

With his theory of psychoanalysis, Sigmund Freud (1856–1939) has exerted a lasting influence not only on medicine but also on our culture generally. In 1896, he coined the term "psychoanalysis". According to Freud, the unconscious psyche, driven by certain instincts and impulses, in particular the sexual instinct (libido), is the main engine behind all our conscious and unconscious actions. An imbalance in the psychological system, so Freud suggested, could lead to very serious emotional disorders and might result in severe mental disturbance.

Various objects used by Sigmund Freud

❸ Burgtheater

The Burgtheater is one of the most prestigious stages in the German-speaking world. The original theatre, built in Maria Theresa's reign, was replaced in 1888 by today's Italian Renaissance-style building by Karl von Hasenauer and Gottfried Semper. In 1897, after the discovery that the auditorium had several seats with no view of the stage, it closed for refurbishment. A bomb devastated the building in 1945, leaving only the side wings and Grand Staircases intact, but subsequent restoration was so successful that today the damage is hard to see.

Busts of Playwrights
Lining the walls of the Grand Staircases are busts of playwrights whose works are still performed here, including this one of Johann Nepomuk Nestroy *(left)* by Hans Knesl.

JOHANN NESTROY 1801–1862

★ Grand Staircases
The two majestic gala staircases in the side wings are the only original parts of the building that escaped destruction in World War II.

Main entrance on Universitätsring

KEY

① **Ceiling frescoes** by the Klimt brothers, Gustav and Ernst, and Franz Matsch cover the north and south wings.

② **Statue of the muse, Melpomene**

③ **Statue of the muse, Thalia**

Foyer
The walls of the curving first-floor foyer are lined with the portraits of famous actors and actresses.

Auditorium
During rebuilding after the war, the original layout was kept in the auditorium with the imperial colours of red, gold and cream. It seats over 1,000 spectators.

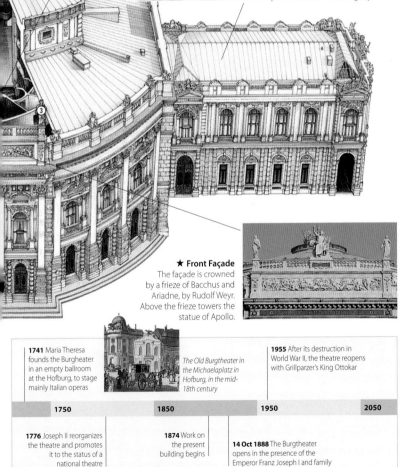

VISITORS' CHECKLIST

Practical Information
Universitätsring.
Map 2 A3.
Tel 51 444 41 40.
Open Guided tours 3pm daily; performances: Sep–Jun; tickets: 8am–6pm Mon–Fri, 9am–noon Sat, Sun & hol. 🦽 📷
Ⓦ burgtheater.at

Transport
Ⓤ Herrengasse, Rathaus, Schottentor. 🚊 1, 2, 71, D.

★ Der Thespiskarren
The ceiling frescoes in the side wings are by the Klimt brothers and Franz Matsch. This one, by Gustav Klimt, depicts the cart of Thespis, first performer of a Greek tragedy.

★ Front Façade
The façade is crowned by a frieze of Bacchus and Ariadne, by Rudolf Weyr. Above the frieze towers the statue of Apollo.

1741 Maria Theresa founds the Burgtheater in an empty ballroom at the Hofburg, to stage mainly Italian operas

The Old Burgtheater in the Michaelaplatz in Hofburg, in the mid-18th century

1955 After its destruction in World War II, the theatre reopens with Grillparzer's King Ottokar

1750	1850	1950	2050

1776 Joseph II reorganizes the theatre and promotes it to the status of a national theatre

1874 Work on the present building begins

14 Oct 1888 The Burgtheater opens in the presence of the Emperor Franz Joseph I and family

❾ Dreifaltigkeits-kirche der Minoriten

Alser Strasse 17. **Map** 1 B2. **Tel** 40 57 225. Ⓤ Rathaus. 🚋 5, 33, 43, 44. **Open** 7:30am–noon Mon–Fri, Sun, 7:30–8:30am Sat.

Built between 1685 and 1727, the church of the Holy Trinity is a typical Baroque structure, with a twin-tower façade. It contains an altarpiece (1708) in the north aisle by the painter Martino Altomonte, and a beautiful crucifix in the south aisle from the workshop of Veit Stoss.

In 1827, the body of the composer Ludwig van Beethoven was brought to this church, from Schwarzspanierhaus in neighbouring Garnisonsgasse where he had died. Following the funeral service, attended by his contemporaries (including Schubert and the playwright Franz Grillparzer), the cortège conveyed his coffin to its final resting place, the cemetery in Währing, on the city outskirts.

16th-century crucifix in the Dreifaltigkeitskirche

❿ Museum für Volkskunde

Laudongasse 15–19. **Map** 1 B3. **Tel** 40 68 905. Ⓤ Rathaus. 🚋 5, 33, 43, 44. 🚌 13A. **Open** 10am–5pm Tue–Sun. 🅿 ♿ 🆆 volkskundemuseum.at

Near a quiet park stands the charming Austrian Folklore Museum. Founded in 1895, it moved in 1917 to its present

Entrance to the Museum für Volkskunde, Schönborn Palace

premises, the former Schönborn Palace, built in 1706–11 to designs by Johann Lukas von Hildebrandt as a homely two-storey mansion, and altered in 1760 by court architect, Isidor Canevale. The building has a rather imposing façade with statues running along its top.

In the museum you will find artifacts reflecting popular culture in Austria and neighbouring countries that were once part of the Habsburg Empire. The collection includes furniture, textiles and ceramics, household and work tools, religious objects and two complete living rooms that illustrate the lifestyle, customs and rituals in the various regions. The core of the collection consists of objects from the 17th to 19th centuries.

On Lange Gasse, a couple of blocks along towards Josefstädter Strasse, you will pass the **Alte Backstube**, at No. 34. This old bakery is one of the loveliest town houses in Vienna. It was built in 1697 by the jeweller Hans Bernhard Leopold and was in continuous use until 1963. The rooms have been lovingly restored, retaining the old baking ovens, and house a traditional restaurant and café, and a small baking museum where baking equipment from the early 18th century can be seen.

⓫ Maria-Treu-Kirche

Jodok-Fink-Platz. **Map** 1 B3. **Tel** 40 50 425. Ⓤ Rathaus. 🚋 2. 🚌 13A. **Open** during mass or by appointment.

Originally designed by Johann Lukas von Hildebrandt in 1716, Maria Treu Kirche (church of Mary the Faithful) acquired its present form in the mid-19th century, when twin towers were added.

The church, as well as the adjacent monastic buildings, was founded by fathers of the Piarist Order, one of whose main aims is education; they also founded a primary and a secondary school next door. The homely cellar of the former monastery is today a pleasant restaurant.

The interior of the church is one of the best preserved in Vienna. Its Baroque ceiling frescoes, the work of the great Austrian painter Franz Anton Maulbertsch, are very lovely. They depict scenes from the life of the Virgin Mary and events from the Old and New Testaments. In one of the chapels, to the left of the presbytery, you can see an altarpiece of the crucifixion, also painted by Franz Anton Maulbertsch.

The Chapel of Our Lady of Sorrows contains the *pietà* known as Our Lady from Malta, which was brought here by the Knights of Malta.

In front of the church is a striking Baroque pillar, topped with a statue of the Madonna (1713), one of many such plague columns erected in Vienna as thanksgiving at the end of the plague era. In this case the column commemorates the epidemic of 1713.

Baroque frescoes in Maria-Treu-Kirche

For hotels and restaurants in this area see p293 and pp312–13

The opulent auditorium of Theater in der Josefstadt

⓬ Theater in der Josefstadt

Josefstädter Strasse 26. **Map** 1 B4.
Tel 42 700. Ⓤ Rathaus. 2. 13A.
🌐 josefstadt.org

This intimate theatre, one of the oldest still standing in Vienna, has enjoyed a glorious history. First established in 1788, the theatre was later much altered. After renovation by Joseph Kornhäusel, for its reopening in 1822, Ludwig van Beethoven composed his overture *The Consecration of the House*, conducting it himself at the reopening gala.

In 1924, the directorship of the theatre was given to Max Reinhardt, one of the most outstanding theatre directors and reformers, who supervised its further restoration and introduced an ambitious modern repertoire as well as magnificent productions of classic drama. He transformed what was once a middle-of-the-road provincial theatre into the most exciting stage in the German-speaking world.

The theatre is worth a visit for viewing its interior alone. As the lights slowly dim, the crystal chandeliers float gently to the ceiling. It offers excellent productions of Austrian plays, with an emphasis on comedy, classics and the occasional musical.

⓭ Palais Trautson

Museumstrasse 7. **Map** 1 C4.
Ⓤ Volkstheater. 49. 48A.
Closed to the public.

The Baroque Trautson Palace, built between 1710 and 1712 for Prince Johann Leopold Donat Trautson, to a design by Johann Bernhard Fischer von Erlach, was acquired by Maria Theresa in 1760. She then donated it to the Royal Hungarian Bodyguard, which she had founded.

The Neo-Classical façade, with rows of Doric columns, is heavily ornamented. Its finest sculptures, including that of Apollo playing the lyre, tower above the first-floor windows. The palace has a beautiful staircase, decorated with carvings of the sphinx, and columns of male figures who support the ceiling, by the sculptor Giovanni Giuliani. Since 1961 the palace has housed the Ministry of Justice, so there is no public access.

⓮ Volkstheater

Neustiftgasse 1. **Map** 1 C5.
Tel 52 111-0; tickets 52 111-400.
Ⓤ Volkstheater. 1, 2, 46, 49, 71, D.
48A. 🌐 **volkstheater.at**

Famed as a venue able to combine classic and modern drama with popular Viennese plays, the Volkstheater (People's Theatre) was, for many years, a staging post for directors and actors on their way from the provincial theatres to the estimable Burgtheater. Today, classic and modern, or even experimental drama dominate the repertoire. The Volkstheater presents many plays for the first time, or for the first time in the German language.

The Volkstheater was built in 1889 by the Austrian architects Ferdinand Fellner and Hermann Helmer. They employed the latest in theatre technology, including electric lighting throughout, and many theatre designers later copied their work. The auditorium, with more than 1,000 seats, is one of the largest in a theatre devoted to German-language drama, and is a great example of Viennese *fin-de-siècle* architecture. In front of the theatre stands a statue (1898) of the dramatist Ferdinand Raimund.

The majestic entrance to the 19th-century Volkstheater

The dinosaur room in the Naturhistorisches Museum

⓯ Naturhistorisches Museum

Burgring 7. **Map** 2 A5. **Tel** 52 177-0.
Ⓤ Volkstheater. 🚋 1, 2, 46, 49, 71, D.
🚌 48A. **Open** 9am–6:30pm Thu–
Mon, 9am–9pm Wed. **Closed** Tue,
1 Jan, 1 May, 1 Nov, 25 Dec. ♿ &
🆆 nhm-wien.ac.at

On two sides of Maria-Theresien-Platz are two identical buildings, designed by Gottfried Semper and Karl von Hasenauer. They were both built as museums at the time of Franz Joseph I, as part of the Ringstrasse development. Today, one is an art museum (Kunsthistorisches Museum, *see pp88–91*), the other the Natural History Museum, home to one of the richest and most wide-ranging collections in the world.

Many exhibits originally belonged to Maria Theresa's husband, Francis Stephen of Lorraine. The present permanent exhibition occupies two floors and consists of archaeological and anthropological displays, reconstructed specimens of extinct animals and one of the best gem collections in the world.

Among the most famous exhibits are the Hallstatt archaeological finds, dating from the early Iron Age, and the famous Venus of Willendorf – a 25,000-year-old stone statuette of a woman.

The Natural History Museum plays a very important role within the education system and its temporary exhibitions are organized mainly with schools in mind. The once famous exhibition showing the imaginary life of dinosaurs toured much of the world in the wake of Steven Spielberg's famous film *Jurassic Park*.

The museum holds several casts of dinosaur skeletons in its palaeontology department.

In the square between the buildings stands an imposing monument of Maria Theresa (1888) by Kaspar von Zumbusch. It shows the empress clasping the Pragmatic Section of 1713, enabling women to ascend to the throne. Below her are her generals and her principal nobles and advisors.

⓰ Kunsthistorisches Museum

See pp88–91.

⓱ MuseumsQuartier

Museumsplatz 1. **Map** 1 C5.
Tel 52 35 881. Ⓤ MuseumsQuartier,
Volkstheater. 🚋 1, 2, 46, 49, 71, D. 🚌
48A. Information: **Open** 10am–7pm
daily. 🆆 mqpoint.at. Museum of
Modern Art: **Open** 2–7pm Mon, 10am–
7pm Tue–Sun (to 9pm Thu). ♿
Admission free 26 Oct. 🆆 mumok.at
Leopold Museum: **Open** 10am–6pm
daily (to 9pm Thu). **Closed** Tue, public
holidays. ♿ 🆆 leopoldmuseum.org
Kunsthalle Wien: **Open** 10am–7pm
Mon–Sat (to 9pm Thu). ♿ &
🆆 kunsthallewien.at

Johann Bernhard Fischer von Erlach was commissioned by Emperor Karl VI to build the imperial stables on the escarpment behind the old town fortifications. In 1921, these Baroque buildings became a venue for fairs, and in the 1980s they were converted into a museum complex to designs by Laurids and Manfred Ortner. They changed the furnishings of the existing structures and added new ones, resulting in one of the world's largest cultural centres.

The MuseumsQuartier (Museum District) includes the **Kunsthalle Wien** (Vienna Art Hall) opposite the main entrance, behind the former premises of the Spanish Riding School. Vienna's main showcase for international contemporary art, the Kunsthalle is one of the city's most important art spaces, focusing on transdisciplinary work including photography, video, film and new media, as well as modern-art retrospectives.

To the left of the Kunsthalle is the white limestone façade of the **Leopold Museum**, which houses the art collection of Rudolph Leopold. This encompasses over 5,000 works of art, including major pieces by Gustav Klimt, together with the world's largest Egon Schiele collection.

The **Museum of Modern Art Ludwig Foundation Vienna**, or **MUMOK**, to the right of the Kunsthalle, is clad in contrasting dark basalt. It contains one of the largest European collections of modern art, from American Pop to Cubism, Expressionism and Viennese Actionism, as well as contemporary art from Central and Eastern Europe.

The **Architektur Zentrum Wien** is a venue for interesting temporary exhibitions of modern architecture and architectural history. Its permanent exhibition features 20th-century Austrian architecture.

The **Tanzquartier Wien** is dedicated to dance, providing facilities and training to performers and choreographers, and presenting various types of dance and other performances to the public. The MuseumsQuartier also has archives and facilities for lectures, workshops and

Rossbändiger (1892), the tamer of horses, near the MuseumsQuartier

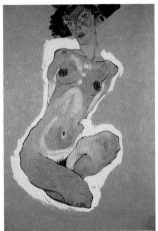

Schiele's *Kneeling Female Nude* (1910), Museum of Modern Art, MuseumsQuartier

seminars, as well as Austria's first centre for museum and exhibition studies. Children can play, explore and learn about a variety of subjects in the **ZOOM Kindermuseum**, an unconventional centre.

Amid this extraordinary cultural setting, numerous cafés, bars, green spaces, shops and bookstores invite visitors to relax.

⓫ Mariahilfer Strasse

Map 4 A1, B1. Ⓤ Westbahnhof, Zieglergasse, Neubaugasse, MuseumsQuartier. 🚌 2A, 13A.

Mariahilfer Strasse is one of the longest streets in Vienna, a main artery running west from the town centre to the area around Schönbrunn.

The part between Getreidemarkt (Grain Market) and Westbahnhof (the Western Railway Station) is also the busiest shopping street in this part of the city. Here you will find Vienna's largest department stores and its best window displays. Shopping tends to be better value here than in Kärntner Strasse, but is still more costly than in Meidling or Favoriten, for instance. Mariahilfer Strasse took its name from the church of

St Mary, Our Lady of Perpetual Succour, built in the late 17th century on the site of an older church, but was not consecrated until 1730. Its façade is an austere pyramidal structure, rising to a bulbous steeple, and there are lively Rococo reliefs set in its walls. In front of the church stands a monument to the composer Joseph Haydn *(see p28)*, who lived at this address for 12 years.

Mariahilfer Strasse No. 45 is the longest and most famous double-exit house in Vienna, the birthplace in 1790 of the popular Austrian playwright Ferdinand Raimund.

⓭ Spittelberg

Map 1 C5. Ⓤ Volkstheater. 🚋 49. 🚌 48A. Amerlinghaus: Stiftgasse 8. **Tel** 52 36 475. **Open** during events. 🏠 Ⓦ amerlinghaus.at

Spittelberg is the oldest and most colourful part of the elegant 7th District. In the 17th century, the cluster of streets between Siebensterngasse and Burggasse, around Spittelberggasse, was Vienna's first immigrant worker district. Its inhabitants were mainly craftsmen, merchants and servants from Croatia and Hungary, brought here to work at the court. Today, the district's crafts heritage lives on in the

street market, held on the first weekend of each month and prior to Christmas. Among the stalls with wood carvings, tie-dyed fabrics and silver jewellery, waiters from the local bars negotiate the busy crowds; there are some 58 bars in this small area, which contains just 138 houses. The number of bars may change from one week to the next, but the bustling, festive party atmosphere can be experienced almost every evening. The Spittelberg area also comprises small art galleries, and artists display their work in the restaurants.

At one time, attractive bar maids offered "additional services", and legend has it that Emperor Joseph II once decided to explore the Spittelberg district for himself. However, when, in disguise, he entered the Witwe Bolte (Widow Bolte) restaurant, still open today, he was unceremoniously thrown out.

Nos. 18 and 20 Spittelberggasse are fine Baroque houses.

The beautifully restored **Amerlinghaus**, in which the painter Friedrich Amerling (1803–87) was born, is now a cultural and community centre, and a restaurant.

A little further along, between Siebensterngasse and Mariahilfer Strasse, is an enclosed area around former barracks now housing the Military Academy, and the Stiftkirche, topped with an onion-shaped cupola, which serves as a garrison church. Its walls are lined with very expressive Rococo reliefs.

Community centre in Amerlinghaus, Spittelberg

⑯ Kunsthistorisches Museum

The world's fourth largest gallery, the Museum of Art History houses a collection based on works amassed over the centuries by generations of Habsburg monarchs. The public was given access to these art treasures when two museums were built in Ringstrasse to designs by Karl von Hasenauer and Gottfried Semper. One was to house the art collection, a second, identical building the Natural History Museum *(see p86)*. Both opened in 1891. The art museum's lavish interior complements its exhibits, today seen by more than one and a half million people each year.

Second floor

First floor

Ground floor

★ **Hunters in the Snow (1565)**
The last in a cycle of seasonal paintings by Pieter Bruegel the Elder, this winter scene graces a gallery room containing the world's largest collection of this artist's work.

Salt Cellar
Benvenuto Cellini made this sumptuous *Saliera* of the sea god Neptune and an earth goddess for the French King François I.

Museum Guide

The ground floor area to the right of the main entrance displays artifacts from the ancient civilizations of Egypt, Greece, Rome and the Near East. The area to the left houses the Kunstkammer, with a collection of sculpture and decorative arts. The picture gallery takes up the entire first floor, while the second floor houses the impressive coin collection as well as temporary exhibitions.

Key

- ▨ Egyptian and Near Eastern collection
- ▨ Collection of Greek and Roman Antiquities
- ▨ Kunstkammer Wien
- ▨ Picture gallery
- ▨ Coin cabinets
- ▨ Non-exhibition space

★ **The Artist's Studio (1665)**
This painting, one of the most famous by Vermeer, is believed by some to be a self-portrait of the artist at work.

★ **Velázquez's Infanta**
The Spanish artist Diego Velázquez immortalized the eight-year-old Margarita Teresa (1659), the future wife of Emperor Leopold I.

★ **Gemma Augustea**
The famous Roman cameo, carved in great precision from onyx, shows the goddess Roma and Emperor Augustus welcoming his son Tiberius after his heroic victory over the barbarians in Pannonia.

Rooms
1–7

King Thutmosis III
This king from the 18th Dynasty (c.1500 BC) was one of the foremost warriors of ancient Egypt. He is depicted in the style typical of the Late Kingdom period.

Hippopotamus
This blue ceramic figure from Middle-Kingdom Egypt (around 2000 BC) was placed in the tombs of important persons, to mark their status in society.

Decoration of the Museum

The museums built in Ringstrasse in the 1890s were among the first to be designed with particular collections in mind. Many prominent artists were employed to decorate the interiors. Their great masterpiece is the main staircase in the Museum of Art History. Hans Makart created the symbolic scenes above the windows, while Gustav and Ernst Klimt painted frescoes depicting stages in the development of art. The *Apotheosis of the Renaissance* (1890) is the fabulous *trompe l'oeil* ceiling fresco by Michael Munkácsy.

Apotheosis of the Renaissance

Exploring the Kunsthistorisches Museum

The Museum of Art History has a fine collection of Egyptian, Greek and Roman objects, which provide an intriguing record of the world's earliest civilizations. The European sculpture and decorative art in the Kunstkammer Wien dates from the 15th to the 18th centuries. This period is also the focus of the picture gallery, which largely reflects the personal tastes of its Habsburg founders. Venetian and 17th-century Flemish paintings are well represented, and there is an excellent display of works by earlier Dutch and German artists. There is also a vast coin collection.

Oriental and Egyptian Antiquities

At the core of this collection are the objects unearthed by Austrian archaeologists in Giza. Particularly fascinating are the well-preserved relics from the tomb of Ka-Ni-Nisut, dating from the Early Kingdom era, including a meticulously reconstructed burial chamber. The blue ceramic figure of a hippopotamus dates from the Middle Kingdom era. Such animal figures were placed in the tombs to mark the social status of the deceased – the hippopotamus was regarded as a royal beast and could be hunted only with the pharaoh's permission.

The exhibits from the Late Kingdom, mainly associated with the mortuary cult, include a papyrus book of the dead, the mummified corpses of people and animals, sarcophagi and Canopic jars used to preserve the entrails of mummified corpses.

Near-Eastern antiquities are represented in the museum collections by the Babylonian reliefs, a lion made of red ceramic brick and various exhibits from Arabia.

Greek and Roman Antiquities

Only part of the museum's Greek and Roman collection is housed in the main building; the finds from Ephesus and on Samothrace are on display in the Ephesus Museum in Neue Burg (see p70). The main building in Burgring has a beautiful collection of early Greek urns, in a variety of shapes, including vessels presented to winners at the Panathenaean Games. The sculpture rooms house many examples of early Greek and Roman art. Some are of outstanding quality: for example, the Youth from Magdalensburg, a cast of a lost Roman statue found buried in an Austrian field; the huge Head of Athena, probably from the school of Phidias; and fragments of a frieze with a dying Amazon. The Hellenic era is represented by the magnificent Head of a Philosopher, likely to have been that of Aristotle. One of the most precious items in the entire collection of antiquities is Gemma Augustea, a Roman

cameo depicting Emperor Augustus welcoming his son Tiberius on his return from war, together with Roma, the goddess of Rome.

The antiquities section also contains some Etruscan ceramics and statuettes from Tanagra. Early Coptic, Byzantine and German items are shown in the other rooms, but the true jewel among the antiquities is the Treasure of Nagyszentmiklós, a collection of 9th-century golden vessels with stunning reliefs, showing Far-Eastern influences, found in Romania in 1799.

Kunstkammer Wien

This museum within a museum is spread over twenty galleries filled with magnificent works of art bought or commissioned by successive Habsburg rulers, scientific instruments and clocks regarded as masterpieces of applied art, and curiosities and artifacts from the rulers' Kunstkammern (chambers of art). Some of the royals worked in the studio; exhibits include, for example, glass blown by Archduke Ferdinand II and embroidery by Maria Theresa.

Some of the most intriguing items, however, are splendid examples of craftsmanship, including pieces of jewellery and items made from gold. The showpiece of the collection is the golden Saliera or Salt Cellar (see p88), made by the Italian goldsmith and sculptor Benvenuto Cellini for the French King, François I.

Other gems in these rooms include the magnificent chalice from the collegiate church in Wilten and the precious Burgundy cup of Friedrich III.

A separate section is devoted to wood and stone sculptures from the Middle Ages, mainly of religious subjects, among them the amazing Madonna from Krumlowa (c.1400), the poignant Virgin with Child

Virgin with Child (c.1495) by Tilman Riemenschneider

Room I of the Egyptian galleries

Susanna and the Elders (1555) by Tintoretto

by Tilman Riemenschneider (c.1495) and stone statues from the cathedral churches of Bamberg and Naumburg.

Highlights of the Italian Renaissance and Baroque rooms are the marble bust of a laughing boy, by Desiderio da Settignano, a marble relief of Bacchus and Ariadne, and a fine bronze and gilt figurine known as *Venus Felix*, after an antique marble statue.

The collection of decorative arts also includes fine pieces of furniture and tapestries, gilded table ornaments and vases, a number of statuettes and figurines, miniature clocks and jewellery.

Picture Collection

Exhibits in the painting galleries are mostly hung according to regional schools or styles of

Summer (1563) by Italian painter, Giuseppe Arcimboldo

painting, and arranged chronologically. Paintings go back as far as the 16th century, and include several works by early Flemish masters, such as Rogier van der Weyden, Hans Memling and Jan van Eyck. The highlight is the collection of Pieter Bruegel the Elder's surviving works, the largest collection of his work and the museum's greatest treasure.

Two rooms are devoted to Rubens, with large-scale religious works and an intimate portrait of his wife. Antony van Dyck is represented by some outstanding works, and there are paintings by Dutch genre painters. All the Rembrandts on show are portraits. The only painting by Johannes Vermeer is *The Artist's Studio*, an enigmatic work.

The Italian collection of 16th-century paintings from Venice and the Veneto include works by Titian, from his early *Gypsy Madonna* (1510) to the late *Nymph and Shepherd* (1570–75). Other highlights are Giovanni Bellini's graceful *Young Woman at her Toilette* (1515) and Tintoretto's *Susanna and the Elders*, one of the major works of Venetian Mannerism. There is a series of allegorical portrait heads representing the elements and the seasons by Giuseppe Arcimboldo. Italian Baroque painting includes works

by Annibale Carracci and Michelangelo Merisi da Caravaggio, including the huge *Madonna of the Rosary* (1606–7).

French treasures include the formal court portrait of the youthful Charles IX of France (1569) by François Clouet, and *The Destruction of the Temple in Jerusalem* (1638) by Nicolas Poussin.

Among the few British works are the *Landscape of Suffolk* (around 1750) by Thomas Gainsborough and paintings by Reynolds. The German collection contains several works by Albrecht Dürer, including his *Madonna with the Pear* (1512), and by Lucas Cranach the Elder and Hans Holbein the Younger.

There are several fine portraits of the Spanish royal family by Diego Velázquez, including his *Portrait of the Infanta* (1659).

Coin Cabinets

The coin and medal collection of the Museum of Art History comprises 500,000 individual items, making it one of the most extensive numismatic collections in the world. Its first inventory was compiled in 1547. The nucleus of the collection derives from the former possessions of the Habsburgs, but has been added to by modern curators. The exhibits illustrate the history of money, with coins from ancient Egypt, Greece and Rome, examples of Celtic, Byzantine, medieval and Renaissance money, right up to present-day Austrian currency.

Medal of Ulrich II Molitor (1581)

Also on display is a collection of 19th- and 20th-century medals, with portraits that are often outstanding miniature works of art. Particularly noteworthy are the silver and gilt medals of Ulrich II Molitor, the Abbot of Heiligenkreuz, and the silver medallion engraved by Bertrand Andrieu and minted to commemorate the baptism of Napoleon's son, showing the emperor as proud father.

SOUTH OF THE RING

This part of town is an area of great diversity, ranging from the stateliness of the Opera House to the raucous modernity of bustling Karlsplatz, from the magnificence of Karlskirche, one of Johann Bernhard Fischer von Erlach's greatest churches, to the secular attractions of the Belvedere. Once Prince Eugene of Savoy's palace, the Belvedere is now the home of the Gallery of Austrian Art, which includes works by Gustav Klimt. The district also has beautiful buildings with façades decorated in the Vienna Secession style. The stalls of the bustling Naschmarkt are also a popular attraction.

Sights at a Glance

Streets and Squares
- ⑬ Schwarzenbergplatz

Historic Buildings
- ① Hotel Sacher
- ② Staatsoper
- ⑤ Theater an der Wien
- ⑦ Technische Universität
- ⑨ Karlsplatz Pavilions
- ⑪ Musikverein

Museums and Galleries
- ③ Academy of Fine Arts
- ④ Secession Building
- ⑩ Künstlerhaus
- ⑫ Wien Museum Karlsplatz
- ⑮ Belvedere see pp102–3

Markets
- ⑥ Naschmarkt

Churches
- ⑧ Karlskirche see pp98–9

Parks
- ⑭ Stadtpark

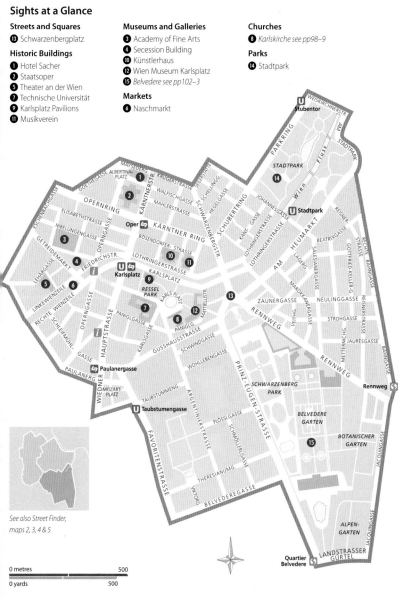

See also Street Finder, maps 2, 3, 4 & 5

0 metres   500
0 yards   500

◀ The opulent interior of the State Opera House

For map symbols *see back flap*

Street-by-Street: Around the Opera

Between two of Vienna's key landmarks, the Opera House and Karlskirche, lies an area that typifies the varied cultural vitality of the city as a whole. Here, you will find cultural monuments such as an 18th-century theatre, a 19th-century art academy and the superb Secession Building, mixed in with emblems of the Viennese devotion to good living: the Hotel Sacher and the Café Museum, both as popular today as ever, and the colourful Naschmarkt, Vienna's best market for vegetables and exotic fruits.

3 Academy of Fine Arts
This Italianate building is home to one of the best collections of old masters in Vienna.

The Goethe Statue

The Schiller Statue dominates the park in front of the Academy of Fine Arts.

4 ★ Secession Building
This delightful structure, built in 1898 as a showroom for the Secession artists, houses Gustav Klimt's *Beethoven Frieze*, created for an exhibition in honour of the great composer.

5 Theater an der Wien
The 18th-century theatre on the banks of the Wien river is a prime operatic venue in a historic setting. Their programme also includes ballet and concerts.

SCHILLERPLATZ

NIBELU

EL

MAKARTGASSE

GETREIDEMARKT

LINKE WIENZEILE

6 ★ Naschmarkt
Fresh produce is sold here Monday to Saturday, and a flea market operates on Saturday mornings.

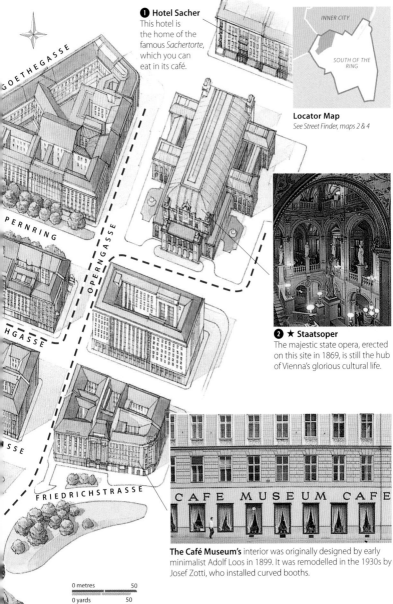

GOETHEGASSE

1 Hotel Sacher
This hotel is the home of the famous *Sachertorte*, which you can eat in its café.

Locator Map
See Street Finder, maps 2 & 4

INNER CITY

SOUTH OF THE RING

PERNRING

OPERNGASSE

H GASSE

SSE

FRIEDRICHSTRASSE

2 ★ Staatsoper
The majestic state opera, erected on this site in 1869, is still the hub of Vienna's glorious cultural life.

CAFE MUSEUM CAFE

The Café Museum's interior was originally designed by early minimalist Adolf Loos in 1899. It was remodelled in the 1930s by Josef Zotti, who installed curved booths.

0 metres 50
0 yards 50

Key
— Suggested route

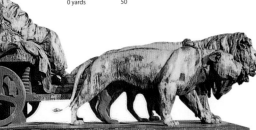

The Mark Anthony Statue (1899), alongside the Secession Building, is a gloriously decadent bronze statue by Arthur Strasser. It depicts the Roman leader sitting in a chariot drawn by lions.

The imposing building of the Vienna State Opera House

❶ Hotel Sacher

Philharmonikerstrasse 4. **Map** 2 B5.
Tel 51 45 60. Ⓤ Karlsplatz. 🚋 1, 2, 71,
D. 🚌 2A. 🆆 sacher.com

The Hotel Sacher is one of the
"must-see" places in Vienna.
It was founded by the son of
Franz Sacher, who was said
to have created the famous
Sachertorte in 1832. Although
this cake can now be bought
in any café, the genuine article
is still the best.

The hotel came into its
own under Anna Sacher, the
founder's cigar-smoking
daughter-in-law, who ran
the hotel from 1892 until her
death in 1930. She collected
autographs, and, to this day, a
vast white tablecloth signed
by Emperor Franz Joseph I is
on display. During her time,
the Sacher became a venue
for the extra-marital affairs of
the rich and noble. It is still a
discreetly sumptuous hotel
with red velvet sofas, draped
curtains and stylish furniture.

❷ Staatsoper

Opernring 2. **Map** 2 B5. **Tel** 51 444-
2250. Ⓤ Karlsplatz. 🚋 1, 2, 71, D.
🚌 2A. 🆆 wiener-staatsoper.at

In May 1869, when Vienna's
State Opera House opened to
the strains of Mozart's *Don
Giovanni*, music lovers rejoiced
that it would no longer be
necessary to travel to Paris in
order to hear good opera. Built
in Neo-Renaissance style, the
Opera House initially failed to
impress the Viennese. The
distressed interior designer,
Eduard van der Nüll, committed
suicide, and two months later,
the architect, August Sicard
von Sicardsburg, also died. Yet,
when the opera was hit by an
allied bomb in 1945, the event
was seen as a symbolic blow
to the city. With a new state-of-
the-art auditorium and stage,
the Opera House eventually
reopened on 5 November
1955 with a performance of
Beethoven's *Fidelio*. Its illustrious
directors have included Gustav

Mahler, Richard Strauss and
Herbert von Karajan.

Each year, on the last
Thursday of Carnival, the stage
is extended to create a vast
dance floor for the Vienna
Opera Ball. This prestigious
high-society event opens
when Vienna's youth – well-
to-do girls clad in white and
their smartly dressed escorts –
take to the floor.

❸ Academy of Fine Arts

Schillerplatz 3. **Map** 4 C1. **Tel** 588 16
22 22. Ⓤ Karlsplatz. 🚋 1, 2, 71, D.
🚌 57A, 59A. **Open** 10am–6pm Tue–
Sun and public holidays. **Closed** 1 Jan,
1 May, 24, 25, 31 Dec.
🆆 akademiegalerie.at

The Academy of Fine Arts
is not only an educational
establishment, but also one
of the finest galleries of Old
Masters. It was built in 1872–6,
by Theophil Hansen, as a school
and museum. In 1907, Adolf
Hitler applied to be admitted
but was refused a place on the
grounds that he lacked talent.

Today, the gallery shows
changing exhibitions. Its pride
is late-Gothic and early-
Renaissance works, including
some pieces by Rubens, a
winged altarpiece by Hieronymus
Bosch depicting the Last
Judgement and works by Titian,
Cranach and Botticelli. It also
has some 17th-century Dutch
and Flemish landscapes and
an Austrian collection.

❹ Secession Building

Friedrichstrasse 12. **Map** 4 C1.
Tel 58 75 307. Ⓤ Karlsplatz. 🚋 1, 2,
62, 71, D. 🚌 57A, 59A. **Open** 10am–
6pm Tue–Sun & hols. **Closed** 25 Dec.
🅿 🆆 secession.at

The unusual Secession Building
was designed in *Jugendstil* style
by Joseph Maria Olbrich, as a
showcase for the Secessionist
artists, including Gustav Klimt,
Koloman Moser and Otto Wagner,
who broke away from Vienna's
traditional art scene. The almost
windowless building, with its

Otto Wagner (1841–1918)

The most prominent architect at the turn of
the 20th century, Wagner studied in Vienna
and Berlin. Initially, he was associated with
the historicist style, but in time he became
the foremost representative of the Austrian
Secession. He prepared plans for the re-routing
of the Wien river and the modernization of
the town's transport system. His most outstanding
works include the **Majolikahaus** *(see Naschmarkt,
opposite)*, train stations *(see p100)*, the Post Office
Savings Bank building, a hospital and the Kirche
am Steinhof *(see p112)*.

Detail of Otto
Wagner's design

Façade of the Secession Building, with its golden filigree dome

filigree globe of entwined laurel leaves on the roof, is a squat cube with four towers. Gustav Klimt's *Beethoven Frieze* (1902) is its best known exhibit. Designed as a decorative painting running along three walls, it shows interrelated groups of figures thought to be a commentary on Beethoven's *Ninth Symphony*.

The Secession Building is Vienna's oldest independent exhibition space dedicated to showing contemporary and experimental Austrian and international art.

❺ Theater an der Wien

Linke Wienzeile 6. **Map** 4 C1.
Tel 58 83 06 65/58 885 (tickets).
Ⓤ Kettenbrückengasse. 🚌 59A.
Ⓦ theater-wien.at

The "Theatre on the Wien River", one of the oldest theatres in Vienna, was founded by Emanuel Schikaneder. A statue above the entrance shows him playing Papageno in the premiere of Mozart's *Magic Flute*. Schikaneder, who had written the libretto for this

same opera, was the theatre's first director. The premiere of Beethoven's *Fidelio* was staged here in 1805, and for a while the composer lived in the theatre. Many plays by prominent playwrights such as Kleist, Grillparzer and Nestroy, and many Viennese operettas were premiered here, too, including works by Johann Strauss (son), Zeller, Lehár and Kalman. After many years as a venue for musicals, the Theater an der Wien now stages only opera.

The Neo-Classical entrance to the Theater an der Wien

❻ Naschmarkt

Map 4 C1. Ⓤ Kettenbrückengasse, Pilgramgasse. 🚌 59A. **Open** 6am–7pm Mon–Fri, 6am–5pm Sat. Schubert Memorial Apartment: **Tel** 58 16 730. **Open** 10am–1pm, 2pm–6pm Wed & Thu. **Closed** 1 Jan, 1 May & 25 Dec. 🅿️

The Naschmarkt is Vienna's liveliest market, selling all types of market goods as well as delicatessen food. The weekly Saturday flea market is particularly popular.

Nearby, at Kettenbrückengasse No. 6, is the simple apartment where the composer Franz Schubert died in 1828. It displays facsimiles, prints and a piano.

Overlooking Naschmarkt, at Linke Wienzeile Nos. 38 and 40, are two remarkable apartment blocks. Designed by Otto Wagner in 1899 and known as the Wagner Apartments, they represent the peak of *Jugendstil* style. No. 38 has sparkling gilt ornament, mostly by Koloman Moser. No. 40 is known as **Majolikahaus**, after the glazed pottery used to weather-proof the walls. Its façade has subtle flower patterns in pink, blue and green, and even the sills are moulded and decorated.

❼ Technische Universität

Karlsplatz 13. **Map** 5 D1.
Tel 588 01–0. Ⓤ Karlsplatz.
🚋 1, 2, 62, 71, D. 🚌 2A, 4A, 59A.

Vienna's Technical University has a Neo-Classical façade, beautiful colonnades and attic statues by Joseph Klieber. It was built in 1816 by Joseph Schemerl von Leytenbach, to the designs of the Imperial Office of Public Works. Klieber also created the eight stone heads flanking the main entrance, featuring some of the university's famous professors.

Inside, the most beautiful room is the Assembly Hall, with carved wall panelling.

The University fronts on to Resselpark, which contains many busts and statues of Austria's most important scientists and engineers.

❶ Karlskirche

During Vienna's plague epidemic of 1713, Emperor Karl VI vowed that as soon as the city was delivered from its plight he would build a church dedicated to St Charles Borromeo (1538–84), the patron saint of the plague. Johann Bernhard Fischer von Erlach created a richly eclectic building, later completed by his son. At 72 m (236 ft), it is the tallest Baroque church in Vienna. The Neo-Classical giant dome and portico are flanked by two minaret-like towers and the Oriental-style gatehouses. The most striking features inside are the beautiful cupola frescoes, high altar and side altarpieces painted by the foremost artists of the day, Martino Altomonte, Daniel Gran and Sebastiano Ricci.

The Pulpit
Two putti crown the canopy of the richly gilded pulpit, adorned with rocailles and flower garlands.

★ High Altar
A stucco relief by Albert Camesina shows St Charles Borromeo being assumed into heaven on a cloud laden with angels and putti.

Main entrance

KEY

① **Pediment reliefs** by Giovanni Stanetti show the suffering of the Viennese population during the 1713 plague.

② **The two gatehouses** leading into the side entrances of the church seem to combine the architecture of Roman triumphal arches with that of Chinese pavilions.

③ **Stairway** (closed to the public).

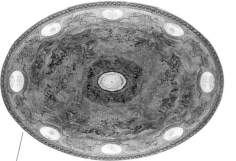

★ **Cupola Frescoes**
Johann Michael Rottmayr's frescoes, painted in 1725–30, depict the Apotheosis of St Charles Borromeo. This was the painter's last commission.

Johann Bernhard Fischer von Erlach

An outstanding architect of the Austrian Baroque, Fischer von Erlach (1656–1723) designed many of Vienna's finest buildings, including the palaces of Schönbrunn, Prince Eugene of Savoy and the Trautson family. He died before he finished the Karlskirche; his son, Joseph Emanuel, completed it in 1737, and also took over as court architect.

★ **The Two Columns**
Inspired by Trajan's Column in Rome, these two columns feature scenes from the life of St Charles Borromeo, illustrating the qualities of Steadfastness and Courage.

St Charles Borromeo
Lorenzo Mattielli's statue of the patron saint and protector from the plague crowns the pediment.

Sunflower motif on the façade of the Karlsplatz Pavilions

❾ Karlsplatz Pavilions

Karlsplatz. **Map** 5 D1. Ⓤ Karlsplatz.
🚊 1, 2, 62, 71, D. 🚌 2A, 4A, 59A.
🚋 Kärntner Ring. **Tel** 50 58 /47-85
177. **Open** Apr–Oct: 10am–6pm Tue–
Sun & public hols. **Closed** 1 May.

Otto Wagner *(see p96)* was
responsible for designing and
engineering many aspects of
Vienna's light urban railway, the
Stadtbahn, in the late 19th
century. A few of Wagner's
stations remain to this day – it is
worth looking at the stations in
Stadtpark, Kettenbrückengasse
and Schönbrunn, for example –
but none can match his stylish
pair of railway exit pavilions
(1898–9) alongside Karlsplatz.
The patina-green copper roofs
and the ornamentation
complement the Karlskirche
beyond. Gilt patterns are
stamped onto the white marble
cladding and eaves, with
repetitions of Wagner's beloved
sunflower motif. The greatest
impact is made by the buildings'
elegantly curving rooflines.
Today the western pavilion
holds an exhibition devoted to
the architect and urban planner.
It covers his most important
designs including the Kirche am
Steinhof *(see p112)* and the
revolutionary Stadtbahn, as well
as his theories of design, which
were radical for the time. The
eastern pavilion houses a café.

❿ Künstlerhaus

Karlsplatz 5. **Map** 5 D1. **Tel** 58 79 663.
Ⓤ Karlsplatz. 🚊 1, 2, 62, 71, D.
🚌 2A, 4A, 59A. **Open** 10am–6pm
daily (to 9pm Thu). 🅿 🌐 **k-haus.at**

Commissioned by the Vienna
Artists' Society as an exhibition
hall for its members, the
Künstlerhaus (Artists' House) was
completed in 1868. The society
favoured grandiose, academic
styles of painting in tune with
the historicist Ringstrasse architecture which was also being
developed around that time.
The Artists' House itself is typical
of this style. Designed by
August Weber (1836–1903) to
look like a Renaissance *palazzo*,
it is decorated with marble
statues of the masters of art,
including Albrecht Dürer,
Michelangelo, Raphael, Peter Paul
Rubens, Leonardo da Vinci, Diego
Velázquez and Titian, symbolizing
the timeless value of art.
Today, the Künstlerhaus
still serves as an exhibition
space, focusing on architecture,
interdisciplinary themes and
international cooperation.
There is also a space for live
performances, a cinema,
theatre and restaurant.

⓫ Musikverein

Bösendorferstrasse 12. **Map** 5 D1.
Tel 50 58 190. Ⓤ Karlsplatz. 🚊 1, 2,
62, 71, D. 🚌 2A, 4A, 59A. **Open**
guided tours: please phone for details;
box office: 9am–8pm Mon–Fri, 9am–
1pm Sat and 1hr before concerts.

Next to the Künstlerhaus is
the Musikverein, headquarters
of the Society of the Friends
of Music. It was designed by
Theophil Hansen in 1867–9
and features terracotta statues
and balustrades.
The Musikverein is the
home of the famous Vienna
Philharmonic Orchestra, which
performs both here and in
the Opera House. The concert
hall, seating almost 2,000, has
excellent acoustics and superb
decor. The balcony is supported
by vast columns; the gilded
ceiling shows nine muses
and Apollo; along the walls
are the statues of various
famous musicians.
The most famous annual
event here is the New Year's
Day concert, which is broadcast
live around the world.

The monumental, historicist façade of the Musikverein

⑫ Wien Museum Karlsplatz

Karlsplatz 8. **Map** 5 D1. **Tel** 50 58 747.
Ⓤ Karlsplatz. 🚋 1, 2, 62, 71, D. 🚌 2A,
4A, 59A. **Open** 10am–6pm Tue–Sun &
hols. **Closed** 1 Jan, 1 May, 25 Dec. 🏛
Ⓦ wienmuseum.at

Visitors to the Historical Museum
of the City of Vienna are greeted
by a vast model of the city from
the era when the Ringstrasse
was developed. The exhibition
covers nearly 3,000 years of
urban history. It illustrates the
lives of its first settlers and life in
the Roman camp of Vindobona,
and it chronicles the threat
from Turkish invaders and the
subsequent rise of Vienna to
the magnificent capital of a
great empire.

The museum has collections
of memorabilia of many of
Vienna's famous citizens. Perhaps
the most interesting of these
are the reconstructed apartments of the writer Franz
Grillparzer (1791–1872) and
the architect Adolf Loos
(1870–1933).

⑬ Schwarzenberg-platz

Map 5 E1. Ⓤ Karlsplatz. 🚋 71.
🚌 4A.

The elongated Schwarzenberg
Square, one of the city's grandest
spaces, is best seen from the
Ringstrasse, from where several
important structures come into
view together. In the foreground
is the equestrian statue of Prince
Karl Philipp Fürst zu Schwarzenberg, who commanded the
Austrian and allied armies in the
Battle of Leipzig in 1813 against
the French army under Napoleon.

The Hochstrahlbrunnen (high
jet fountain) was built in 1873 to
mark the connection of Vienna's
first Alpine water supply. The
fountain is floodlit in summer.
Once the focal point of the
square, it now partly obscures the
heroic-style Soviet monument to
the Red Army that commemorates the Russian liberation of
Vienna. Beyond the Russian
monument, the beautiful
Schwarzenberg Palace can be
seen. It was built in 1697 by

Fountain and Soviet Monument at Schwarzenbergplatz

Johann Lukas von Hildebrandt
and altered by the Fischer von
Erlachs, Johann Bernhard and
Joseph Emanuel. One wing
houses the Swiss Embassy and
there are plans for a casino in
the rest of the palace.

⑭ Stadtpark

Map 3 D5. Ⓤ Stadtpark, Stubentor,
Landstrasse–Wien Mitte. Ⓢ Wien
Mitte. 🚋 2. 🚌 3A, 74A.

On the Weihburggasse side
of the municipal park stands
one of the most photographed
sights in Vienna, the gilded
statue of the King of Waltz,
Johann Strauss the Younger.
It was designed by Edmund
Hellmer in the Neo-Romantic
style of the 1920s. The park,
opened in 1862, also contains
the statues of the composers
Franz Schubert and Franz Lehár,
the painter Hans Makart and
portraitist Friedrich von Amerling.
Parallel to the Ringstrasse,

along the Wien River, runs
an attractive promenade
designed in Secession style by
Friedrich Ohmann. It includes
several magnificent portals,
part of a project to regulate the
flow of the Wien river, as well as
several pavilions, bridges and
stone playgrounds.

A Secession-style portal in the Stadtpark,
built in 1903–04

ⓑ Belvedere

The Belvedere was built as the summer
residence of Prince Eugene of Savoy by Johann
Lukas von Hildebrandt. A brilliant military commander
whose strategies helped vanquish the Turks
in 1683, the Prince became a favourite
at the Austrian court and with the
people. Situated on a gently sloping
hill, the Belvedere consists of two palaces
linked by a formal garden designed in the
French style by Dominique Girard. The garden
is laid out on three levels, each conveying a
complicated series of Classical allusions:
the lower part represents the domain of the
Four Elements, the centre is Parnassus and
the upper section Mount Olympus.

Chapel
Prince Eugene's
former chapel is
now part of a gallery
with works by
Caspar David
Friedrich, F. G.
Waldmüller,
Edvard Munch,
Renoir and Monet.

**★ Gustav Klimt
Collection**
Klimt's portrait of
the Old-Testament
figure of *Judith I*
(1901, right) and
his famous *The Kiss*
(1907–08) hang
in this superb
collection.

Main entrance leading
to Lower Belvedere

**Figures from the
Providentia Fountain
(1739)**
The original lead
figures that Georg
Raphael Donner made
for the Providentia
Fountain in Neuer
Markt are displayed
in the Marble Hall; this
central statue shows
Providence. The figures
that now stand in the
market are copies.

Entrance to the Upper Belvedere from Prinz-Eugen-Strasse

★ **Sala Terrena**
One of the finest rooms of the Upper Belvedere, this hall has beautiful stucco work by Santino Bussi and statues by Lorenzo Mattielli.

VISITORS' CHECKLIST

Practical Information
Map 5 E2, F2, F3.
Lower Belvedere & Orangery: Rennweg 6. **Open** 10am–6pm daily (until 9pm Wed). Upper Belvedere: Prinz-Eugen-Strasse 27. **Tel** 795 57 134. **Open** 10am–6pm daily. Stables: **Open** 10am–noon daily. **W** **belvedere.at**

Transport
Lower Belvedere: 71. 4A. Upper Belvedere: Quartier Belvedere. 18, D, O. 69A.

Statues of Sphinxes
With their lion bodies and human heads, the imposing Sphinx statues adorning the Belvedere gardens represent strength and intelligence.

★ **Hall of Mirrors**
A statue of Prince Eugene by Balthasar Permoser stands in this richly ornamented Baroque room, whose walls are covered with huge gilt-framed mirrors.

KEY

① **Upper cascade**

② **Main gate** leading to the Upper Belvedere.

③ **Upper Belvedere**

④ **The Orangerie** houses temporary exhibitions.

⑤ **Palace Stables** house the collection of Medieval Art (Study Collection).

FURTHER AFIELD

For a city of over 1.7 million inhabitants, Vienna is surprisingly compact. Nonetheless, some of the most interesting sights are a fair distance from the historic city centre. At Schönbrunn sprawls the vast Neo-Classical palace of the same name, with its Rococo state rooms and superb gardens. The Habsburgs' summer residence, it was greatly beloved by Maria Theresa. It is also worth going to

Kahlenberg, which offers the most splendid panoramic views of Vienna. You should spend at least one evening tasting the new-vintage wines in one of the *Heurigen* in Grinzing. Many parks and gardens, including the Prater, featured in the film *The Third Man* and one of Europe's best funfairs, as well as the Lainzer Tiergarten, are former Habsburg domains now open to the public.

Sights at a Glance

Historic Buildings
3 Karl-Marx-Hof
4 Liechtenstein Garden Palace
5 Augarten
9 Hundertwasser-Haus
11 Amalienbad
15 *Schönbrunn see pp114–15*
17 Wagner Villas

Museums and Galleries
10 Heeresgeschichtliches Museum
13 Haydnhaus
14 Museum of Technology

Parks and Gardens
6 Donauinsel
8 Prater
18 Lainzer Tiergarten

Interesting Districts
1 Kahlenberg
2 Grinzing
7 UNO-City

Churches
16 Kirche am Steinhof
19 Wotrubakirche

Cemeteries
12 *Zentralfriedhof see pp110–11*

Key
▦ Central Vienna
▦ Greater Vienna
═ Motorway
⋯ Motorway tunnel
▬ Major road
═ Other road

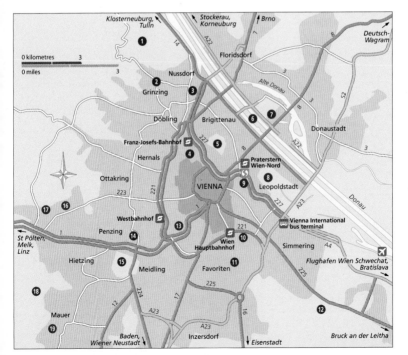

◀ A section of the façade of the eccentric Hundertwasser Haus, created in 1985   **For map symbols** *see back flap*

Cobenzlgasse, one of the charming streets in Grinzing

❶ Kahlenberg

🚌 38A.

North of the city, on the edge of the Vienna Woods, rise two almost identical peaks. The lower of the two, with ruins visible on top, is Leopoldsberg, the former seat of Margrave Leopold who ruled Austria in the 12th century. The second, with a television mast and the outline of a white church at the top, is Kahlenberg, the highest peak in Vienna.

It was from here, on the 12 September 1683, that the Polish King Jan III Sobieski led his troops to relieve the besieged city. Pope Innocent III's papal legate celebrated a thanksgiving mass in the ruins of the church that had been destroyed by the Turks.

The restored St Josefkirche on Kahlenberg is now maintained by Polish monks. Two tablets beside the church door commemorate the battle and the visit by Pope John Paul II, in 1983. Inside the church is a chapel with frescoes by the Polish artist, Jen Henryk de Rosen, and a display of the coats of arms of families whose members took part in the battle.

A short distance behind the church is an observation terrace and a restaurant. The views over the vineyards below and the city beyond are fabulous, with the Danube bridges to the left and the Vienna Woods to the right. No wonder then that Kahlenberg is a popular weekend destination.

❷ Grinzing

🚋 38. 🚌 38A.

The quiet villages scattered among the vineyards on the slopes of the Vienna Woods usually come to life during the wine-making season, when large groups of tourists descend on them to sample the new vintage *Heuriger*. Originally, the vintners were licensed to sell their own wine, while snacks were offered for free. This tradition developed into today's *Heurigen* – new-vintage wine taverns, typical of Vienna.

Today, of course, such hospitality is no longer offered for free. At *Heurigen* inns, wine and other drinks are served at the table and food is available from self-service buffets. Guests sit on benches around wide wooden tables, where they can drink and enjoy themselves until the early hours. There are

A plaque on No. 31 Himmelstrasse in Grinzing

many such villages in the area around Vienna, but undoubtedly the most famous of all is Grinzing. Although it may have lost some of its original charm, this is still a nice place to spend an evening.

On the way to Grinzing, it is worth taking the time to visit the Heiligenstädter Testament-Haus at No. 6 in the narrow Probusgasse, Ludwig van Beethoven's most famous home in Vienna. It was here that the great composer tried to find a cure for his worsening deafness; when he failed, he wrote a dramatic letter to his brothers, known as *The Testament*.

❸ Karl-Marx-Hof

Heiligenstädterstrasse 82–92. Ⓤ Heiligenstadt. 🚋 D. 🚌 5A, 10A, 11A, 38A, 39A.

In the 1920s, Vienna was governed by a social-democratic town council, elected mainly thanks to the votes of first-time women voters, a period known as Red Vienna. The council formed the ambitious plan to build houses for its entire working population. As a result, between 1923 and 1933 more than 60,000 new apartments, well-appointed for the time, were built. The programme was financed by a luxury tax imposed on wealthy citizens. Its execution was so strict that the municipal finance director, Hugo Breitner, earned himself the nickname the "financial vampire". Karl-Marx-Hof is an

The peach- and salmon-coloured façade of the Karl-Marx-Hof

The Baroque building of the Wiener Porzellanmanufaktur

immense complex of 1,382 council apartments and recreational facilities, and is the most celebrated of the municipal housing developments of that period. The project's architect, Karl Ehn, was a pupil of Austrian architect, Otto Wagner.

The delightful ceiling frescoes in the Liechtenstein Garden Palace

❹ Liechtenstein Garden Palace

Fürstengasse 1. **Map** 2 A1. **Tel** 319 57 67-158. Ⓤ Friedensbrücke. 🚌 40A. 🚋 D. **Open** for groups by appointment only.

Completed in 1692 to designs by Domenico Martinelli in the Rococo style, this was the Liechtenstein family's summer palace. It has a monumental façade, with tall pilasters and typically Baroque windows.

Inside, the colourful ceiling paintings in the vast ground-floor room are the work of Johann Michael Rottmayr. Vault paintings by Antonio Belucci can be seen on both sides of the stairway. The grand hall is

decorated with frescoes by Andrea Pozzo, a masterpiece of Baroque interior design.

The palace houses the art collection of Prince Hans-Adam II von und zu Liechtenstein – one of the richest private collections in the world. The collection is centred on the Baroque with special focus on Rubens, and ranges from the Renaissance (for example, Raphael and the Bruegels) through to the early 19th century (Waldmüller and Füger). The Liechtenstein family also acquired many masterpieces of modern art, dating from the early 20th century. The palace stands in an extensive garden, which was remodelled in the 19th century in the English style.

❺ Augarten

Obere Augartenstrasse 1. **Map** 3 D1. **Tel** 21 12 418. Ⓤ U-Taborstrasse. 🚌 5A, 5B. 🚋 2, 5, 31. Augarten Palace: **Open** guided tours 10:15am & 11:30am Mon–Fri (manufactory), 10am–6pm Mon–Sat (museum). **Closed** Sun & public hols.

There has been a palace on this site since the days of Leopold I, but it was destroyed by the Turks in 1683 and then rebuilt around 1700 to designs attributed to Johann Bernhard Fischer von Erlach. Since 1948 it has been the home of the world-famous Vienna Boys' Choir and is consequently closed to the public.

The surrounding park is one of the oldest in Vienna; it was first planted in 1650 by Emperor Ferdinand III, later renewed and opened to the public in 1775. Topiary lines long paths; the handsome gates were designed by Isidor Canevale. Mozart, Beethoven and Johann Strauss (father) all gave concerts in the

park pavilion, which was once the imperial porcelain factory.

Renovated in 2011, the **Augarten Palace** now houses the Porcelain Museum. This museum illustrates the history of Vienna porcelain. Several exhibits on display highlight the craftsmanship and techniques. The manufactory is open to the public for guided tours.

❻ Donauinsel

Ⓤ Donauinsel, Handelskai.

The numerous side-arms and rivulets of the Danube river regularly flooded the town until it was first canalized between 1870 and 1875. The second period of canalization in the Vienna region began in 1972 and was completed in 1987. The New Danube, a 5-km (3-mile) canal that acts as an "overflow", dates from this period.

The wooded island created between the Danube and its canals by the first stage of canalization is known as Donauinsel, or Danube Island. It is Vienna's largest recreation area and a favourite with the local population, who come here to swim and sunbathe in the summer. The vast park is criss-crossed by dozens of avenues, walking and cycling paths, picnic areas with built-in barbecues as well as nudist areas. Even water-skiing and surfing are possible. Once the weather warms up, the Copa Cagrana entertainment centre attracts visitors with its array of bars, restaurants, discos and the popular *Heurigen*.

The island hosts an annual festival, with open-air pop concerts and other events.

The vast, modern complex of UNO-City on the Danube

❼ UNO-City

Wagramerstrasse 5. **Tel** 26060-5596.
Ⓤ Kaisermühlen, Vienna International
Center. 🚌 20A, 92A, 92B. 🚋 11am,
2pm, 3:30pm Mon–Fri (plus 12:30pm
Jul & Aug); ID required. Donauturm:
Tel 263 35 72. 🅦 unvienna.org

On the left bank of the Danube
is UNO-City, one of only three
United Nations headquarters.
The complex stands on international, non-Austrian territory;
its post office uses its own special
postage stamps and UN post-
marks. UNO-City consists of four
vast semicircular buildings and
a large congress hall, one of the
most strikingly modern pieces of
architecture in Europe, designed
by the architect Johann Staber
and opened in 1979. Today,
visitors can join one of the regular
guided tours of the complex.

UNO-City is surrounded by a
green park, covering an area of
over 600,000 sq m (700,000 sq yds),
with excellent recreational
facilities. One of the main attractions is the **Donauturm**, a TV
tower rising to 252 m (827 ft),
with two revolving restaurants
and an observation platform.

❽ Prater

Tel Praterverband 728 05 16. Ferris
Wheel 72 95 430. Ⓤ Praterstern. 🚌
5B, 80A. 🚋 5, O. Ⓢ Wien Nord. **Open**
Funfair mid-Mar–Oct: 10am–midnight
daily. 🅦 praterwien.com

Originally an imperial
hunting ground, the
woods and meadows
between the Danube and
its canal were opened
to the public by Joseph II
in 1766. The Hauptallee
(central avenue) was for
a long time the preserve
of the nobility and their
footmen. During the 19th
century, the northwestern
end of Prater became a massive
funfair with booths, sideshows,
shooting galleries, merry-go-
rounds and beer gardens. Today,
the Wurstelprater, as the funfair
is called, is one of Europe's best-
equipped amusement parks.
Its most famous attraction is the
giant Riesenrad (ferris wheel) built
in 1896 by the English engineer
Walter Basset. The setting for the
tense final scene in Carol Reed's
film *The Third Man* (1949), it is
now one of the city's symbols.

The Prater is also a vast sports
park, home to a soccer and a
trotting stadium, the Freudenau
Racetrack, swimming pools,
tennis courts, a golf course
and cycling trails, as well as
a planetarium and open-air
restaurants and bars.

Nearby are the pavilions
and vast grounds of the annual
Vienna Fair for numerous
temporary exhibitions.

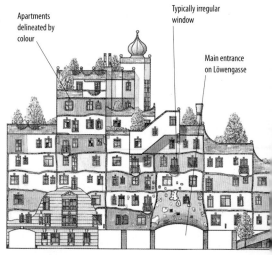

The Wurstelprater funfair at night

❾ Hundertwasser-Haus

Löwengasse/Kegelgasse.
Ⓤ Landstrasse. 🚋 1.
Closed no admission to the public.
Kunsthaus Wien: **Tel** 712 0491.
Open 10am–7pm daily. 🅦 das-
hundertwasser-haus.at

Hundertwasser-Haus is a
municipal apartment block
created in 1985 by the artist
Friedensreich Hundertwasser. An
eclectic-style building, combining
the elements of a Moorish
mosque with features of Spanish
villages and Venetian palaces, it
has become one of Vienna's main
attractions. The shopping centre
opposite was designed by the
artist, whose work is on show at
the **Kunsthaus Wien**, Untere
Weissgerberstrasse 13.

Apartments
delineated by
colour

Typically irregular
window

Main entrance
on Löwengasse

For hotels and restaurants in this area see p294 and pp314–16

⑩ Heeresgeschicht-liches Museum

Ghegastrasse Arsenal, Objekt 18.
Tel 79 56 10. Ⓤ Südtiroler Platz,
Schlachthausgasse. Ⓢ Quartier
Belvedere. 🚌 13A, 69A. 🚊 18, O & D.
Open 9am–5pm daily. Guided tours
(in English), call 0664 622 2248.
Closed 1 Jan, Easter Sunday, 1 May, All
Saints, 25 & 31 Dec. 🚫 Ⓦ hgm.or.at

The impressive Museum of
Army History is housed in the
military complex known as the
Arsenal, built as a fortress in
1856. The museum, which
chronicles Austria's military
prowess from the 16th century,
was designed by Theophil
Hansen and Ludwig Foerster.

Exhibits relate to the Turkish
Siege of Vienna in 1683, the
French Revolution and the
Napoleonic wars. There are
documents relating to the battles
fought by the Habsburgs, a
collection of arms, banners,
uniforms and military vehicles.
Among the most fascinating
exhibits are memorabilia relating
to Prince Eugene of Savoy,
as well as a collection of model
ships that illustrates the past
glories of imperial power at sea –
since it is landlocked, it is easy
to forget that Austria was once
a formidable naval power.
A separate section is devoted to
the events in Sarajevo on 28 June

Decorative tiling from the 1920s in Amalienbad

1914, when Archduke Franz
Ferdinand and his wife Sophie
von Hohenberg were assassinated by a Serbian nationalist,
provoking a crisis that led to the
outbreak of World War I.

⑪ Amalienbad

Reumannplatz 23. **Tel** 60 74 747.
Ⓤ Reumannplatz. 🚌 7A, 65A, 66A,
67A, 68A, 68B, 70A. 🚊 6, 67. **Open**
9am–6pm Tue, 9am–9:30pm Wed, Fri,
7am–9:30pm Thu, 7am–8pm Sat,
7am–6pm Sun.

Public baths may not seem like
an obvious tourist attraction,
but the *Jugendstil* Amalienbad
(1923–6) is a fine example of a
far-sighted municipal authority

providing essential public
facilities for the local working
population, and doing so with
style and panache. Named after
one of the councillors, Amalie
Pölzer, the baths were designed
by Otto Nadel and Karl
Schmalhofer, employees of the
city's architectural department.

The magnificent main pool,
overlooked by galleries, is covered
by a glass roof that can be
opened in minutes. There are
saunas, baths and therapeutic
pools. When first opened, the
baths were one of the largest of
their kind in Europe. The interior is
enlivened by fabulous Secession
tile decorations. The baths were
damaged in World War II but have
been impeccably restored.

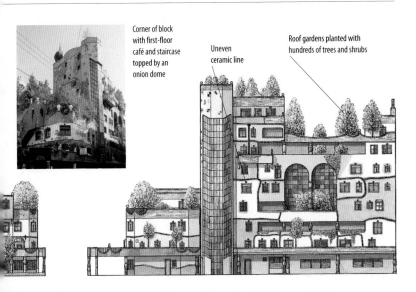

Corner of block
with first-floor
café and staircase
topped by an
onion dome

Uneven
ceramic line

Roof gardens planted with
hundreds of trees and shrubs

⑫ Zentralfriedhof

Austria's largest burial ground, containing 300,000 graves and covering over 2.5 sq km (1 sq mile), was opened in 1874. The central section includes the graves of artists, composers, architects, writers and local politicians. Funerals in Vienna are often quite lavish affairs, and the cemetery contains a vast array of funerary monuments, from the humble to the ostentatious, paying tribute to the city's enduring obsession with death.

★ **Friedhofskirche zum Heiligen Karl Borromäus**
This Art Nouveau church is decorated with Egyptian elements.

KEY

① **Presidential Vault** contains the remains of Dr Karl Renner, the first President of the Austrian Republic after World War II.

② **Arcades** around the cemetery's Secession church.

③ **Monument (1894) to Dr Johann Nepomuk Prix**, mayor of Vienna, by Viktor Tilgner.

④ **The main entrance** to the cemetery is from Simmeringer Hauptstrasse, with the Secession-style Gate II, designed by Max Hegele in 1905.

Cemetery Layout

The cemetery is divided into numbered sections: apart from the central garden of honour (reached via gate II), where VIPs are buried, there are old (gate I) and new (gate IV) Jewish cemeteries, a Protestant cemetery (gate III), a Russian Orthodox section, and various war graves and memorials. It is easiest to explore the cemetery on board the circulating minibus.

The Monument to the Dead of World War I is a powerful representation of a grieving mother by Anton Hanak.

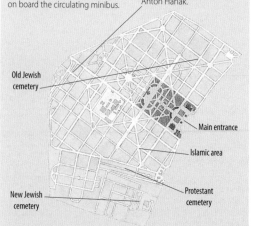

Old Jewish cemetery

Main entrance

Islamic area

New Jewish cemetery

Protestant cemetery

Arnold Schönberg's Cube
The grave of the modernist composer Arnold Schönberg, creator of dodecaphonic music, is marked with this bold cube by Fritz Wotruba.

Theophil Hansen's Grave
A Danish architect, Theophil Hansen, made Vienna his home and designed the city's Parliament building. He died in 1891.

VISITORS' CHECKLIST

Practical Information
Simmeringer Hauptstrasse 234.
Tel 534 69-28405.
Open Nov–Feb: 8am–5pm daily; Mar & Oct: 7am–6pm daily; Apr–Sep: 7am–7pm daily (until 8pm Thu May–Aug).

Transport
🄎 Zentralfriedhof. 🚋 6, 71.

The Arcades
Some spectacular monuments can be seen carved in the semi-circular arcades facing the main entrance, including this memorial (1848) to the miner August Zang. It shows the entrance to a mine.

★ Graves of the Musicians
The musicians buried here include Johann Strauss father and son (shown left), Brahms, Beethoven and Schubert. There is also a monument to Mozart.

Russian Orthodox Chapel
This small chapel, built in traditional Russian Orthodox style in 1894, is used by Vienna's Russian community.

Brahms' Room in the Haydnhaus

⑬ Haydnhaus

Haydngasse 19. **Tel** 59 61 307.
Ⓤ Zieglergasse. ☒ 57A. **Open** 10am–
1pm, 2–6pm Tue–Sun. **Closed** 1 Jan,
1 May, 25 Dec. ◪

Haydn built this house in what
was then a new suburb with
money that he had earned on
his successful trips to London
between 1791 and 1795.
He lived in the house from
1797 until his death in 1809,
and composed many major
works here, including *The
Seasons* and *The Creation*.
   The museum was extensively
renovated and reopened in 2009
to commemorate the 200-year
anniversary of Haydn's death.
The exhibits include portraits,
documents and original scores
as well as Haydn's clavichord,
which was bought by Johannes
Brahms. The museum's garden,
in the middle of Mariahilfer
Strasse, is open to the public.

⑭ Museum of Technology

Mariahilfer Strasse 212. **Tel** 89 998-0.
Ⓤ Schönbrunn, Johnstrasse. ☒ 10,
52, 58. ☒ 10A, 57A. **Open** 9am–
6pm Mon–Fri, 10am–6pm Sat, Sun
and hols. **Closed** 1 Jan, 1 May, 1 Nov,
25 & 31 Dec. ☒ tmw.at

Originally founded by Franz
Joseph I in 1908, Vienna's
Museum of Technology was
completely renovated during
the late 1990s, and now
covers a massive area.
   The museum documents
technical progress over the
past centuries, from domestic
appliances to heavy industry,
with a particular emphasis on
Austrian engineers and scientists.
Exhibits include the world's first

sewing machine
(Madersperger, 1830),
the oldest typewriter
(Mitterhofer, 1860),
the ship's propeller,
designed by Ressel in
1875, and the first
petrol-driven car built
in the same year by
Siegfried Marcus.
A major section
features displays on
computer technology
and oil and gas refining, as well
as a reconstructed coal mine.
   The Railway Museum, which is
an integral part of the museum,
houses a large collection of
imperial railway carriages and
engines. Its prize exhibit is the
carriage used by Franz Joseph I's
wife, the Empress Elisabeth.
The Post Office Museum displays
the world's first postcard – an
Austrian invention.
   A huge lighthouse at the
entrance recalls the Habsburg
Empire's once formidable extent,
from the Tatra Mountains to
the Atlantic Ocean.

⑮ Schönbrunn

See pp114–15.

⑯ Kirche am Steinhof

Baumgartner Höhe 1. **Tel** 91 060-11007.
Open 4–5pm Sat, noon–4pm Sun.
☒ 47A, 48A. ◪ (free on Sat). ◪ 3pm
Sat, 4pm Sun & by appointment.

At the edge of the Vienna Woods
rises the conspicuous copper
dome of the astonishing Church
at Steinhof. Built in 1902–7 by
Otto Wagner, the church is
considered to be one of the most
important works of the Secession.
It is an integral part of the large
mental hospital complex, also
designed by Wagner, who laid
out the church to facilitate access
for disabled churchgoers.
   The church, dedicated to
St Leonard, is clad in marble
with copper nailhead ornament,
and has spindly screw-shaped
pillars topped by wreaths
supporting the porch, and four
stone columns. The light and airy
interior is a single space with
shallow side chapels. Its main
decoration consists of gold and
white friezes as well as gilt
nailhead and beautiful blue
stained-glass windows by
Koloman Moser. The altar mosaics
are by Rudolf Jettmar.

The Secession-style interior of the Kirche am Steinhof

Hermesvilla in Lainzer Tiergarten, retreat of the imperial family

and elegance; Franz Joseph's were much more spartan. The villa, named after a marble statue of Hermes, was fully equipped with electricity. Bathtubs and toilets were added by the Empress in the 1890s. Attractive murals show scenes from Shakespeare's *A Midsummer Night's Dream*, designed by Hans Makart and painted by the young Gustav Klimt.

Today, Hermesvilla holds exhibitions, while the stables act as summer quarters for the Lipizzaner horses from the Spanish Riding School.

⓱ Wagner Villas

Hüttelbergstrasse 26 & 28. **Tel** 914 85 75. **Ⓤ** Hütteldorf. 🚌 43B, 52A, 52B. Ernst Fuchs-Museum: **Open** 10am–4pm Tue–Sat, by appointment Mon & Sun. 🅿 📷

Hidden behind dense, leafy greenery, at the start of a road to Kahlenberg, stand two villas built by the architect Otto Wagner. The oldest, built for himself, still has some Classical elements such as Ionic columns, once favoured by Wagner. It was meticulously restored by the present owner, the painter Ernst Fuchs, who added his own colours and established a museum. The villa is now a famous meeting place for Vienna's artistic community as well as a venue for fund-raising auctions. The second villa, built some 20 years later, was completed in pure Secession style. Privately owned, it can be viewed only from outside.

⓲ Lainzer Tiergarten

Hermesstrasse. 🚃 60 to Hermesstrasse, then 🚌 55A. **Open** daily. Hermesvilla: **Tel** 80 41 324. **Open** Apr–Oct: 10am–6pm Tue–Sun & hols. **Closed** between exhibitions. 🅿 **W wienmuseum.at** **W lainzer-tiergarten.at**

The Lainzer Tiergarten in the Vienna Woods, once an imperial hunting ground, was enclosed within a 25-km (16-mile) long wall on the orders of Maria Theresa. The wall still stands today and successfully stops herds of deer

and wild boar escaping. It also prevents modern building developments from encroaching on this beautiful space.

The Tiergarten was opened to the public in 1923, and in 1941 the entire area was declared a nature reserve. Walks in the woods and meadows of this large park will transport the visitor into another world. It is forbidden to disturb the animals; bikes and dogs are banned, turning the reserve into a true haven for wildlife.

There are now also bars and cafés here. From the observation platform on top of Kaltbründlberg, there are great views over Vienna and the Vienna Woods.

Detail on the stables in Hermesvilla

A 15-minute walk along paths brings you to the **Hermesvilla**. In 1885, the Emperor Franz Joseph I ordered a hunting lodge to be built here and presented it to his wife Elisabeth, in the hope that this would keep her close to the court and stop her from perpetually seeking to escape the clamour of the city. He did not succeed, but the beautiful Hermesvilla was built by Karl von Hasenauer as a retreat for the imperial family. The couple's rooms were on the first floor; Elisabeth's quarters were designed with flourish

⓳ Wotrubakirche

Georgsgasse/Rysergasse. **Tel** 888 61 47. 🚌 60A. **Open** 2–8pm Sat, 9am–4:30pm Sun and public holidays. 📷 by appointment.

Standing on a hillside close to the Vienna Woods, this church was designed in uncompromisingly modern style in 1965 by the Austrian sculptor Fritz Wotruba (1907–75), after whom it is named. It was built in 1974–6 by Fritz Gerhard Mayr. The church is made up of a pile of uneven concrete slabs and glass panels that provide its principal lighting and views for the congregation out onto the hills.

The building is raw in style, but powerful and compact. The church looks different from every angle and has a strong sculptural quality. The central section, consisting of 152 concrete blocks, can accommodate a congregation of up to 250.

The sculptural Wotrubakirche

⑮ Schönbrunn

In 1695, Emperor Leopold I asked Johann Bernhard Fischer von Erlach to rebuild the former summer residence of the imperial family. However, it was not until the reign of Maria Theresa that the project was completed by Nikolaus Pacassi (1744–9). It is to him that the palace owes the magnificent Rococo decorations of its state rooms. Schönbrunn has been the scene of many important historic events.

Round Chinese Cabinet
Maria Theresa used this room for private discussions with her State Chancellor, Prince Kaunitz. The walls of the white-and-gold room are adorned with lacquered panels.

★ Great Gallery
Used for imperial banquets, this room has a lovely ceiling fresco by Gregorio Guglielmi.

A hidden staircase leads to the apartment of the State Chancellor, above which he had secret conferences with the Empress.

Blue Chinese Salon
The last Austrian emperor, Karl I, signed his abdication in 1918 in this Rococo room with Chinese scenes.

Napoleon Room

Millionen-Zimmer
(Millions Room) was Maria Theresa's conference room.

★ Vieux-Lacque Room
During her widowhood Maria Theresa lived in this room, which is decorated with exquisite oriental lacquered panels.

Main entrance

Miniatures Cabinet
The paintings on the wall of Maria Theresa's breakfast room are copies of Dutch and German paintings by Franz Stephan and his daughters Maria Anna, Maria Christine and Maria Antonia.

VISITORS' CHECKLIST

Practical Information
Schönbrunner Schlossstrasse 47.
Tel 81 11 32 39.
Palace: **Open** Apr–Jun, Sep–Oct: 8:30am–5:30pm daily; Jul–Aug: 8:30am–6:30pm daily; Nov–Mar: 8:30am–5pm daily. Gardens: **Open** morning till dusk.
W schoenbrunn.at

Transport
U Schönbrunn, Hietzing. 10, 58, 60. 10A, 56A, 56B, 58A.

Large Rosa Room
This is one of three rooms decorated with monumental Swiss and Italian landscape paintings by Josef Rosa, after whom the room is named.

Palace Guide
On the first floor, the suite of rooms to the right of the Blue Staircase was occupied by Emperor Franz Joseph I and his wife Elisabeth. The rooms in the east wing include Maria Theresa's bedroom and rooms used by Archduke Franz Karl.

The Blue Staircase leads to the entrance for all tours of the state rooms.

The Coach Museum
One wing of Schönbrunn Palace, formerly housing the Winter Riding School, now contains a marvellous collection of coaches – one of the most interesting in the world. It includes over 60 carriages dating back to the 17th century, as well as riding uniforms, horse tackle, saddles, coachman liveries, and paintings and drawings of horses and carriages. The pride of the collection is the coronation coach of Emperor Karl VI. Other exhibits include sleighs and sedan chairs belonging to Maria Theresa, among others.

Coronation coach of Karl VI

Key
- Franz Joseph I's apartments
- Empress Elisabeth's apartments
- Ceremonial and reception rooms
- Maria Theresa's rooms
- Archduke Franz Karl's rooms
- Closed to visitors

SHOPPING IN VIENNA

Since Vienna is a compact city, it is a pleasant place to shop. The main shopping area is pedestrianized and you can browse around at a leisurely pace. Austrian glassware, food and traditional crafts are all good buys. However, the shops tend to cater for fairly mature tastes and full purses. Vienna has a number of markets selling anything from produce to trinkets. The pedestrian shopping areas of Kärntner Strasse, Graben and Kohlmarkt have more expensive shops. There are also several shopping centres in the suburbs, including Wien Mitte Landstrasse, Stadion Center and BahnhofCity West. These can all be reached on the U-Bahn.

Where to Shop

The most elegant shops are found within the Ring, and the most attractive window displays can be seen in Kärntner Strasse, Graben, Kohlmarkt and the central shopping passage connecting Kärntner Strasse with Weihburggasse. The shops here are also the more expensive ones. You will find smaller shops, tastefully decorated, offering goods of guaranteed quality and which are often truly unique. This applies to clothes, glass and porcelain, as well as to confectionery, books and decorative items. On Graben and Kärntner Strasse, you will also find a number of chain stores such as H&M and Mango.

The shops along Mariahilfer Strasse are more middle-of-the-range; this is where you will find many of the multi-national chains, as well as large shoe shops, stationery and bookshops, and a variety of food shops. A similar range of goods, but at lower prices, can be found in Meidlinger Hauptstrasse, and even less costly ones are on sale in Favoritenstrasse.

All of Vienna's shopping areas can easily be explored by public transport.

Opening Hours

Shops generally open at 8:30 or 9am and close at 6 or 7pm. Almost all stay open till 5pm on Saturday and close on Sundays and public holidays.

The supermarket chain Billa is open on Sundays at the main railway stations and Vienna airport. Most bakeries are also open. It is possible to buy some items at petrol stations too.

How to Pay

In Vienna, most stores accept major credit cards, including Visa, MasterCard and American Express. Debit cards are also usually accepted, however, it is still wise to carry some cash. Visitors normally resident outside the EU are entitled to claim back the VAT (Mehrwertsteuer – MwSt) if the total value of goods purchased in any one shop exceeds €73. Take your passport when shopping and ask the shopkeeper to complete the

A chest of drawers with chocolates from Altman & Kühne

appropriate form; keep the receipts. The VAT rate is 20 per cent and the goods listed in the form must be unused and available for inspection by Customs officers.

Rights and Services

If you have purchased goods that turn out to be defective, you are usually entitled to a refund, provided you have kept the receipt. This is not always the case with goods bought in the sales – inspect them carefully before you buy. Many shops in Vienna will pack goods for you – and often gift-wrap them at no extra charge – and send them anywhere in the world.

Antiques and Art

A pawnshop established by Emperor Joseph I in 1703 has been transformed into Austria's largest auction house, **Dorotheum,** one of the best known in the world. Items auctioned here include mainly antique furniture and objects of decorative value. Its vast

Opulent glassware in a shop on Kärntner Strasse

store at Dorotheergasse No. 17 is open to the public and also conducts a non-auction sale. Dorotheum has several branches all over the city.

Lovely second-hand and antique items can also be bought at the flea markets that take place regularly in various parts of town; the largest of them, but also the most expensive, is held on Saturday at the **Naschmarkt** *(see p97)*.

Food and Drink

Vienna is justly famous for its cakes, pastries and *Torten*, and any good *Café-Konditorei* (cake shop and café) will post cakes back home for you. In the pre-Christmas period, try the buttery Advent *Stollen* from **Meinl am Graben**, or the original *Sachertorte*, directly from the **Hotel Sacher**, at any time of year. The specialist chocolate shops are also worth a visit if you have a sweet tooth. And look out for *Eiswein*, a delicious dessert wine made from grapes left on the vine after the first frosts.

Souvenirs

There are many things you can buy to remind you of Austria,

Kohlmarkt, one of Vienna's most fashionable shopping streets

from the kitsch, such as the giant Ferris Wheel in a snow-storm or drinking glasses playing *O du lieber Augustin* (Oh, you dear Augustin), to the classy, such as Biedermeier-style flower posies, pretty handbags embroidered with folkloric designs or exquisite figurines and tableware from the famous **Augarten** porcelain factory. There are also cups with

the profile of Romy Schneider in her role as Sissi, or pictures of the young Franz Joseph I. Traditional Austrian clothes or *Trachten* are sold by **Witzky Landhausmode**. Products here include *Loden*, a felt-like fabric used to make warm coats, jackets and capes, and *Dirndls* (dresses). **Zauberklingl** is the place for practical jokers, with great party jokes.

DIRECTORY

Antiques & Art

Dorotheum
Dorotheergasse 17.
Map 2 B4. **Tel** 515 600.
w dorotheum.com

Galerie Rauhenstein
Rauhensteingasse 3.
Map 2 C4.
Tel 513 30 09.

Kunst- und Antikmarkt
At the Salztorbrücke.
Map 2 C3.
Open May–Sep: 2–6pm Sat, 10am–8pm Sun.
Am Hof.
Map 2 B3.
Open 10am–7pm Fri, Sat.

Naschmarkt
Map 4 C1.
Open 6am–7pm Mon–Fri, 6am–6pm Sat. Flea market: 6am–2pm Sat.

Food & Drink

Altmann & Kühne
Graben 30.
Map 2 B4.
Tel 533 09 27.

Delikatessen Böhle
Wollzeile 30.
Map 2 B4.
Tel 512 31 55.

Hotel Sacher
Philharmonikerstrasse 4.
Map 2 B5.
Tel 514 560.

Meinl am Graben
Graben 19.
Map 2 B4.
Tel 532 33 34.

Vinothek St. Stephan
Stephansplatz 6.
Map 2 C4.
Tel 512 68 58.

Zum Schwarzen Kameel
Bognergasse 5.
Map 2 B3.
Tel 533 81 25.

Souvenirs

Augarten
Spiegelgasse 3. **Map** 2 C4.
Tel 512 14 94.

J. & L. Lobmeyr
Kärntner Strasse 26.
Map 2 C5.
Tel 512 05 08-88.

Kalke Village
Kegelgasse 37–39.
Tel 710 46 16.

Lebzelterei Pirker
Stephansplatz 7.
Map 2 C4.
Tel 512 03 69.

Maria Stransky
Hofburg Passage 2.
Map 2 B4.
Tel 533 60 98.

Österreichische Werkstätten
Kärntner Strasse 6.
Map 2 C4.
Tel 512 24 18.

Petit Point
Kärntner Strasse 16.
Map 2 C4.
Tel 512 48 86.

Witzky Landhausmode
Stephansplatz 7.
Map 2 C4.
Tel 512 48 43.

Zauberklingl
Führichgasse 4.
Map 2 C4.
Tel 512 68 68.

ENTERTAINMENT IN VIENNA

Vienna offers a wide range of entertainment of every kind, from street theatre in the famous Wurstelprater funfair to classical drama in one of the opulent theatres. But most of all, Vienna is a musical town. There is grand opera at the Staatsoper, or the latest musical at the Theater an der Wien; dignified orchestral music and elegant waltzes; relaxed dances in the Stadtpark and free open-air concerts. Even the famous Lipizzaner horses perform to Viennese music. The city also takes pride in its Burgtheater, one of the most foremost stages in the German-speaking world, as well as its many smaller dramatic theatres. There are two excellent theatres performing in English and several cinemas which specialize in classic films. Restaurants tend to close early but you can still be entertained around the clock at one of the many nightspots; jazz clubs, discos, casinos and bars with live music all beckon within the Ringstrasse. Or you can end your day sipping coffee and indulging in the gorgeous pastries at one of the late-night cafés.

The giant Ferris wheel in the Wurstelprater funfair

Practical Information

Listings of current events and theatre, concert and cinema programmes can be found in most daily newspapers; check *Neue Kronen Zeitung, Die Presse, Standard* or *Kurier*. The weekly guide *Der Falter* (www.falter.at) is entirely devoted to the arts. The Vienna Tourist Office (Wiener Tourismusverband) publishes a monthly guide with listings of art and sports events taking place that month, and every hotel has a range of free leaflets with details of concerts, theatre performances and other artistic events. You can also check the fat round billboard columns all over the city, which have posters advertising the latest events. Most theatres, concert halls and public buildings have been specially adapted to accommodate disabled spectators (ramps, lifts), and many museums also offer wheelchairs for hire. All have at least one disabled toilet.

Booking Tickets

You can buy tickets directly from the appropriate box office, or reserve them by telephone or via the Internet. Hotel receptions can often help. Buy tickets to major theatre and classical music performances at the **Bundes-theaterkassen**, which is run by the state. You can also reserve tickets through **Vienna Classic** and the **Vienna Ticket Office**.

Theatres offer various concessions and the opera house sells cheap tickets for standing-only places. Tickets bought in advance tend to be up to 10 per cent cheaper than those bought just before the start of a performance.

Music

The principal venues for classical concerts, including the ever-popular waltzes, are the **Staatsoper** (State Opera), the concert halls of the **Musikverein**, where the Wiener Philharmoniker perform, and the **Konzerthaus**. Here you can hear the world's greatest performers. Classical music concerts are also held in many churches. Open-air concerts are very popular during the summer season. Another Viennese favourite is the **Wiener Kursalon**, where you can enjoy old and new tunes while over-looking the Stadtpark.

The **Donauinselfestival**, staged in the summer on the Danube island, is a great way to hear free concerts by some of the world's most popular performers. During local festivals, in wine bars and cafés you can often hear Viennese folk music called *Schrammelmusik*. Kärntner Strasse is another kind of music venue – many street

A young street musician entertaining with his cello

performers and buskers here hope for hand-outs from the generally well-to-do passers-by.

Theatre

Vienna's Staatsoper enjoys an excellent international reputation. Opera is also shown in the **Wiener Volksoper** (Vienna People's Opera) and the **Wiener Kammeroper** (Vienna Chamber Opera). The **Raimund Theater** is one of the best places for musicals. The **Theater an der Wien** specializes in opera productions. The **Burgtheater** is still regarded by many as one of the most interesting theatres; a smaller and more intimate stage is called **Akademietheater**. The **Volkstheater** stages modern plays and the occasional classic drama, while the **Theater in der Josefstadt** specializes in subtle takes on comedy, both old and new, as well as performances of past and contemporary Austrian drama.

Cinema

Most films are dubbed and shown in German; those that can be watched in their original language

The famous Vienna State Opera Ball

Billboard column

are always advertised as such in the programme. Some cinemas specialize in foreign films. The **Österreichisches Filmmuseum,** based in the Albertina building, screens classics of the silver screen, while the **Votivkino** and the **Filmhaus Stöbergasse** cinemas often put on a season of films devoted to one artist or subject; it is usually these arthouse and repertory cinemas that show the most interesting films in the city.

Casinos

Casino Wien is set in the fabulous Baroque Esterházy Palace, where you can play French or American roulette, baccarat and poker.

After a Night Out

At night, public transport is provided by a network of half-hourly buses, departing from the central points at Schwedenplatz, Franz-Josef-Kai and the opera. It is worth buying a ticket in advance from the kiosk, as these are cheaper than the ones sold on the bus. The U-Bahn runs all night on weekends and the night before a public holiday. Taxis can be found outside all major venues and at taxi ranks.

DIRECTORY

Bookings

Bundestheaterkassen
Operngasse 2. **Map** 2 B5.
Tel 51 444-7880. **Open** 8am–6pm Mon–Fri, 9am–noon Sat, Sun.

Vienna Classic
Tel (01) 1 982 13 51.
W viennaclassic.com

Vienna Ticket Office
W viennaticketoffice.com

Music

Donauinselfestival
W donauinsel fest.at

Konzerthaus
Lothringerstrasse 20.
Map 5 D1. **Tel** 24 20 02.
W konzerthaus.at.

Musikverein
Bösendorferstrasse 12.
Map 5 D1. **Tel** 50 58 190.
W musikverein.at.

Staatsoper
Opernring 2. **Map** 2 B5.
Tel 51 444-2250.
W wiener-staatsoper.at.

Wiener Kursalon
Johannesgasse 33.
Map 3 D5. **Tel** 51 257 90.

Theatre

Akademietheater
Lisztstrasse 1. **Map** 5 E1.
Tickets: Opernring 2.
Tel 51 444–4140.

Burgtheater
Universitätsring 2.
Map 2 A3.
Tel 51 444–4400.

Raimund Theater
Wallgasse 18–20.
Tel 588 85.

Theater an der Wien
Linke Wienzeile 6. **Map** 4 C1. **Tel** 588 301 010.

Theater in der Josefstadt
Josefstädter Strasse 26.
Map 1 B4. **Tel** 42 700.

Volkstheater
Neustiftgasse 1.
Map 1 C5.
Tel 52 111-400.

Wiener Kammeroper
Fleischmarkt 24. **Map** 3 D3. **Tel** 58 885.

Wiener Volksoper
Währingerstrasse 78.
Map 1 C1.
Tel 51 444–3670.

Cinema

Filmhaus Stöbergasse
Stöbergasse 11–15.
Map 4 A 4/5.
Tel 54 666–30.

Österreichisches Filmmuseum
Augustinerstrasse 1.
Members only.
Map 2 B5. **Tel** 53 370 54.

Votivkino
Währingerstrasse 12.
Map 2 A2. **Tel** 31 735 71.

Casinos

Casino Wien
Kärntner Strasse 41.
Map 2 B5. **Tel** 51 248 36.

VIENNA STREET FINDER

The map references given for all the sights, hotels, restaurants, bars, shops and entertainment venues described in this book refer to the maps in this section. Most of the city's famous sights, historic buildings, tram, bus, U-Bahn and railway stations, and river landing-stages have been marked on the map. Others are indicated by symbols, which are explained in the key below. The names of the streets and squares on the map are given in German. The word *Strasse* (Str.) translates as street, while *Gasse* is a smaller street, *Platz* means square, *Hof* means a courtyard, *Brücke* translates as bridge and a *Bahnhof* is a railway station.

Key to Street Finder

Major sight

Place of interest

Other building

U-Bahn station

Bundesbahn station

Schnellbahn station

Badner Bahn stop

Tourist information office

Hospital with casualty unit

Police station

Church

Synagogue

Railway line

Pedestrianized street

Scale of Maps 1–5

0 metres 200

0 yards 200

1:11,500

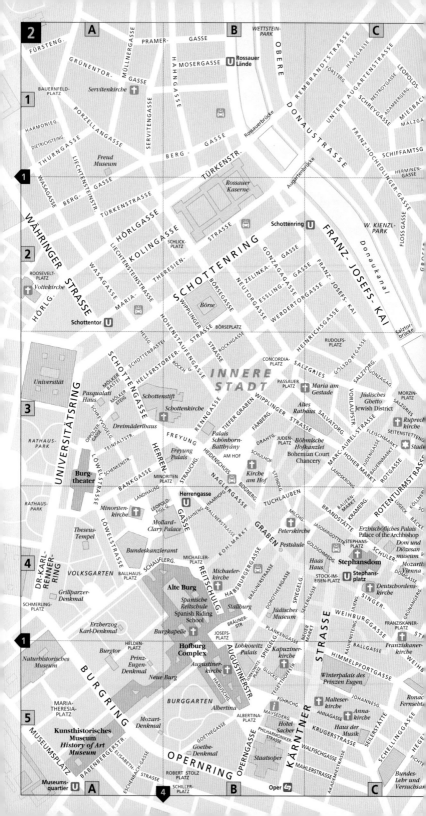

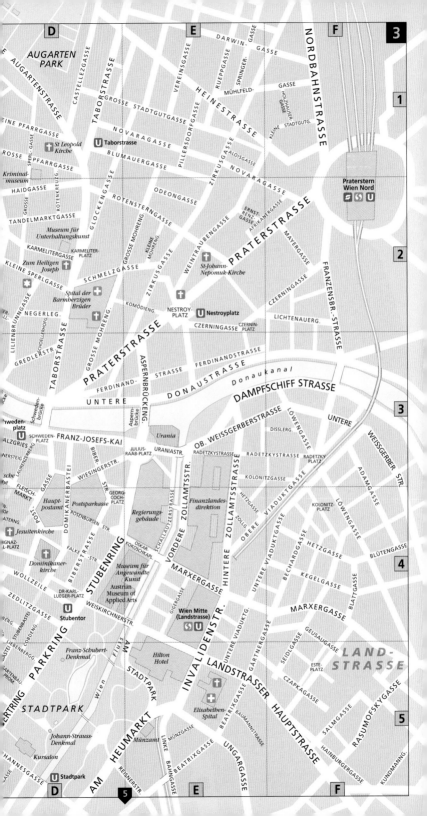

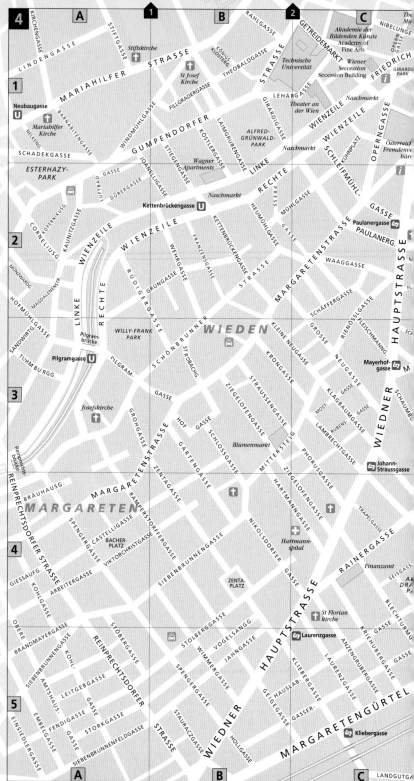

Street Finder Index

AUSTRIA REGION BY REGION

Austria at a Glance

This modest-sized country situated at the heart of Europe is a true paradise for visitors. There is beautiful countryside – from Neusiedler Lake in the east, surrounded by vast, flat steppes, to the fertile plains of the Danube Valley; the scenic Vienna Woods; and three majestic Alpine ranges that cut across the country from west to east. These glorious settings provide stunning backdrops for the historic sites and art treasures that form Austria's cultural highlights, and the names of great artists and Habsburg rulers will follow you wherever you go. There are also grand Baroque abbeys, and everywhere you can enjoy the work of Austria's outstanding musicians – Mozart, Strauss, Haydn and Beethoven, an adopted citizen of Vienna.

The Mirabell Palace in Salzburg was built in the 17th century for Salome Alt, the mistress of Archbishop Wolf Dietrich von Raitenau. The magnificent stairway is adorned with sculptures by Raphael Donner.

Innsbruck, with its picturesque Old Town and church spires rising against the majestic backdrop of the snow-covered Alps, is the capital of the Tyrol, the picture-postcard province most popular with visitors.

UPPER
AUSTRIA
(see pp190 21?

Salzburg

Lofer

Wörgl

Bregenz   Reutte

Schwaz

Zell am See   Radsta

TYROL AND
VORARLBERG   Innsbruck   SALZBURGER LAND
Bludenz   (see pp238–67)   (see pp214–37)

Lienz   CARINTHIA
AND EAST TYRC
(see pp268–85)

Villa

Houses in Bregenz, capital of the Vorarlberg province, are decorated with early heraldic paintings and the figures of saints.

Schloss Bruck in Lienz, in East Tyrol, was built in 1252–77 for the Görz family. Today, it is home to a museum with a fine collection of 19th- and 20th-century Austrian art and folklore items.

Hauptplatz in Linz, capital of Upper Austria, is one of the most beautiful architectural sights in Central Europe. In the centre of the square stands the marble column of the Holy Trinity (1723).

A Monument to Strauss and Lanner was erected in the spa park of Baden, a sleepy town close to Vienna, famous for its sulphuric baths and casino, one of the oldest in Austria.

Gmünd

Hollabrunn

LOWER AUSTRIA AND BURGENLAND
(see pp132–59)

Stockerau

VIENNA
(see pp54–127)

Linz

Melk   St Pölten

Steyr

Baden

Mitterbach

Wiener Neustadt

Eisenstadt

Oberpullendorf

Leoben

STYRIA
(Ssee pp160–89)

Murau

Graz

Wolfsberg

Leibnitz

Klagenfurt

The Zeughaus in Graz, capital of Styria province, is an impressive display of the city's armoury and former power.

The Landhaus in Klagenfurt, seat of the Carinthian provincial government, was built in the 16th century in an Italianate style, and is one of Klagenfurt's most attractive buildings. Its glorious galleried inner courtyard remains intact to this day.

0 kilometres   50

0 miles   50

LOWER AUSTRIA & BURGENLAND

Lower Austria is the largest province in Austria, both in terms of area and population. It surrounds the Austrian capital, Vienna, which for many years doubled as capital of the province. Following a plebiscite in 1986, the provincial capital was moved to St Pölten. At the edge of Lower Austria, bordering Hungary along one side, is the low-lying province of Burgenland, with its capital Eisenstadt.

Lower Austria, together with Upper Austria, covers the area that was once the cradle of the country. The low-lying and gently undulating terrain make this region easily accessible. During Roman times, its southern reaches belonged to the provinces of Noricum and Pannonia, while the areas north of the Danube frequently changed hands as Slav and German tribes fought over them. From AD 791, Lower Austria belonged to the Franks and, in AD 970, it was given the name Ostmark (Eastern Margravate). Today, it occupies an area of 19,163 sq km (6,930 sq miles) and stretches along the Danube valley, from the German border in the west, to Hungary in the east. In the south it reaches the slopes of the limestone Rax Mountains, with their highest peak, Schneeberg, and the popular winter resort of Semmering.

Lower Austria's most important towns, beside St Pölten, are Krems, Mödling, Wiener Neustadt, Klosterneuburg and Baden bei Wien. In the north of the province, adjoining the Czech Republic and Slovakia, lies the vine-growing region of Weinviertel. Further west is the wooded Waldviertel.

To the southeast of Lower Austria, from Neusiedler See downwards, is the long province of Burgenland, covering an area of 3,965 sq km (1,530 sq miles), with a population of 278,000. Historically, it was a part of Hungary, but after the Turkish wars (1529–1791) it was settled by Germans and Croats, and finally included in Austria in 1921.

The main town in Burgenland is Eisenstadt, where the mighty Esterházy family established their seat; to this day they continue to play an important role in the region's development.

The ornate 19th-century casino in the spa town of Baden bei Wien

◄ Beautiful spiral staircase with *trompe l'oeil* moulding, Melk Abbey

Exploring Lower Austria and Burgenland

The Wachau, a narrow stretch of the Danube valley, forms the heart of Lower Austria, famous for its fertile plains, its vineyards and picturesque villages. Formidable fortresses, castles and fortified abbeys rise along the high banks of the river, including the imposing Benedictine Abbey in Melk. Further east, the *Wienerwald* (Vienna Woods) is perfect for walking and cycling. Burgenland Province has its own unique flora and fauna around Neusiedler See. It produces the finest red wines in Austria and celebrates the memory of Joseph Haydn, former court musician to the Esterházy family in Eisenstadt.

Gossiping Women at Herrenplatz in St Pölten

The Gothic parish church in Spitz, overlooking the picturesque Wachau valley

0 kilometres 20
0 miles 20

16th-century Teisenhoferhof, with its attractive galleried courtyard,
now home of the Wachaumuseum, Weissenkirchen

Jihlawa

Brno

Laa an der
Thaya

erndorf

Poysdorf

Hohenau

Hollabrunn

Mistelbach

ÖSTERREICH

Dürnkrut

Stockerau

Wolkersdorf

LN

4 KORNEUBURG

Gänserndorf

3 KLOSTERNEUBURG

ersdorf

SCHLOSS HOF

VIENNA

28

Donau (Danube)

27 HAINBURG

Schwechat

Petronell

Mödling

9

5 LAXENBURG

26 ROHRAU

WIENER
WALD

8

7 BADEN

25 BRUCK AN DER LEITHA

Ebreichsdorf

Neusiedl am See

Győr

orf

Podersdorf

EISENSTADT

Frauenkirchen

WIENER
USTADT

6

24 Rust

23 NEUSIEDLER SEE

berg

BURGENLAND

Ilmitz

22 BURG
FORCHTENSTEIN

Neunkirchen

ggnitz

Aspang Markt

Deutschkreutz

Oberpullendorf

Mannersdorf
an der Rabnitz

Pinkafeld

Oberwart

Szombathely

Grosspetersdorf

Graz

Güssing

Jennersdorf

The mock-Gothic Franzensburg Castle,
Laxenburg

Key

Motorway

Major road

Minor road

Scenic route

Main railway

Minor railway

International border

Province border

Getting Around

Flights to both provinces depart from Vienna-Schwechat
International Airport, which is served by every major airline.
St Pölten is a major railway and road hub, situated on the route
of the Westbahn line, with branch lines to Mariazell, Krems,
Tulln and Gaming. St Pölten is also served by the Westautobahn
(motorway) and the road connecting Vienna and Salzburg.
The entire region is covered by a dense road network.

For map symbols see back flap

❶ St Pölten

The capital of Lower Austria since 1986, St Pölten was the first Austrian city to be granted municipal rights, in 1159. Its history dates back to Roman times, and it achieved considerable status under the Augustinian orders in the 8th century. St Pölten's fastest period of growth, however, was during the Baroque period, when outstanding masters of that era, such as the architect Jakob Prandtauer and the painters Daniel Gran, Paul Troger and Bartolomeo Altomonte, made their home here. Economically, St Pölten became the most important city in Lower Austria when trade switched from the Danube waterways to overland roads.

Rathausplatz in St Pölten, with the Holy Trinity column

Exploring St Pölten

The beautiful Baroque centre, with several older buildings, lies to the south of the railway station between Domplatz, Riemerplatz and Rathausplatz. The town centre is compact and easy to explore on foot, being largely pedestrianized. Apart from fascinating Baroque buildings and those associated with the town's administrative role, St Pölten also has more recent architecture of interest.

🏛 Domkirche Mariä Himmelfahrt

Domplatz 1. **Tel** (02742) 353 402.
Diocesan Museum: **Tel** (02742) 324 331. **Open** May–Oct: 10am–noon, 2–5pm Tue–Fri, 10am–1pm Sat. 📷

In the 12th century, a church dedicated to St Hippolytus stood on this site. After a devastating fire in 1278, the church was renovated and practically rebuilt in Baroque style to designs by Jakob Prandtauer. Deceptively plain on the outside, the cathedral's interior is a typical example of exuberant Baroque ornamentation. Daniel Gran and Bartolomeo Altomonte created the large wall and ceiling paintings, depicting scenes from the life of Jesus. Adjoining the cathedral is the Bishops' Palace, once an abbey, with a lovely staircase, also by Prandtauer, and a magnificent library decorated by Paul Troger.

The **Diocesan Museum** houses a collection of sculptures, paintings and decorative art objects dating from the Gothic and Baroque periods. Behind the palace, at No. 1 Klostergasse, is the apartment of Jakob Prandtauer.

A detail on the cathedral door

🏛 Franziskanerkirche

Rathausplatz.
The Franciscan church of the Holy Trinity, together with its friary, occupies the narrow, northern end of the square. A Rococo church with a delightful pink façade, it is unusual because it has no tower. The church interior, also decorated in Rococo style, features an altarpiece by Andreas Gruber. There are four wing paintings by another well-known Austrian Baroque artist, Martin Johann Schmidt, known as Kremser Schmidt.

🏛 Rathaus

Rathausplatz 1.
Tel (02742) 333 3000.
The present town hall was built in the 16th century by combining two Gothic buildings in a mishmash of incongruous styles. The niches of the Gothic entrance gate abut a Renaissance portal, the Gothic tower has a Baroque onion dome on top, and the entire structure has been concealed behind a Baroque façade. Inside, however, it is worth seeing the ceiling stuccowork in the Mayor's Chamber and sculptures by Christoph Kirschner.

The town hall occupies the southern side of Rathausplatz, once considered the most beautiful square in Austria. Today, it is lined with modern buildings, and has lost some of its Baroque charm. Next to the town hall you can see the house where Austrian composer Franz Schubert once lived, and at No. 5 is the Montecuccoli Palace. The façades of both buildings were created by Prandtauer's nephew, Joseph Munggenast.

At the centre of the square stands the marble column of the Holy Trinity, with a fountain and statues of saints.

Portraits line the walls in the Mayor's Chamber, Rathaus

🏛 Institut der Englischen Fräulein
Linzer Strasse 9–11.
Tel (02742) 3521 88–0.
Church: **Open** 10am–5pm daily.

The Institute of the English Ladies, founded by the English Catholic nun Mary Ward, established several schools in St Pölten to educate the girls of aristocratic families. The institute, one of the most beautiful Baroque buildings in Lower Austria, was begun in 1715 and enlarged some 50 years later. Prandtauer created the beautiful white and pink façade, punctuated by black wrought-iron grills on the windows, with three groups of sculptures on two floors.

A statue on the façade of the Institut der Englischen Fräulein

St Mary column, in the centre of the Baroque Herrenplatz

🏛 Riemerplatz
Riemerplatz is another beautiful Baroque square, lined with exquisite buildings such as the striking Herberstein Palace, at the wider end of Wiener Strasse. In Kremser Gasse, which runs north from the square, at No. 41, stands the delightful Stöhr-Haus with its breathtakingly beautiful Art Nouveau façade. It is the work of the architect Joseph Maria Olbrich, who also designed the superb Secession Building in Vienna.

🏛 Herrenplatz
This is yet another attractive Baroque square in the city; its most outstanding features are the Baroque façades of the buildings around the square. Mostly attributed to Jakob Prandtauer, these façades often hide much earlier medieval niches and arcaded courtyards. On top of the house at No. 2 is a lovely sculpture by Georg Raphael Donner, called *Dispersing of Darkness by Light*. At the centre of the square stands St Mary's Column (1718).

🏛 Wiener Strasse
Wiener Strasse, adjacent to Herrenplatz, has been a main thoroughfare since Roman times, as is still obvious today from its many inns. There are a number of interesting historical buildings in this road, including St Pölten's oldest pharmacy, at No. 1, dating back to 1595. Its façade, built in 1727 by Joseph Munggenast, still displays the pharmacist's original coat of arms from 1607 and the 19th-century sign "Zum Goldenen Löwen" (To the Golden Lion).

St Pölten City Centre
① Domkirche Mariä Himmelfahrt
② Franziskanerkirche
③ Rathaus
④ Institut der Englischen Fräulein
⑤ Riemerplatz
⑥ Herrenplatz
⑦ Wiener Strasse

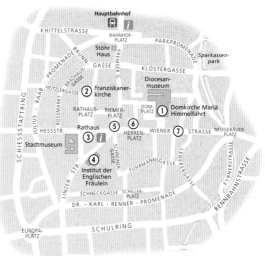

0 metres 250
0 yards 250

The 13th-century funerary chapel of the Three Wise Men in Tulln

❷ Tulln

Road map F3. 🏛 16,000. 🆂 🚌
🚉 🄸 Tourismusverband Tullner Donauraum, Minoritenplatz 2 (02272) 67 566-0. 🆆 tulln.at

Tulln, on the right bank of the Danube river, was the site of the Roman camp of Comagena. Two structures remain from that period: the 3rd-century Roman Tower, probably the oldest structure in Austria, and a milestone.

Tulln is famous as the birthplace of Egon Schiele, one of the foremost painters of the turn of the 20th century, best known for his provocative nudes. The **Egon-Schiele-Museum**, housed in an old prison on the banks of the Danube, shows 90 original works by the artists and the permanent exhibition *Egon Schiele and his Times*.

The former monastery, Minoritenkloster, houses Tulln's town hall, as well as the **Zuckermuseum**, on the top floor, which is devoted to the history of sugar.

The Romanesque **Pfarrkirche St Stephan**, the parish church of St. Stephen, was built in the 12th century, but subsequently altered, first in Gothic, then in Baroque style. It has an interesting Romanesque portal with 12 reliefs, probably representing the apostles. Next to the church is the 13th-century mortuary, one of the more interesting historic sites in town. It holds the cemetery chapel of the Three Wise Men,

the largest and most famous in Austria, combining elements of late-Romanesque style with early Gothic, and featuring a beautifully decorated portal and well-preserved murals.

The remains of the old city walls are also still preserved.

🏛 **Egon-Schiele-Museum**
Donaulände 28. **Tel** (02272) 645 70.
Open Apr–Oct: 10am–5pm Tue–Sun & hols. 🄲 on request.
🆆 egon-schiele.eu

🏛 **Zuckermuseum**
Minoritenplatz 1. **Tel** (02272) 602 11 237. **Open** 8am–3:30pm Mon, Tue & Wed, 8am–7pm Thu, 8am–noon Fri. 🄲

❸ Klosterneuburg

Road map G3. 🏛 26,000. 🆂 🚌 🚉
🄸 Niedermarkt 4 (02243) 320 38 600.
🆆 klosterneuburg.at.

This small town, just outside Vienna, was once the main seat of the Babenberg rulers. In the early 12th century, Margrave Leopold III built his castle here, and later the collegiate church, the magnificent **Stift Klosterneuburg**, supposedly in atonement for an act of treason he committed against Heinrich V.

The Romanesque church of the Augustinian Abbey was altered many times until the 17th and 18th centuries, when it acquired its present Baroque interior, designed by Joseph Fischer von Erlach and Donato Felice d'Allio, among others. Original features include the early-Gothic cloister and burial chapel of Leopold III; the latter contains the town's greatest treasure, an altarpiece by Nicolas of Verdun, a goldsmith and master of enamel from Lorraine. In 1181, the church acquired its altar, with 45 gilded and enamelled tiles depicting Bible scenes. The chapel also has fine stained-glass windows.

The museum in the former imperial residence

A wine barrel in Klosterneuburg

holds a valuable collection of paintings and Gothic and Baroque sculptures. A highlight is the **Essl Collection**, an important museum specializing in Austrian art since 1945.

A small museum in nearby **Kierling** is devoted to the writer Franz Kafka, based in the former Hoffmann Sanatorium where he died.

🏰 **Stift Klosterneuburg**
Tel (02243) 411-212. **Open** May–mid-Nov: 9am–6pm daily; mid-Nov–Apr: 10am–5pm. **Closed** 25, 26, 31 Dec. 🄲

🏰 **Essl Collection of Contemporary Art**
An der Donau-Au 1. **Tel** (02243) 370 50 150. **Open** 10am–6pm Tue–Sun, 10am–9pm Wed. 🄲
🆆 essl.museum

❹ Korneuburg

Road map G3. 🏛 12,000.
🆆 korneuburg.qv.at

Korneuburg once formed a single town with Klosterneuburg. In 1298 it became independent, and grew into an important trading and administrative centre.

Hauptplatz, the main square, is surrounded by houses with late-Gothic, Renaissance and Baroque façades. Other interesting sights include the late-Gothic St-Ägidius-Kirche (church of St Giles) and the Rococo Augustinerkirche (church of St Augustine), whose

The main altarpiece in Korneuburg

Franzensburg Castle, a mock-Gothic folly in Laxenburg

main altarpiece shows the sky resting on four columns, with God the Father sitting on his throne, holding the Earth in his hand. The altar painting of the *Last Supper* is the work of Franz Anton Maulbertsch.

Burg Kreuzenstein, on the road to Stockerau, is a fascinating folly of a Gothic castle. Built in the 19th century by Count Johann Nepomuk Graf Wilczek, on the site of a former fortress (1140) that was almost entirely destroyed by Swedish forces during the Thirty Years' War, it holds the count's extensive collection of late-Gothic art and handicrafts.

❺ Laxenburg

Road map G3. 🚗 ℹ️ Gemeindeamt (02236) 71101. **Fax** 73150.
🌐 laxenburg.at

This small town, situated 15 km (9 miles) outside Vienna, is a favourite place for day-trips from the capital. It began as a hunting lodge, Lachsenburg, around which a settlement grew. Destroyed during the last Turkish wars, but restored and enlarged in the 17th century, it became a favourite retreat for Maria Theresa and other members of the imperial family. Laxenburg was chosen as a venue for the signing of many important state treaties, including the Pragmatic Sanction which made it possible for a woman, Maria Theresa, to accede to the throne. Today, the former imperial palace is the seat of the

International Institute for Applied Systems Analysis (IIASA), and it also houses the Austrian Film Archives. The palace is surrounded by a landscaped, English-style **Schlosspark**, one of the grandest such palace parks in Europe at the time of Emperor Joseph II.

The park is dotted with many follies, and one particularly worth visiting is the early 19th-century **Franzensburg**, a mock-Gothic castle, built on an island in an artificial lake within the palace grounds at the height of the fashion for all things historic. It was furnished with original objects collected and pillaged from all over the empire, such as the 12th-century columns with capitals in the chapel, from Klosterneuburg, or the ceiling in the Hungarian Coronation Room from the Hungarian town of Eger. In the summer, open-air theatre performances take place on the castle island.

❻ Wiener Neustadt

Road map G3. 🚻 42,000. 🚌 🚉
ℹ️ Neunkirchner Strasse 17 (02622) 373-311. 🌐 **wiener-neustadt.at**

This large town, some 40 km (25 miles) south of Vienna, is an industrial city and an important road and rail transport hub, and also the largest shopping city of Lower Austria.

In the centre of the town is the attractive Hauptplatz, with a part-Gothic **Rathaus** (town hall) rebuilt in Baroque style. Gothic houses line the northern side of the square, and the St Mary's Column (1678) stands in the centre. The **Dom** (Cathedral Church of the Ascension of Our Lady) was built in the 13th century. Its outstanding features include 12 wooden statues of the apostles by the columns of the central nave, and the Baroque main altar. The Brautportal (Portal of the Betrothed) dates from 1230.

In **Stift Neukloster** (Holy Trinity church) you can see a beautifully carved stone on the tomb of Eleanor of Portugal, wife of Emperor Friedrich III, by Niklas Gerhaert of Leyden, dating from 1467.

The former castle now houses the prestigious Military Academy, once commanded by General Rommel. In its west wing is the 15th-century **St-Georgs-Kathedrale** (St George's Cathedral), with the tomb of Maximilian I under the main altar. A corner tower, a remnant of the old fortified city walls, now houses a criminology museum and a gruesome exhibition of instruments of torture.

The town hall in Hauptplatz, Wiener Neustadt

One of the many attractive villas in Baden bei Wien

❼ Baden bei Wien

Road map G3. 🏘 25,000. 🚉 🚌 🚆
ℹ️ Brusattiplatz 3 (02252) 22 600–600.
🎭 Festival of Roses (Jun).
🌐 **baden.at**

The spa town of Baden, on the eastern slopes of the Vienna Woods, was already known in Roman times, when it was called *Aquae Pannoniae*, and Emperor Marcus Aurelius praised its sulphuric springs. Today, its 15 hot springs make Baden a popular destination with older patients, but taking a hot sulphur bath is a relaxing experience for younger visitors too. In summer, you can swim in the open-air Art-Deco baths.

The small town was completely rebuilt after a fire in 1812, and many of its attractive Neo-Classical town houses and Biedermeier-style villas hail from this period. The main architect at the time, Joseph Kornhäusel (1786–1860), largely shaped the look of the town.

At one time, the list of Baden visitors read like a *Who's Who* of the rich and famous, and included such luminaries as Wolfgang Amadeus Mozart, who composed his *Ave Verum* here; Franz Schubert; and, most importantly, Ludwig van Beethoven. It was here that he composed his *Ninth Symphony*. Baden was frequented by the maestros of Viennese operetta as well: Strauss (father and son), Lanner and Zeller. Napoleon also holidayed here with his wife Marie Louise.

❾ Wienerwald Tour

The Vienna Woods (Wienerwald), to the west of the capital, are a favourite weekend destination for the Viennese. Crossed by numerous walking and cycling tracks, the wooded hills covering an area of 1,250 sq km (480 sq miles) are a perfect place for recreation. The main towns in the area are Klosterneuburg, former capital of the Babenbergs, Tulln *(see p138)* and Baden, one of Europe's most famous spa towns. There are also some interesting works of art and unique scenery worth seeing.

② Heiligenkreuz
The Cistercian Abbey (1133) at Heiligenkreuz, founded by Leopold III of Babenberg, has retained its fine Romanesque-Gothic character and some Baroque furnishings to this day.

Key

━━ Suggested route
━━ Scenic road
═══ Other road
═══ River, lake

③ Mayerling
After the suspected double suicide of Rudolf and Mary von Vetsera, Franz Joseph I had the famous hunting lodge converted into a Carmelite chapel of atonement.

The Mayerling Mystery

Rudolf, the only son of Franz Joseph I and Elisabeth, was a restless man, unable to adjust to the rigours of court. After a fierce quarrel with his father, he went to Mayerling with his mistress, Mary von Vetsera. On 30 January, the two lovers' bodies were found in the lodge. Both had been shot. Had they been murdered, was it joint suicide, or did Rudolf kill Mary and then turn the gun on himself? The reason behind the tragedy also remains a mystery to this day.

The tombstone of Mary von Vetsera

For hotels and restaurants in this region see p295 and pp316–18

① Burg Liechtenstein
The castle in Maria Enzersdorf, originally built in 1166, has been altered many times and now resembles a Gothic castle, with imposing towers and battlements.

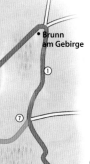

⑦ Mödling
This small, picturesque town, once a retreat for artists, is situated in beautiful natural scenery of limestone rocks.

```
0 kilometres          3
0 miles               3
```

⑥ Gumpoldskirchen
This small wine-making town has become famous for its countless *Heurigen* wine bars and cheerful restaurants.

⑤ Bad Vöslau
Poised on the southern slopes of the Vienna Woods, this village has two claims to fame: its wines and its baths (1837), built by Count Moritz von Fries, with crystal-clear natural mineral water.

Tips for Drivers

Length of the route: 60 km (37 miles).
Stopping places: most of the best restaurants can be found in Gumpoldskirchen and Baden.
Suggestions: visit the abbey in Heiligenkreuz. **Tel** (02258) 8703-0; take a boat excursion on the underground lake in Seegrotte Hinterbrühl. **Tel** (02236) 26364.

④ Baden bei Wien
Frauenbad, one of the original 19th-century baths, is today no longer in use but makes an interesting historic sight.

The magnificent organ in Stift Göttweig

❾ Stift Göttweig

Road map F3. 🚌 🚆 **Tel** (02732) 85 581-0. **Open** mid-Mar–Oct: 8am–6pm daily. Museum: **Open** mid-Mar–Oct: 10am–6pm daily (from 9am Jun–Sep). 🎫 📷 (02732) 85 581-231 to book. 💻 🌐 stiftgoettweig.or.at

Stift Göttweig, a Benedictine abbey, crowns a hilltop on the south bank of the Danube, near Krems. Founded in 1083, it was inhabited by Benedictine monks from St Blasien in the Black Forest in 1094. Stift Göttweig is sometimes referred to as the Austrian Monte Cassino because, superficially, it resembles the Benedictine mother abbey. The abbey was rebuilt after a fire in 1718, according to plans by Johann Lukas von Hildebrandt. The project was never completed, however, and the present abbey has an interesting but somewhat asymmetrical outline, with a Neo-Classical façade. In 1739, a magnificent flight of stairs, known as Kaiserstiege (imperial staircase) was added to the western section of the abbey. The stairs are lined with statues representing the four seasons and the twelve months of the year. Inside, the abbey is adorned with a fresco by Paul Troger, depicting the

Exhibit from the Wine Museum in Krems

apotheosis of Karl VI. The abbey has an interesting collection of sculptures, paintings and graphic art. The abbey restaurant affords great views of the surroundings.

❿ Krems

Road map F3. 🅰 24,000. 🚆 🚌 ℹ️ Utzstrasse 1 (02732) 82676. 🎭 Donaufestival (late Apr/early May), Folklore Festival (Jul). 🌐 krems.gv.at

During the 11th and 12th centuries, Krems, then known as *Chremis*, was a serious rival to Vienna. Today, this attractive town, together with neigh-bouring Stein, is a popular destination. Visitors are enchanted by the beautiful architecture of its town houses and courtyards, which give Krems a southern, Italian feel. There are remains of the old town walls, but the greatest attraction is the late-Gothic **Piaristenkirche**, an imposing Piarist church built on the foundations of an older church. It boasts a beautiful Baroque altarpiece by the local artist Johann Martin Schmidt, known as Kremser Schmidt. The **Veitskirche**, the parish church of St Veit, is the earliest Baroque church in Austria, the work of the Cypriano Biasino. The

former Dominican abbey has a lovely early-Gothic cloister; it is now the History Museum. Krems also has a Renaissance town hall and the vast, 13th-century **Gozzoburg**, a palace built by Judge Gozzo.

The Minoritenkirche, the Church of the Minorite Monks in Stein dates from the same period. It is adorned with 14th-century paintings of the Virgin Mary on a throne. The parish church of St Nicholas has beautiful ceiling frescoes and an altarpiece painted by Kremser Schmidt.

⓫ Waldviertel Tour

See pp144–5.

⓬ Dürnstein

Road map F3. 🅰 900. 🚆 🚌 🌐 duernstein.at

Much of the popularity of the idyllically situated town of Dürnstein is due to the adventures of the English King, Richard the Lionheart. On the Third Crusade, undertaken with the French King Philip August and the Austrian Margrave Leopold V, Richard fell out with his fellow crusaders. On his journey home through Babenberg territories, in 1192, he was imprisoned in Kuenringer castle above Dürnstein, whose ruins can still be seen today. As legend has it, the King's faithful French minstrel, Jean Blondel, discovered him with a song known only to the two of them. A ransom of 35,000 kg (77,100 lbs) silver was paid and Richard released. The Babenbergs used the money to fortify Enns, Hainburg, Wiener Neustadt and Vienna, while the name of the faithful servant lives on in many of Dürnstein's establishments.

The Baroque silhouette of the **Stiftskirche** (Collegiate Church of the Assumption of the Virgin Mary) towering above the town was created by the masters of the day. The courtyard is probably the work of Jakob Prandtauer; the entrance is embellished with lovely, decorated portals. The former convent of St Claire is now an inn; the Renaissance castle a hotel.

The Baroque tower of the Pfarrkirche in Dürnstein

⓭ Weissenkirchen

Road map F3. 🚶 1,500. 🚌 🚉
Tel (02715) 2600.

The small village in the heart of the Wachau Valley has attracted artists since 1900, who come to paint the magnificent scenery of the Danube gorge and to enjoy the cosy inns. Today, their works can be seen in the **Wachaumuseum**, in the Teisenhoferhof, a Renaissance mansion. Another attraction is the Wehrkirche Mariä Himmelfahrt (Church of the Assumption of the Virgin Mary), on a hilltop, fortified against Turkish raiders. The well-preserved defence towers are remains of those fortifications. The main entrance to the church is through the western portal, which has fine mouldings. Inside, on the rainbow arch, is a beautiful painting (1520) of the Madonna, from the Danube School.

🏛 Wachaumuseum
Tel (02715) 2268. **Open** Apr–Oct: 10am–5pm Tue–Sun. 🖼

Environs: Situated between Weissenkirchen and Spitz is the small village of **St Michael**, with another example of a fortified church. A few miles beyond

Spitz is **Willendorf**, where the famous statuette of the *Venus of Willendorf* was found. This representation of female fertility is believed to be over 25,000 years old. The figure itself is now kept in Vienna's Natural History Museum (*see p86*), while an over-life-sized copy stands in a field near Willendorf.

⓮ Spitz

Road map F3. 🚶 1,600. 🚌 🚉
Tel (02713) 23 63.

On the banks of the River Danube at the foot of the Tausendeimerberg (thousand bucket hill, so called because of the amount of wine it was said to produce), nestles the enchanting town of Spitz an der Donau. The river was once important to the town's economic life, and the **Schifffahrtsmuseum** tells the story of the Danube navigation.
Another famous sight is the **Pfarrkirche**, the early-Gothic parish church of St Maurice, furnished in late-Gothic style. The church has a presbytery (1508), criss-cross vaulting and elaborate window lacework. The altar painting is by Kremser Schmidt. Lovely wooden statues from around 1380, showing Christ and the apostles, are set in niches along the Gothic gallery.
High above the town looms the ruin of Hinterhaus Castle, with its Gothic bulwark and Renaissance fortifications.

🏛 Schifffahrtsmuseum
Auf der Wehr 21. **Tel** (02713) 2246.
Open Apr–Oct: 10am–noon, 2–4pm Mon–Sat, 10am–4pm Sun & hols.

Ruins of the formidable 12th-century Burg Aggstein

⓯ Burg Aggstein

Road map F3. 🚉

The impressive ruins of Burg Aggstein, built into the rock, are poised high above the banks of the river. Today the castle lies in ruin, but once it measured some 100 m (330 ft) in length, with tall stairs leading to the Upper Castle. Built by the notorious Kuenringers, a band of robber barons, it served to repel attacks by Turks and Swedes during the 16th and 17th centuries, thus cementing its rank as one of the most important fortresses in the region.
Many gruesome stories are told about the castle's early days. Its owner, an unmitigated thief, was said to have laid in wait for passing barges and demanded a hefty toll to allow them passage. Those who refused to pay were imprisoned in the Rosengärtlein, a rose garden set on a rocky shelf, where they would either die of hunger or jump to their death.
Today, the picturesque Burg Aggstein and its café are popular destinations for a day trip from Vienna.

The romantic ruins of Hinterhaus Castle in Spitz

⓫ Waldviertel Tour

Bitterly fought over by Germans and Slavs, who both wanted to settle here and exploit the area's natural resources, Austria's northwest boasts numerous historic sights, from abbeys built as defensive structures to the magnificent residences of the nobility built during times of peace. The wooded region became known as an idyllic spot for hunting trips and excursions, and today it is still its natural beauty and recreational facilities which draw most visitors; the traditional crafts practised in the area's numerous villages are another attraction.

① Gmünd
This town, on the Czech border, has a fascinating glass and stone museum. To the north is the Naturpark Blockheide-Eibenstein, with its vast granite rock formations and an unusual open-air exhibition of minerals.

② Rosenau
First built in 1590 as a Renaissance palace, Rosenau was remodelled some 150 years later in Baroque style. Its owner, Leopold Schallenberg, set aside some rooms for use as a Masonic lodge; today, it is a Masonic museum.

Jihlawa

Waidhofen an der Thaya

Schrems

Weitra

Linz

Key
▬ Suggested route
═ Other road
― River, lake

```
0 kilometres        500
0 miles             500
```

Linz

Ybbs

Kre...

③ Zwettl
This lovely old town boasts several original Baroque houses with interesting pediments. Nearby is one of the region's gems, the magnificent Cistercian monastery (1137–8), with a Gothic church and Baroque interior.

Tips for Drivers
Length of the tour: 210 km (336 miles).
Stopping places: numerous places offer accommodation at reasonable rates in the region.
Suggestions: visits to Altenburg Abbey and Schloss Greillenstein; falconry shows at Schloss Rosenburg.

⑦ Greillenstein
Set in woodland in the Kamp river valley, this Renaissance castle features a beautiful arcaded courtyard and several tall chimneys.

⑥ Eggenburg
A small, medieval town, Eggenburg has two attractions: 1,900 m (6,200 ft) of original town walls and towers, and the Rollipop museum, which is dedicated to scooters, motorbikes and tiny cars.

Stockerau

⑤ Rosenburg
One of Austria's most famous castles, Schloss Rosenburg was rebuilt in Neo-Classical style after a fire. The former state rooms house a splendid museum of old furniture, paintings and arms.

Stockerau

Stockerau

Krems

④ Altenburg
This gorgeous Benedictine Abbey (1144) has a great library, a treasury and, above all, a crypt entirely covered in stunning ceiling paintings depicting the dance of death.

Freemasonry in Austria

Francis Stephen, future husband of Maria Theresa, introduced freemasonry to Austria from Holland. In the late 18th and early 19th centuries, it played a very important role in the Austro-Hungarian empire, with many prominent politicians and artists being counted among its members. An increasing desire for national self-determination and liberal thought slowly removed the masons from power. In 1945, the Grand Masonic Lodge of Austria renewed its activities. Today, it has some 2,400 members in 52 lodges, including many public figures, financiers and artists.

Masonic Lodge in Rosenau

⑯ Melk Abbey

The town and abbey of Melk, the original seat of the Babenbergs, tower above the left bank of the Danube, some 60 km (37 miles) west of Vienna. In the 11th century, Leopold II invited the Benedictines from Lambach to Melk and granted them land and the castle, which the monks turned into a fortified abbey. Almost completely destroyed by fire in 1297, the abbey was rebuilt many times. In the 16th century, it had to withstand a Turkish invasion. In 1702, Abbot Berthold Dietmayr began a thorough remodelling of the complex. Jakob Prandtauer, Johann Michael Rottmayr, Joseph Munggenast and other renowned artists of the day helped to give the present abbey its magnificent Baroque form.

Stairwell
A spiral staircase with ornamental balustrade connects the library with the Stiftskirche, the monastery church of St Peter and St Paul.

★ Library
The impressive library holds some 100,000 volumes, including 2,000 manuscripts and 1,600 incunabula. It is decorated with a beautiful ceiling fresco by Paul Troger.

Crowning with the Crown of Thorns
This powerful painting by Jörg Breu (1502) is exhibited in the Abbey Museum.

KEY

① **Marble Hall**, a magnificent room decorated with a painting by Paul Troger, was once used for receptions and ceremonies.

② **Convent courtyard**

③ **17th-century two-tiered fountain**

④ **The grand staircase** leading to the imperial apartments, with putti and sculptures.

★ Stiftskirche
The splendid Baroque monastery church has a ceiling fresco by Johann Michael Rottmayr. The main altar features the figures of the church's patron saints, the apostles St Peter and St Paul.

VISITORS' CHECKLIST

Practical Information
Road map F3. 🚗 5,000.
ℹ️ Kremser Strasse 5, (02752) 555-232. 🎭 Melker Sommerspiele (Jul, Aug). Melk Abbey: **Open** May–Sep: 9am–5:30pm; Apr & Oct: 9am–4:30pm. 🦽 🎫 by appointment. Nov–Mar: guided tours only. 🅦 **stiftmelk.at**

Transport
🚌 🚆 🚐

Prelates' Courtyard
The courtyard is surrounded by imposing buildings crowned with statues of the prophets and frescoes showing the cardinal virtues.

★ Melk Crucifixes
The abbey holds two important crucifixes – one is Romanesque (c.1200, shown here), the other from the 14th century, containing gems and a piece of Christ's cross.

The View
Austria's most magnificent Baroque monastery, Melk Abbey is a vast yellow building perched dramatically on a high bluff overlooking the Danube.

A figure decorating an elevation of Schallaburg Castle

⓱ Schallaburg

Road map F3. 💻 **Tel** (02754) 6317-0. **Open** 9am–5pm Mon–Fri, 9am–6pm Sat, Sun, public holidays. 🅿 🆆 schallaburg.at

Schallaburg Castle counts as one of the most beautiful Renaissance castles in Lower Austria. It has some early remains of medieval Romanesque and Gothic architecture, but these are overshadowed by later additions. Particularly impressive are the Renaissance courtyard and the two-storey red and white terracotta arcades, the work of Jakob Bernecker. Carved terracotta atlantes support the second-storey arcades; sculptures and terracotta masks decorate the lower niches and walls of the castle. One of the best of these is the mask of a court jester holding a wand. Wilhelm von Losenstein, who owned the castle when the arcades were created, was a Protestant and a Humanist, a fact that is reflected in the works commissioned by him.

At the end of World War II, Schallaburg Castle was totally destroyed by the Russians, and it was not until 1970, when it came into state administration, that work began in order to return the castle to its former splendour.

Today, the Schallaburg houses Lower Austria's Cultural and Educational Centre, and serves as a venue for excellent exhibitions and lectures.

⓲ Amstetten

Road map E3. 🗺 23,000. 🚌 💻 **Tel** (07472) 601 454.

A major transport hub, the town of Amstetten is situated on the Ybbs River near the border with Upper Austria. Originally known as Amistein, the town witnessed the arrival of Illyrian, Celts and Roman settlers over time. It is the largest town in the Mostviertel region and boasts an attractive town hall, the 15th-century parish church of St Stephen with frescoes depicting the Last Judgement, and the Gothic Church of St Agatha. The **Mostviertler Bauernmuseum**, set in a former farmhouse, covers traditional country life.

🏛 **Mostviertler Bauernmuseum** Gigerreith 39. **Tel** (07479) 73 34-1. **Open** call ahead. 🅿 ⬜

Environs: Some 6 km (4 miles) southwest of the town is the medieval **Burg Ulmerfeld**, first recorded in the 10th century. From the 14th century until 1803, the castle belonged to the bishops of Freising. Later transformed into a paper-mill, it is now an important cultural centre and has a collection of arms.

⓳ Waidhofen an der Ybbs

Road map E3. 🗺 11,000. 🚌 💻 **Tel** (07442) 511255.

In the 16th century, this little town in the Ybbs valley was an important centre of iron processing and arms production. Its medieval old town is dominated by church spires and two towers, remains of the medieval fortifications: the 13th-century Ybbsturm and the Stadtturm, which was raised by 50 m (164 ft) in 1534 to celebrate the town's victory over the Turks. Since then, the clock on its north side has shown 11.45am, the hour of victory. The former Capuchin church has an interesting painting by Kremser Schmidt from 1762. Another great attraction is

Attractive houses and onion-dome spires in Waidhofen an der Ybbs

the city's **5e Museum**, one of the most modern in Lower Austria.

🏛 **5e Museum** Oberer Stadtplatz 32. **Tel** (07442) 511 255. **Open** 10am–5pm daily. 🅿 🆆 5e-waidhofen.at

Environs: The Carthusian Marienthron Monastery in **Gaming**, the most important structure of its kind in Central Europe, was founded in 1332 by Prince Albrecht II. The monks' cells and the fortified walls with round turrets remain to this day. Its Baroque library has frescoes by the Prague painter Wenzel Lorenz Reiner, his only work on display outside his Czech homeland. Today, the Carthusian monastery is used as a venue for cultural events. One of the best Austrian concert halls, it is much-liked by pianists, and the annual Chopin Festival is held at Marienthron in late summer.

The town also has an interesting Baroque church, several early buildings, St Mary's column and a pillory.

The Marienthron Monastery in Gaming, seen from the Prelates' Courtyard

Benedictine Abbeys

Benedictine monasticism was established in the 6th century, in Italy, by St Benedict of Nursia, and its mother abbey was Monte Cassino. The first Benedictine abbey in Austria was instituted in the 8th century, in Salzburg, but it was not until the 11th century that the order became a major force. Its growth was linked to the increased importance given to the Austrian state under the rule of the Babenbergs, whose history was chronicled by the Benedictines. Fortified abbeys were built on unassailable hilltops, and rural settlements grew up in the shadow, and under the protection, of the abbeys. The beautiful silhouettes of the abbeys tower over their surroundings. Stunningly decorated inside, they boast marvellous libraries that house outstanding records of the past.

Altenburg Abbey, *(see p145)* from the 12th century, was altered in Baroque style in the 18th century. Its façade is adorned with statues and paintings.

Kremsmünster Abbey *(see p204)* houses a tombstone with the figure of Knight Gunther. The inscription tells the legend of how his father founded the abbey in 777, following his son's death.

St Paul im Lavanttal Abbey *(see p272)* houses one of the most extensive Benedictine libraries with over 40,000 volumes and manuscripts.

The grand imperial staircase in Stift Göttweig *(see p142)*, lined with statues, was designed by F. A. Pilgram in 1739.

The family tree of the Babenberg dynasty, who brought the Benedictine monks to their seat in the stunning monastery of Melk, can be studied in Klosterneuburg Abbey *(see p138)*, just outside Vienna.

In front of the Stiftskirche in Melk *(see pp146–7)*, one of the most magnificent abbeys in Austria, extends a terrace affording fabulous views far across the Danube and the surrounding countryside.

⑳ Neuhofen an der Ybbs

Road map E3. 🏠 2,900. 🚌
Tel (07475) 52700-40.
ⓦ neuhofen-ybbs.at

Neuhofen is a small town on the Ybbs River, in the foothills of the Alps. Its centre is occupied by a Gothic church with a tall spire. The town was once a stopping place for pilgrims travelling to nearby Sonntagberg, whose basilica is the central place of worship for followers of the cult of the Virgin Mary.

Today, the **Ostarrichi Kulturhof**, a museum of Austrian history on the outskirts of the village, is the town's top attraction. The modern building was erected in 1980 to designs by Ernst Beneder, who also landscaped the surroundings in an attempt to make new and old blend in a single composition. The museum was built in record time, at a cost of 28.8 million shillings, and in 1996 it became the focus of Austria's 1,000th anniversary celebrations.

The most important exhibit, from which the centre has taken its name, is the facsimile of a document which first mentions the term *Ostarrichi* (the original document is kept in archives in Munich). In this document, dated 1 November

Facsimile of the 996 document, Ostarrichi Kulturhof, Neuhofen an der Ybbs

996, Emperor Otto III, ruler of the German Roman Empire, presented the land around Niuvanhof (present-day Neuhofen), known as *Ostarrichi* in the local language, to Gottschalk, Bishop of Freising in Bavaria. It was the first time that this name was used to describe the land that was controlled by the Babenbergs and which eventually, in the 11th–12th centuries, would become Austria. The Bishops of Freising had owned estates in this district from as early as the 9th century, and they regularly toured their territories. The names "Osterriche" and "Osterland", which appeared later, referred to the land east of the Enns River. It is fairly likely that originally the name referred to the entire country of Eastern Franconia. With time, Niuvanhof became Neuhofen, and if etymologists are to be believed, the present name of

Austria (Österreich) derives from *Ostarrichi*. According to the most widely believed interpretation, it meant "eastern territories", but an alternative view also exists: at the time when the name *Ostarrichi* first appeared, the area in this part of the Danube valley was still populated by Slav tribes, and the names of many surrounding towns and villages reveal a Slav origin. *Ostarrichi*, as it was then, could come from the Slav word "ostrik", meaning a hill.

Whichever interpretation is accurate, the year 996 is recognized here as the beginning of Austrian history, and the Neuhofen Museum informatively presents the story of the remarkable rise of a small German duchy to the heights of European power as the multi-ethnic Habsburg empire, and the tangled web of history that eventually, in 1918, led to the creation of the Austrian Republic.

The permanent exhibition in the Kulturhof consists of three parts. The first shows a facsimile of the *Ostarrichi* document in the original Latin version and in its German translation, together with photographs. The second exhibition is devoted to the etymological changes that the term has gone through, including its geographical, linguistic and political transformations. The third part of the exhibition is devoted to present-day Austria and its provinces. It illustrates how the distinct areas grew together into the Austrian Republic of today, and how each province has managed to preserve its own regional identity, customs, traditions, arts and culture.

🏛 **Ostarrichi Kulturhof**
Millenniumsplatz 1. **Tel** (07475) 5270040. **Open** mid-Apr–Oct: 9am–noon Mon, Tue, Thu & Fri; 10am–noon, 1–5pm Sat, Sun & hols. 🅿
ⓦ ostarrichi-kulturhof.at

The Gothic church in the centre of Neuhofen an der Ybbs

㉑ Schneeberg Tour

Both the Schneeberg and Raxalpen mountain ranges are popular with the Viennese for short winter breaks. Situated some 100 km (60 miles) from the capital, they offer excellent and well-developed skiing areas as well as many attractive walking trails for summer outings. The world's first high-mountain railway line was laid here, through the town of Semmering. To this day a ride on the railway is a thrilling experience.

Tips for Drivers

Length of the route: 130 km (80 miles). **Stopping places:** hotels and restaurants can be found in Puchberg, Semmering, and at the upper station on Schneeberg. **Suggestions:** ride on the railway from Puchberg to Schneeberg (mid-Apr–Oct).
🛈 (02742) 360 99 099.
Ⓦ schneebergbahn.at

④ Schneeberg
The highest peak in the range and in Lower Austria, whose distinctive silhouette is clearly visible from the motorway between Vienna and Graz, rises to 2,076 m (6,811 ft). The summit affords magnificent views of the Raxalpe range.

⑤ Höllental – Hell Valley
The ravine along the Schwarza River starts from the slopes of Hirschwang, where the first-ever cable car in the world was built in 1926.

① Puchberg am Schneeberg
A rack-railway links Schneeberg with Puchberg, a popular resort which also boasts an old castle.

Kernhof

Schwarzau im Gebirge

㉑

27

ariazell

Terz

⑤

Höllental

④

Schneeberg

③

Wiener Neustadt

26

Wiener Neustadt

①

Mürz

Raxalpen

②

Mürzsteg

Kapellen

Schwarza

Gloggnitz

23

Mürzzuschlag

S6

⑥

⑥ Semmering
A popular health resort since the early 19th century, this town is known for its long sunshine hours, great views and interesting architecture.

Key

━━ Suggested route
━━ Scenic road
══ Other road
── River, lake

```
0 kilometres      5
0 miles           5
```

② Neunkirchen
One of the oldest towns in Lower Austria, Neunkirchen has original Renaissance buildings and a church with late-Romanesque details.

③ Ternitz
This small town, in the Sierningbach valley, is a resort as well as a nature reserve. It has a modern church with a large mosaic.

For additional map symbols see back flap

㉒ Burg Forchtenstein

Road map G3. 🚉 Mattersburg. 🚌
ℹ Hauptstrasse 31 (02626) 631 23.
Castle: **Tel** (02626) 81212. **Open** Apr–Oct: 10am–6pm daily; Nov–Mar: groups by appointment. 📷
🅦 esterházy.at

Perched unassailably on the rocky slopes of Rosaliengebirge stands Forchtenstein Castle, built in the 14th century by the Mattersdorfer family. Bought and extended by the Esterházys, it now houses a private collection of arms, one of the most magnificent and extensive in Austria. The castle armoury exhibits arms and war trophies dating from the 16th to 19th centuries as well as memorabilia and pictures from the wars with Turkey, France and Prussia. Forchtenstein Castle was one of the fortresses that defended the Habsburg state during the Turkish raids of 1529 and 1683. Other trophies from that period include a captured Turkish tent, one of the major attractions, as well as vast paintings of battle scenes and a tank, dug 142 m (466 ft) deep into the castle courtyard by the captive Turks. Having played its part in repelling the Turkish threat, the heavily fortified castle became a museum in 1815.

The equestrian statue in the courtyard is of Paul, the first Prince of the Esterházy family, which

The birthplace of Franz Liszt in Raiding near Forchtenstein

still owns the castle today. In summer the castle hosts a popular festival.

Environs: In the village of Raiding, 24 km (15 miles) to the south of Forchtenstein, is a lovely cottage, the birthplace of the composer Franz Liszt (the **Liszt-Haus**). The house has been turned into a museum.

🏛 Liszt-Haus
Lisztstrasse 46. **Tel** (02619) 510 47-16. **Open** mid-Mar–May: 9am–5pm Tue–Sat; Jun–mid-Nov: 9am–5pm Mon–Sat, 10am–5pm Sun & hols.

㉓ Neusiedler See
See pp156–7.

㉔ Eisenstadt
See pp158–9.

㉕ Bruck an der Leitha

Road map G3. 🚊 7,500. 🚉 🚌
ℹ Hauptplatz 16 (02162) 622 21.

This small town, situated 30 km (19 miles) east of Vienna, was established as a Babenberg fortress in 1230, and formed the main border point between Austria and Hungary. Its present form dates mainly from the turn of the 17th century, but the remains of the medieval fortifications from the 13th century, as well as several old houses, remain in the main square today.

In Hauptplatz, the main square, stands an attractive town hall with a Rococo balcony and an arcaded courtyard. Also here is the Baroque Pfarrkirche, built by Heinrich Hoffmann. In Friedrich-Schiller-Gasse

Imposing 14th-century Burg Forchtenstein on the slopes of Rosaliengebirge

◀ The tranquil waters of Neusiedler See, the jewel of Burgenland stands the Kapuzinerkloster, the Capuchin Friary with its church dating from 1629.

The town's greatest architectural attraction, however, is the Prugg, a 13th-century castle with an original early-Gothic turret. In 1707, Johan Lukas von Hildebrandt altered the castle in the Baroque style. The chapel also dates from this period.

The Stadtmuseum Ungarturm, located in a 13th-century tower on Burgenlandstrasse, exhibits prehistorical and Roman finds, along with armaments and handicrafts. It also provides background on the town's past.

㉖ Rohrau

Road map G3. ![icon] 1,600.
![icon] Bad Deutsch Altenburg, Petronell.

East of Vienna lies the small town of Rohrau, with two attractions: Haydn's birthplace and the Harrach family castle, **Schloss Rohrau**. The pretty house in which the composer and his brother Michael were born, is now a small museum, the **Haydn-Geburtshaus**, devoted to both composers.

The nearby Schloss Rohrau contains one of the most beautiful private art galleries in Austria with a splendid collection of 17th- and 18th-century paintings, mainly from Spain and Naples, but also some work from the Netherlands. There are also interesting porcelain pieces. The castle dates from the 16th century but was rebuilt in the 18th century.

![icon] **Haydn-Geburtshaus**
Tel (02164) 2268. **Open** 10am–4pm Tue–Sun & hols. **Closed** 1 Jan, 24 Dec.
![icon] ![icon] haydngeburtshaus.at

![icon] **Schloss Rohrau**
Tel (02164) 2253 16. **Open** Easter–Oct: 10am–5pm Fri–Sun. ![icon]
![icon] schloss-rohrau.at

㉗ Hainburg

Road map G3. ![icon] 6,000. ![icon]
![icon] Ungarstrasse 3 (02165) 62 111 23.

Hainburg on the Danube was once a fortified border town of the Eastern Margravate, and it is

The Heathen's Gate in the Carnuntum Archaeological Park near Hainburg

still a gateway into Austria from the east. The ruins of an 11th-century castle and three substantial town gates remain from this period. The small town has many historic sights, such as the Romanesque cemetery chapel and the Rococo Marian column in Hauptplatz. The best way to travel to Hainburg is along the Danube. The marshy area around the town is a nature reserve, and home to rare bird species no longer seen elsewhere. The area west of Hainburg is preserved as a unique nature reserve.

Environs: 38 km (24 miles) east of Vienna is the village of Petronell-Carnuntum, where archaeologists unearthed a Roman town, Carnuntum, and the remains of a military camp.

The sights open to visitors in the **Archaeological Park Carnuntum** include a Roman triumphal arch known as Heidentor (gate), public baths, a reconstructed town villa and two huge amphitheatres. The ruins of ancient Carnuntum,

the former capital of the Roman province of Pannonia, extend to nearby Bad Deutsch-Altenburg, where many of the unearthed objects are on display in the **Museum Carnuntinum**.

![icon] **Archaeological Park Carnuntum**
![icon] Petronell Carnuntum, Hauptstrasse 296 (02163) 33 77-0. **Open** mid-Mar–mid-Nov: 9am–5pm daily. ![icon]
![icon] carnuntum.co.at

![icon] **Museum Carnuntinum**
Bad Deutsch-Altenburg, Badgasse 40–46. **Tel** (02163) 33 77-0. **Open** mid-Mar–mid-Nov: 9am–6pm daily. ![icon]
![icon] carnuntum.co.at

㉘ Schloss Hof

Road map G3. Imperial Festival Palace Hof. **Tel** (02285) 20 000. ![icon]
Open mid-Mar–Oct: 10am–6pm daily.
![icon] schlosshof.at

After extensive renovation, Schloss Hof is now one of the most appealing destinations for an excursion from Vienna. From 1725 Prince Eugene of Savoy made it into his principal country seat and laid out a formal country garden which survives to this day.

Extended a generation later under Empress Maria Theresa, the palace contains state and private rooms from both these periods. The Schloss Hof complex also includes an idyllic Manor Farm with herb gardens, craft workshops, and numerous attractions for the young such as rare breeds and pony and carriage rides.

The enchanting nature reserve around Hainburg

㉓ Neusiedler See

The jewel of Burgenland, Neusiedler See is the largest steppe lake in Central Europe. On the border between Austria and Hungary (a small section – around one-fifth of its total area – at the southern end belongs to Hungary) it covers an area of 320 sq km (124 sq miles) and has no natural in- or outlets apart from the Wulka River. The water is slightly saline and never more than 2 m (6½ ft) deep, so it warms up quickly in summer. The banks are densely overgrown with reeds which make ideal nesting grounds for birds, while the lakeside beaches are popular with visitors. In 2001, the lake and the surrounding countryside were declared a World Heritage Site by UNESCO.

Neusiedler See
Neusiedler See, Vienna's "seaside", attracts visitors with its wide range of water sports facilities and enchanting, melancholy landscapes.

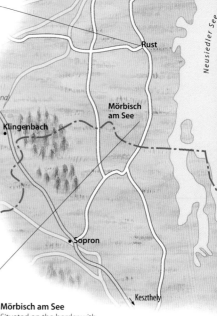

★ Rust
This attractive town on the western lake-shore has a perfectly preserved old town with many Renaissance and Baroque buildings. Star sights include the town hall and Fischerkirche.

Mörbisch am See
Situated on the border with Hungary, this village produces an excellent white wine. Its charming, whitewashed houses, laden with flowers, create a truly unique atmosphere.

For hotels and restaurants in this region see p295 and pp316–18

Neusiedl am See

A well-known resort and agricultural centre, Neusiedl is situated at the northern end of Neusiedler See. It has a museum devoted to local fauna and flora, and a small ruin.

VISITORS' CHECKLIST

Practical Information
Road map G3.
ℹ Rust (02685) 502; Neusiedl am See (02167) 2229; Illmitz, National Park Information Centre (02175) 3442; Neusiedlersee Tourismus (02167) 8600.
ⓦ neusiedlersee.com

Transport
🚆 🚌 🚌 🚢

★ Podersdorf

With its access to the water unencumbered by the wide band of reeds that separates other villages from the lake, and with swimming, boating and windsurfing facilities, Podersdorf is the most popular resort on the lake's eastern shores.

Illmitz

Situated amid the marshes of the Seewinkel national park, this is a good base for exploring the surrounding grass- and wetlands.

Seewinkel

This national park, a naturalist's paradise of reedbeds, small lakes and marshes, is home to over 250 different bird species.

Key

- ▦▦ Motorway
- ▭ Major road
- ▭ Minor road
- ꞏ ▪ Walking route
- ▬▪▬ National border
- ⋯⋯ River

0 kilometres 5

0 miles 5

㉔ Eisenstadt

This small town in Burgenland lies on the southern slopes of the Leitha Hills, 50 km (31 miles) south of Vienna. It became the capital of Burgenland province in 1925, when the larger and more notable Ödenburg – today the Hungarian town of Sopron – ended up on the other side of the border. From this date the town underwent a remarkable growth, and today it is an important transport hub, and wine-making centre. Eisenstadt is mainly associated with the Hungarian Esterházy family and their famous choirmaster, Joseph Haydn. Another great musician, Franz Liszt, was born on the Esterházys' estate, in the village of Raiding *(see p154)*.

Ornamental grille on Joseph Haydn's tomb in the Bergkirche

Exploring Eisenstadt

Above all, Eisenstadt is the town of Haydn, and the main tourist trails retrace his footsteps. Most of the town's historic sights are clustered around the inner town centre, south of Schlosspark. Only the Bergkirche, with its calvary, and the Jewish quarter of Unterberg are situated further to the west.

🏠 Bergkirche

Joseph-Haydn-Platz 1.
Haydnmausoleum **Open** Apr–Oct:
9am–5pm daily. 🎟

In 1715, Prince Paul Esterházy ordered a hill to be created to the west of the Schloss and of Eisenstadt's centre. He then had a church built on top of that hill, dedicated to the Visitation of the Virgin Mary, with a Way of the Cross made up of 24 stations. The Passion figures are life-size and each tableau stands in a specially laid out room. The rather theatrical, Baroque-style figures are carved from wood or

stone. The north tower of the church contains the most-visited attraction of the church: the tomb of Joseph Haydn. In 1932, on the 200th anniversary of the composer's death, a small mausoleum was built here by the Esterházys for the marble sarcophagus containing Haydn's remains.

🕍 Jüdischer Friedhof

Unterbergstrasse. Jewish Museum:
Unterbergstrasse 6. **Tel** (02682) 65145.
Open May–Oct: 10am–5pm Tue–Sun;
Nov–May: 9am–4pm Mon–Thu,
9am–1pm Fri; groups only.
Closed 24 Dec–6 Jan.

Until 1938, the Unterberg district of Eisenstadt was the base of the Jewish population, established in the 17th century by the Esterházys. It remained under their protection and played an important role in the life of the town. Inhabitants of the district included the Chief Rabbi of the Hungarian Jewry, banker Samson Wertheimer, and Sandor Wolf, a famous art collector. Eisenstadt was one of a handful of towns where

old traditions were still observed, such as the closing of the district for Sabbath, and the chains that were once used for that purpose are preserved to this day. The two Jewish cemeteries in Eisenstadt are among the best-preserved in Austria. The adjacent house, which once belonged to Samson Wertheimer, now houses the Jewish Museum.

🏛 Landesmuseum Burgenland

Museumgasse 1–5. **Tel** (02682) 719-4000. **Open** Timings vary, check website for opening timings.
🌐 landesmuseum-burgenland.at

This museum houses a large collection of objects associated with the history and art of the Burgenland province. Its geological collection comprises minerals and exhibits on the local Ice Age fauna. Archaeological findings include the Drassburg Venus, items from burial mounds in Siegendorf and objects which represent the Hallstatt and Roman cultures.

🏰 Schloss Esterházy

Esterházyplatz. **Tel** (02682) 63 004-7600. **Open** May–Sep: 10am–6pm daily; Apr & Oct: 10am–5pm daily; Nov–Mar: 10am–5pm Fri–Sun & hols.
🎟 🎥 🌐 esterhazy.at

The Esterházy Castle was built around 1390, on the site of earlier fortifications, remains of which were discovered in the course of excavations. In 1663–72, Carlo Martino Carlone transformed the castle into a magnificent Baroque palace. The main attraction inside is the Haydnsaal, a concert hall beautifully decorated with

Tombstones in one of the Jewish cemeteries in Unterberg

Prince's apartments in Esterházy Castle

frescoes and boasting truly amazing acoustics. Joseph Haydn once used to conduct the castle orchestra here.

Today, the larger part of the castle is leased to the Burgenland provincial authorities. The castle is surrounded by a beautiful English-style park.

⬆ Domkirche

Domplatz 1a.
This late-Gothic church was built in the 15th century on the site of an earlier medieval structure. As with many other churches in this part of Austria, its builders were conscious of the permanent threat of Turkish invasion, and its lofty steeple is therefore full of loopholes which leave no doubt as to their purpose.

The eclectic-style interior features some medieval tomb-stones and a relief in the church's vestibule depicting the Mount of Olives. The pulpit and the beautiful organ are Baroque, as are the two altar paintings by Stephan Dorfmeister. The large bronze sculpture of the Pietà is the work of Anton Hanak. The Domkirche was given cathedral status in 1960.

⬆ Franziskanerkirche

Joseph-Haydn-Gasse.
The Franciscan church of St Michael was built between 1625 and 1630, but its interior hails from a later period. The magnificent reliefs in the altarpiece date from 1630. Beneath the church you will find the crypt of the powerful local dynasty, the Esterházy family.

⬛ Haydn-Haus

Joseph-Haydn-Gasse 21. **Tel** (02682) 719 6000. **Open** Apr & May: Tue–Sat; Jun–mid-Nov: daily. 🅿
W haydn-haus.at
The house where Joseph Haydn lived in 1766–78 is now a small museum displaying a number of the composer's possessions. From 1761, Haydn was employed by the Esterházy family as their

Kapellmeister (music director), and in the evening he conducted the court orchestra for performances of his own music. Many of his beautiful compositions were first heard in Eisenstadt.

Haydn's home for 12 years, now a museum devoted to the composer

Eisenstadt City Centre

0 metres 250
0 yards 250

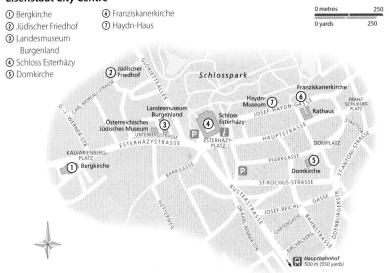

STYRIA

Austria's second-largest province, in the country's southeast, Styria has a population of 1.2 million. It is dominated by forests, meadows and vineyards covering some three-quarters of its total area of 16,387 sq km (6,327 sq miles). It is also an area of iron ore extraction and processing, and Erzberg (Iron Ore Mountain), glittering in every hue of red and brown, is a major tourist attraction.

Iron ore was already extracted by the Romans, who had named this part of Austria the Roman province of Noricum. The mineral shaped the history of this province through the centuries, and its traces survive to this day. Following the highs and lows of the early Middle Ages, Styria fell into the hands of the Habsburg dynasty in the 13th century and shared in its fate and fortunes. The province was repeatedly ravaged by Hungarians and Turks, and, after having staved off the Turkish threat, also became susceptible to attacks by the French.

A legacy of these times are its numerous hilltop castle strongholds and imposing fortified abbeys. Some have survived intact, others have been meticulously restored to their former splendour to capture the imagination of visitors to the region.

Styria's great attractions include the south-facing slopes of Raxalpen, its gentle climate and its rural idylls – it is known as "the green heart" of Austria. In the west, along its border with the Salzburger Land, the area is dominated by the lofty peaks of the Salzburg Alps and Lower Tauern. Here you will find excellent winter sport centres around Schladming, and at the foot of Dachstein, the highest peak in the region, with the best cross-country-skiing trails.

The Salzkammergut in the north is a stunningly beautiful lake district. The province's main rivers are the Mur, which flows through Graz, its tributary the Mürz, and the Salza.

Bad Blumau, an architectural complex based on Franz Hundertwasser's designs

◀ Steep, terraced vineyards near Gamlitz

Exploring Styria

Styria, or Steiermark, is rich in attractions and its capital, Graz, is Austria's second largest city. The west of the province offers excellent winter sports facilities; in the north lie the beautiful Mur and Mürz valleys, and many lakes. The quiet, agricultural southeast is covered with vineyards. Special sights are the National Austrian Open-Air Museum in Stübing, the Lipizzaner stud Piber, and the Mariazell Basilica, the country's largest Marian sanctuary.

Tobacco, one of the products grown in eastern Styria

One of the grand villas in the spa town of Bad Gleichenberg

For hotels and restaurants in this region see pp295–6 and pp318–20

Getting There

Graz has a passenger airport, though most international flights go to Vienna. The Province of Styria extends either side of the main road and rail connections crossing Austria from north to south. Local rail and road networks are also fairly well developed.

Watermill in Mureck on the Mur river

Statue of St Roch in the Wine Museum in Kitzeck, near Graz

30 MARIAZELL BASILICA
Gußwerk
Seewiesen
MÜRZZUSCHLAG 6
Krieglach
Aflenz Kurort
Kindberg
Kapfenberg
5 BRUCK AN DER MUR
Birkfeld
4 FROHNLEITEN
Anger
belbach
3 LURGROTTE
Weiz
2 STÜBING
atwein
1 GRAZ
eiersberg
och
Kalsdorf
undersdorf
Wildon
Stainz
Leibnitz
utsch-dsberg
14
Wies
Ehrenhausen
Neunkirchen
Wiener Neustadt
VORAU 7
Hartberg
8 PÖLLAU
HERBERSTEIN
9
Pischelsdorf
Gleisdorf
Bad Waltersdorf
10 BAD BLUMAU
Fürstenfeld
SCHLOSS RIEGERSBURG 11
Feldbach
Fehring
BAD GLEICHENBERG 12
Straden
BAD RADKERSBURG
13
Mureck
Maribor
Murska Sobota

Key
- Motorway
- Major road
- Minor road
- Scenic route
- Main railway
- Minor railway
- International border
- Province border
- △ Summit

Sights at a Glance

1. Graz pp164–9
2. Stübing pp170–71
3. Lurgrotte
4. Frohnleiten
5. Bruck an der Mur
6. Mürzzuschlag
7. Vorau
8. Pöllau
9. Herberstein
10. Bad Blumau
11. Castle Riegersburg
12. Bad Gleichenberg
13. Bad Radkersburg
15. Piber
16. Judenburg
17. St Lambrecht
18. Turracher Höhe
19. Murau
20. Oberwölz
21. Schladminger Tauern
22. Ramsau
23. Bad Aussee
24. Admont
25. Hohentauern
26. Eisenerzer Alpen
27. Seckau
28. Leoben
30. Mariazell Basilica pp188–9

Tours
14. Steirische Weinstrasse Tour
29. Salzatal Tour

❶ Graz: Street-by-Street

Graz, the capital of Styria, is the second largest city in Austria. During the Middle Ages it was the seat of a junior branch of the Habsburg family, and later of Emperor Friedrich III. The legacy of the Habsburgs is Graz's lovely Altstadt (old town), one of the best preserved in Central Europe and a UNESCO World Heritage Site. Graz was also a stronghold against Turkish attack.

The modern city extends from the foot of Schlossberg (Castle Mountain), on both sides of the Mur river. Graz is famed for its universities, architecture, cultural attractions and culinary traditions. It hosts two classical music festivals each year, one in the summer at the Music College and the "Styriarte", as well as the avant-garde "Styrian Autumn".

Haus am Luegg
This town house at Nos 11 & 12 Hauptplatz (c.1690) has a striking façade, with Renaissance frescoes and early Baroque stucco work.

Rathaus
The new town hall, built in the late 19th century on the southern side of Rathausplatz, replaced the smaller Renaissance palace that previously stood on the same site.

Hauptplatz
The Old Town's triangular main square is surrounded by 17th-century town houses.

FÄRBERGASS

HERRENGASSE

ALBRECHTGASSE

LANDHAUSGASSE

SCHMIEDGA

★ **Landhaus**
The inner courtyard of this government building has three magnificent storeys of arcaded Renaissance galleries.

★ **Landeszeughaus**
The jewel of this old armoury, the largest in the world that has been preserved intact, is the collection of weapons from Austria's 16th- and 17th-century Turkish wars (see pp168–9).

Key
— Suggested route

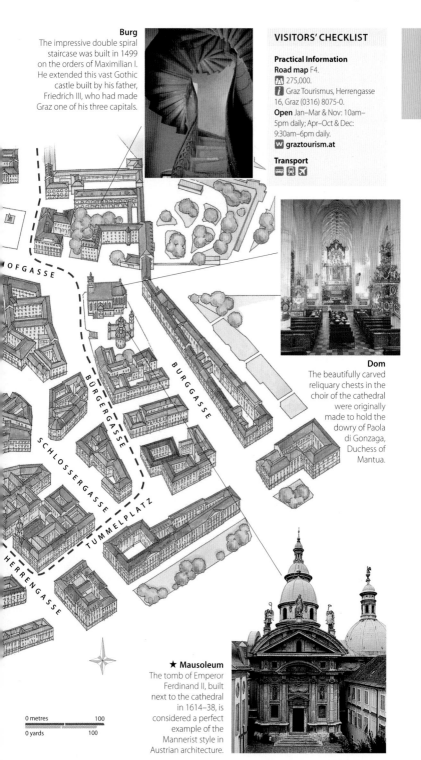

Burg
The impressive double spiral staircase was built in 1499 on the orders of Maximilian I. He extended this vast Gothic castle built by his father, Friedrich III, who had made Graz one of his three capitals.

Dom
The beautifully carved reliquary chests in the choir of the cathedral were originally made to hold the dowry of Paola di Gonzaga, Duchess of Mantua.

★ **Mausoleum**
The tomb of Emperor Ferdinand II, built next to the cathedral in 1614–38, is considered a perfect example of the Mannerist style in Austrian architecture.

0 metres   100
0 yards   100

View of the city of Graz and Mur river from the Clock Tower

Exploring Graz
The town is built on both banks of the Mur river; the Altstadt, with most of the tourist sights, is on the left bank. It can be reached by tram from the railway and bus stations. The Island in the Mur is Graz's newest attraction.

⌂ Schlossberg
Hofgasse.
At the north of the Altstadt rises the 473-m (1552-ft) high Schloss-berg. The top can be reached by a funicular or by a 20-minute walk. The 28-m (92-ft) high Clock Tower (1561), one of the symbols of Graz, offers splendid views over the city. It houses a museum.

⌂ Dom
Hofgasse.
The cathedral is a former castle church, built between 1439 and 1464 for Emperor Friedrich III. Its west portal bears the Emperor's coat of arms and his famous motto, AEIOU (see p42). Originally, the cathedral was built as a defensive church on the outskirts of town. It has survived almost intact to this day and the interior still features some original elements, including Gothic frescoes showing life during the plague, although most of the decorations stem from the Baroque period.

⌂ Franziskanerkirche
Franziskanerplatz.
The church once belonged to the Minorite Friars, but in 1515 it was handed over to the Franciscans.

Inside, the St James's chapel dates from 1320–30, and there are also Gothic cloisters with beautiful tombstones. The interior was redesigned after World War II, and the combination of the restored vault and modern stained-glass windows with earlier details creates a very striking effect. Next to the church is a monastery with a distinctive tower. Both the church and monastery are in an unusually shaped square, surrounded by many interesting buildings with Baroque façades.

⌂ Hauptplatz
The triangular square at the heart of the Old Town is an excellent starting point for exploring the city of Graz. It is surrounded by many original town houses from different periods, including the

Ducal coronet from the Joanneum collection

famous Haus am Luegg with its Renaissance and Baroque façade decorations. To the north of the square, at No. 4, stands Graz's oldest pharmacy, in a house dating from 1534 with some earlier features. The south side of the square is occupied by the neo-Renaissance town hall, built in the 1880s. In the middle of the square stands the fountain of Archduke Johann, who contributed much to the city's development. The four female figures around it symbolize Styria's four main rivers: the Mur, the Enns, the Drau and the Sann.

⌂ Universalmuseum Joanneum
Old Gallery in Schloss Eggenberg (see below). **Tel** (0316) 8017 9560. New Gallery: Joanneumviertel entrance Kalchberggasse. **Tel** (0316) 8017 9100. **Open** 10am–5pm Tue–Sun. Schloss Eggenberg: Eggenberger Allee 90. **Open** Apr–Oct: 10am–5pm Wed–Sun; Nov–Mar: Sun & hols as part of a tour. **W museum-joanneum.at**

The memory of Archduke Johann remains alive in Graz to this day. The grandson of Maria Theresa, he played an important role in the political life of the country and participated in military campaigns, until he finally settled in Graz to devote time to his favourite pursuit of scientific research. He founded the Technical University as well as the Joanneum, Austria's first public museum, which is named

Hauptplatz, the distinctive triangular main square in Graz's centre

The Italianate galleried courtyard in the Landhaus

after him. Today the Joanneum has 17 departments and holds several exhibitions, some bequeathed by the Archduke.

The Old Gallery, the most interesting display, is located in the lovely Baroque Eggenberg Palace, 3 km (2 miles) west of Graz, and contains some magnificent medieval paintings by Cranach, Pieter Bruegel the Younger, and Styrian 17th- and 18th-century artists. Another department, holding a collection of coins and medals and various interesting historic objects is also to be found there. The most valuable exhibit in the museum is the Strettweg chariot, which dates from the 7th century BC. Another department houses an interesting collection of coins and medals.

Reopened in 2013, the Natural History Museum provides an insight into the geological and mineralogical history of Styria.

The New Gallery, a collection of 19th- and 20th-century paintings, drawings and sculptures, previously housed in the Rococo Herberstein Palace, is now part of the Joanneum Quarter.

🏛 Landhaus
Herrengasse 16.
The Landhaus, one of the most beautiful Renaissance buildings in Styria, was once the seat of the Styrian diet which under Habsburg rule also covered areas that are now part of Slovenia and Italy. Today it houses the provincial parliament.

The building was altered in the 16th century by the Italian military architect Domenico dell'Allio. The stairs on the north-

western side of the courtyard are the work of another Italian, Bartolomeo di Bosio. The front, with its loggia and vast arched windows, is kept in the Venetian style. Well worth seeing is the beautiful courtyard with its three storeys of balustraded galleries linked by a raised walkway, and a fountain topped with a forged bronze cupola. In summer months it serves as a venue for festival events. Inside the Landhaus is the Baroque Landtag conference room, which has beautifully carved doors crowned by allegorical scenes, and ceiling stucco work by Johann Fromentini, depicting scenes from Styrian history. Also worth seeing is the Knight's Hall, which was decorated by the same artist.

🏛 Mausoleum
Hofgasse.
This small building, commissioned by Emperor Ferdinand II (1578–1637) as a tomb for himself and his family, is one of the most unusual and magnificent in Graz. A devout Catholic, the Emperor became especially notorious for the extremely harsh measures he took to introduce the Counter-Reformation in his territories, as well as for provoking the outbreak of the Thirty Years' War.

The mausoleum is one of the foremost examples of Austrian Mannerism, successfully blending various different styles. It was designed by an Italian architect, Pietro de Pomis, and completed by another Italian, Pietro Valnegro, who also built the belfry by the eastern apse.

Its narrow façade, exuberantly decorated with sculptures, consists of several architectural planes that create an exceptionally harmonious composition. The interior design is the work of Johann Bernhard Fischer von Erlach, who was born in Graz and began his life and career here.

🏛 Palais Attems
Sackstrasse 17.
Palais Attems is the city's most attractive Baroque palace. Built in 1702–16, it was designed by Johann Joachim Carlone. The palace's main features are its monumental staircase with frescoes and stucco ornaments, and its richly ornamented façades (inside and out, beyond the drive). The uniform furnishing of the rooms, with ceiling stuccos and lovely fireplaces and tiled stoves, is considered to be testimony to the Austrian aristocracy's standard of living during the Baroque period.

🏛 Grazer Congress
Albrechtgasse 1. **Tel** (0316) 8088-400.
Next to the town hall stands an old palace which, in 1980, was transformed into a modern congress centre with multiple facilities for arts performances. The building has two magnificent conference suites as well as contemporary entertainment venues furnished with state-of-the art technology. It also houses the city's largest concert hall, the Stefaniensaal.

The opulent main hall and stairs of the Grazer Congress

Landeszeughaus

The Landeszeughaus, or armoury, was built between 1642 and 1645 as a stock of arms to be handed to the local population in the fight against the Turks. Graz was in the vanguard of defending and guarding access to the threatened Austrian provinces of Styria, Carinthia and Carniola, which gave its armoury great importance. With a collection of over 32,000 objects, the Graz armoury today ranks as the world's best-preserved early arsenal. The museum's beautiful Renaissance façade was designed by the Italian Antonio Solari.

Minerva Statue
The Minerva statue in a niche to the right of the entrance, like the Mars statue on the left, is the work of Giovanni Mamolo.

17th-century Muskets
These front-loading firearms, with smooth barrels, were widely used in Europe throughout the 16th and 17th centuries.

Museum Guide

The first floor is devoted to heavy guns, flintlock pistols and rifles. The second floor holds the store of armour used by infantry and cavalry units, and pistols. The third floor displays the armour used by nobles and in tournaments. The fourth floor is devoted to staffs and edged weapons. The cloakroom, toilets and museum shop are located on the ground floor.

Cannons
The first-floor exhibition includes field guns and old naval deck guns.

Wheel-lock Pistol
This type of pistol, with a spherical barrel-end, was introduced to the German and Austrian cavalry in the 17th century.

★ Helmets
Most of the 16th-century helmets adorning the third floor ceiling were made in the Nuremberg and Augsburg workshops.

★ Hungarian Sabres
The 16th-century sabres are the pride of the side-arms collection exhibited on the fourth floor.

Fluted Armour
Made in a Nuremberg workshop during the 16th century, this suit of armour is one of the earliest in the collection.

Key

First floor
Second floor
Third floor
Fourth floor

★ Horse Armour
Dating from 1505, this armour hails from the workshop of Konrad Seusenhofer, master armourer of Innsbruck.

❷ Stübing

After several earlier attempts, the Österreichische Freilichtmuseum (Austrian Open-Air Museum) was started in 1962, when work was begun in the Styrian village of Stübing by the renowned scholar Professor Viktor Herbert Pöttler. It now occupies an area of 66 ha (24 acres), only 15 km (10 miles) north of Graz. The museum displays are buildings that have been moved here from other parts of Austria. This journey across the country, from east to west, from Burgenland to Vorarlberg, reveals remarkable regional differences in architecture, furnishings and workrooms, and document the everyday life of the houses' former inhabitants.

Farmstead from Alpbach
This Tyrolean farm is called Hanslerhof and dates from 1660. It unites all the essential areas of a farmstead under one single roof.

Pigsty from Gstadtterboden in the Enns valley

0 metres 50
0 yards 50

Granary (1620) from Hintertux in Tyrol

Chapel from Haag in Upper Austria

8th-century farm buildings from Waldviertel in Lower Austria

Residential House
St Walburg in southern Tyrol is the original location of this house. It was reconstructed in its present form following a fire in 1811.

House from Schwarzenberg
This 17th-century building is typical of the rural architecture in Bregenzer Wald (the Bregenz Forest) in Vorarlberg.

Brenner Kreuz
A brick shrine from Ebene Reichenau in Carinthia, this little chapel houses a statue of St Florian, the patron saint of fire fighters, who is invoked against fire.

Museum Activities

Every day, the Open-Air Museum offers activities associated with traditional customs and crafts, in which visitors are invited to participate. You can try your hand at lace-making, or on special days sing folk songs or listen with children to classic fairy tales. *Erlebnistag*, or adventure day, held every year on the last Sunday in September, combines a picnic with instruction into the secrets of traditional craft skills, customs and entertainments.

Traditional needlework display in Stübing

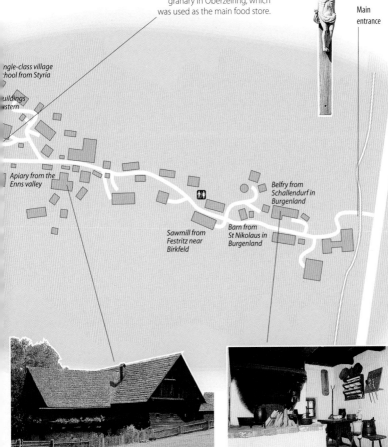

Crucifix
This cross was taken from a granary in Oberzeiring, which was used as the main food store.

Main entrance

ngle-class village chool from Styria

uildings astern

Apiary from the Enns valley

Belfry from Schallendurf in Burgenland

Sawmill from Festritz near Birkfeld

Barn from St Nikolaus in Burgenland

★ **Farmstead from Western Styria**
The main room in the 16th-century part of this house is the large "black room", where the entire family used to gather around the hearth and stove to cook, eat and socialize.

★ **Kitchen**
This typical kitchen from a house in the Burgenland province, is whitewashed and chimneyless, with an open hearth and traditional bread oven.

The astonishing Lurgrotte caves close to Peggau

❸ Lurgrotte

Road map F4. 🚗 ℹ (03127) 2580. **Open** Apr–Oct: 10am–4pm daily (3pm at from Peggau). 🎟 🚶 on the hour (more frequently in summer); Adventure Tours in winter by request (0680 232 4281). 🖥 **lurgrotte.com**

The Lurgrotte is the largest and most interesting cave in Austria, with superb stalactites and stalagmites. Starting at the entrance at either Peggau or Semriach, guides lead visitors through this world of icy wonders, along an underground stream. The largest dripstone, 13 m (43 ft) tall, is nicknamed the "Giant" (der Riese). A railway takes you there from Semriach.

❹ Frohnleiten

Road map F4. 🏠 6,500. 🚗 🚌 ℹ (03126) 2374. 🖥 **frohnleiten.or.at**

Set among gentle hills on the Mur river, the town of Frohnleiten is surrounded by a network of clearly marked rambling trails which invite visitors to take long walks.

At one time Frohnleiten was an important transhipment post on the Mur. In 1763, the town almost burned to the ground in a fire. Sights worth visiting include the Servite monastery and the parish church with Rococo figures in the altarpiece by Veit Königer and ceiling frescoes by Josef Adam von Mölk.

Frohnleiten has won several awards for its impressive flower displays, and it has a splendid Alpine garden on 90,000 sq m (107,000 sq ft) of land, stocked with some 10,000 species from around the world.

Environs: A short way to the west, in Adriach, is the **St Georgskirche**, church of St George, with an altarpiece of the martyrdom of St George and four frescoes in the main nave by Josef Adam von Mölk.

❺ Bruck an der Mur

Road map F4. 🏠 16,000. 🚗 🚌 ℹ Koloman-Wallisch-Platz 1 (03862) 890-121. 🎭 Murenschalk (2nd Thu and Fri in Aug).

This major industrial centre lies at the mouth of the Mürz river, where it flows into the Mur. Bruck flourished during the 14th and 15th centuries, thanks to its trade with Venice, when it had the right to store grain and salt. The small but attractive old town in the fork of the Mürz and Mur rivers dates from this period. Bruck was once a town of blacksmiths and their works are now its chief historical attractions. On the main square stands an iron well (1626) by the local master, Hans Prasser, sporting an intricate wrought-iron canopy. The **parish church of Mariä Geburt** features an interesting door (1500) to the vestry, a beautiful example of Styrian metalwork. This Gothic church was later altered in the Baroque style. The former Minorite church has several important 14th-century frescoes. In the main square, Koloman-Wallisch-Platz, stands the town hall with an attractive arcaded courtyard, in a former ducal residence. The town's loveliest building is the late-Gothic **Kornmesserhaus**, built for the ironmonger Kornmess. It has open arcades on the ground floor and a first-floor loggia.

A small distance away, on the other side of the Mur, stands St Rupert's church, with a superb *Last Judgement* fresco (1420), uncovered in the 1930s. Above the town rise the ruins of **Landskron** fortress, whose only remaining feature is the bell tower.

Poster from the Winter Sports Museum in Mürzzuschlag

❻ Mürzzuschlag

Road map F4. 🏠 9,000. 🚗 ℹ Wiener Strasse 9 (03852) 3399.

This town on the Mürz at the foot of Semmering Mountain is Austria's oldest winter sports resort. In 1893, Mürzzuschlag hosted the first skiing competitions in the Alps, and in 1934 it was the venue for the Nordic Games that later became the Winter Olympics. The town's first historic records date from 1469,

Ruins of Landskron Castle rising above Bruck an der Mur

The richly ornamented library in the 12th-century Augustinian Vorau Abbey

when Emperor Friedrich III ordered it to be burned to the ground, following a rebellion led by Count Andreas Baumkircher. Today its main sights of interest are the parish church with a lovely Renaissance altarpiece and its picturesque old houses, including **the house of Johannes Brahms** at No. 4 Wiener Strasse. Also worth visiting is the **Winter Sports Museum** which has the world's largest collection of objects and memorabilia relating to all aspects of winter sports.

🏛 **Winter Sports Museum**
Wiener Strasse 13. **Open** 9am–12:30pm & 2–5pm Tue–Sun. **Closed** 1 Jan, Shrove Tuesday, 1 Nov, 24–25 Dec, 31 Dec.

❼ Vorau

Road map F4. 👥 4,800.
ℹ Stift Vorau (03337) 2351.

On a remote hill stands the 12th-century Augustinian **Vorau Abbey**. In the 15th century, the abbey was turned into a fortress; its present form is the result of alterations made throughout the 17th and 18th centuries. The main entrance has symmetrical wings on both sides, adjoining

two identical towers. One wing contains the cloister; in the other wing are the prelacy and the magnificent fresco- and stucco-adorned library with its low barrel-vault ceiling. On the floor above is the cabinet of manuscripts, decorated with ceiling paintings of the Gods, the Virtues and The Immaculate. It contains some 415 valuable manuscripts, including the oldest annals of poetry in the German language – the Vorauer Handschrift and the famous Kaiserchronik.

Bust of Johannes Brahms, who lived in Mürzzuschlag

The abbey church, dedicated to St Thomas, acquired its sumptuous decor in 1700–1705. It has a main altarpiece by Matthias Steinl, who also created the beautifully ornamented pulpit.

The small nearby town of Vorau also has an **Open-air Museum** (Freilichtmuseum) with a fascinating collection of typical homes and public buildings (school, pharmacy, smithy) from the neighbouring villages, complete with their distinctive furnishings.

🏛 **Open-air Museum**
Tel (03337) 3466. **Open** Apr–Oct: 10am–5pm daily (Jul & Aug: 9am–5pm daily).

❽ Pöllau

Road map F4. 👥 6,000.
ℹ (03335) 4210.
🌐 naturpark-poellauertal.at

Pöllau lies at the centre of a national park, surrounded by woodland, vineyards and walking trails. The town's main attraction is the former **Augustinian Abbey** and, above all, the lovely **St Veit's church**. Built between 1701 and 1712 by Joachim Carlone of the famous family of architects from Graz, this is a splendid example of Styrian Baroque. The building is vast: the main nave and presbytery measures 62 m (203 ft), the transept 37 m (121 ft) and the dome is 42 m (138 ft) high. The vaults and the inside of the dome are decorated with *trompe l'oeil* frescoes by Mathias von Görz, depicting the four fathers of the church, two Augustinian saints and the 12 apostles. The main altarpiece has a monumental painting by Josef Adam von Mölk showing the martyrdom of the patron saint St Veit.

Environs: About 6 km (4 miles) northeast of Pöllau, high up on Pöllauberg, stands the 14th-century Gothic pilgrimage church of **Maria-Lebing**, with vault frescoes by Mölk and two statues of the Virgin Mary – from the 15th and 17th centuries.

🟊 Herberstein

Road map F4. 🏛 300. 🚌 **Tel** (03176) 88250. **Open** Mar–Apr: 10am–4pm daily; May–Sep: 9am–5pm daily; Oct–Mar: 10am–4pm daily. 🅿
🌐 **herberstein.co.at**

Schloss Herberstein, perched on a steep rock amid wild countryside, has remained in the hands of the same family since 1290. Since the Herbersteins still live in the castle, a visit feels a bit like peeping through a keyhole at history.

The medieval fortress, rebuilt numerous times, achieved its present form in the late 16th century. Its most magnificent part is the Florence Courtyard, a lovely arcaded enclosure more reminiscent of Renaissance Italian palaces than of northern European fortresses. Once the castle was a venue for knightly tournaments.

The rooms that are open to visitors today display many items relating to the Herberstein family, and an exhibition that gives a unique insight into aristocratic life in the 18th and 19th centuries. There is even an original kitchen from the 16th century. Temporary exhibitions are organized during the summer.

One of the most interesting places within the castle grounds is the nature reserve, **Tierwelt Herberstein**, which is home to wild plants and animals. Its origins can be traced back to the 16th century, when the castle was inhabited by Count Sigmund von Herberstein, the author of pioneering works on the agriculture and geography of Eastern Europe.

The Bad Blumau resort, designed by Friedensreich Hundertwasser

🌿 **Tierwelt Herberstein**
Open mid-Mar–Apr & Oct: 10am–4pm daily; May–Sep: 9am–5pm daily; Nov–mid-Mar: 10am–3:30pm Thu–Sun & hols. 🅿 🌐 **tierwelt-herberstein.at**

🔟 Bad Blumau

Road map F4. 🏛 1,600. 🚌 🚉
ℹ Rogner–Bad Blumau (03383) 51000. 🌐 **blumau.com**

In eastern Styria, in an area that has long been famed for its crystal-clear mineral waters, is a spa resort that is certainly worth a detour or even a few days' visit. The entire resort of Bad Blumau was designed by the painter and architect Friedensreich Hundertwasser, in a style similar to his building in Vienna (*see pp108–109*). You will see rounded façades, rippling roofs, colourful walls and irregularly shaped terraces and balconies which transport you into a strange and surreal fairyland.

The outside of the complex can be seen with a guided tour. As you stroll along an avenue lined with trees and shrubs that represent the Chinese horoscope, you suddenly realize that the grass you are walking on grows on the roof of a building below.

The main reason for a visit to the spa is, of course, taking the waters. Admission to the complex is available for half and full days, and will prove both an artistic experience and a pleasant way to while away some time.

⓫ Castle Riegersburg

Road map F5. 🏛 5,000. 🚌
Tel (03153) 8670. **Open** Apr & Oct: 10am–6pm daily; May–Sep: 9am–6pm daily. 🌐 **riegersburg.com**

On a steep basaltic rock high above the Grazbach stream stands Schloss Riegersburg, a mighty medieval fortress, once Styria's most easterly outpost against raiders from Hungary, and then Turkey, and, more recently,

The medieval fortress of Riegersburg, rebuilt in the 17th century

For hotels and restaurants in this region see pp295–6 and pp318–20

a German stronghold during World War II. The present castle dates from the 17th century. The fortress is surrounded and defended by a 3-km (2-mile) long wall with eleven bastions, seven gates and two moats, and can only be approached by a long steep climb. The castle buildings begin beyond the sixth gate. The first building is the former armoury with a collection of arms and war machines used in the defence of the fortress during a siege. In the courtyard stands a monument to soldiers killed during World War II. Beyond the second moat are the buildings of the castle proper, which houses a museum dedicated to the Liechtenstein family, now owners of the castle and who played an important role in the turbulent history of Austria and Europe.

In the inner courtyard you will find a well surrounded by an intricate wrought-iron enclosure featuring a horseshoe. Is it said that those who succeed in tracing the horseshoe among the intricate decorations may count on good luck. The twelve castle rooms housing the Witches' Museum are devoted to those horrendous times in medieval European history when many women (and some men) were tortured, burned at the stake and otherwise persecuted. The museum has many fascinating exhibits recounting the most gruesome of tales.

⑫ Bad Gleichenberg

Road map F5. 🏠 5,500.
🚌 **Tel** (03159) 2203.

Once the most popular health resort in Styria, Bad Gleichenberg was developed in 1834 by Matthias Constantin Capello Graf von Wickenburg. When the therapeutic properties of the local spring waters – already known to the Romans – were brought to his attention, he set about developing them. A shrewd businessman, he soon turned this quiet corner of southeastern Styria into a modern resort that attracted visitors with its promise of painless treatments for heart disease, circulatory and respiratory ailments, problems of the digestive tract and rheumatic conditions. Consequently, Bad Gleichenberg became one of the most popular destinations for the health-conscious Austrian aristocracy, who also congregated on the local promenade, and in the magnificent park, which now displays statues of its former visitors hidden among the shrubbery. The town has many surviving villas and Secession-style palaces; one of the most beautiful is the old theatre, now housing a cinema.

The octagonal tower of the late-Gothic town hall, Bad Radkersburg

Environs: A short way north of the spa town, in Gleichenberg village, stands the medieval **Schloss Kornberg**. Built as a fortress in the 13th century, it was transformed into a residential palace in the 17th century. Today it is a two-storey castle complex with four towers, and a magnificent Renaissance courtyard.

⑬ Bad Radkersburg

Road map F5. 🏠 3,100. 🚌 🚉
Tel (03476) 25450.

Bad Radkersburg, on the Slovenian border, was founded as a town in 1265 by the Bohemian King Ottokar. Once a fortified border post as well as an important trade centre and transhipment harbour on the Mur river, today it is a peaceful small town, which still bears many signs of its former glory. In the main square stands the late-Gothic town hall with its octagonal clock tower topped by a belfry. The Marian or Plague Column in the square dates from 1681, and the surrounding houses with their patios and shaded galleries are the former homes of noblemen and rich citizens. The house at No. 9 once belonged to the von Eggenbergs, one of Styria's most powerful families.

Like many of its neighbours, Bad Radkersburg is also a spa town and health resort whose health-giving mineral waters attract numerous visitors.

Statue of Graf von Wickenburg, Bad Gleichenberg

The Plague Column on Hauptplatz in Bad Radkersburg

⓮ Steirische Weinstrasse

Much of southern Styria is given over to vineyards, with vines planted on steep, south-facing slopes. The roads along the foot of the hills run through fields of maize, the region's second crop. The third crop is pumpkins, and pumpkin seeds are used to make *Kürbiskernöl*, a popular salad oil. Visitors following the Styrian wine routes will find many pleasant places to stop for a meal, but more importantly, a chance to sample the local wine and learn about the grape varieties that cloak the gardens of the restaurants.

① Gundersdorf

At the entrance to the village stands a high pole with four vanes clattering in the wind. This is the *Klapotetz*, a scarecrow that guards the vineyards against birds. There are many such devices throughout the region, but the one in Gundersdorf is the largest.

② Stainz

This town owes its former wealth to the wine trade. The Augustinian Abbey was converted into a palace by Archduke Johann and now houses part of the Graz Joanneum musuem, dedicated to the history of farming and hunting in the region.

③ Bad Gams

A health resort with iron-rich mineral waters, Bag Gams owes its fame mainly to its superb pottery products.

④ Deutschlandsberg

This village is the centre of production for Schilcher rosé wine. It is dominated by the ruins of a former castle, whose remaining 12th-century turret affords spectacular views over the valley.

0 kilometres   5

0 miles   5

Key

━━ Suggested route

══ Other road

── River, lake

Map labels: Klagenfurt, Graz, 76, Eibiswald, Schwarze Sulm, 74

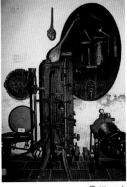

⑤ Kitzeck

In the centre of town, in an old inn between the church and the pub, is a fascinating wine museum. Kitzeck also boasts the highest vineyards in Europe, growing on steep slopes, at an altitude of 564 m (1,850 ft).

Austrian Wines

Austria can boast some truly excellent wines, in particular its white wines can take their place among the best in the world, and production meets almost the entire domestic demand. The largest wine-producing area is Lower Austria, particularly the Weinviertel and the Wachau Valley. Burgenland, southern Styria and the environs of Vienna are also key regions. The most popular white wines are Grüner Veltliner, Welschriesling and Weissburgunder. The land around Neusiedler See produces white wines, but is famous for its reds: Zweigelt and the full-bodied Blaufränkisch. The light Schilcher comes from Deutschlandsberg in Styria. The sweet dessert wine Eiswein, made from grapes picked after the first frosts, is also produced in Austria.

Label for Austrian red wine from Gumpoldskirchen

⑥ Leibnitz

Several traces reveal earlier Roman settlements in the town of Leibnitz. The archaeological finds are now on display in nearby Seggau Castle.

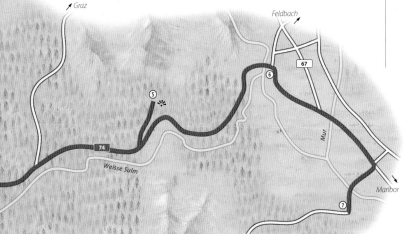

⑦ Ehrenhausen

This historic town makes a good starting point for exploring much of the Styrian wine route. Its greatest attraction is the mausoleum of Rupert von Eggenberg (died 1611), a hero of the Turkish wars, with an interior designed by Johann Bernhard Fischer von Erlach.

Tips for Drivers

Length of route: 66 km (41 miles).
Stopping places: inns and rooms to rent are dotted along the route.
Suggestions: a visit to the Steirisches Weinmuseum (wine museum) Kitzeck, Steinriegel 15.
Tel (03456) 3000.
Open Apr–Oct: 10am–noon, 2–5pm daily; Nov–Mar: 9am–noon Mon–Fri.

⓯ Piber

Road map F4. 🚉 Köflach. 🚌
🏘 500. **Tel** (03144) 72 777-0. Stud:
Tel (03144) 3323-100. **Open** Apr–Oct:
9:30am–5pm daily; Nov–Mar: guided
tours only. 🐎 🎦 Apr–Oct: 10am,
11am, 1pm, 2pm, 3pm, 4pm daily;
Nov–Mar: 11am, 2pm daily.

Piber houses the stud farm
for the Spanish Riding School
horses. When the town of
Lipizza was incorporated into
Slovenia after World War I, it
was in a former castle in Piber,
a small Styrian village, that the
famous Lipizzaner horses found
a new home. The horses are a
complex mixture of six different
breeds. Born dark-chestnut or
black, they acquire their famous
white colour between the ages
of four and ten. In Piber the
initial selection of 5 out of 40
stallions takes place: they are
assessed for their suitability and
stage talents before five years
of training at the Spanish Riding
School in Vienna. You can visit
the stables here, and watch a
film on the history of the stud.

⓰ Judenburg

Road map E4. 🏘 10,000. 🚌 🚉
Tel (03572) 85000. 🌐 **judenburg.com**

This town at the fork of a road is
an old mercantile centre that took
its name from the *Juden*, or Jews,
who once lived and traded here.
When Emperor Maximilian
expelled the Jews in 1496, the
town went into decline. Not much
remains of the medieval Jewish
quarters, but it is worth visiting
Nikolauskirche, the church of St
Nicholas. The only original feature

is the presbytery. Rebuilt in 1673
in the Baroque style, the church
was subsequently given a Neo-
Renaissance facelift during the
Neo-Classicist period. Inside are
statues of the 12 apostles by the
local artist Balthasar Brandstätter.
One of the side altars contains a
small wooden statue of the
Madonna and Child, dating from
1500. The Magdalenenkirche,
church of St Mary Magdalene,
features lovingly restored
Gothic stained-glass windows.
Judenburg also has a town
museum devoted mainly to the
region's history and art.

Environs: East of the
town, on the ledge
of a rock, stand the
ruins of an old
Liechtenstein **castle**
that was once acces-
sible only by step
ladder. In the
environs of
Judenburg are
some of the
most interesting
archaeological
sites dating from
prehistoric times. The famous
chariot that is now displayed
in the Joanneum museum in
Eggenberg castle in Graz was
unearthed in nearby **Strettweg**.

⓱ St Lambrecht

Road map E4. 🏘 1,900. 🚌
🚉 **Tel** (03585) 2305.

St Lambrecht, a Benedictine
Abbey, was founded in the
12th century by Henry III, Duke
of Carinthia. The monastery
complex was built in 1640 to

designs by Domenico Sciassia.
The church dates from the
14th century, but it was rebuilt
in the Baroque style and today
it is a triple-nave basilica with
medieval frescoes on the walls
and presbytery ceiling, and
statues of the church's fathers
in the organ enclosure. The
main altar (1632) by Valentin
Khautt is 16 m (52 ft) high.

North of the church, by the
cemetery, stands a 12th-century
Romanesque chapel. The abbey
also has a magnificent library
and an interesting museum
with a collection of the
old furnishings of
church and
abbey, including
Romanesque
sculptures, a
15th-century votive
painting, *The Mount
of Olives*, by Hans
von Tübingen,
and 15th-and
16th-century
stained-glass
panels. The gem
of the museum,
however, is its

Image of the patron saint of
St Lambrecht Abbey

collection of birds. Some 1,500
species were assembled in the
19th century by the amateur
collector Blasius Hanf.

🏛 **St Lambrecht Abbey Museum**
Hauptstrasse 1–2. **Tel** (03585) 2305-29.
Open for guided tours only mid-May–
mid-Oct: 10:45am, 2:30pm Mon–Sat,
2:30pm Sun & hols.

⓲ Turracher Höhe

Road map E5. 🏘 100. 🚌
Tel (04275) 8392.

This small ski resort nestles at
an altitude of 1,700 m (5,575 ft)
high in the Nockbergen (Nock
Mountains), one of Austria's
most scenic Alpine ranges on
the border between Styria and
Carinthia. The town makes a
great base for year-round walks
in the woods and mountain
meadows. Nearby are the
remains of an old iron-smelting
plant. The blast furnace ended
its operation in the early 20th
century, but the remains of
heavy industry create a very
striking feature set against the

The world-famous Lipizzaner horses in a paddock near Piber

Splendid autumn colours in the woods around Turracher Höhe

backdrop of the pistes and the beautiful snow-covered hills of the ski resort.

⑲ Murau

Road map E4. 🚠 3,700. 🚌 🚉
Tel (03532) 2720. 🌐 murau.at

Murau sprang up in the 13th century at a crossroads of trading routes on the scenic Mur river and became a local centre for commerce and industry. The historic town centre of Murau lies on the left bank of the Mur river. Its Renaissance houses are dominated by the Gothic **Matthäuskirche**, the church of St Matthew, consecrated in the 13th century and later altered in the Baroque style. The church contains some interesting epitaphs of the Liechtenstein

family but its star attraction is the main altar (1655), a magnificent work by local Baroque masters, incorporating a Gothic painting of the Crucifixion (c.1500). Also worth seeing are the medieval frescoes of St Anthony in the transept, and the Entombment of Christ and Annunciation in the main nave.

The castle behind the church, **Schloss Murau**, was founded by the Liechtenstein family and later passed into the hands of the Schwarzenbergs. It has an interesting museum of metallurgy. In the vaults of **Elisabethkirche**, at No. 4 Marktgasse, is a Diocesan Protestant Museum that holds documents relating to the events around the Reformation and Counter-Reformation in these parts of Austria.

Historic buildings in the old town of Murau on the Mur River

⑳ Oberwölz

Road map E4. 🚠 3,000.
Tel (03581) 8420.

This small town, which grew rich through its trade in salt and the smelting of silver excavated in the surrounding hills, has preserved some of its former glory. In the surrounding area many archaeological finds from the Hallstatt period have been unearthed, revealing a long history. Oberwölz once belonged to the bishopric of Freising and up to the time of the Napoleonic wars its envoy resided in the neighbouring **Schloss Rothenfels**.

The town has some well-preserved remains of medieval fortifications, including three turrets and two town gates. Its pride is the Gothic **Stadtpfarrkirche St Martin**, the parish church of St Martin, a triple-nave basilica with an early-Gothic chapel and a 15th-century Gothic vestibule. In 1777, J. A. von Mölk painted the ceiling frescoes in the chapel vault. On the external south wall is a relief from 1500, showing the Last Judgement. Next to the church stands the 14th-century chapel of St Sigismund, with the Way of the Cross by Johann Lederwasch from the turn of the 18th century. In the Cultural Centre is a regional museum with a collection of archaeological finds from the area, and a museum of wind instruments.

㉑ Schladminger Tauern

The small town of Schladming lies at the foot of the Niedere (Lower) Tauern that extend along the Enns Valley. Rising to 2,800 m (9,200 ft), their gentle slopes provide excellent conditions for downhill skiers, from the beginner to the professional. The scenery is superb, excellent for walking in summer, with an efficient bus network, cable cars and ski lifts in winter. If you are looking for more of a challenge, you can find this in the Dachstein massif close by. But for a relaxing break it is still worth going down to Schladming, with its tempting restaurants and cosy cafés lining the broad promenade.

★ **Schladming**
The little town of Schladming has a rich history. Once a centre of peasant revolts, it remains to this day the centre of Austrian Protestantism.

★ **Ennstal – the Enns Valley**
One of Austria's major rivers, the Enns, separates the Niedere Tauern from the Dachstein massif.

0 kilometres   5

0 miles   5

KEY

① **The ascent** by cable car from the small village of Ramsau am Dachstein (*see p184*) takes visitors to the tops of Dachstein and Hunerkogel. Climbing instructors also give advice to rock climbers.

② **Gröbming** has an attractive late-medieval church of the Assumption of the Virgin Mary, with a winged altar (1520).

③ **Hochgolling**, rising to 2,863 m (9,393 ft), is the highest peak in the Schladminger Tauern. The long, arduous climb rewards with stunning views of the mountains from the top.

Filzmoos

Hunerkogel

Ramsau am Dachstein

Schladming

ENNSTAL

E651

320

Rohrmoos

Radstadt

Hochwurzen

Forstaubach

99

Klagenfurt

Rohrmoos
This resort, just outside Schladming, is a good base for climbing the neighbouring Hochwurzen and Planai summits.

◀ Traditional huts in an Alpine village, Goeriachtal Valley

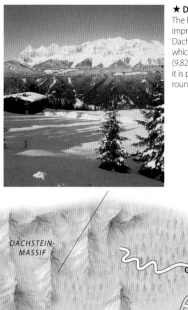

★ **Dachstein Massif**
The highest, most impressive peak is Dachstein itself, which rises to 2,995 m (9,826 ft). A glacier, it is perfect for year-round skiing.

VISITORS' CHECKLIST

Practical Information
Road map D4, E4.
🛈 Schladming, Ramsauerstrasse 756, (03687) 23 310.
🔲 schladming-dachstein.at

Transport
🚉 🚌

Haus
A resort and winter sports centre, Haus has a beautiful Baroque church. It is a good starting point for mountain walks to the nearby scenic lakes, including Bodensee, Hüttensee and Obersee.

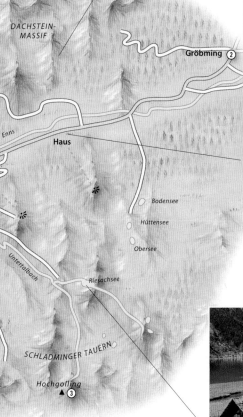

DACHSTEIN-MASSIF

Gröbming ②

Enns

Haus

○ Bodensee

○ Hüttensee

○ Obersee

Untertalbach

Riesachsee

SCHLADMINGER TAUERN

Hochgolling ▲ ③

Key

═══ Major road

═══ Minor road

···· Mountain railway

═══ River

Riesachsee
One of many mountain lakes set amid beautiful scenery, the Riesachsee lies at an altitude of 1,333 m (4,373 ft). It is a perfect spot for trout fishing.

The resort of Ramsau, famed for cross-country skiing

❷ Ramsau

Road map D4. 🏔 2,800. 🚌
Tel (03687) 81 833. 🌐 ramsau.com

At an altitude of 1,000 m (3,280 ft) lies the small town of Ramsau am Dachstein, renowned for its superb cross-country ski runs, extending over some 230 km (143 miles). Snow is almost guaranteed from November until March and the efficient inter-connecting system of lifts, cable cars, trains and buses also puts more difficult runs within easy reach. The peaks opposite the Dachstein massif have slopes that are perfectly suited to moderately skilled downhill skiers. In the summer the *Loipen* or cross-country ski runs turn into excellent long-distance walking routes.

From the Ramsau side visitors can ascend the famous Dachstein south face by cable car. Cable cars also travel up Hunerkogel (2,694 m/8,836 ft), from where a lovely panoramic view of the area unfolds. The descent takes you to nearby Filzmoos, a resort with views of the spectacular Bischofsmütze (Bishop's Mitre).

There are many attractions on offer in Ramsau, such as feeding alpine animals and night tobog-gan runs. The **Alpinmuseum** illustrates the history of mountaineering in the region. The **Wassermühle Rössing** is one of several waterwheels that has been built in the area since the 17th century. It lies at the foot of Sattelberg, near the start of the children's *via ferrata*, the

Kali-Kinderklettersteig. The old waterwheel creaks into motion on Friday afternoons.

🏛 Alpinmuseum
Tel (03687) 70 63 836. **Open** May–Oct: 10am–4pm daily. 📷 on request.

🏚 Wassermühle Rössing
Tel (03687) 81 874. **Open** mid-Jun–Sep.

❸ Bad Aussee

Road map D4. 🏔 4,800. 🚌
🚉 **Tel** (03622) 54040-0.

Bad Aussee, the main town in the Styrian part of the Salzkammergut, lies at the fork of the Traun river, which cuts a scenic gorge between the Dachstein massif and the Totes Gebirge (Dead Mountains). The region's original wealth was founded on its salt deposits. Later, Bad Aussee achieved renewed fame when, in 1827, Archduke Johann married

Anna Plochl, daughter of the local postmaster. The Archduke, who made many important contributions to the life of Styria, was a grandson of Maria Theresa, the 13th child of future Emperor Leopold II.

The former seat of the Salt Office, in Chlumeckyplatz, is a lovely 14th-century building which now houses the city's regional museum with its exhibition on salt mining. The 13th-century, Romanesque St Paul's church has a notable stone statue of the Madonna.

Environs: A scenic road northwest of Bad Aussee will take you to **Altausseer See** and the Loser peak. On the road is an old salt mine, open to the public. During World War II it was reputedly used to hide works of art.

❹ Admont

Road map E4. 🏔 5,000. 🚌
🚉 **Tel** (03613) 21160-10 .

At the centre of the village of Admont stands a **Benedictine abbey** whose importance once reached far beyond the region. Built in the 11th century and often rebuilt, it burned down in 1865, but the fire spared its priceless collection: with nearly 160,000 volumes, it is said to hold the world's largest monastic library. The library's magnificent Rococo interior, dating from 1773, was designed by the Viennese architect Josef Hueber. The large hall holding two-storey cabinets is 72 m

A picturesque street in Bad Aussee

Richly ornamented interior of Admont library

26 Eisenerzer Alpen

Road map E4. Eisenerz: 4,300.
ℹ️ Dr-Theodor-Körner-Platz 1, (03848) 2511-81.

You can reach the Eisenerzer Alpen (iron-ore alps) by following the steep, narrow valley of the Enns river. This gorge, called Gesäuse, begins a short distance from Admont, near Hieflau. The entrance to the gorge presents great views of the river and the Hochtor massif, rising 2,369 m (7,772 ft) above. The surrounding area is used as a training ground for advanced mountaineering and as a base for expeditions to the neighbouring peaks. Easily the most famous mountain in the Eisenerzer Alpen is **Erzberg**, which has has been exploited for its large iron ore deposits since ancient times. It looks like a stepped pyramid, the red pigment contrasting with the green forests and meadows.

The area around Erzberg is the largest iron ore basin in this part of Europe. In **Eisenerz**, an old mining town at the foot of Erzberg, visitors can join an underground tour at **Abenteuer Erzberg**, which includes a ride on a mammoth dumptruck. The village also has a lovely old town and the fine fortified 16th-century church of St Oswald.

🏛️ Abenteuer Erzberg
Erzberg 1. **Tel** (03848) 3200.
Open May–Oct daily.
🕐 10am–3pm; obligatory.
🌐 **abenteuer-erzberg.at**

The shimmering Erzberg – the red iron-ore mountain in the Eisenerzer Alpen

(236 ft) long. The ceiling frescoes by Bartolomeo Altomonte show vast allegorical scenes of the arts, the natural sciences and religion. The abbey's south wing has been converted into a museum showcasing both historic treasures and modern art.

🏛️ Benedictine Abbey
Tel (03613) 2312-604. Library & Museum: **Open** mid-Mar–Oct: 10am–5pm daily; Nov–Feb: on request. 🌐 **stiftadmont.at**

Environs: 5 km (3 miles) beyond Admont, high above the Enns river, stands the 15th-century pilgrimage church **Frauenberg**, rebuilt in the Baroque style. It has a beautiful altarpiece by Josef Stammel.

25 Hohentauern

Road map E4. 430.
Tel (03618) 335.

Hohentauern (1,274 m/ 4,180 ft) is the highest village in the Rottenmanner Tauern, surrounded by more than 20 peaks higher than 2,000 m (6,560 ft). This mountain range is part of the Niedere (Lower) Tauern, which extend also to Salzburger Land. Other ranges in the Niedere Tauern include Radstädter (see p232), Schladminger (see pp182–3) and Wölzer Tauern.

Hohentauern was founded by the Celts. From the 12th century it became important as a commercial centre along Hohentauernpass, the mountain pass connecting the Enns and Mur valleys. St. Bartolomäus Church has magnificent carvings by Josef Stammel.

The Hohentauernpass crosses the range at 1,260 m (4,134 ft) height. A drive along Hohentauernpassstrasse is one of the best ways to enjoy the superb mountain scenery.

From the north, you pass through **Rottenmann** with its old city walls; **Möderbrugg**, a former centre of the metal industry; **Oberzeiring** and its disused salt mine; and **Hanfelden**, with its large ruined castle. Nearby is the ruined **Schloss Reifenstein**.

㉙ Salzatal Tour

The small Salza river, a tributary of the upper Enns, cuts its way across the eastern end of the High Limestone Alps. A journey along the Salza Valley is an expedition through a thinly populated area of entrancing beauty. The trail leads along the foothills of the Hochschwab massif, beside wild mountain streams, small barrier lakes and through dense woodlands. The river flows through virgin mountain terrains and its waters are so crystal clear that you can see every detail reflected in its stream.

Brunnsee ②
Beyond the village of Wildalpen, a magnificent view opens onto the valley and the lake at the very heart of the Hochschwab massif. The northern slopes of the mountains present themselves in their full glory.

Prescenyklause ③
Beyond a rock gate is an old dam that once held back the waters of the Salza river so rafts could carry timber to the valleys.

Hieflau ①
This former centre of the metal industry is hidden amid dense forests. The local village museum displays objects associated with the region's history.

0 kilometres 5

0 miles 5

Key

▬ Suggested route

▬ Scenic road

═ Other road

┄ River, lake

Hochschwab ⑤
The highest summit in this vast mountain range is the 2,277-m (7,470-ft) high Hochschwab, the destination of both summer and winter excursions.

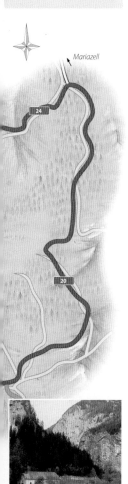

Mariazell

The main nave of the abbey church in Seckau Abbey

ⓐ Seckau

Road map E4. ⓜ 1,300. 🚍 🚉
Tel (03514) 5205-3.

The small town of Seckau, established in the 13th century, has some interesting houses and the late-Gothic chapel of St Lucia in the town square. But the main claim to fame lies with **Seckau Abbey**, originally Augustinian and taken over by the Benedictines in the 19th century. Its present shape, dating from the 17th century, is the work of Pietro Francesco Carlone, but the abbey's basilica of the Assumption of the Virgin Mary has maintained its original late-Gothic character. Among its treasures is the Crucifixion group in the presbytery, highly expressive figures from the 12th and 13th centuries. The lion figures in the portal and the Madonna and Child in the church vestibule are Romanesque or early Gothic, and on the south wall, 13th-century frescoes were discovered.

ⓐ Leoben

Road map F4. ⓜ 25,000. 🚍 🚉
ⓘ Hauptplatz 3 (03842) 48148-0.

Leoben, Styria's second largest town, is an industrial and academic centre. Beautiful mansion houses line Hauptplatz (main square), and the adjacent streets bear witness to the town's early wealth derived from the local iron deposits. There is a lovely old town hall with coats of arms, and the Hacklhaus has a glittering red façade.

Also worth seeing in the old town is the **Pfarrkirche St Xaver**, the church of St Xaver, built in the 17th century by the Jesuits, with its beautiful Baroque main altar and a Romanesque crucifix on the south wall. On the other side of the bridge across the Mur river stands the Gothic church of **Maria am Waasen**, with original stained-glass windows in the presbytery. On the southern outskirts, in the district of Göss, stands Styria's first Benedictine **Abbey**, built around 1000 by Archbishop Aribo. It is mainly 16th-century with some earlier elements. The church's main nave is a monument to Styria's late-Gothic architecture. Other original features include 14th-century frescoes in the presbytery and an 11th-century, early-Romanesque crypt.

Austria's most famous brewery, Gösser, a short way from the abbey, is also open to the public. In the city centre, at No. 6 Kirchgasse, is the **Kunsthalle Leoben**, a museum of fine arts.

Weichselboden ④
It is worth stopping off in this small village, one of very few along this route, to visit its lime-tree-shaded church. A very small old hotel invites visitors to stay.

The elegant Baroque façade of the Hacklhaus in Leoben

⑳ Mariazell Basilica

The earliest records of the church devoted to the Birth of the Virgin Mary date from 1243, but it is believed to have been established in 1157 and its 850th anniversary was celebrated in 2007. Mariazell is the main pilgrimage centre for the Roman Catholic population in this part of Europe. Pilgrims arrive all year, but highpoints are Assumption (15 Aug) and the Birth of the Virgin (8 Sep). Mariazell became famous in the 14th century, when King Louis of Hungary founded the Gnadenkapelle (chapel of mercy) to give thanks for his victory over the Turks.

View of the Church
In the 17th century, the church was extended to accommodate the growing number of pilgrims, and the central tower was supplemented by two Baroque side towers.

Church Interior
The basilica was originally a Gothic hall church, which is still apparent despite the Baroque-style alterations carried out in the late 17th century by Domenico Sciassia.

KEY

① **14th-century Gothic tower**

② **Vault frescoes** by Giovanni Rocco Bertoletti

★ **Treasury**
The treasury is home to various precious objects, including liturgical vessels, a wooden statuette of the Madonna and Child and an ivory relief – both from the 14th century.

Main entrance

Madonna and Child
Magna Mater Austriae – the Great Mother of Austria, a late-Romanesque statue of the Madonna and Child – is the main object of veneration by pilgrims to Mariazell.

VISITORS' CHECKLIST

Practical Information
Road map F4.
Kardinal-Tisserant-Platz 1, Mariazell.
Tel (03882) 2595. **Open** May–Oct: 7:45am–8pm daily (until 9pm Sat); Nov–Apr: 7:45am– 7:15pm daily. Treasury: **Open** May–Oct: 10am–3pm Tue–Sat, 11am–4pm Sun & hols; Advent: 1–5pm Fri–Sun.
W **basilika-mariazell.at**

★ Main Altar
The monumental altar showing the Crucifixion is the work of Johann Bernhard Fischer von Erlach. The silver figures on the altar were created by Lorenzo Mattielli.

Cardinal Joseph Mindszenty (1892–1975)

The Hungarian Primate, imprisoned for his opposition to the communist regime, was released in the 1956 uprising. When this was crushed, he took refuge in the US Embassy in Budapest for 15 years. He later lived in Austria and was buried in Mariazell. His body is now in Hungary.

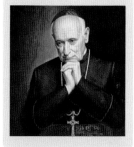

★ Gnadenkapelle
The chapel, with a statue of the Virgin Mary, was probably founded by King Louis of Hungary and was decorated in Baroque style by Fischer von Erlach the Younger and Lorenzo Mattielli.

UPPER AUSTRIA

Upper Austria, so called because of its location in the upper reaches of the Austrian Danube, occupies an area of about 12,000 sq km (4,600 sq miles) and has 1.4 million inhabitants. Its borders are marked by the rivers Enns to the east and Inn to the west. To the north, the Czech Republic is its neighbour, to the south there are Styria and the Salzburger Land, to the west is Germany.

Upper Austria is, after Vienna, the most industrialized Austrian province and has remained the richest area of the country since the time when Austria was part of the Roman province of Noricum. In later years, Upper Austria joined Bavaria. Then, under Babenberg rule in the 13th century, it became the cradle of the great future empire, in conjunction with neighbouring Lower Austria.

Historically, the province of Upper Austria is divided into five districts: Mühlviertel, which stretches south to the Danube and occupies the Czech Massif, with Freistadt its largest town; the westernmost district of Innviertel, which lies in the foothills of the Alps, and includes the towns of Ried and Braunau; the Hausruckviertel is named after the

Hausruck Massif and Vöcklabruck is its largest town; and the Traunviertel, which includes the Salzkammergut, one of the most picturesque and popular natural areas in Austria. The Danube Valley is generally considered to be a separate region, with scores of small towns, lofty fortresses and magnificent abbeys, including the most glorious of them all, St Florian, a jewel of Austrian Baroque architecture.

The province's capital, Linz, is Austria's third largest city, comprising an important industrial centre, the largest Austrian Danube port, and a major transport hub. It is beautifully situated in an extensive valley, surrounded by gently rolling hills, and has a charming old town district.

View from the Krippenstein peak across to the imposing Dachstein massif

◄ Houses located on the banks of the glorious Hallstätter See, Hallstatt

Exploring Upper Austria

Upper Austria is an exceptionally diverse province, with something to interest everyone. Linz, the capital city, has both the oldest church in Austria and a state-of-the-art virtual technology museum. On the banks of the rivers Danube and Enns rise the magnificent abbeys in Kremsmünster, Steyr and St Florian. The caves in the Dachstein range are fascinating natural monuments. However, Upper Austria's greatest attraction are its glorious lakes set amid limestone peaks in the beautiful Salzkammergut. The mild climate and therapeutic facilities attract visitors to small resorts, and Bad Ischl was once the summer home of the Emperor.

Steyr's trademark – the Gothic Bummerlhaus with its steeply pitched roof

Sights at a Glance

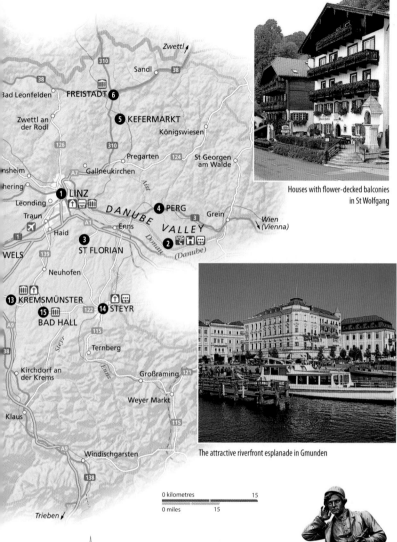

Houses with flower-decked balconies
in St Wolfgang

The attractive riverfront esplanade in Gmunden

0 kilometres   15

0 miles   15

Getting There

Although Linz-Hörsching Airport
is served by some international
flights, most visitors fly to Vienna.
Linz lies on the Vienna–Salzburg
railway line and the A1 motorway, which traverses the province,
east to west, and also connects
with the southern A9 motorway.
There is a dense network of
roads and bus routes throughout. From spring until autumn,
boats on the Danube River
connect Passau with Linz and
Linz with the Wachau Valley.

Statue in front of the Kaiservilla,
in Bad Ischl

For map symbols *see back flap*

Key

━━━ Motorway

━━ Major road

┄┄┄ Minor road

━━ Scenic route

╍╍╍ Main railway

── Minor railway

▦▦▦ International border

▬▬▬ Province border

❶ Linz

Straddling the Danube in a scenic spot, Linz owes its former importance and wealth to its location at an intersection of waterways – salt and iron ore were transported along the rivers Traun and Enns, and further along raw materials and finished products travelled down the Danube to Vienna or Passau. This strategic position led the Romans to found a substantial settlement called Lentia on the site. Since the 15th century, Linz has been the capital of Upper Austria. A major industrial centre, it is also a hub of culture with numerous galleries, museums, and the futurist Ars Electronica Center. The composer Anton Bruckner was also associated with Linz in his early career.

A birds-eye view of the town on the banks of the Danube

Exploring Linz

The town of Linz sprawls across both banks of the Danube, with the historic old town on the right (south) bank, in the bend of the river. The vast Hauptplatz is regarded as one of Austria's most beautiful architectural complexes. It is also worth taking a trip to a nearby hill, the Pöstlingberg, from where there are splendid views over the town and river. The Ars Electronica Center is situated on the left (north) bank of the Danube.

🏛 Martinskirche

Römerstrasse/Martinsgasse.
Tel (0732) 777454.
A modest façade hides Austria's oldest surviving church, dedicated to St Martin. It was first mentioned in the 8th century, during the times of Charlemagne, as part of the Carolingians' former royal residence. The Gothic windows and portals date

from the 8th century. There was an older Roman wall on the same site, and ten Roman tombstones, together with other ancient stones, were used as building material to erect the church. The interior also dates from the Carolingian period, the only later addition being the Neo-Gothic presbytery. The rainbow arch that separates the nave from the presbytery and the north wall of the church are adorned with 15th-century frescoes of the Virgin Mary on a throne. Much of the interior can only be seen with a guide.

The tiny Martinskirche, Austria's oldest church

🏛 Linzer Schloss

Schlossberg 1. **Tel** (0732) 774419-0.
Open 9am–6pm
Tue–Fri, 10am–5pm Sat, Sun,
public holidays. 🅿

In the 15th century, Emperor Friedrich III built his residence on the Römerberg (Roman Mountain), on the foundations of an earlier structure. The castle acquired its present shape between 1600 and 1607, and its distinctive silhouette has become one of the most famous sights in Linz. Since 1966, this former imperial residence has housed a branch of the Oberöster-reichisches Landesmuseum. Exhibits include paintings and sculptures from early medieval times to the 19th century and the Secession, 12th–18th-century arms, 16th–19th-century musical instruments, furniture and handicrafts, golden, ceramic and glass objects, and a permanent archaeological exhibition. Part of the museum is devoted to folk traditions; there's a recon-structed physics laboratory from the Jesuit school in Linz and the Schloss Weinberg pharmacy˜ (c.1700). From the castle, there are superb views over Linz.

🏛 Landhaus

Theatergasse 1. **Tel** (0732) 77200.
The regional government is based in a Renaissance palace built on the site of a former Minorite monastery. Its north portal, from Klosterstrasse, is a beautiful marble work by Renaissance artists. The inner courtyard is surrounded by a colonnade. Here you will find Planetenbrunnen (Fountain of the Planets), built to com-memorate the outstanding astronomer and mathematician Johannes Kepler who stayed in Linz and lectured at the college, then based in the Landhaus, for 14 years (1612–26). The seven figures on the fountain's bronze plinth show the planets known at the time. Close by is the Minoritenkirche, a former Minorite Church, the earliest documented record of which is in the town chronicles of 1288. Altered in the

The Planet Fountain in the inner courtyard of the Landhaus

Baroque style in 1751–8, the church has an unusual façade with oval telescopes between the storeys. The lovely Rococo interior is decorated with charming stuccowork and paintings by Martin Johann Schmidt and Bartolomeo Altomonte.

🚌 Hauptplatz

Hauptplatz, in Linz's Old Town, is one of Austria's finest squares and considered to be one of the foremost achievements of town planning. It is 220 m (720 ft) long and 60 m (200 ft) wide, and overall it creates a much stronger impression than its component parts would suggest, although many of its buildings are worth a closer look. The Gothic Altes Rathaus (Old Town Hall) at No. 1 was built around 1513, and still has the original octagonal tower with an astronomical clock. In the 17th century, the town hall was given a new façade supported by columns. Other interesting buildings are the Gothic and Baroque houses, including Feichtingerhaus, a former mail inn (No. 21), a Gothic building with an early-Baroque façade. The Plague Column (1723) in the centre of the square was funded jointly by the local council and all citizens, in thanksgiving for sparing Linz and the Linzers from three deadly disasters: war, fire and the Black Death plague.

VISITORS' CHECKLIST

Practical Information
Road map E3.
🗺 195,000. 🏛 Hauptplatz 1, (0732) 7070-2009.
🎭 Pflasterspektakel (end Jul); Brucknerfest (Sep); Ars electronica (Sep). 🌐 linz.at

Transport
✈ 🚌 🚆 🚢

Hauptplatz with its Baroque Plague Column

Linz City Centre

① Martinskirche
② Schloss
③ Landhaus
④ Hauptplatz
⑤ Alter Dom
⑥ Stadtpfarrkirche
⑦ Landesmuseum
⑧ Stadtmuseum Nordico
⑨ Seminarkirche
⑩ Neuer Dom
⑪ Ars Electronica Center

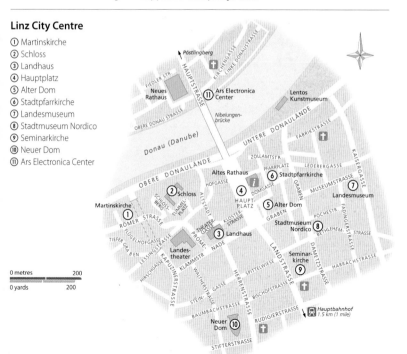

0 metres 200
0 yards 200

For map symbols see back flap

The towers of Alter Dom in Domgasse

☖ Alter Dom

Domgasse 3. **Tel** (0732) 770866-0.
Open 7:30am–6:30pm daily.

Thanks to reforms, the capital of the archbishopric of Upper Austria was established at Linz, and in 1785 the former Jesuit church was chosen as the cathedral. Ignatiuskirche, the church of St Ignatius, was built in the second half of the 17th century to designs by Pietro Francesco Carlone, and today its green façade and onion-dome–topped twin towers are distinctive features in the town panorama. The simple, modest elevation of the church conceals a beguiling Baroque interior. The wide main nave has three side chapels on each side. Particularly fascinating are the beautifully engraved stalls in the presbytery, where local artists carved the figures of dwarfs and monsters peeping out from behind the backrests and armrests.

From 1856 until 1868 the composer Anton Bruckner was the cathedral's organist. The present organ, by the famous master Krismann, was altered according to Bruckner's own instructions.

☖ Stadtpfarrkirche

Pfarrplatz 4. **Tel** (0732) 776120.
The parish church of the Assumption of the Virgin Mary (Mariä Himmelfahrt) was built in the 13th century as a triple-nave basilica with Gothic presbytery, and altered in the 17th century,

when it received a new interior and further chapels. The presbytery includes the tombstone of Emperor Friedrich III, who resided in Linz for a while. The urn containing his heart is concealed behind a marble slab in the church wall to the right of the altar. In the eastern end of the south nave is the chapel of St John of Nepomuk. Its lovely Baroque interior is decorated with frescoes and an altar by Bartolomeo Altomonte. St John of Nepomuk was one of the most revered saints in the Austrian empire. Many towns erected statues to him, and the Stadtpfarrkirche in Linz houses two of these. In the external chapel by the presbytery is a figure, probably created by Georg Raphael Donner. The chapel's architecture and dome shape are the work of another Austrian master of the Baroque, Johann Lukas von Hildebrandt.

▥ Landesmuseum

Museumstrasse 14. **Tel** (0732) 7720-52200. **Open** 9am–6pm Tue, Wed & Fri, 9am–9pm Thu, 10am–5pm Sat, Sun & hols. ◪

The Landesmuseum building is reminiscent of the Viennese houses along Ringstrasse, which is hardly surprising since they were built at the same time and designed in the same spirit of historicism. The museum's architect was a German from

Illumination in a Psalter, Landesmuseum

Düsseldorf, Bruno Schmitz. The museum was named Francisco-Carolinum Museum in honour of Archduke Francis Karl. Originally it was meant to house the collection of the Museum Society of Upper Austria, established in 1833 by Anton Ritter von Spaun. Today, the museum shows mainly modern Austrian art, with a particular emphasis on artists from Upper Austria. It also holds a collection of works by the renowned Bohemian illustrator, Alfred Kubin, and presents exhibitions of its natural history treasures or relating to the province's past.

▥ Stadtmuseum Nordico

Dametzstrasse 23. **Tel** (0732) 7070-1912. **Open** 10am–6pm Tue–Sun (to 9pm Thu). ◪ ▥ **nordico.at**

In 1675, this 17th-century Baroque complex was the home of the college known as "Nordisches Stift", which had as its aim the education of young boys from nordic countries – hence the name – and their transformation into good Catholics. Today, this imposing building, now owned by the council, houses the Nordico Town Museum, with its collection of objects relating to the history of Linz from ancient times onwards, including a model of the town from 1740. The top floor is given over to temporary exhibitions, mainly of Modern art.

☖ Seminarkirche

Harrachstrasse 7.
Tel (0732) 771205.
Open 7am–5pm daily.

The former Deutsch-ordenkirche (church of the Teutonic Order) is now a seminary church. Artistically, this is the most valuable historic church building in Linz. It was built in the early 18th century, to a design by Johann Lukas Hildebrandt. Its beautiful Baroque façade is topped with the decorative coats of arms of the Harrach family. The tower, crowned with a distinctive flattened dome, is surrounded by

The impressive Neuer Dom, Austria's largest cathedral

towns or see a flying saucer disappear into space. There is also a 3D virtual space in the basement where you can explore other worlds with special headsets.

🏛 Lentos Kunstmuseum

Ernst-Koref-Promenade 1. **Tel** (0732) 7070 3614. **Open** 10am–6pm Tue–Sun (to 9pm Thu). **Closed** 1 Jan, 24–25 Dec. 🅿 🆆 **lentos.at**

This brand-new museum on the south bank of the Danube houses a major collection of paintings, sculptures and prints, concentrating on international and Austrian art from the early 20th century to the present day, featuring Expressionism (Kokoschka, Klimt), Op and Pop Art (Warhol), Pluralism and Austrian photography.

Pöstlingberg

A short distance from the centre of Linz, on the extensive plateau of Urfahr on the north bank of the Danube, rises the 537-m (1,762-ft) Pöstlingberg. The electric mountain train, built in 1898, that climbs almost to the top, was once acclaimed as a wonder of technology. The route is 2.9 km (2 miles) long, and the incline reaches a staggering 10.6 per cent.

On the mountain's summit stands the Wallfahrtskirche zu den Sieben Schmerzen Mariens, the pilgrimage church of Our Lady of Seven Sorrows, which is regarded as one of the main symbols of Linz.

sandstone statues depicting the virtues expected of a Knight of the Order. The interior is in the shape of an ellipse and is covered with an oval dome. The Crucifixion in the main altar is the work of Martino Altomonte. To the right of the entrance stands a statue of St John of Nepomuk, facing which is a painting of the death of St Joseph. The beautiful ceiling relief shows God the Father reigning among a host of angels on a sky adorned with filigree leaf ornaments.

🏛 Neuer Dom

Herrenstrasse 26.
Tel (0732) 946100.
Open 7:30am–7pm
Mon–Sat, 8am–7pm Sun.

Construction of the New Cathedral started in 1862, but it was not completed until 1924. Its architect was Vincenz Statz, the builder of Cologne cathedral. The Neo-Gothic Neuer Dom is Austria's largest sacred structure, with a capacity of 20,000 faithful. It is said that only one condition was stipulated by the local council, and that was that the steeple must not be taller than that of the Stephansdom in Vienna (*see p62*). Statz complied

Sebastian, mascot of Pöstlingberg's train

with the request and the tower in Linz is 134 m (440 ft) high – 3 m (10 ft) lower than its counterpart. The interior was designed by Josef Gasser. The most interesting features of the cathedral are its modern, colourful stained-glass windows, which depict often complex scenes, such as the history of the city.

🏛 Ars Electronica Center

Ars-Electronica-Strasse 1. **Tel** (0732) 7272-0. **Open** 9am–5pm Tue, Wed, Fri, 9am–9pm Thu, 10am–6pm Sat, Sun & hols. 🆆 **aec.at**

At the entrance to the Nibelungenbrücke (Bridge of the Nibelungs), on the north bank of the Danube, stands one of Austria's most unusual museums, or rather exhibition centres. The Ars Electronica Center is a highly original museum of virtual worlds, created with the help of modern computer technology. It demonstrates the latest computer wizardry and virtual-reality simulations of space and time travel. Visitors can, for example, journey inside various parts of the universe, visit imaginary Renaissance

Pilgrimage church built between 1738–47 on Pöstlingberg

❷ The Danube Valley

The beautiful blue Danube, extolled by writers and composers, is an extraordinary river. It passes through eight countries, and four capital cities have been built on its banks. The Danube enters Austria as a mountain river right after Passau at Achleiten and leaves 360 km (240 miles) further along, beyond the Hainburg marshes, heading for Bratislava. In Upper Austria, many magnificent towns have been built along its routes; historically, scores of fortresses, abbeys and churches arose on its steep banks (Clam, Melk). The majestic river is an important transport route, and to visitors it offers an excellent network of bicycle routes, with special hotels for cyclists alongside.

Burg Clam
The romantic silhouette of Clam Castle rising above a deep ravine has remained virtually unchanged since the 12th century.

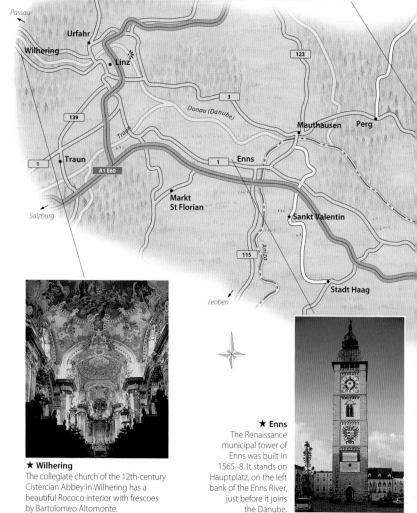

★ Wilhering
The collegiate church of the 12th-century Cistercian Abbey in Wilhering has a beautiful Rococo interior with frescoes by Bartolomeo Altomonte.

★ Enns
The Renaissance municipal tower of Enns was built in 1565–8. It stands on Hauptplatz, on the left bank of the Enns River, just before it joins the Danube.

Grein
In the town hall is an original Rococo theatre, but Grein's most popular sight is its late-Gothic castle, extended in the 17th century.

St Nikola an der Donau
The Danube ends its journey through Upper Austria near St Nikola, an area of outstanding natural beauty.

Concentration Camps

During the Third Reich, more than 50 concentration camps were built on Austrian territory. Most were destroyed immediately after the war, but some commemorative plaques and symbolic sites have been preserved: there is a memorial crematorium at Gusen, and in Ebensee the cemetery and underground mine tunnels where prisoners once worked can be seen. The most important memorial, however, is the former camp at Mauthausen, where the quarry, original buildings and the "ash dump" have been preserved. Just outside the camp is a visitors' centre and musuem operated by the Austrian Government. Each year the liberation is celebrated on the Sunday nearest 8 May.

Mauthausen Todesstiege (Stairway of Death) between quarry and camp

0 kilometres 5
0 miles 5

Key

▬▬▬ Motorway

═══ Major road

⁓⁓⁓ Minor road

⁓⁓ River

•─• Bundesland (province) border

For additional map symbols see back flap

One of the magnificent emperor's rooms in St Florian Abbey

❸ St Florian

Road map E3. 🏛 6,000. 🚌
Tel (07224) 5690. **Open** Stift: Guided
tours: 11am, 1, 3pm. Bruckner organ:
mid-May–mid-Oct: 2:30pm Wed–Fri,
Sun, Mon. 🅿

Florian, the prefect of the Roman
Noricum Province, converted
to Christianity and was tortured
and thrown into the Enns river
as a result in 304.
His body was
retrieved and, in
the 11th century,
a magnificent
abbey and a
church were built
on the site of his
burial place by
Augustinian monks;
they remain the

Alter Codex from
the library of St Florian

keepers of St Florian to this day.
The present appearance of the
abbey and church is the work
of two outstanding Baroque
architects: Carlo Carlone and
Jakob Prandtauer.

St Florian is an impressive
complex of buildings, with
monks' quarters, reception
rooms and a church with an
adjoining chapel of the Virgin
Mary. The main feature in
the large courtyard is the
Adlerbrunnen (Eagle Well), built
in 1603. The east wing houses
the library with its vast collection
of over 140,000 volumes,

incunabula and manuscripts.
The ceiling painting by
Bartolomeo Altomonte shows
the marriage of Virtue with
Knowledge. Next to the library is
the Marble Hall with its vast
columns, designed by Jakob
Prandtauer. The grand staircase
in the west wing, also by
Prandtauer, leads to the emperor's
apartments where important
guests stayed.
Adjacent is the
room of Anton
Bruckner, who
was associated
with St Florian for
many years.
Carlo Carlone
remodelled the
abbey church – his
great masterpiece.
Worth seeing inside are the
stained-glass windows, the lovely
pulpit and the main altar with a
painting of the Assumption of
the Virgin Mary flanked by
columns of pink Salzburg marble.
The abbey also has an art gallery.

❹ Perg

Road map E3. 🏛 8,000. 🚌 🚆
Tel (07262) 53150.

Perg, a small town with a long
history situated 30 km (19 miles)
east of Linz, was once owned
by the mighty von Perg family,

whose last member died in the
12th century, during the Third
Crusade. Until the 19th century
Perg was the largest centre of
millstone production; it is also
the home of Manner, the largest
manufacturer of sweet wafers in
the world. Worth seeing today
are some attractive houses on
Herrengasse, a 1683 Baroque
pillory in the main square and
St Jacob's church (1416), which
has retained its Gothic interior.

In Perg's environs, graves and
numerous remains of the
Hallstatt civilization have been
unearthed. The Heimathaus
at No. 1 Stifterstrasse exhibits
finds from that period. It also
documents the production of
millstones and has an interesting
collection of 16th–17th-century
ceramics, decorated using a
special local technique.

❺ Kefermarkt

Road map E3. 🏛 2,000. 🚌
Tel (07947) 75 700.

The main attraction in this
little town is its 15th-century
Wallfahrtskirche (pilgrimage
church), built by Christoph
von Zelking, the master of
Kefermarkt's castle, Schloss
Weinberg. He also commis-
sioned its altar dedicated to his
favourite saint, St Wolfgang
(died 994), Bishop of Regensburg
and Henry II's tutor. We do not
know who created the altar, but
the result is a masterpiece of
medieval art. Entirely carved
from limewood, it was probably
once painted, but now the
original texture and colour of
the wood are revealed. Its centre
is made up of the figures of
Saints Peter, Wolfgang and
Christopher. On the wings of
the altar the unknown artist
has placed scenes of the
Annunciation, the Birth of
Christ, the Adoration of the
Magi and the Death of Mary.
The altar was once riddled
with woodworm and only
narrowly escaped total destruction. It was carefully restored in
1852–5, under the supervision
of Adalbert Stifter, a writer and
school inspector for Upper
Austria. It is to his dedication

and appreciation of great art that we owe the altar's survival. There is also an interesting permanent exhibition in the church called "Jesus on the road".

A statue on the splendid wooden altar in Kefermarkt church

❻ Freistadt

Road map E3. 🚉 7,500. 🚌 🚆
Tel (07942) 75700-30.

Freistadt, the largest town in the Mühlviertel region, was once the last border fortress on the route leading from the Alpine countries to Bohemia. Much of the medieval **town wall** has survived to this day, including several bastions and two impressive gateways; one of these, the late-Gothic Linzer Tor, is the symbol of the town. The focal point of the old town centre, the rectangular Hauptplatz, is lined with historic houses. On its east side

stands the town hall, with a carved fountain.

The 15th-century **Katharinenmünster**, the church of St Catherine, on the southwest side of the square, was altered in the Baroque style by Johann Michael Prunner. The altar paintings are the work of Carlo Carlone. The castle, not far from the main square, was built in 1397 for the widow of Prince Albert III. It was devastated by a fire in 1888 and subsequently turned into a military barracks. The building now houses the **Schlossmuseum**, a regional museum holding Austria's largest collection of glass paintings.

🏛 Schlossmuseum
Schlosshof 2.
Tel (07942) 72 274.
Open 9am–noon, 2–5pm Mon–Fri, 2–5pm Sat, Sun & public holidays. 🖼

Jakob Prandtauer (1660–1726)

Austria's outstanding architect of the Baroque, Prandtauer specialized in sacred buildings and shaped the present look of several medieval abbeys. His greatest masterpiece is generally agreed to be the Benedictine Abbey in Melk. He also created the church of the Carmelite nuns in St Pölten, and gave a Baroque face to the Augustinian abbey in St Florian and the Benedictine abbey in Kremsmünster. Distinctive features of his work are the variety of forms he used, and the vigorous way in which he blended architecture with the surrounding countryside.

Jakob Prandtauer

❼ Schärding

Road map D3. 🚉 4,900. 🚌
Tel (07712) 4300. 🌐 schaerding.at

This town on the banks of the Inn River was, until 1779, owned by the Bavarian family of Wittelsbach, whose influence can be seen in the local architecture. Schärding's most beautiful feature is its **Stadtplatz**, the central square cut in half by buildings.

At the north end of the upper square, **Silberzeile** is a row of beautiful houses with gabled roofs. It is overshadowed by the vast Church of St George's with a grand steeple. Little apart from the gateway and moat remains of the old castle here. The gateway houses a regional museum with a late-Gothic Madonna, a beautiful crucifix and sculptures by Johann Peter Schwanthaler the Elder (1720–95).

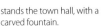

Silberzeile, a row of pretty and colourful gabled houses in the Stadtplatz in Schärding

Baroque house façades in Obernberg

❽ Obernberg am Inn

Road map D3. 🏔 1,500. 🚌
Tel (07723) 8555.

Until the late 18th century, Obernberg belonged to Bavaria and was ruled by the bishops of Passau. In 1779, it transferred to Austria. The old market town has preserved its lovely **Marktplatz**, the central town square, lined with pretty houses with exceptionally beautiful, richly ornamented stucco façades. Particularly interesting are the façades of the houses at Nos 37, 38 and 57, with decorations attributed to the prominent Bavarian artist, Johann Baptist Modler. A fountain in the centre of the square is surrounded by sculptures. When visiting the Annakapelle, the parish church of Obernberg, it is worth taking a closer look at the 16th-century wood-carving of the Holy Family.

A castle, once owned by the bishops of Passau, has stood in Obernberg since the 12th century, but little remains of it.

Environs: Near Obernberg, 15 km (9 miles) to the southwest, is the largest town of the province, **Ried im Innkreis**, an agri-cultural centre and the home town of the Schwanthaler family of sculptors. Many members of the family

Figure from fountain in Obernberg town square

were outstanding artists, active in the region from 1632 to 1838. The local museum, at No. 13 Kirchenplatz, exhibits some of their works.

❾ Braunau am Inn

Road map D3. 🏔 16,000. 🚌 🚉
ℹ Stadtplatz 2 (07722) 62 644.
🌐 **tourismus-braunau.at**

Braunau is a substantial border town on the Inn River and one of the prettiest spots in the entire region. It was built by the dukes of Lower Bavaria, who ruled it for a long time. Originally intended as a bridgehead in their battles with the East, the town remained one of the best-fortified towns in this part of Europe until the 17th century. In 1779 it passed to Austria, together with the rest of the province. The Baroque fortifications were dismantled by Napoleon, but some sections survived, including the remains of several medieval buildings.

The centre of this Gothic town is occupied by the unusually elon-gated **Stadtplatz**, surrounded by historic houses. At No. 18 Johann-Fischer-Gasse, built in 1385, an old bell-foundry has survived almost intact. Together with the former ducal castle at No. 10 Altstadt next door, it is now the home of the regional museum, showing art, handicrafts and traditions of the Inn region.

The town's symbol is the stone tower of the **Stephanskirche** (parish church of St Stephen) which is nearly 100 m (330 ft) tall. Construction began in 1492, but the Baroque cupola dates from a later period. Inside the church is a lovely stone pulpit. The only surviving parts of the original altarpiece by Michael Zürn are figures of the Madonna with Child and Saints Stephen and Laurence. The altar itself dates from 1906; it is a Neo-Gothic copy of Michael Pacher's altar in St Wolfgang *(see p210)*. Among the tombs outside the church is one of Hans Staininger, who is shown with a curly beard that reaches to his toes – and was said to have been the cause of his untimely death.

Braunau was also the birthplace of Adolf Hitler, who lived at No. 15 Salzburger Vorstadt until he was two.

The birthplace of Adolf Hitler in Braunau am Inn

❿ Schmiding Zoo

Road map D3. **Tel** (07249) 46 272.
🚌 🚉 Haiding. **Open** Mar–Nov: 9am–5:30pm daily. 🅿
🌐 **zooschmiding.com**

Upper Austria's largest zoo, covering an area of some 120,000 sq m (30 acres), is based at Schmiding, 7 km (4 miles) north of Wels. This modern zoo, with giraffes, monkeys, crocodiles, exotic birds and 1,500 other animal species, is famous for its walk-in aviary with birds of prey – the world's largest. A huge tropical house, an African savannah and Austria's

Flamingoes in the zoo at Schmiding

biggest colony of flamingoes are further highlights of the zoo. Children love the 5-m (16-ft) high platform which allows them to come face to face with the giraffes.

The park lies at the foot of a castle dating from 1405. After World War II the castle served as a military hospital; it has since been restored and converted into apartments.

⓫ Lambach

Road map D3. 🕂 3,400. 🚌 🚆
Tel (07245) 283550.

Lambach, conveniently located on the left bank of the Traun River, grew rich in the Middle Ages thanks to the flourishing salt trade. Around 1040 Count Arnold II von Wels-Lambach and his wife Regilinda transformed the family seat into a monastery. Their son, Bishop Adalbero of Würzburg, who was later canonized, invited Benedictine monks here in 1089. In the same year, the Lambach monks established a second monastery at Melk which, eventually, was to surpass the mother abbey in terms of status and beauty. The abbey church was mostly rebuilt in the 17th century; rebuilding of the abbey itself was completed 50 years later.

The Baroque interior of the church is very beautiful, but Lambach owes its fame primarily to the Romanesque frescoes, probably dating from the 11th century. Unique in Austria, they are considered to be one of Europe's most resplendent examples of Romanesque art. At their centre is the Madonna with Child, to the left the Adoration of the Magi, who present gifts to the Holy Infant. The south vault depicts Jerusalem and Herod's palace. The abbey treasury also holds the Romanesque chalice of Bishop Adalbero and precious monstrances and chasubles. Also on view are ceiling paintings by Martino Altomonte and Martin Johann Schmidt. The musical archives hold a copy of Mozart's *Lambacher Symphonie*, which the composer reputedly created while staying here. Lambach also has a beautifully preserved Rococo theatre.

Romanesque frescoes in Lambach Abbey

⓬ Wels

Road map E3. 🕂 59,000. 🚌 🚆
ℹ Stadtplatz 44 (07242) 67 722-0.
🅦 wels.at

The history of Wels dates back to Roman days, as testified by numerous excavations. Some of the objects discovered are on display in the former Minorites' Abbey, including the famous Wels Venus, a bronze statuette from the 1st–2nd century AD and the oldest early-Christian epitaph in Austria, from the first half of the 4th century.

Today Wels is a centre of agriculture and industry, and the venue of Agraria, a biennial agricultural fair of international importance. Many historic features have also been preserved. **Stadtplatz**, the main square in the old town, is entered through a Baroque gate, the **Ledererturm**. Many houses in Stadtplatz have attractive façades, such as the Rococo **Kremsmünstererhof** with its arcaded courtyard, which for 400 years belonged to Kremsmünster Abbey. Adjacent to it stands a water tower (1577) and a two-house complex forming the late-Baroque town hall.

Also in Stadtplatz is the Stadtpfarrkirche, the parish church of St John the Evangelist, with an original Romanesque portal and magnificent 14th-century stained-glass windows in the presbytery. **Burg Wels**, the imperial palace first documented in 776, is now a lively cultural centre and home of the regional museum.

The galleried courtyard of Kremsmünsterhof in Stadtplatz, Wels

⓭ Kremsmünster

Road map E3. A-4450 Kremsmünster.
🚌 🚉 **Tel** (07583) 5275-0. **Open** May–
Oct: guided tours 10am, 11:30am,
2pm, 4pm daily; Nov–Jan & Mar:
11am, 2pm, 3:30pm Tue–Sun.
Sternwarte: ◼ May–Aug: 10am, 2pm,
4pm daily; Sep & Oct: 2pm Mon–Fri,
10am, 2pm Sat & Sun. Call ahead for
tours in English (min four people).
🅿 ⓦ stift-kremsmuenster.at

Perched high above the Krems
river stands the 8th-century
Benedictine Abbey of
Kremsmünster, its present
appearance dating mostly from
the 17th century. The
abbey was completed
by Jakob Prandtauer,
to designs by Carlo
Carlone. Two of its most
remarkable features are
the 17th-century fish
ponds, surrounded by
columns, corridors and
sculptural fountains,
and the unusual
Sternwarte, a 50-m
(165-ft) high observa-
tion tower, which
holds collections of
palaeontology, physics,
anthropology, astronomy and
zoology. The **Stiftskirche**
(abbey church) has rich stucco
decorations and angel statues.
The abbey museum comprises
works by Austrian and Dutch
masters from the Baroque and
Renaissance periods, wood
carvings and gold objects.

The Tassilo Chalice in
Kremsmünster

The pride of Kremsmünster are
its earliest exhibits; these include
the gilded-copper chalice and
candelabras of Duke Tassilo, the
legendary founder of the abbey,
and the *Codex millenarius* (c.800),
an illuminated manuscript.

⓮ Steyr

Road map E3. 🏔 38,000. 🚌 🚉
ⓘ Stadtplatz 27 (07252) 53 229.

Steyr, one of Austria's largest
industrial centres, is also a
very attractive town which has
managed to preserve its old
town almost intact.
The townscape is
punctuated in the
north by the turrets
of the castle and in
the south by the towers
of the Stadtpfarrkirche,
the parish church at
Brucknerplatz. The centre
of town is the elongated
Stadtplatz (town
square) with most of
the historic sights. The
Bummerlhaus (1497)
at No. 32, is a well preserved
Gothic house with a high-
pitched roof and three arcaded
courtyards, that is now a bank.
The Rococo **Rathaus** (town hall),
with its slender steeple, was
designed by Johann Gotthard
Hayberger. The inner courtyards
of houses around the square
are also worth seeing. The
Stadtpfarrkirche, built in

1443, was remodelled in the
Neo-Gothic style, but it has
preserved some elements of
its original 15th-century decor,
the work of Hans Puchsbaum,
builder of the Stephansdom in
Vienna, as well as some lovely
wrought-iron grilles. The south
wall has magnificent 15th-cen-
tury stained-glass windows; the
sculptures in the north portal
and the former cemetery chapel
of St Margaret (1430), also by
Hans Puchsbaum, date from
the same period.

The **Schloss** (castle), first
mentioned in 10th-century
annals, stands in the oldest
part of the town. Today it has
a Baroque façade and a mostly
Rococo interior. The house at
No. 26 Grünmarkt, formerly a
granary, is now a museum.

Environs: In **Gleink**, a northern
suburb of Steyr, stands a worthy
Benedictine Abbey. Some 3 km
(2 miles) west of the town centre,
in the suburb of **Christkindl**, is
the church of the same name
(meaning "Infant Christ"), the
joint work of Giovanni Battista
Carlone and Jakob Prandtauer.
In 1695, a devout person placed
a wax figure of the Infant Jesus
in the hollow of a tree and
prayed there every day for a
cure. His prayers were answered
and soon the crowds of pilgrims
drawn to the site of the miracle
were so large that in 1702 the
abbot from nearby Garsten

Steyr town panorama as seen from the river

decided to build a church. The main object of adoration is the wax figurine of Jesus, kept in a beautifully decorated glass cabinet. The cabinet itself is part of a composition symbolizing the Holy Trinity. Christkindl has its own post office, using the coveted "Christkindl" postmark showing the Infant Jesus. It operates only in the pre-Christmas period, and millions of letters, supposedly from the Infant Jesus, are sent around the world from here.

The lovely scenery around the resort of Bad Hall

🏛 **Christkindl Church**
Christkindlweg 69. **Tel** (07252) 54 622.

The façade of the Christkindl church, on the outskirts of Steyr

🅯 Bad Hall

Road map E3. 🏠 4,900. 🚌
🛈 Kurpromenade 1 (07258) 7200-0.

Bad Hall, a health resort between Steyr and Kremsmünster, lies on the so-called "Romantic Route", but the idyllic scenery is just one of its attractions: it also boasts the richest iodine springs in Central Europe. A highly modern resort surrounds the springs, which are used to treat eye, circulatory and heart diseases. The lovely Kurpark (spa park), with its excellent sports facilities, makes convalescence a real treat. There is also a Rococo church which belongs to the abbey at Kremsmünster.

Another sight worth visiting is the fascinating **Forum Hall Museum**, which holds a superb collection devoted to the development of traditional folk handicrafts in Upper Austria, as well as to the history of the local springs.

🏛 **Forum Hall Museum**
Eduard-Bach-Strasse 4. **Tel** (07258) 4888. **Open** Apr–Nov: 2–6pm Thu–Sun. 🅿

🅰 Stadl-Paura

Road map D3. 🏠 4,900. 🚌 🚃
🛈 Marktplatz 1 (07245) 28 011-0

Stadl-Paura, a small town on the right bank of the Traun River 2 km (1 mile) south of Lambach, has an imposing **Dreifaltigkeitskirche** (church of the Holy Trinity). Construction of the church was started in 1714 in thanksgiving for the sparing of the town from the plague. In its design, the church

The Dreifaltigkeitskirche, pilgrimage church of the Holy Trinity in Stadl-Paura

represents the Holy Trinity – everything is in triplicate. There are three façades, three portals, three towers and three altars. The church was built by the Linz architect, Johann Michael Prunner. In the design of the interior decorations some clever false architectural perspectives have been incorporated, creating unusual effects. The paintings in the altarpieces are by Carlo Carlone, Martino Altomonte and Domenico Parodi.

The house at No. 13 Fabrikstrasse, once an orphanage for the children of sailors who lost their lives in the waters of the Traun river, is now a museum of shipping, **Schiffleutmuseum**, which is open on Sundays and holidays in summer.

🅱 Schwanenstadt

Road map D3. 🏠 4,000. 🚌 🚃
🛈 Stadtplatz 54 (07673) 2255-22.

This small town, situated between Lambach and Vöcklabruck, is today an important economic centre. In the centre of town stands a Neo-Gothic parish church with a 78-m (256-ft) spire, built in 1900 on the site of an earlier Gothic church. Worth seeing inside are a late-Gothic statue of the Virgin Mary, a 15th-century relief of the Mourning for Christ and 18th-century Baroque statues of the 12 apostles.

In front of the town hall is a 13th-century well, which is set on an attractive square lined with houses with Renaissance and Baroque façades.

The riverside townscape of the health resort of Gmunden, on the banks of the Traun river

⑱ Vöcklabruck

Road map D3. 🅜 12,000. 🚌 🚊
ℹ️ Graben 8 (07672) 26 644.

The name of this town was first documented in 1134 as Pons (bridge) Veckelahe. Soon after, a trading settlement sprang up on the banks of the Vöckla River. The only original structures to have survived from this period are two medieval towers.

At the centre of town stands the small, 15th-century, late-Gothic **St Ulrichkirche** (church of St Ulrich), which has a Baroque interior. The site of the 12th-century hospital and chapel is occupied by the magnificent Baroque **St Ägidiuskirche**, designed by Carlo Carlone, with sculptures by Giovanni Battista Carlone. The ceiling frescoes depict scenes from the lives of Christ and the Virgin Mary.

The former parish house, at No. 10 Hinterstadt, now houses a regional museum with a room devoted to Anton Bruckner.

The south of the town is dominated by the silhouette of **Wallfahrtskirche Maria Schöndorf**, a church of pilgrimage. It has a Neo-Gothic altarpiece with a beautiful 15th-century statue of the Virgin Mary, and pretty stained-glass windows behind the main altar from the same period.

Environs: West of Vöcklabruck, about 12 km (7 miles) away, is the small town of **Gampern**. Its Remigiuskirche (church of St Remigius) has an attractive late-Gothic polyptych (1507) carved in wood.

⑲ Gmunden

Road map D3. 🅜 13,000. 🚌 🚊
ℹ️ Rathausplatz 1 (07612) 65 752.

This lakeside town, on the northern end of Traunsee, established itself as a trading post in the salt trade. Today, it is a popular and well-run health resort, and it is also known for its fine ceramics. Gmunden's old town centre is situated between the lake and the left (western) bank of the Traun river. Its Hauptplatz boasts a Renaissance town hall with a small, arcaded tower and a carillon that plays a regular tune. The **Stadtpfarrkirche** (parish church) has a two-fold dedication: the Virgin Mary and the Three Kings. The Magi are also depicted in the main altarpiece, one of the most beautiful works by Thomas Schwanthaler.

A detail from Gmunden town hall

The figures of Saints Elizabeth and Zacharias were carved by Michael Zürn. Each year on Epiphany Eve (5 Jan), a barge travels along the Traun river, bringing the Three Kings to town, who solemnly proceed to "their" church. A ceramic fountain decorated with a figure of a salt miner stands adjacent to the church.

The **Gmunden K-Hof Museum**, based in the Renaissance building of the former Salt Mines Authorities, has exhibits on the history of the town and its salt production, a room on the astronomer and mathematician Johannes von Gmunden, and a section dedicated to the history of sanitation, which includes displays of locally made toilet bowls and chamber pots.

In Traunsee stands the water fortress of **Lake Castle Ort**, built in the 15th and 16th centuries and rebuilt inn 1634. It has an enchanting triangular, arcaded courtyard and remnants of Renaissance frescoes. A popular TV series is set in the castle.

🏛 **Gmunden K-Hof Museum**
Kammerhofgasse 8. **Tel** (07612) 794 420. **Open** 10am–5pm Wed–Sun (also Tue Jun–Aug). 🦽

⑳ Traunkirchen

Road map D3. 🅜 1,600. 🚌
ℹ️ Ortsplatz 1 (07617) 2234.

Precariously perched on a rocky promontory, the small village of Traunkirchen is one of the most popular tourist destinations in Salzkammergut (see p213). It creates a lovely picture, clinging to the west shore of Traunsee,

Johannesbergkapelle above Traunsee in Traunkirchen

Austria's deepest lake, with views of the lake's wild southern shore and the Traunstein peak on the eastern shore, the highest mountain of the region rising to 1,691 m (5,548 ft). Above the village towers the pretty Johannesbergkapelle. On the northern end of the headland stands the Jesuit **Pfarrkirche**, rebuilt after a fire in 1632. It has an unusual fishermen's pulpit shaped like a fishing boat, with the apostles drawing nets filled with fish. Since 1632, Traunkirchen has also hosted the annual Corpus Christi boat procession.

㉑ Salzkammergut Lakes

See pp210–11.

The steam mountain railway leading to the top of Schafberg

㉒ Schafberg

Road map D4.

One of the most picturesque peaks in the area, Schafberg (Sheep Mountain) rises to 1,783 m (5,850 ft) between Attersee and Wolfgangsee. A mountain railway with steam locomotives takes visitors to the summit, although you have to walk the last bit.

The views from the top are truly unforgettable, embracing the most beautiful lakes of the Salzkammergut: Mondsee, Attersee and Wolfgangsee. Visible in the background are the towering mountain ranges running up to the Dachstein massif in the south, and, beyond Salzburg, you can see the Bavarian Alps on the German-Austrian border.

㉓ St Wolfgang

Road map D4. 🏔 2,800. 🚌 🛈 Au 140 (06138) 8003. 🌐 stwolfgang.at

On the northern shore of Wolfgangsee lies the popular town of St Wolfgang. According to legend it arose around a chapel built by Wolfgang (died 994), Bishop of Regensburg in Germany and teacher of Emperor Henry II. Although he died a hermit, Wolfgang was an extremely popular figure in his day, and was later canonized. His chapel became a much-visited place of pilgrimage. In the 15th century it was replaced by a church with room for a much larger number of pilgrims. It was around that time that the Abbot of Mondsee commissioned the famed South Tyrolean artist, Michael Pacher, to create an altar for the **pilgrimage church**.

Pacher's high altar, combining sculpture, painting and architecture, is acclaimed as one of the most beautiful works of the late-Gothic era. The four scenes visible on the wings of the altarpiece when they are closed (on weekdays) depict events from the life of St Wolfgang, patron saint of the church. The saint is shown holding a model of the church and is flanked by the figures of the Saints George and Florian. On Sundays, the wings of the altar are opened to reveal eight painted scenes from the life of Christ. They are striking in their coloration, the dynamics of their life-like figures and, above all, in the architectural perspective employed by the artist. The brightly gilded, sculpted centrepiece depicts the Coronation of the Virgin

Mary attended by Christ, St Benedict and St Wolfgang.

The church of St Wolfgang also has a lovely Baroque altarpiece by Thomas Schwanthaler, depicting the Holy Family on their journey to Jerusalem. The three side altarpieces on the north wall and the magnificently ornate pulpit are the works of a Mondsee master, Meinrad Guggenbichler.

St Wolfgang is also popular with tourists who come to see the hotel "Weisses Rössl" which inspired an operetta of the same name, *White Horse Inn*, by Ralph Benatzky.

㉔ Bad Ischl

Road map D4. 🏔 14,000. 🚌 🚆 🛈 Auböckplatz 5 (06132) 27 757-0. 🌐 badischl.com

Unusually potent saltwater springs were discovered in this region as early as the 16th century, but Bad Ischl did not become a popular health resort until the early 1800s, when the court doctor ordered saline treatments for the infertile Archduchess Sophie. Soon, she started producing babies. The most famous of these was Franz Joseph I, the future emperor, who spent all his summer holidays with his wife Elizabeth at the **Kaiservilla**. It was also here that he signed the declaration of war with Serbia, on 1 August 1914, signalling the start of World War I.

Many aristocrats and artists have been attracted to the spa, among them the composer Franz Lehár, who lived at No. 8 Franz-Lehár-Kai, which is now a museum devoted to him.

The imposing Spa House in the popular resort of Bad Ischl

For hotels and restaurants in this region see pp296–7 and pp320–21

㉑ Salzkammergut Lakes

This corner of Austria, which belongs to the Salzkammergut region, is worth visiting at any time of the year. With more than 70 lakes surrounded by mountains, it boasts breathtaking scenery as well as a unique climate, and offers excellent facilities for winter and summer holidays. This is also one of the few areas in Europe to preserve many original folk customs, including the tradition of placing a crib in front of the house at Christmas.

Mondsee
The warmest of the Salzkammergut lakes, at the foot of craggy mountains, is famous for its windsurfing. The little town of the same name arose around a Benedictine abbey, which dominates it to this day.

★ St Wolfgang
The main attraction in this charming small town and holiday resort is the parish church with its beautiful altarpiece by Michael Pacher *(see p209)*.

Braunau

St Georgen

A1 E55 E60

Salzburg

Mondsee

Mondsee

154

151

Unterach

Burggrabenklam

Wolfgangsee

St Wolfg

Politicians and Artists on Holiday

The shores of the Salzkammergut lakes have seen many famous visitors. The house that witnessed the engagement of Emperor Franz Joseph I to Elizabeth of Bavaria in 1853 is now a museum with memorabilia of famous guests in Bad Ischl. There were scores of them: crowned heads and high-ranking aristocrats were joined by artists. Franz Lehár, composer of operettas such as *The Merry Widow* and *The Land of Smiles*, had his villa here; so did the actor Alexander Girardi and the actress Katharina Schratt, the long-term mistress of Franz Joseph I. Other regular visitors included the writer and actor Johannes Nepomuk Nestroy, the painter Rudolf von Alt, and musicians Johannes Brahms, Anton Bruckner, Johann Strauss and Imre Kálmán. In the late 20th century many politicians spent their holidays in St Wolfgang, including both the former Austrian and German Chancellors.

Franz Joseph I and his hunting party

Key

- ▬▬ Motorway
- ▭▭ Major road
- ⋯⋯ Minor road
- ⋯ River
- – – Bundesland (province) border

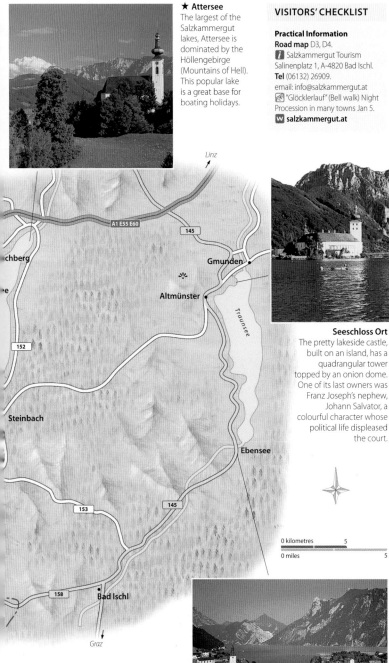

★ Attersee
The largest of the Salzkammergut lakes, Attersee is dominated by the Höllengebirge (Mountains of Hell). This popular lake is a great base for boating holidays.

VISITORS' CHECKLIST

Practical Information
Road map D3, D4.
🛈 Salzkammergut Tourism Salinenplatz 1, A-4820 Bad Ischl.
Tel (06132) 26909.
email: info@salzkammergut.at
🗓 "Glöcklerlauf" (Bell walk) Night Procession in many towns Jan 5.
🖥 salzkammergut.at

Linz

Seeschloss Ort
The pretty lakeside castle, built on an island, has a quadrangular tower topped by an onion dome. One of its last owners was Franz Joseph's nephew, Johann Salvator, a colourful character whose political life displeased the court.

Graz

Ebensee
This town, a centre of the salt industry scenically located at the southern end of Traunsee at the bottom of Höllengebirge, is famous for its carnival festivities.

For additional map symbols *see back flap*

Bronze-age finds in Hallstatt's World Heritage Museum

㉕ Hallstatt

Road map D4. 🏔 800. 🚌 🚉 🚢
ℹ️ Seestrasse 99 (06134) 8208.
🆆 hallstatt.net

The small town of Hallstatt is one of the loveliest tourist destinations in the Salzkammergut. The steep drop of the Dachstein massif provides a scenic backdrop for the town and adjacent Hallstätter See. The houses are clustered together so tightly that many are accessible only from the lakeside, while the old street runs above the rooftops. Even the local Corpus Christi procession is held on the lake, in festive, decorated boats.

Rising above the town on a rocky headland is the pagoda-like roof of the **Pfarrkirche**. Its stepped dome dates from a later period, but the church was built in the 15th century and to this day contains many original features, including the carved wooden altarpiece of the Virgin Mary, sometimes compared to Pacher's altar in St Wolfgang (*see p209*). The figure of the Madonna at its centre is flanked

Painted skulls in the Beinhaus chapel of Hallstatt's Pfarrkirche

by the Saints Barbara, patron of miners, and Catherine, revered by woodcutters. Depicted on the inner wings are scenes from the lives of Mary and Jesus. The altar is guarded by the statues of two knightly saints, George and Florian.

In the cemetery surrounding the church stands the **Beinhaus**, a chapel that serves as a storehouse for some very bizarre objects. This former mortuary now holds some 1,200 human skulls, painted with floral designs and in many cases inscribed with the name, date and cause of death of the deceased. Shortage of space in the graveyard had meant that some ten years after a funeral, when a body had decomposed, the remains were moved to the chapel to make room for the next coffin to be buried, resulting in this unusual depository.

A short distance below the Catholic Pfarrkirche stands a Neo-Gothic Protestant church, with a slender steeple.

Vertically above the town, about 500 m (1,640 ft) higher, is **Salzwelten Hallstatt**, probably the oldest salt mine in the world, which can be reached by cable car. Salt was mined here as early as 3,000 BC and then transported to the Baltic Sea and the Mediterranean.

In 1846, a large cemetery yielding some 2,000 graves was uncovered in Hallstatt. Rich burial objects dated mainly from the Iron Age but some dated even further back in time, to the Bronze Age. The Hallstatt finds proved so important archaeologically that the Celtic culture of that period (800–400 BC)

was named the Hallstatt civilization. Its influence reached far into France, the Slav countries and Hungary.

Today, Hallstatt treasures can be seen in many Austrian museums, with the bulk of them held at Schloss Eggenberg, near Graz (*see p166*). The few finds that stayed in Hallstatt are kept in the **World Heritage Museum**. The entire Hallstatt region has been declared a World Heritage Site by UNESCO.

🏛 **Salzwelten Hallstatt**
Lahnstrasse 21. **Tel** (06132) 200 2400. **Open** late Apr–mid-Sep: 9:30am–4:30pm daily; mid-Sep–Oct: 9:30am–3pm daily. 🅿️ 🅰️ 📷
🆆 salzwelten.at

🏛 **World Heritage Museum**
Seestrasse 56. **Tel** (06134) 828015. **Open** Nov–Mar: 11am–3pm Wed–Sun; Apr, Oct: 10am–4pm daily; May–Sep: 10am–6pm daily. 🅿️ 🅰️
🆆 museum-hallstatt.at

㉖ Gosauseen

Road map D4. 🚌
ℹ️ Gosau (06136) 8295.

You cannot truly appreciate the unique charms of the Salzkammergut without visiting this outstandingly beautiful Alpine area. The Gosauseen are three small mountain lakes – Vorderer Gosausee, Gosaulacke and Hinterer Gosausee – both are beautifully situated in limestone rocks intercut with deep gorges. Vorderer Gosausee lies at an altitude of 933 m (3,061 ft). An undemanding walk around the lake will reward you with superb views of the surrounding mountains and over the Dachstein range with its many glaciers.

The most picturesque mountain, with zigzag peaks and a sheer drop, is Gosaukamm (2,459 m/8,068 ft high). This is the easternmost part of the Alps where the snow stays on the ground all year round. The road to Hinterer Gosausee climbs steeply among thick forest. From this lake, 1,154 m (3,786 ft) high, you can climb some of the adjacent peaks.

A mountain stream racing through a gorge in the Dachstein range

⑳ Dachsteinhöhlen

Road map D4. 🛈 Winkl 34, Obertraun am Hallstättersee (06131) 351.
🌐 dachstein-salzkammergut.com

The caves in the slopes of the Dachstein range are among Austria's most beautiful and fascinating natural monuments. The vast caves, one of the largest systems on Earth and millions of years old, are covered by 500-year-old permafrost. After the last Ice Age, underground waters created strange ice mountains, glaciers and frozen waterfalls. The most interesting of these is the **Rieseneishöhle** (Giant Ice Cave). The caverns in this surreal underground ice-world are named after King Arthur and the Celtic heroes, Parsifal and Tristan. The most arresting cavern formation is the so-called Ice Chapel.

The Salzkammergut

For centuries, the name Salzkammergut applied only to the area around the Hallstätter See and Traunsee lakes, and to the towns of Bad Ischl, Hallstatt and Gmunden. Salt has been excavated here since prehistoric times, ensuring the long-term wealth and development of the entire region. Salt mines exist in the area to this day. In the second half of the 19th century the area became famous for its therapeutic springs, and with time the term Salzkammergut came to refer to the entire land of lakes and mountains that is now Austria's most popular tourist destination. It includes the eastern part of the Salzburg Alps, with the picturesque mountain ranges of Dachstein (eastern part), Totes Gebirge (Dead Mountains) and Höllengebirge (Mountains of Hell). Between the mountains lie 76 lakes, the largest and most famous of which are Traunsee, Mondsee, Attersee, Hallstätter See and Wolfgangsee. For historical reasons, the "land of salt" straddles three Austrian provinces. The largest part is in Upper Austria, a small area in the south belongs to Styria, whilst almost all of Wolfgangsee and the St Gilgen resort are part of the Salzburger Land.

The much-loved Salzkammergut, land of lakes and mountains

A little further along, also in a limestone wall of Dachstein, is the entrance to a second system of caves, known as **Mammuthöhle** (Mammoth Caves), so named because of their size rather than after the prehistoric mammal. These caves do not have ice formations, but there is a spectacular light show.

Both networks of caves can be reached via paths starting from the first cable-car station. The sightseeing route leads through a labyrinthine network of tunnels, gorges and chambers that stretch over 44 km (27 miles), with a 1,200 m (4,000 ft) change in altitude. Individual caverns have been given evocative names such as the Realm of Shadows or Midnight Cathedral. Also worth seeing is a third cave, **Koppenbrüllerhöhle**, which has a giant water source and is considered to be the largest water cave in the Dachstein massif.

All caves are open to the public only during the spring and summer seasons (May to Oct; Koppenbrüllerhöhle May to Sep). When visiting the caves, especially the ice caves, make sure you take plenty of warm clothing.

Dachstein ice caves in Obertraun

SALZBURGER LAND

The province of Salzburg, a region of high mountains, covers an area of 7,154 sq km (2,762 sq miles) and has 450,000 inhabitants. Its neighbours are Germany and the Austrian provinces of Tyrol, Upper Austria, Styria and Carinthia. A narrow wedge of land along the peaks of the Hohe Tauern mountains reaches as far as the Italian border in the south.

Salzburger Land is divided into five regions: Flachgau, Tennengebirge, Pongau, Pinzgau and Lungau. History has made them different in character and traditions; all are great for sports.

Colonization of the Salzach Valley goes back to prehistoric times. The mineral deposits – copper, precious metals and, above all, salt (*Salz* in German) from which both the town and province take their names – were being exploited as early as 1000 BC. It was salt which created the basis for the development of the so-called Hallstatt civilization that spread from here. The Celtic town of Noricum established in the Alpine region ultimately became a Roman province of the same name. Christianity arrived here early, and its turbulent progress was halted only by the great Migration of Nations in 5th-century Europe. It was not until the 7th century that monks settled in Mönchsburg, the future Salzburg, which became first a bishopric and then an archbishopric. The entire province was an independent principality for many centuries, governed by an ecclesiastical ruler acting as sovereign prince and, depending on political circumstance and personal preference, associating himself with the Holy Roman Empire, the Austrian Habsburgs or Rome. Following the Congress of Vienna, in 1815, Salzburg became part of Austria. Today, the beauty of Salzburg, inextricably linked with Mozart, makes this province a visitor magnet second only to Vienna.

The Hochkönig Alpine meadows in Salzburger Land

◀ Spectacular church domes towering over the Baroque buildings, Salzburg

Exploring Salzburger Land

Most of the province lies in the Salzach river basin, at a
relatively high altitude, offering excellent conditions for both
winter sports and summer mountain walks. Austria's most
scenic mountain road, the Grossglockner Hochalpenstrasse
(see pp284–5), crosses the southern part of the province. The
region abounds in mineral springs and waterfalls, and boasts
one of the world's largest caves. Salzburg, an administrative
centre, is also the cultural and artistic capital of the province,
the city of Mozart and home of the annual Salzburg Festival.

Alpine meadows near Lungötz, typical of Salzburger Land

Sights at a Glance

1. Salzburg pp218–27
2. Hellbrunn
3. Anif
4. St Gilgen
5. Hallein
6. Golling
7. Abtenau
8. Werfen
9. Bischofshofen
10. Radstadt
11. St Johann im Pongau
12. Wagrain
13. Mauterndorf
14. Moosham
15. Tamsweg
16. Gasteinertal pp234–5
17. Kaprun
18. Zell am See
19. Saalbach
20. Lofer
21. Mittersill
22. Krimmler Wasserfälle

Eisriesenwelt near Werfen, the largest ice
caves on earth

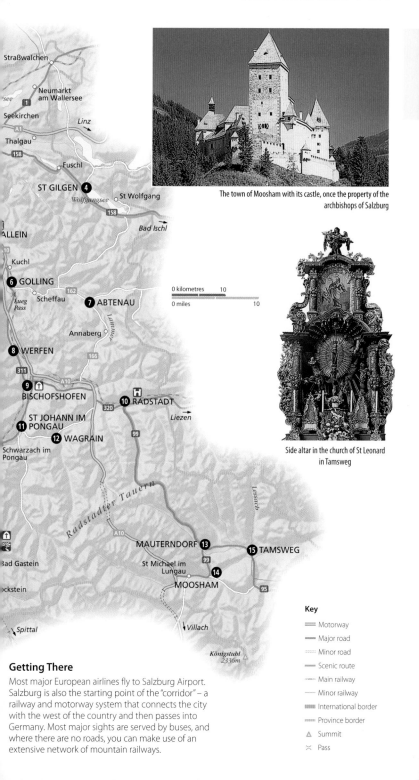

Straßwalchen
Neumarkt
am Wallersee
see
Seekirchen
Linz
A1
Thalgau
158
Fuschl
ST GILGEN **4**
Wolfgangsee   St Wolfgang
158
ALLEIN
Bad Ischl
Kuchl
6 GOLLING
Lueg Pass   Scheffau
162
7 ABTENAU
Annaberg
Lammer
8 WERFEN
166
311
9 BISCHOFSHOFEN
A10
320
10 RADSTADT
ST JOHANN IM PONGAU **11**
Liezen
12 WAGRAIN
99
Schwarzach im Pongau
Radstädter Tauern
Lessach
A10
MAUTERNDORF **13**
15 TAMSWEG
99
St Michael im Lungau
14
Bad Gastein
MOOSHAM
95
ockstein
Spittal
Villach
Königstuhl 2336m

The town of Moosham with its castle, once the property of the archbishops of Salzburg

0 kilometres   10
0 miles   10

Side altar in the church of St Leonard in Tamsweg

Getting There

Most major European airlines fly to Salzburg Airport. Salzburg is also the starting point of the "corridor" – a railway and motorway system that connects the city with the west of the country and then passes into Germany. Most major sights are served by buses, and where there are no roads, you can make use of an extensive network of mountain railways.

Key

━━ Motorway
━━ Major road
┈┈ Minor road
━━ Scenic route
╍╍ Main railway
── Minor railway
▬▬ International border
▭▭ Province border
△ Summit
⤬ Pass

❶ Salzburg

According to legend, Salzburg was founded by Bishop Rupert, who arrived with Benedictine monks, and by the Irish Bishop Virgil, who built the town's first cathedral. Salzburg, however, owes its glory and its present appearance to the three archbishops who ruled here after them, between 1587 and 1653: Wolf Dietrich von Raitenau, Marcus Sitticus and Paris von Lodron. The most famous creator of the Austrian Baroque, Johann Bernhard Fischer von Erlach, began his career as an architect in Salzburg. It is also the town of Mozart, who was born here in 1756. Today, the prestigious Salzburg Festival attracts participants from around the world.

Tanzmeisterhaus, once the home of Wolfgang Amadeus Mozart

View over the churches of Salzburg and Hohensalzburg fortress

Exploring Salzburg

Salzburg is divided into three distinct areas of interest. The first, including the finest churches, the archbishop's residence and Mozart's birthplace, is on the left bank of the Salzach river. The second area, on the right bank of the Salzach, is the New Town. Its most interesting sights are the Mirabell Palace, the Mozart Conservatoire and Kapuzinerberg. The third area is the mighty former fortress of Hohensalzburg.

🎹 Makartplatz

Mozart-Wohnhaus
Makartplatz 8. **Tel** (0662) 874227-40.
Open Sep–Jun: 9am–5:30pm daily,
July–Aug: 9am–7pm daily. 🏛

This square was given its current name in memory of the Salzburg-born painter, Hans Makart, whose work greatly influenced contemporary fashion, architecture and interior design in the mid-19th century.

The Tanzmeisterhaus at No. 8 was Wolfgang Amadeus Mozart's home in 1773–87. The original house, destroyed in World War II, was rebuilt, and is a small museum dedicated to the composer.

The Dreifaltigkeitskirche (church of the Holy Trinity), in the northeast corner of the square, dates from 1694 and is one of the earliest works of Johann Bernhard Fischer von Erlach. Built shortly after his return from Italy, it shows signs of Roman influence. Its façade is crowned with sculptures of Faith, Love, Hope and the Church by Michael Bernhard Mandl. The frescoes in the dome vault are by Johann Michael Rottmayr.

⛪ Sebastiansfriedhof

Linzer Gasse 41. **Tel** (0662) 875208.
Open 9am–4pm daily (until 6:30pm in summer).

The St Sebastian cemetery lies just below the church of the same name. All that remains of the old church is a Rococo portal with the bust of its patron saint, and the wrought-iron grille by Philipp Hinterseer. The present, much more modest building, dates from the early 19th century. The cemetery is older, dating from the 15th century. It was designed along the lines of Italian *campo santo*, with burial sites surrounded by columns, and has magnificent sculptures and tombstones. Next to the entrance, beside the church, is the tomb of the philosopher, physician and father of pharmacology, Paracelsus, who died in Salzburg in 1541.

At the centre of the cemetery stands the chapel of the Archangel St Gabriel that doubles as Archbishop Wolf Dietrich von Raitenau's mausoleum. Nearby are the graves of Mozart's father Leopold, and his wife Constanze.

Kapuzinerberg

Kapuzinerberg, a hill on the right bank of the Salzach river opposite the historic Old Town, drops almost down to the river. Two hundred and fifty steep steps, known as the Imbergstiege, climb up from Linzer Gasse. At the halfway point stands the church of St Johannes am Imberg, built in 1681. Its main altarpiece has a painting of the Baptism of Christ. Another interesting feature is the carved pulpit by Johann Georg Hitzl.

A gilded figure from the church of St Sebastian

For hotels and restaurants in this region see pp297–8 and pp322–3

A small castle once stood on top of the hill and formed part of the medieval fortifications; later it was partly incorporated into the Capuchin monastery complex whose church was completed in 1602. The monastery has a carved oak door made from the medieval stalls of the earlier cathedral. A short distance away stands a villa that was once the home of the Austrian writer, Stefan Zweig. Below the church, from the top of an old tower, the Hettwer Bastei, you can enjoy superb views over the many domes and spires of Salzburg and its immediate environs.

Putti on the Angels Staircase in Mirabell

she is said to have borne the archbishop 15 children. Dietrich referred to her as his wife and loved her to the end of his life. In 1727, Johann Lukas von Hildebrandt rebuilt the palace for Archbishop Franz Anton Fürst von Harrach as a truly royal Baroque home. A fire in 1818 destroyed part of the building, but fortunately the superb Angels Staircase, with sculptures by Georg Raphael Donner, and the gilt-stuccoed Marble Hall, where a young Wolfgang Mozart performed with his sister Nanneri, were spared.

🏠 Schloss Mirabell
Mirabellplatz. **Tel** (0662) 80720.
Open 8am–4pm Mon, Wed & Thu, 1–4pm Tue & Fri.

The site of the present Mirabell Palace was originally used by Archbishop Wolf Dietrich von Raitenau in 1606 to erect a much more modest mansion, which he intended as a home for his mistress Salome Alt. The daughter of a Jewish merchant,

VISITORS' CHECKLIST

Practical Information
Road map D3. 🔼 145,000.
ℹ️ Mozartplatz 5 (0662) 88987330. 🎭 Salzburger Festspiele (late Jul–late Aug).
🌐 **salzburg.info.at**

Transport
✈️ Innsbrucker Bundesstrasse 95 (0662) 85800. 🚉 Hauptbahnhof, Südtirolerplatz (0662) 930 003161.

The palace is now a civic administration building. It is surrounded by attractive gardens designed by Johann Bernhard Fischer von Erlach, with groups of sculptures and fountains.

The beautiful gardens of Schloss Mirabell

Salzburg City Centre

1. Kapuzinerberg
2. Makartplatz
3. Sebastiansfriedhof
4. Schloss Mirabell
5. Mozarteum
6. Haus der Natur
7. Carolino Augusteum
8. Festspielhäuser
9. Mozart Geburtshaus
10. Kollegienkirche
11. Franziskanerkirche
12. Residenzplatz
13. Stift St Peter
14. Dom
15. Stift Nonnberg

0 metres 500
0 yards 500

For map symbols *see back flap*

Street-by-Street: Old Town

Salzburg's beautiful Old Town occupies the area
between Mönchsberg (Monks' Mountain) and
the Salzach river. It has been designated a World
Cultural Heritage Site by UNESCO. The town that
grew up on the left bank of the Salzach was
built almost entirely in the Baroque style and is
unusually uniform in appearance. Its ubiquitous
Baroque period designs have been faultlessly
and seamlessly blended with both earlier and
modern architecture.

GRIESGASSE

GETREIDEGASSE

REINHARD
PLATZ

S. HAFFNER-GAS

★ Getreidegasse
One of the longest
and busiest streets
in Salzburg's Old
Town, Getreidegasse
accommodates present
commerce in medieval
settings. No. 9 is
the house where
Wolfgang Amadeus
Mozart was born
and lived until he
was 17; it is now
a museum of the
composer's life.

Kollegienkirche
The university
church is one of
the earliest works
of Johann Bernhard
Fischer von Erlach.
The high altar in
the transept is the
work of Johann
Michael Rottmayr.

Key

— Suggested route

★ Franziskanerkirche
The Franciscan
church has a Baroque
altarpiece by Johann
Bernhard Fischer von
Erlach, which has as
its centre an exquisite
figure of the Madonna
and Child.

0 metres	50
0 yards	50

Altes Rathaus
The angular tower of the 15th-century Old Town Hall comes into view at the end of a narrow medieval alleyway.

★ Residenz
The most opulent building in town, this former home of the Archbishop clearly reveals his wealth and power.

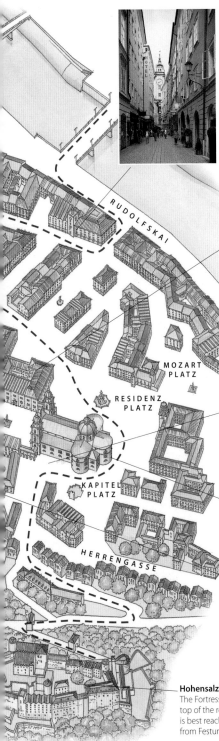

Kapitelplatz
The bustling market square has one of Salzburg's most attractive fountains, and offers outdoor games and fun for everyone.

Dom
The cathedral church of St Rupert & St Virgil was first built in 774, and was subsequently altered many times.

Stift St Peter
This 12th-century Benedictine church is dedicated to St Peter, whose statue adorns the fountain (1673) in front of the church.

Hohensalzburg
The Fortress (*see pp226–7*), on top of the rocky Mönchsberg, is best reached by the funicular from Festungsgasse.

The Mozarteum building, Salzburg's Conservatoire

🎵 Mozarteum

Schwarzstrasse 26. **Tel** (0662) 88 940-0.

In 1842 Mozart's home town erected a monument to the composer and, in 1870, the International Foundation of Mozarteum was established here to promote his music. Today, the Mozarteum holds a collection of his letters, and it is also one of the foremost music schools in Europe.

In the grounds of the conservatoire stands the cottage in which Mozart wrote the opera *The Magic Flute*, brought here from Vienna. The main building of the Mozarteum was designed by the architect Richard Berndl, and built in 1910–14. Some departments are housed in the completely rebuilt former palace of Archbishop Lodron next to the Foundation gardens.

🏛 Haus der Natur

Museumsplatz 5. **Tel** (0662) 842653. **Open** 9am–5pm daily. 🅿

W hausdernatur.at

The quarters that were once occupied by the Ursuline Sisters are now the home of the Natural History Museum, one of the most interesting and fun places to visit in Salzburg. The vast complex, consisting of more than 90 rooms arranged on five floors, houses a great variety of fauna.

Individual sections of the museum are arranged thematically. In "Sea World", a gigantic aquarium recreates the conditions that closely resemble the natural habitat of various water creatures. The "Reptile Zoo's" 33 terraria house some of the most exciting snakes from around the world. There are also huge rooms simulating the natural habitat of Mississippi alligators and the lost worlds of Jurassic creatures, including ever-popular dinosaurs. Other themes include "men and animals in myths and fairy tales", "the cosmos" and "forest animals". Finally, the treasury room displays equipment needed for gold-panning, as well as crystalline forms of precious gems and stones.

🏛 Salzburg Museum

Neue Residenz Mozartplatz 1. **Tel** (0662) 620808-700. **Open** 9am–5pm Tue–Sun. 🅿

W salzburgmuseum.at

This History Museum was founded in 1834 by the amateur collector and treasury official, Vinzenz Maria Süss, who donated his collections to the town. It was named after the Bavarian Princess Caroline Augusta, who, in 1850, took over the stewardship of the museum's collections.

The most exciting items on display date back to Celtic times and include a Celtic pitcher from the Dürnberg area and a Bronze-age helmet from the Lueg Pass. The exhibits from Roman Salzburg, or *Juvavum*, are also interesting; there are fragments of mosaics, including one depicting the abduction of Europa, and numerous architectural features and statues.

Also worth seeing are paintings by the Baroque masters, Paul Troger and Johann Michael Rottmayr, as well as those by Hans Makart, who was born in Salzburg in 1840. Separate departments are devoted to handicrafts, coins and musical instruments.

🎵 Grosses Festspielhaus

Hofstallgasse 1. **Tel** (0662) 80450. **Open** 2pm daily for guided tours only.

In 1606, Archbishop Wolf Dietrich von Raitenau started building the palace stables on the site of the former barracks. The north façade was designed by Johann Bernhard Fischer von Erlach. The marble fountain, or Pferdeschwemme (horses' trough), in the stable yard, was built in 1695.

In 1917, it was decided that Salzburg should host a theatre and opera

The Pferdeschwemme (horses' trough) fountain in the Grosses Festspielhaus

festival, and the stables were converted into the Small and Grand Festival Theatres. One of Austria's most outstanding architects, Clemens Holzmeister, designed the Small Festival Theatre during the 1920s, and then from 1956 until 1960 supervised the rebuilding of the Grand Festival Theatre. The building incorporates the original façade of the former stables and is one of the largest opera houses in the world. Its vast stage is 100-m (328-ft) wide and is carved deep into the rockface of Mönchsberg. The auditorium can easily accommodate up to 2,180 spectators.

Mozarts Geburtshaus

Getreidegasse 9. **Tel** (0662) 844313. **Open** Sep–Jun: 9am–5:30pm daily; Jul & Aug: 8:30am–7pm daily.

Hagenauerhaus, at No. 9 of the narrow Getreidegasse, is the house where Wolfgang Amadeus Mozart was born on 27 January 1756. The composer's family occupied only one floor of the house. In 1880, the Mozarteum-Stiftung (International Mozart Foundation) helped to establish a museum here, featuring a collection of Mozart's memorabilia, including family portraits, documents and his first instruments. On the second floor is a delightful exhibition on the theatrical staging of Mozart's operas.

Kollegienkirche

Universitätsplatz. **Tel** (0662) 841327. **Open** 9am–dusk daily.

The Collegiate Church, consecrated in 1707, is one of Salzburg's finest Baroque structures. It was designed by Johann Bernhard Fischer von Erlach, who achieved fantastic and unusual effects by letting natural light shine through windows of various shapes. The paintings on two side altars of the church are by Johann Michael Rottmayr. Italian artisans produced the beautiful stucco work, which decorates the church walls, to a design by Johann Bernhard Fischer von Erlach. The very ornate main altarpiece shows the

university as a temple of art and science. It features winged figures symbolizing music, poetry, painting, architecture, theology, philosophy, law and medicine.

The Romanesque south portal of Franziskanerkirche

Franziskanerkirche

Franziskanergasse 5. **Tel** (0662) 843629. **Open** 6:30am–8:30pm daily.

The Franciscan Church seems somewhat out of place in Baroque Salzburg. Repeated attempts at refashioning it in the Baroque style have failed to disguise its Romanesque origins, mixed with Gothic. The 13th-century Romanesque portal leading to the presbytery is particularly fine, with a figure of Christ on the throne flanked by St Rupert and St Peter. The presbytery, with its tall tower and magnificent star-vault, is Gothic. In the 16th century, when the Franciscan Church was temporarily used as a cathedral, it gained an additional Baroque portal, a ring of chapels and many rich interior furnishings. The creator of the new altar, Johann Bernhard Fischer von Erlach, preserved the central statue of the

Madonna from the earlier Gothic altar made by Michael Pacher, the outstanding artist of the late-Gothic. The St Francis Chapel has frescoes by Johann Michael Rottmayr, with scenes from the life of its patron saint. On the opposite side of the street are the monastery buildings, which are connected with the church by a bridge.

Residenz

Residenz: Residenzplatz 1. **Tel** (0662) 8042-2690. **Open** Sep–Jun: 10am–5pm Wed–Mon; Jul & Aug: 10am–5pm daily. Residenzgalerie: **Tel** (0662) 840451. **Open** same hours as Residenz.

The **Residenz**, seat of the Prince-Archbishop, the religious and secular ruler of the entire province, was built for Archbishop Wolf Dietrich von Raitenau. His successors further extended the building. Following secularization, the building became the seat of the administration. Now one part of the building houses central government agencies and university offices, while the upper storeys are occupied by the **Residenzgalerie**, which exhibits artworks from the 16th to 19th centuries. Not much remains of its erstwhile decor, but the interior decorations, completed under Johann Lukas von Hildebrandt and carried out by the most prominent artists of the Baroque era, including Johann Michael Rottmayr and Martino Altomonte, still charm visitors to this day. On the forecourt of the palace is the Baroque Residence Fountain, with Tritons and horses spouting water. On the opposite side of the square stands the Neue Residenz (New Residence), used as a temporary abode while the bishop's seat was being rebuilt. It has a carillon – the bells can be heard at 7am, 11am and 6pm from Mozartplatz, where a statue of the great composer stands.

Statue of Mozart in Mozartplatz

Sculptures decorating the façade of the Dom

🔼 Stift St Peter

St Peter Bezirk 1/2. **Tel** (0662) 844576-0.
Open 8am–noon, 2:30–6:30pm.

Salzburg's Benedictine Abbey was founded in the 7th century by St Rupert, who is said to have resurrected the town after the Great Migration of Nations. It is the only abbey in this part of Europe that has survived intact since then. The present church and monastery complexes were built in the 12th and 13th centuries, but remodelled during the Baroque era, in the 17th and 18th centuries. However, some of the old sculptures have survived, including the early 15th-century *Beautiful Madonna*. The majority of Baroque altar paintings are by Kremser Schmidt. The abbey interior is an impressive display of Baroque opulence.

In the cemetery, Salzburg's oldest, are the final resting places of Mozart's sister Nannerl and of Johann Michael Haydn, brother of Joseph.

🔼 Dom

Cathedral: Domplatz 1a. **Tel** (0662) 80477950. Cathedral Museum:
Tel (0662) 80471860. **Open** Oct–Nov: 8am–6pm Mon–Sat, 1–6pm Sun (until 5pm Jan, Feb & Nov); May–Sep: 8am–7pm Mon–Sat, 1–7pm Sun.

The first cathedral church in Salzburg, the Dom was built in the 8th century. Following several remodellings and a fire in 1598, the archbishops set out to build an almost entirely new church, designed by the Italian architect, Santino Solari, on the site of the earlier one. The new cathedral, consecrated in 1628, became a model of Baroque

church architecture north of the Alps. The façade is decorated with the vast sculpted figures of the cathedral's patron saints, Rupert and Virgil, and Saints Peter and Paul. The cathedral was designed to accommodate 10,000 worshippers, more than the entire population of Salzburg at the time. Its monumental interior is still impressive today. Stairs lead from the transept to the crypt where several prince-archbishops have been laid to rest. Mozart himself played the Baroque organ here. Today, the great Mozarteum choir often holds concerts of his music in the cathedral. The church's treasures are on show in the **Cathedral Museum**.

🔼 Stift Nonnberg

Nonnberggasse 2. **Tel** (0662) 841607.
Open Summer: 7am–7pm daily; winter: 7am–5pm.

The Benedictine nunnery on the slope of Mönchsberg, now known as Nonnberg (Nuns' Hill),

The pilgrimage church Maria Plain on Plainberg

was founded in 714 by St Rupert, who established his niece, St Erentrude, as Mother Superior. Her tomb lies in the crypt of the church. Emperor Henry II and his wife Kunegunde had the convent and the church extended in the 11th century. A fire in 1423 destroyed most of the buildings and, in the 15th century, a new convent was built on the same site, with a church devoted to the Assumption of the Virgin Mary and to St Erentrude. The Roman tympanum above the main door shows the Virgin Mary accompanied by John the Baptist and St Erentrude.

Fresco (1150) in Stift Nonnberg

A true jewel of Nonnberg is its late-Gothic main altarpiece, brought from Scheffau and reputedly produced to sketches by Albrecht Dürer. Behind the main altar, in the central window of the apsis, is an interesting stained-glass panel by Peter Hemmel von Andlau, one of the most renowned stained-glass artists in the late-Gothic style. Original 12th-century Romanesque frescoes are preserved in the niches. The adjacent chapel of St John has a Gothic altarpiece taken from the earlier cathedral; its creator was visibly influenced by the school of Veit Stoss.

Environs

On top of Plainberg, a hill north of Salzburg, stands the pilgrimage church of **Maria Plain**, built by Giovanni Antonio Dario and consecrated in 1674. In 1779, Mozart composed the *Coronation Mass* in celebration of the miraculous picture of the Madonna and Child. The interior was designed by famous Austrian Baroque artists, including Kremser Schmidt and Thomas and Franz Schwanthaler.

Further north, in the village of **Oberndorf**, the carol *Silent Night* was first performed in 1818. Franz Xaver Gruber, a local teacher and organist, wrote the music, and Joseph Mohr the words.

The Salzburg Festival

The Salzburger Festspiele, the largest and most important opera and theatre festival in Europe, was initiated by three people. The eminent writer, Hugo von Hofmannsthal, the composer and conductor Richard Strauss, and the greatest theatrical innovator of the 20th century, the director Max Reinhardt, decided to honour the memory of Mozart by organizing a festival devoted to his work. It was to be held in his home town and be a celebration of theatre and opera. The first festival was held in Salzburg in 1920. Today, it is the most all-embracing event of its type in Europe. The festival programme has become increasingly rich, and the former court stables were converted to create two festival theatres. Performances are held in the Makartplatz theatre, in Schloss Mirabell and in many open-air venues around town. Theatre troupes come from all over the world, often with original performances prepared specifically for the festival. Tickets tend to be sold out several months in advance *(see pp334–5)*.

Herbert von Karajan (1908–89), born in Salzburg and one of the most outstanding 20th-century conductors of symphonies and operas, was the musical director of the Salzburg Festivals for almost 30 years.

The Grosses Festspielhaus is adorned with a Baroque portal by Johann Bernhard Fischer von Erlach. The modern building of the Grand Festival Theatre was completed in 1960 by Clemens Holzmeister *(see pp222–3)*.

The stage in front of the cathedral in Salzburg is where the Salzburger Festspiele performances begin each July. Max Reinhardt pioneered the idea of open-air performances at the festival, and theatre troops now play to large audiences.

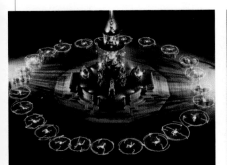

The Fire Dance is one of the most beautiful performances staged regularly during the Salzburg Festival. As soon as night falls, the whole town comes alive with the lights of the spectacle.

Since its very first staging the festival has opened with a performance of Hugo von Hofmannsthal's morality play *Jedermann* ("Everyman").

Hohensalzburg Fortress

Hohensalzburg, the fortress perched on the rocky peak of Festungsberg, was built in the 11th century, during the wars between the Holy Roman Empire and the Papacy, and was gradually extended. The castle served as a refuge for Salzburg's archbishops whenever they felt threatened. Archbishop Leonhard von Keutschach gave it its present look in the 16th century; Archbishop Paris von Lodron introduced further architectural changes. A military barracks in the late 19th century, it is today a major tourist attraction.

Early Cannons
Aimed at the town, many cannons can be seen among the numerous bastions, bulwarks and walkways.

Salzburg Coat of Arms
The coat of arms is placed above the wicket leading to the inner courtyard in front of the old castle.

KEY

① **The Glockenturm**, through which the castle's residential quarters can be reached, has a bell case created by Hans Reichert in 1505.

② **The well**, dating back from 1539, is an interesting feature in the fortress courtyard.

Archbishop
Johann Jakob Khuen von Belasi (1560–86) carried out the final remodelling of the old fortress. His portrait hangs in one of the rooms of the old castle.

Schulhaus and Kuchlturm
Schoolhouse and Kitchen Tower are the remains of fortifications built outside the castle in the 16th century during a revolt against the archbishops.

VISITORS' CHECKLIST

Practical Information
Mönchsberg 34.
Tel (0662) 842430-11.
W salzburg-burgen.at
Open Jan–Apr & Oct–Dec:
9:30am–5pm; Easter & Advent
weekend: 9am–6pm; May–Sep:
9am–7pm.

★ **Goldene Stube**
The richly ornamented Golden Chamber, with its large tiled stove in Gothic style, is one of the loveliest rooms in the castle.

Small Courtyard
In a small square on the castle ramparts stand an old salt warehouse (former stables), and two towers, Hasenturm (Hares' Tower) and Schwefelturm (Sulphur Tower).

★ **Torture Chamber**
Reckturm, the corner tower, was once a prison and torture chamber. Prisoners were still being tortured at Hohensalzburg up until 1893.

Portrait of Archbishop Marcus Sitticus in Schloss Hellbrunn

❷ Hellbrunn

Road map D4. 🚌 🚉 **Tel** (0662) 820372-0. **Open** Apr–Oct: 9am–4:30pm daily; May–Sep: 9am–5:30pm daily (until 6pm Jul–Aug; trick fountains until 9pm). 🚶 🌐 hellbrunn.at

Schloss Hellbrunn, once a summer residence of Salzburg's Archbishop Marcus Sitticus, stands about 4 km (2 miles) south of Salzburg. Sitticus was a nephew of Wolf Dietrich von Raitenau, with an Italian mother. He spent most of his life in Italy, and so it is hardly surprising that his small, suburban castle resembles a Venetian villa. It has an interesting state room with architectural paintings and a tall, octagonal music room. However, the most interesting and popular feature is its garden with ornamental fountains and scenic grottoes, including a mechanical theatre, with trick fountains and moving figures powered by water.

❸ Anif

Road map D4. 🚌 4,000. 🚌 🚉 **Tel** (06246) 72365.

Another 2 km (1 mile) beyond Hellbrunn, also south of Salzburg, stands the small Neo-Gothic castle of Anif. Once a suburban residence, it now lies virtually within the limits of the town Anif. Its earliest historic records

date from the 15th century, but it bears signs of an earlier, late-Gothic structure. Once the summer estate of the Salzburg rulers, it belonged to the Chiemsee bishops from 1693 to 1803. After the secularization of the province, it was put up for sale and passed to Count Aloys Arco-Stepperg. This new owner had the summer residence converted into a romantic English-style Neo-Gothic castle that has survived unchanged to this day. Its rectangular turret is proudly mirrored in the waters of the lake; the interior is furnished in the English fashion of the day. At the end of World War I, on 13 November 1918, the last king of Bavaria, Ludwig III, signed his abdication in Anif. As the castle is privately owned, visitors can only see its high outside walls.

❹ St Gilgen

Road map D4. 🚌 3,800. 🚌 ℹ️ Mondsee, Bundesstrasse 1A (06227) 2348.

St Gilgen is the largest resort in the Salzburg area of the Salzkammergut. Set on the western shores of the warm Wolfgangsee, amid mountain scenery, this is one of the most attractive health resorts in Austria. St Gilgen was the birthplace of Mozart's mother, Anna-Maria Pertl. Later, the composer's sister, Nannerl, lived here with her husband, a local office worker. These Mozart-related facts are commemorated by a plaque on the court building. In 1927, the Mozart Fountain was erected in the town square.

The local church of St Giles (St Ägidius) shows hints of an earlier structure. It was extended in the 18th century and given three Rococo altars with paintings by Peter Lorenzoni.

St Gilgen is a major water sports centre and harbour, with cruises on Wolfgangsee aboard the steamer *Kaiser Franz Josef I* that has been in continuous service since 1873. Not far from St Gilgen, on the shores of the neighbouring

Fuschlsee, stands **Schloss Fuschl**, a small hunting lodge that now houses a luxury hotel.

❺ Hallein

Road map D4. 🚌 20,000. 🚌 🚉 ℹ️ Mauttorpromenade 6 (06245) 85394.

The town of Hallein was founded in the 13th century, but salt was mined here way back in prehistoric times. The long association with the salt trade is apparent from the town's name: *hall* is the Celtic word for "salt". The "white gold", as it was called, brought wealth to the entire region for many centuries, until the 18th-century Counter-Reformation led to the emigration of the predominantly Protestant salt miners.

Hallein's Old Town, on the left bank of the Salzach river, is mainly 18th-century in appearance, following much remodelling. The church of St Antonius has a Gothic presbytery, but the rest is much newer. The painting of the Birth of Christ in the main altarpiece is by the last court painter of the Salzburg rulers, the Neo-Classical Andreas Nesselthaler. Hallein was the home of Franz Xaver Gruber who wrote *Silent Night*, and he is buried here. His house at No. 1 Gruberplatz is now a small museum. The most interesting sight in Hallein, however, is the **Keltenmuseum** with its unique

Poster of the fascinating Keltenmuseum in Hallein

collection of Celtic objects which relate to the history of salt-mining in the area.

⑪ Keltenmuseum
Pflegerplatz 5. **Tel** (06245) 80783.
Open 9am–5pm daily. 🅿

Environs: From the southern end of Hallein you can drive to the top of Dürrnberg, which has some of the most interesting prehistoric finds in Austria. The remains of the settlements that grew up around the rich local salt deposits can be seen to this day.

The spa of **Bad Dürrnberg** has a show-mine open specifically for tourists, who are offered rides on an underground salt lake.

In the village stands a 14th-century Marian church, now a Baroque struc-ture. The altar-piece contains a miraculous picture of the Madonna, once visited by pilgrims.

Logo of salt mine in Dürrnberg

❻ Golling

Road map D4. 🗻 4,200. 🚌 🚉
Tel (06244) 4356.

South of Hallein lies the small town of Golling. At its centre stands the Church of St John the Baptist and St John the Evangelist, with a Gothic main nave and remodelled Baroque side naves. A small medieval castle, devoid of any ornaments and adjoined by a chapel with a Rococo altar, now houses a regional museum.

Environs: There are many natural features of interest near Golling, including the **Lueg Pass** with the spectacular, 100-m (328-ft) deep Salzach river gorge, and the Schwarzbacher Wasserfall, better known as **Gollinger Wasserfall** (100 m/328 ft), much beloved by romantic painters of natural scenes. Also worth a detour is a visit to two interesting churches in the vicinity – St Ulrich's in

The Gollinger Wasserfall, a favourite theme for painters

Scheffau and the late-Gothic St Nicholas's Church near **Torren**, which stands high up on a rocky shelf.

❼ Abtenau

Road map D4. 🗻 5,600. 🚌 🚉
ℹ Markt 165 (06243) 4040.

Abtenau, a summer resort situated in the Salzburg Dolomites, is surrounded by the mighty peaks of the Tennengebirge. The church in the valley was built around 1500. Its main nave is guarded by figures of St George and St Florian. On the north wall, an original late-Gothic fresco can be seen, but the new main altar and side altars are built in the Baroque style. It is worth taking a walk upstream along the

Lammer river, which cuts a scenic valley between the Tennengebirge and the craggy wall of the Dachstein.

❽ Werfen

Road map D4. 🗻 3,000. 🚌 🚉
Tel (06468) 5248. 🗾 eisriesenwelt.at

The little town of Werfen has several interesting churches. St James's Church is mentioned in 14th-century records, but its present style dates from a 17th-century Baroque conversion. The Marian Church was built in the early 18th century.

Environs: There are two fascinating sights near Werfen. Hohenwerfen fortress, built on a rocky outcrop, dates back to the 11th century. Today, it is an interactive museum with many displays, including late-Romanesque frescoes and an exhibition of weapons. It also includes Austria's first museum of falconry.

Eisriesenwelt (giant ice world) is one of the world's largest cave systems. It has dramatic ice formations and superb ice galleries. Some 42 km (26 miles) have been explored so far. A scenic walk or bus or cable car journey will take you from Werfen to the entrance in the western wall of the Hochkögel peak. Inside it is very cold (so take warm clothes). It is open from May to October.

The enchanting winter landscape of Abtenau

❾ Bischofshofen

Road map D4. 🏔 10,000. 🚌
🚆 **Tel** (06462) 2471.

The Celtic settlement that stood on the site of the present Bischofshofen was once a centre of the copper mining trade; the area was also rich in salt mines. Colonization of the region started well before recorded history and traces of ancient cultures can be found everywhere.

The town is dominated by the spire of **St Maximilian's Church**, reputedly built on the site of an older church established by St Rupert, founder of Salzburg. The walls are decorated with 15th-century frescoes, and next to the Neo-Gothic side altarpieces stand the original Gothic figures of St Rupert and St Virgil. In the south arm of the transept stands a Baroque altar with a picture of St Anna attributed to Lienhart Astl (c.1520) and a relief on the predella of Christ and the 12 apostles dating from the same period. The most valuable historic relic in the church is St Rupert's crucifix. This simple, gilded cross, encrusted with precious stones, was given to Bischofshofen in the 12th century by the Archbishop of Salzburg.

Bischofshofen is renowned for its excellent ski-jumping hills. Every year, on 6th January, the final event of the world-famous Four Hills Ski-Jumping event takes place on the largest of the slopes.

St Rupert's Crucifix, Bischofshofen

❿ Radstadt

Road map D4. 🏔 4,800. 🚌 🚆
Tel (06452) 7472.

The small town of Radstadt grew up around a 13th-century fortress on the banks of the Enns river. Its wealth hailed from its propitious location on the road to Venice, and its monopoly position in the wine trade. Radstadt also had a licence to stock iron and salt. Its medieval fortifications, built by the archbishops of Salzburg, have remained intact.

The surrounding area boasts many small, beguiling castles, including the Renaissance **Schloss Tandalier**, southwest of the town. **Schloss Lerchen**, in the centre of town, shows some traces of original, 13th-century architecture; today it houses a regional museum.

Environs: East of Bischofshofen runs **Radstädter Tauernstrasse**, one of the most scenic roads in the Alps. A vast skiing area extends on both sides. The **Rossbrand** (1,770 m/ 5,807 ft), rising north of Radstadt and accessible by car via the Rossbrand Panorama Street, offers astonishing views of more than 150 Alpine summits on a clear day.

⓫ St Johann im Pongau

Road map D4. 🏔 11,000. 🚌
Tel (06412) 6036.

The largest town in the region, St Johann im Pongau is a popular resort, visited for its excellent skiing conditions in winter and its plentiful facilities for swimming and walking in summer.

Little remains of its original buildings due to a series of fires in the 19th century; the present town was almost entirely rebuilt. The Neo-Gothic **Domkirche**, the cathedral of St John the Baptist (1861), is acclaimed as the most outstanding work of Neo-Classicism in the Salzburg area. Its architects were Georg Schneider and Josef Wessiken. The charming carved altarpiece (1530) in adjacent St Anna's Chapel has late-Gothic wooden figures of saints. Some 5 km (3 miles) south of the town run the torrential waters of **Grossarler Ache**, a rapid mountain stream that winds through the scenic **Liechtensteinklamm**.

⓬ Wagrain

Road map D4. 🏔 3,000. 🚌 🚆
Tel (06413) 8448.

Wagrain, situated at an altitude of 800 m (2,625 ft), is the centre of a highly developed winter sports area known as **Ski Alliance**. This vast terrain extends between the Tennengebirge and Radstädter Tauern mountain ranges, and includes several villages connected by good public transport links, funiculars and buses. One ski pass is valid throughout the entire area, giving the holder access to some 260 ski lifts and 860 km (534 miles) of pistes, suitable for intermediates and beginners.

Year-round fun in the water is guaranteed by the Amadé Water World's all-weather pool. The most interesting place is **Zauchensee**, the highest village in the region (1,361 m/4,465 ft).

View of the town and cathedral in St Johann im Pongau

◀ Picture-postcard Hohenwerfen fortress, near Werfen

Rushing stream in the Liechtensteinklamm, near Wagrain

It is also worth going inside the Gothic church in Altenmarkt im Pongau. Wagrain itself has a museum devoted to Joseph Mohr, who wrote the words for *Silent Night*, and to the popular 20th-century Austrian writer and humorist Karl Heinrich Waggerl.

The views from the tops of Schwarzkopf, Rosskopf and Mooskopf are stunning and worth a detour.

⑬ Mauterndorf

Road map D4. 🏔 1,700. 🚌
Tel (06472) 7949.

Strategically positioned on the road connecting Salzburg with the Hohe Tauern passes, this little town owed its former wealth to the road tolls it was able to collect. Mauterndorf's greatest attraction is its **Burg**, built in the 13th century and extended in the 16th century, under Archbishop Leonhard von Keutschach. Scenically located and well proportioned, it is an attractive medieval structure. The rooms are richly decorated with stuccowork and provide interesting interiors. The castle's best feature, however, is the lovely chapel devoted to St Henry (Emperor Henry II), with superb 14th-century frescoes of the

Coronation of the Virgin Mary on the rainbow arch, and a 15th-century carved altarpiece. The castle was well restored in the 20th century, and is now a museum and cultural centre. Mauterndorf also has excellent summer and winter sports facilities.

⑭ Moosham

Road map D4. 🚌 Schloss Moosham 12. **Tel** (06476) 305. **Open** for guided tours only; Apr–Sep: 10 am, 11am, 1pm, 2pm, 3pm & 4pm Tue–Sun (Aug daily); Oct & mid-Dec–Mar: 11am & 2pm Tue–Sun.

Near the southern end of Radstädter Tauernstrasse, high above the Mur river, towers Schloss Moosham, which also belonged to the Archbishops of Salzburg. The structure probably dates from the 13th century and consists of an upper and a lower castle. Following the secularization of the archbishop's principality, the castle fell into ruin. But in 1886 it passed to Count Hans Wilczek, who fully renovated it. Among the remaining original features are the Baroque roadway, Gothic stained-glass windows in the presbytery of the castle chapel and a collection of items relating to the local arts, which are kept in the castle museum. The coach house and the armoury are also of interest. Some rooms are open to the public, such as a torture

Bedchamber in Schloss Moosham

chamber, and a Gothic bed-chamber with a panel listing the supposed characteristic traits of various European nationalities.

Below the castle is the popular resort of St Michael, with an interesting Gothic church.

A stained-glass window in the church of St Leonard in Tamsweg

⑮ Tamsweg

Road map E4. 🏔 5,600. 🚌 🚉
Tel (06474) 2145. 📷 Samson Procession (late Jun, Jul, Aug).

The largest town in the isolated Lungau region, Tamsweg is famous for its curious Samson Processions, when an effigy of Samson and other figures are paraded around town. Tamsweg owes its past wealth to the iron and salt trade. Fine town houses, such as the 15th-century Mesnerhaus and the 16th-century turreted town hall, line the market square. The 18th-century Post House has frescoes by Gregor Lederwasch, who also painted the pictures in Heiliger Jakobus (St James's Church) built in 1741, to a design by Fidelis Hainzl. The original Rococo interior has been preserved. The 15th-century Church of St Leonard, towering above the town, is one of Austria's foremost pilgrimage churches. It has beautiful stained-glass windows, such as the famous Golden Window (1430–50). The interior furnishings are almost entirely late medieval.

⓰ Gasteinertal

The therapeutic properties of the radon-rich mineral springs in and around Bad Gastein were known to the Celts and Romans, and this was when the first settlements grew in the valley of the Gasteiner Ache stream. The valley flourished in late medieval times and more recently it has become a popular spa, with a long list of clients including royalty, politicians and artists. A cure is sought by those suffering from cardiac and gastric ailments, rheumatism and allergies. At the same time, the valley has developed into a fabulous winter sports centre, with skiing for all levels and snowboarding.

Bad Hofgastein
The late-Gothic parish church was built in the 15th and 16th centuries. The carved tombstones found in its niches show the skills of gold- and silversmiths using locally excavated metals.

The Gasteiner Ache
The stream runs along a scenic valley, down from the Hohe Tauern mountains, finishing as a tributary of the Salzach, the principal river of Salzburger Land.

KEY

① **The summit of Schlossalm** has a viewing platform at 2,050 m (6,726 ft), providing panoramic views of the neighbouring peaks. It can be reached by funicular.

② **Gasteinertal**, a well-developed valley surrounded by modest mountains, is a popular skiing, snowboarding and summer walking area.

★ **Sportgastein**
The wide valley near Sportgastein has been transformed into a true mountain gorge, with bridges and viaducts spanning the stream.

②

Bad Hofga

Schlossalm
① ▲
2050

▲
2461

▲
2600

Gasteiner Ache

*Spo
gas*

Dorfgastein
The village of Dorfgastein
has preserved many
traditional, rural customs.

astein

2033

2413

VISITORS' CHECKLIST

Practical Information
Road map D4.
🛈 A-5630-Bad Hofgastein,
Gasteinertal Tourismus GmbH,
Tauernplatz 1; (06432) 3393-0.
W gastein.com

Transport
🚌 🚆

★ Bad Gastein
The most popular
resort in Gasteinertal
is crossed by the
Gasteiner Ache,
which runs right
through its centre in
a series of attractive
waterfalls.

Gasteiner Ache

2324

Key
══ Major road
══ Minor road
···· Funicular
══ River

Bad Gastein

2492

öckstein

★ Böckstein
The altar in the
Neo-Classical
Church of Our Lady
of Good Counsel is
the work of Johann
Baptist Hagenauer.
The medieval mine
where gold was
once excavated
now houses a
sanatorium.

0 kilometres   2

0 miles   2

⓱ Kaprun

Road map D4. 🚠 3,000. 🚌
🅘 (06547) 8080.

Kaprun is a popular winter sports resort. It is also famous for its sophisticated hydroelectric power station, which is acclaimed as a wonder of technology and one of the greatest achievements of human ingenuity. Work on the construction of the Kapruner Ache power station began in 1938, and was completed in 1951. Its highest reservoir is Mooserboden, a lake situated at an altitude of 2,036 m (6,680 ft) and fed by the melting ice of the Pasterze glacier.

Kaprun power station is not only a technological marvel; it is also a tourist attraction. Artificial lakes, weirs and dams, set amid the rocky limestone peaks of the Hohe Tauern mountain range, create a unique natural environment, with numerous trails and attractive scenery for walkers. Following the building of the power station, Kaprun became one of Austria's foremost sports resorts, especially as the nearby glaciers makes year-round skiing possible.

The town of Kaprun itself lies in a valley accessible by road and public transport. It has some of the most modern facilities in Austria, serving the **Kitzsteinhorn** (3,203 m/10,509 ft) to the north, an outpost of Austria's highest mountain range. This summit has year-round pistes and excellent snow. In the year 2000, a fire on the Kitzsteinhornbahn, the funicular railway taking visitors to the slopes, caused a major mountain tragedy. The railway has since been re-routed to run outside the tunnel, providing magnificent views of Austria's highest mountains.

On the western edge of Kaprun stands a 15th-century castle destroyed in the 18th century. The building has been restored and today it is a cultural centre.

Kaprun and neighbouring ski resorts have joined forces to attract visitors to this so-called "Europa Sportregion".

Inside St Hippolytus Church in Zell am See

⓲ Zell am See

Road map C4. 🚠 9,500. 🚉
🚌 **Tel** (06542) 770.

This picture-postcard town on the western shores of Zeller See has a long history. First recorded as the Roman settlement of Bisontio, in medieval times Zell was a mining centre. Among its more interesting historic sights are the 13th-century Vogtturm, and the Church of St Hippolytus (St Hippolyte) that once belonged to the Augustinian Order. There are some interesting medieval frescoes: the figures of Saints George and Florian in the western gallery are by an artist from the Danube School. Zell am See is now considered one of the best developed sports resorts in Austria, with excellent facilities for skiing and water sports, as well as a convenient base for long walks.

Charming, flower-bedecked houses in Saalbach

Environs: South of Zell am See is the **Hohe Tauern** mountain range and national park (see pp282–5), to the north the rugged scenery of the Steinernes Meer (Stone Sea) and to the west the Schmittenhöhe, divided into the Sonnkogel and Hirschkogel regions, with its highest peak rising to over 2,000 m (6,562 ft).

The **Pinzgauer Spaziergang** is one of the most beautiful walking trails in the Austrian Alps, running at an altitude of about 1,000 m (3,280 ft) above the valley floor, from Zell am See to Saalbach, via Schmittenhöhe (a seven-hour walk).

⓳ Saalbach

Road map C4. 🚠 2,900. 🚉 🚌
🅘 Glemmtaler Landesstrasse 550 (06541) 6800-68. 🆆 **saalbach.com**

At the heart of the Glemmtal lies this small town, marking the border between Salzburger Land and Tyrol. A charming winter resort with guaranteed snow, it provides access to 200 km (120 miles) of pistes, with beginner and more challenging runs right to the village centres. There is a wide range of entertainments on offer including extra-wide carving pistes, ungroomed moguls, a GS-race course, facilities for tobogganing and tubing as well as snow bars, huts and flood-lit slope dances.

To the north of Saalbach the Spielberghorn comes into view, while to the south the Schattberg marks the end of the Pinzgauer Spaziergang. This trail, leading across several passes, affords breathtaking views over the neighbouring mountain range. The view from Rohrertörl Pass (1,918 m/6,293 ft) embraces the town of Saalbach and the valley.

⓴ Lofer

Road map C4. 🚠 2,000. 🚉 🚌
🅘 Lofer Nr. 310 (06588) 8321.
🆆 **lofer.com**

The town of Lofer, in the green Salzach Valley, has retained much of the charm of an old mountain village. It is surrounded by the snow-covered rocky summits of the Loferer Steinberge (Stone Mountains). These limestone mountains hide many caves still waiting to be explored. The Lamprechtsofenloch is said to be the deepest aquiferous cave in the world.

Environs: A short distance south of Lofer, outside the village of St Martin, is the pilgrimage church **Maria Kirchenthal**, built between 1693 and 1701 by Johann Bernhard Fischer von Erlach. It is one of the greatest works by this outstanding architect, in which he employed some of the ideas that he had developed earlier in Salzburg.

The building is blended into the rocky mountain scenery of the Saalach Valley, and two white towers are prominent against the distant snowy mountains. The Neo-Baroque altarpiece includes the 15th-century miraculous picture of the Madonna that was once the destination of pilgrims. On one of the two altars, created by Jakob Zanussi from reddish-pink Salzburg marble, the parents of the Virgin Mary, St Jacob and St Anne, are depicted.

㉑ Mittersill

Road map C4. 🏔 5,500. 🚉 🚌
ℹ️ Stadtplatz 1 (06562) 4292.
ⓦ mittersill-tourismus.at

This summer resort at the main crossroads of the Upper Salzach Valley sprang up around a castle. The castle was built in the 12th century and since then has been rebuilt many times, following its destruction during the Peasant Wars and numerous fires. Today it is the seat of the International Protestant Youth Community, a cultural centre and a hotel.

The chapel (1533) features an interesting late-Gothic polyptych attributed to an Aussee Master. St-Leonhard-Kirche was originally Gothic, but was remodelled in the 18th century to a design by Johann Kleber. It contains a heavily ornamented Rococo pulpit and some remains of the old decorations, including an early 15th-century stone statue of Leonard.

Mittersill lies at the Salzburg end of a beautiful mountain trail leading from East Tyrol, among the wild scenery of the Hohe Tauern National Park. The road known as Felberntauernstrasse affords lovely views of the rugged slopes of Grossvenediger.

The scenic Krimmler Wasserfälle

㉒ Krimmler Wasserfälle

Road map C4. 🚌

In the northwestern part of the Hohe Tauern National Park (*see pp282–5*), on the border between the provinces of Salzburger Land and Tyrol, are the famous Krimmler Wasserfälle, the waterfalls of the Krimmler Ache, the stream flowing from the glacier of the same name at an altitude of around 3,000 m (9,850 ft). The water falls in three steps, with a total drop of 380 m (1,247 ft).

The journey to the waterfalls can be made by car, but a walk along the Wasserfallweg (waterfall path) will prove a truly unforgettable experience.

The best starting points for the walk are the Gerlos Pass or Krimmel village. In winter, the waterfalls freeze over.

View of the Hohe Tauern mountains, near Mittersill

TYROL AND VORARLBERG

Both Tyrol and Vorarlberg lie on a narrow stretch of land west of Salzburg. Their main attractions are the Alps – few areas are below 500 m (1,640 ft) – and tourism is their primary source of income. The Tyrol is famous for its magnificent scenery and world-renowned resorts such as Kitzbühel, Seefeld and St Anton, while Vorarlberg draws visitors seeking a more relaxed, rural environment.

The Tyrol occupies an area of 12,648 sq km (4,883 sq miles) and has a population of 722,000. Its neighbours are Bavaria in the north, Italy in the south, Vorarlberg in the west and Salzburger Land in the east. The Inn is the province's main river, winding its way through the Alpine massifs.

In ancient times Tyrol was inhabited by Rhaetian and Illyrian tribes; it came under Roman rule in the 1st century BC, and later fell to the Bavarians and the Lombards.

In the 13th century, it became an independent principality of the Reich. Until 1363 it remained a bone of contention between the Habsburgs and the Bavarians, when it was bequeathed to the Habsburgs. Tyrol was a domain of the family's junior line and as such enjoyed a degree of

independence. To this day it has maintained its unique character, music, dialect and even fashion, which has shaped cultural life in the rest of Austria.

The province of Vorarlberg, in contrast, has for many years been culturally fairly separate, largely orientating itself towards its neighbours Germany, Liechtenstein and Switzerland. After Vienna, it is the smallest Austrian province, covering an area of just 2,601 sq km (1,000 sq miles), with 375,000 inhabitants. It was once inhabited by Aleman tribes.

From the 15th century the area of present-day Vorarlberg passed gradually into the hands of the Habsburgs, and in 1919 it finally became an independent Austrian province.

The beautiful Lünersee in the province of Vorarlberg, hidden between snow-covered Alpine peaks

◀ Lech am Arlberg, a popular ski resort in Vorarlberg

Exploring Tyrol and Vorarlberg

Both provinces, in the far west of Austria, are predominantly winter sports regions, although they also offer excellent facilities for summer activities. Among the popular and world-famous tourist centres of Tyrol are Kitzbühel, the area around the Arlberg Pass, and the hinterland of Innsbruck. The latter has twice played host to the Winter Olympic Games, in 1964 and 1976. The capital of the smaller Vorarlberg province is Bregenz, a somewhat sleepy resort located in a romantic spot on the eastern shores of Lake Constance (Bodensee).

Chairlift and ski runs near Zürs

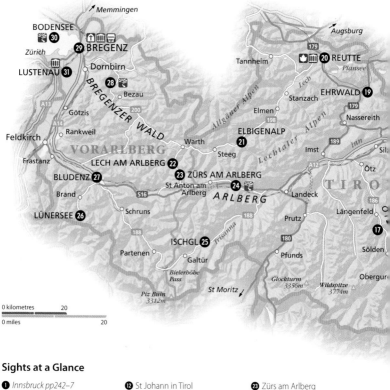

Sights at a Glance

Getting There

From Innsbruck-Kranebitten Airport flights depart to Vienna and most major European cities. Both Tyrol and Vorarlberg are served by the main railway line from Vienna to Bregenz, and the western motorway reaches Bregenz. Austria's first toll road tunnel passes through the Arlberg massif. Both provinces have a good network of bus routes, although many roads may become impassable in winter. From autumn until spring motorists planning excursions to the mountains need to remember to take winter tyres and snow chains.

The Ballunspitze peak, seen from Paznauntal

A coat of arms on the 5th-century town hall in Hall in Tyrol

Chapel in the snow-covered valley of Stubai

Key

━━━ Motorway
━━━ Major road
┅┅┅ Minor road
┅┅┅ Main railway
┄┄┄ Minor railway
▬▬▬ International border
▬▬▬ Province border
△ Summit
╳ Pass

For map symbols see back flap

❶ Innsbruck: Street-by-Street

Innsbruck was built at the confluence of the Sill and Inn rivers and became an important trading post in the Middle Ages. The present district of Wilten was once the site of the Roman camp of Veldidena, but the founders of the city itself are the counts of Andechs, who built a settlement here in 1187. Today Innsbruck is the capital of the province of Tyrol, Austria's most important tourist region. In 1964, and again in 1976, Innsbruck was the host city for the Winter Olympics; many competitions took place in Axamer Lizum, 20 km (14 miles) southwest of the city.

★ Goldenes Dachl
The symbol of Innsbruck, the Golden Roof is an oriel window added in 1500 by Maximilian I to Friedrich IV's former residence. It is covered with 2,657 gilded copper roof tiles.

Herzog-Friedrich-Strasse
The main street of the old town is lined with the attractive façades of numerous Baroque buildings.

Key

— Suggested route

Stadtturm
The 14th-century city tower next to the old town hall acquired its present Renaissance look in 1560. At 56 m (184 ft) high it affords great views.

Helblinghaus
The building with an elegant Regency façade at No. 10 Herzog-Friedrich-Strasse was originally a medieval corner house in the Gothic style. In 1725 it was decorated with opulent Rococo stuccowork.

★ **Dom St Jakob**
The Baroque cathedral has enchanting vault frescoes by Cosmas Damian Asam and a picture of the *Madonna and Child* by Lucas Cranach the Elder.

VISITORS' CHECKLIST

Practical Information
Road map B4. 125,000.
Burggraben 3 (0512) 59850.
Tanzsommer Innsbruck (Jun, Jul) (0512) 561 561, Innsbrucker Festwochen der Alten Musik (Festival of Early Music, Jul, Aug) (0512) 571032.
W innsbruck.info

★ **Hofburg**
The interior of the imperial palace was extensively rebuilt in Rococo style during the reign of Maria Theresa, to designs by Johann Martin Gumpp the Younger and Konstantin Johann von Walter.

RENGASSE

RENNWEG

UNIVERSITÄTS-STRASSE

ANGERZELLGASSE

PROF. F. MAIR-GASSE

Jesuitenkirche

Landesmuseum

Hofkirche
The court church, built in 1553–63 as a mausoleum for Maximilian I and guarded by large statues *(right)*, was remodelled in the Baroque style by Georg Anton Gumpp *(see pp246–7)*.

0 metres   75
0 yards   75

Exploring Innsbruck

Innsbruck straddles the Inn river. Its Old Town is situated on the right bank, close to the river. Leading up to it is the broad Maria-Theresien-Strasse with the tall column of St Anna (1706). The most impressive historic buildings are found on Herzog-Friedrich-Strasse, Stadtplatz, Hofgasse and Rennweg. Other important sights are Schloss Ambras, on the southern outskirts of the city, and the Panorama of the Battle of Bergisel.

🏛 Dom St Jakob

Domplatz. **Tel** (0512) 583902.
St James' Cathedral was built in Baroque style in the early 18th century by Johann Jakob Herkomer. Severely damaged during World War II, it was rebuilt in the 1950s, when the church finally acquired the figures for the niches, as well as the equestrian statue of St Jakob on top of the building, as envisaged in the original designs; the sculptor was Hans André. The fine Baroque interior is the work of Munich artists, the two brothers Cosmas Damian (painter) and Egid Quirin (sculptor) Asam. The vault paintings depict scenes from the life of St James (St Jakob). The picture of *Madonna and Child* in the high altar, which miracles are attributed to, is by Lucas Cranach the Elder.

The old town houses with their rich stucco ornaments, reliefs and frescoes provide an enchanting backdrop to the cathedral, which is regarded as the most magnificent Baroque church building in North Tyrol.

🏛 Hofburg

Rennweg 1. **Tel** (0512) 587186.
Open 9am–5pm daily (Mar–Aug: until 7pm Wed). 🖼
In 1453, Archduke Sigismund embarked on a project to build a princely residence in Innsbruck. His Gothic castle, extended by Maximilian I, survived for several centuries, and to this day the castle dungeons feature the original late-Gothic vaults. A major remodelling took place in 1755,

under Maria Theresa, when the plans for the Baroque south wing were prepared by Johann Martin Gumpp the Younger, who also remodelled the front of the building and the grand staircase. His work was continued by Konstantin Johann von Walter, who is responsible for the palace's uniform, Classicist shape.

The interior of the Hofburg is furnished in Rococo style. The staterooms on the second floor were completed in 1773. The most beautiful of these is the Riesenhalle (the Giants' Hall), embellished with white and gold stucco and a ceiling painting by Franz Anton Maulbertsch, depicting the triumph of the House of Habsburg–Lothringen. The walls are hung with vast portraits of Maria Theresa, her 16 children and other members of the imperial family.

The remaining rooms of the south wing also have original Rococo decorations and furnishings.

Riesenhalle, a stateroom in Hofburg

🏛 Goldenes Dachl

Herzog-Friedrich-Strasse 15.
Tel (0512) 581111. **Open** May–Sep: 10am–6pm daily; Oct–Apr: 10am–5pm, Tue–Sun. 🖼

In about 1500 the tall oriel window, with its numerous gilded copper tiles, was added above the balcony of this former residence of the Tyrolean rulers. It created a viewing box from which Emperor Maximilian I could observe street life on the main square of Innsbruck. The two-storey oriel rests on two slender columns. There are six coats of arms under the first-floor windows and the second-floor balustrade is decorated with reliefs; one of these depicts Maximilian I and his two wives: Maria of Burgundy and Bianca Maria Sforza; the second shows the emperor surrounded by court jesters. The building behind the Goldenes Dachl houses the small Maximilianeum, a museum of the emperor's life.

🏛 Herzog-Friedrich-Strasse

Herzog-Friedrich-Strasse is one of Innsbruck's loveliest streets. Its main historic sights include the Rococo Helblinghaus (No. 10), the Gothic Old Town Hall, dating from the 14th–15th centuries (No. 21), and its adjacent Stadtturm (city tower), with a viewing terrace.

Many of the other houses along the street also warrant a close look. The four-storey Ottoburg at No. 1, close to the Inn river, has four oriels stacked on top of each other and late-Gothic interior vaults.

The richly ornamented pulpit in Dom St Jakob

The Baroque façade of Altes Regierungsgebäude (old governmental building) at No. 3 hides some beautiful rooms including the Claudia-Saal, the Hall of Claudia de Medici, with a late-Renaissance coffered ceiling. At No. 6 is an old inn, *Der Goldene Adler* (Golden Eagle Inn), and the Katzunghaus (at No. 16) has interesting 16th-century reliefs on the oriels.

🏛 Altes Landhaus

Maria-Theresien-Strasse 43.
Tel (0512) 5900. **Closed** to visitors.

This 18th-century house, built in 1725–8 by Georg Anton Gumpp and today the seat of Tyrol's provincial government, is regarded as one of Austria's most beautiful secular structures. It has an attractive inner courtyard and its colourful elevations were embellished by Alessandro Callegari. The niches lining the walls of the monumental internal staircase are filled with marble statues and busts of Greek and Roman gods. Ceiling frescoes depict the Tyrolean eagle with an open map of the country. The most opulent room in the building is the Rococo conference hall. Along the same street the Annasäule (1706) rises in front of the Neues Rathaus.

Georg Anton Gumpp's imposing stairwell in Altes Landhaus

🏛 Tiroler Landesmuseum Ferdinandeum

Museumstrasse 15. **Tel** (0512) 59489.
Open 9am–5pm Tue–Sun.
W tiroler-landesmuseum.at

Together with the former armoury of Maximilian I at No. 1

The impressive, two-tiered 16th-century Schloss Ambras

Zeughausgasse, this 19th-century building houses the collection of the Tiroler Landesmuseum (the Tyrol Regional Museum), named after Archduke Ferdinand II (1529–95), a Tyrolean ruler and a passionate collector. The museum has departments devoted to the natural environment, history, art and handicrafts, and it is also home to a library. Among its most precious exhibits are Gothic panel paintings, sculptures by Michael Pacher, and works by old German and Dutch masters – Lucas Cranach the Elder, Rembrandt, Pieter Bruegel the Younger and others. The museum also exhibits more recent Austrian art, including works by Klimt, Schiele and Kokoschka.

🏰 Schloss Ambras

Schlossstrasse 20. **Tel** (01) 52524-4802.
Open 10am–5pm daily. **Closed** 25 Dec.
🚗 **W** schlossambras-innsbruck.at

The castle, on the southeastern city limits, was once the symbol of Tyrol's power and glory. In the 12th century it was the seat of local rulers.

The present 16th-century building consists of a lower castle with entrance gate and spacious courtyard, and an upper castle built on the site of an earlier structure. The two parts are connected by the early-Renaissance Spanish Hall, built by Giovanni Luchese in 1571, with original coffered ceiling and inlaid doors.

Archduke Ferdinand II established his own museum at Ambras, but the exhibits ended up in various Viennese museums. Nonetheless, there is still plenty to see, including the Rüstkammer (arsenal), the Kunst- und Wunderkammer (chamber of arts and marvels), and the gallery with portraits of members of the Habsburgs by famous artists such as Lucas Cranach, Peter Paul Rubens and Diego Velázquez.

Andreas Hofer (1767–1810)

Andreas Hofer is regarded as Austria's national hero, widely extolled in its literature and poetry. In 1809, he led the Tyrolean uprising against the Bavarian rulers, who were allied with Napoleon's forces. He succeeded in beating the Bavarians, and forced the French army, led by Marshal Lefebvre, to retreat from Tyrol after their defeat on Bergisel, a hill just outside Innsbruck (see p247). Hofer assumed civilian power in Tyrol, but was soon betrayed and captured, and subsequently executed by the French in the town square of Mantua.

Hofkirche

Hofkirche, the court church, was built by Ferdinand I to house the tomb of his grandfather, Emperor Maximilian I. The tomb was designed by Maximilian himself and although his plans were never fully realized, the ensuing structure, completed in 1587, is very impressive indeed and ranks as a masterpiece of Renaissance sculpture. At the centre of the church stands the sarcophagus with a kneeling figure of the emperor. Reliefs on the side panels depict scenes from the emperor's life; the tomb is guarded by larger-than-life cast-iron statues. The tomb is, in fact, empty – Maximilian was laid to rest in Wiener Neustadt, in Lower Austria.

Vaults
The vaults acquired their present form in the early 17th century, when the church was rebuilt in the Baroque style.

★ Tomb of Maximilian I
The cenotaph, at the centre of the church, is guarded by giant figures representing members of Maximilian I's family, including his daughter-in-law, Joanna the Mad, and his spiritual forefathers.

Main Portal
The grand Renaissance portal leading into the church was built in 1553–63 as a tribute to the House of Maximilian I.

Main entrance

KEY

① **Kneeling figure of Emperor Maximilian I**

② **An onion dome** crowns the octagonal tower of the church.

★ Silberne Kapelle
The silver chapel holds the tombs of Archduke Ferdinand II and his beloved wife, Philippine Welser, by the Dutch artist, Alexander Colin.

For hotels and restaurants in this region see pp298–9 and pp323–4

VISITORS' CHECKLIST

Practical Information
Universitätsstrasse 2.
Tel (0512) 584302.
W hofkirche.at
Open 9am–5pm Mon–Sat,
12:30–5pm Sun & hols. 🅿

Charles the Bold
The statue of Charles the Bold, Duke of Burgundy and Maximilian's father-in-law, stands to the right of the tomb, closest to the high altar.

🏛 Wilten

In the southeastern suburb of Wilten stands a lovely Baroque church, the Wilten Basilica, built in 1751–6 on the foundations of a former chapel. The church was intended to provide a worthy setting for the picture of *Our Lady at Four Columns*, which miracles were attributed to. It was designed by Franz de Paula Penz and the interior has been kept in the Rococo style. The altarpiece, with its gold, pink and yellow colour scheme, includes a 14th-century painting of the Madonna. It is surrounded by an intricate canopy resting on slender columns. The ceiling paintings are by an Augsburg artist, Matthäus Günther, and show in the presbytery *Saint Mary Our Advocate* and in the nave *Ester and Judith*.

The Romanesque abbey of Wilten has a church built in the 12th century, devoted to St Lawrence. According to legend, the abbey was built by the giant Haymon, in atonement for the murder of another giant, Thyrsus; both are commemorated by statues. Burned and destroyed several times, the abbey was rebuilt in Baroque style in the 17th–18th centuries.

Bergisel

Tirol Panorama mit Kaiserjäger-museum: Bergisel 1–2. **Tel** (0512) 5948 9611. **Open** 9am–5pm Wed–Mon (until 7pm Thu Jul & Aug). 🅿 ♿

On 13 August 1809, Bergisel, or Isel Mountain, in the south of the city, was the scene of a battle fought by Andreas Hofer *(see p245)* and his army of insurgent highlanders, who defeated the combined occupying forces of Bavarians and French. The hill is a popular place for weekend walks among Innsbruck residents.

A monument to Andreas Hofer and the Kaiserjäger-museum serve as reminders of the 1809 battle as well as of later battles by this famous regiment of imperial fusiliers.

Statue of Andreas Hofer on Bergisel

In 2011, the Riesenrundgemälde, a panoramic painting of the Battle of Bergisel, was moved from its previous home at the bottom of the Hungerburg cable car, to Das Tirol Panorama, a museum on top of Bergisel. Painted by Zeno Diemar in 1896, and measuring 10 x 100 m (33 x 328 ft), the panorama is a *trompe l'oeil* depicting an abbreviated version of the entire battle.

The museum also hosts temporary exhibitions alongside its permanent collection of Tyrolean artifacts.

On Bergiselschanze, one of the competitions in the world-famous Vierschanzentournee (four hills' ski-jumping tournament) is held every year on 4 January.

🦦 Alpenzoo

Weiherburggasse 37A. **Tel** (0512) 292323. **Open** Apr–Oct: 9am–6pm; Nov–Mar: 9am–5pm. 🅿

On the southern slopes of Bergisel is a fascinating Alpine zoo, housing a comprehensive collection of alpine fauna. There are some 2,000 animals here, representing more than 150 species typically found in an alpine habitat, including the alpine ibex and bear, and many local birds, fish and reptiles. A cable car from Hungerburg Talstation takes you to the zoo; the ride is free with an entry ticket to the zoo.

An otter in Alpenzoo, on Bergisel south of Innsbruck

The emblematic Mint Tower of Burg Hasegg in Hall in Tirol

❷ Igls

Road map B4. 🏔 2,000. 🚌
ℹ Hilberstrasse 15 (0512) 377101.

This small town south of
Innsbruck, which had long been
popular as a holiday centre and
winter-sports resort, was given
a new face for the 1976 Winter
Olympic Games when modern
toboggan and bobsleigh
runs were built. The nearby
Patscherkofel (2,247 m/7,372 ft
high) is a popular destination
for winter skiing expeditions
and summer rambles. It is served
by a funicular, a chair lift and
five T-bars. An old salt track,
Römerstrasse, runs above the
Sill Valley, providing views of the
famous Europabrücke (Europe
Bridge) (see p256), which spans
the Alpine gorges and is part of
the busiest motor-
way network
connecting northern
Europe with Italy.

The **Aegidius-
kirche** in Igls, the
church of St Giles,
probably dates
back to the 13th
century but has been
remodelled in the
Baroque period. It has
beautiful vault frescoes
by Josef Michael Schmitzer.

Coat of arms of Hall
in Tirol

Near Igls is the interesting
pilgrimage chapel Heiligwasser
(1662), with attractive stuccowork created in 1720 as well as
a wooden statue of the Virgin
Mary dating back to the early
15th century.

❸ Hall in Tirol

Road map B4. 🏔 13,000. 🚌 🚊
ℹ Wallpachgasse 5 (05223) 455440.
🌐 hall-wattens.at

Hall ranks mostly as a holiday
resort, but the Old Town, with
much of its original architecture
intact, bears testimony to the
town's former glory. The symbol
of Hall is the twelve-sided
tower, known as the Mint Tower,
of **Burg Hasegg**. This castle, with
its beautiful inner courtyard,
once formed a corner section
of the town's fortifications.
It was the seat of the Tyrolean
rulers and, in the 16th century,
it became the mint. Today the
castle houses the town museum.

In the Old Town, the **Town Hall**
with its steep Gothic roof consists
of two parts: the 1406 Königshaus
(Royal House) with a
beautiful debating
hall with exposed-
beam ceiling; and is a
large building on the
south side of Oberer
Stadtplatz, with a
Renaissance portal
and a balcony from
which the town
fathers used to make
their proclamations.
The 14th-century
Nikolauskirche, the church of
St Nicholas, nearby, has a lovely
portal featuring the Sorrowful
Christ, the Virgin Mary and
St Nicholas, and an attractive
Baroque interior. Particularly worth
seeing is the Waldaufkapelle,
which is closed off from the rest

of the church interior by a
wrought-iron grille. It houses a
collection of reliquaries.

❹ Wattens

Road map B4. 🏔 7,700. 🚌 🚊 **Tel**
(05224) 455 440. 🌐 hall-wattens.at

The Swarovski factory of
decorative glass and glass
jewellery and its museum in
Wattens are a unique and
fascinating experience. Here
you can see the world's largest
cut crystal (300,000 carats), and
a crystal wall 11 m (36 ft) high,
with several tons of glittering
semi-precious stones.

🏛 **Swarovski Crystal Worlds**
Kristallweltenstrasse 1. **Tel** (05224)
51080. **Open** 9am–6pm. ♿

Environs
Volders has an unusual church
devoted to St Charles Borromeo,
dating from 1620–54.

The entrance to Swarovski Kristallwelten
in Wattens

❺ Schwaz

Road map C4. 🏔 13,000. 🚌 🚊 ℹ
Münchnerstrasse 11 (05242) 63240.
🌐 silberregion-karwendel.com

During the 16th century, this
busy commercial town in the
Inn river valley was the second
largest in the Tyrol. Schwaz
suffered extensive damage
during the battle of 1809, but
it has preserved some lovely
historic sights. The most impressive of these is the 15th-century
Pfarrkirche, with its high

The imposing Renaissance Schloss Tratzberg

copper-shingled tower and beautiful, crenellated gables. The most striking elements inside are the stone balustrade of the gallery with intricate lacework (c.1520) and an impressive Baroque organ enclosure. The figures of St Anne, St Ursula and St Elizabeth on the altarpiece are original Gothic decorations. The statues of St George and St Florian, the patron saints of Austria, were added at a later date.

The double **cemetery chapel** (1504–7) has a lovely covered staircase leading to the upper chapel, which has a carved wooden altar. The lower chapel has original 16th-century frescoes depicting the Crucifixion and the Mount of Olives.

The late-Gothic **Franziskanerkirche**, the Franciscan church and monastery, has retained its original Gothic interior, clearly visible despite Baroque additions made in the 18th century. The cloister along the south wall of the church was built in 1509–12 by Christoph Reichartinger; it shows a series of 16th-century paintings with Passion scenes.

Schwaz was once a major centre for the production of silver, and one of the mines, the **Silberbergwerk**, is now open to the public and can be explored by train and a guided tour on foot.

▥ Silberbergwerk
Alte Landstrasse 3a. **Tel** (05242) 72 372. **Open** May–Sep: 9am–5pm daily, Oct–Apr: 10am–4pm Wed–Sun.
w silberbergwerk.at

❻ Tratzberg

Road map C4. ▦ ▦ **Tel** (05242) 63 566. **Open** Apr–Oct: 10am–4pm daily.
w schloss-tratzberg.at

A short way from Schwaz, in the Inn river valley, stands the impressive Renaissance Schloss Tratzberg. This castle was once a frontier fortress which guarded Andechs county against the Bavarians. It changed hands many times and is now the private property of the Enzenberg family, with a small museum.

The castle is entered from the west side through a Renaissance portal. The inner courtyard with its heavily decorated low arcades was built in two stages: the first around 1500 and the second in the late 16th century. The most interesting parts of the castle are the armoury, with its tremendous collection of early arms; the Royal Room, with its exposed beam ceiling, once used by Anna of Bohemia, the widow of Duke Henry of

Tyrol; and finally the Habsburg Hall, with the family tree of Emperor Maximilian I and 148 portraits. The room has a red marble column at its centre and is covered by a coffered ceiling. The emperor's room on the second floor retains its original intricately carved wooden ceiling, and the bedroom is decorated by a series of 16th-century paintings of a knightly tournament created by Hans Schäufelein. The Fugger family room still boasts its original Renaissance decor. Its best feature is the richly inlaid door dating from 1515.

❼ Achensee

Road map C4. ▦ ▦

Situated between the Inn and the Isar river basins is Achensee, the largest lake in Tyrol, about 9 km (6 miles) long. On its northern shore the Karwendel mountain range extends up to Innsbruck. On its eastern shore are the Rofan Mountains, with their highest peak, the Rofanspitze, rising to 2,259 m (7,411 ft).

Achensee can be reached by cog-wheel steam train from **Jenbach**. Worth seeing in this village is the church of St Wolfgang, a late-Gothic structure built in 1487–1500 by Gilg Mitterhofer from Schwaz; its Baroque tower is a later addition. Although repeatedly rebuilt, it still has its late-Gothic side portals and ogival windows; one of the side altars has a late-Gothic statue of the Madonna.

Sailing yachts on Achensee, Tyrol's largest lake

Charming flower displays outside the Alpine houses in Alpbach

❽ Alpbach

Road map C4. ⛰ 2,600.
Tel (05337) 21200-30. 🌐 alpbach.at

In a high mountain valley on the Alpbach river lies the town of the same name that once a year becomes the intellectual capital of Europe. Every year since 1945, delegates representing the worlds of science, politics, economics and culture have gathered here to discuss the future of the world. Before the fall of communism in the Eastern bloc countries in 1989, Austria's central position in Europe made this the most appropriate place for people from East and West to meet. Today their discussions are rather more academic, yet Alpbach has retained its great importance on Europe's political and intellectual map.

The floral displays outside the Alpine houses and chalets in Alpbach rank among the best in the country. The little town also has the interesting **Church of St Oswald**. Its earliest records date from 1369, although it was altered in 1500 and the Baroque interior dates from 1724. The naves have ceiling paintings by Christoph Anton Mayr (1751); the sculptures in the presbytery (c.1779) are the work of Franz Xaver Nissl.

❾ Wörgl

Road map C4. ⛰ 13,000.
🛈 Bahnhofstrasse 4a (05332) 76007.

The industrial town of Wörgl, at the fork of Inn river and Brixentaler Ache (a stream), is an important road and rail hub. The earliest settlement on the site, revealed by archaeological finds on the northeastern outskirts of town, date from the Bronze Age. In later years this was the site of a Roman settlement, and in the 4th century a Christian community was founded in the area. In the 13th century Wörgl belonged to Bavaria; during the reign of Maximilian I it finally became incorporated into Tyrol. Wörgl and its environs were the scene of fierce fighting during

Monument to the Battle of 1809 in Wörgl

the Napoleonic wars, when the Tyrolean highlanders fought for their independence from the Bavarians and the French. A monument commemorating the battle now stands in front of **St Lawrence's church**. This church, built in 1748, is Baroque in style and has interesting stucco decorations, vault paintings, a main altar with Baroque sculptures and an attractive medieval statue of the Madonna.

Wörgl's location between the two popular tourist regions of Kaisergebirge and the Kitzbühel Alps makes it a convenient base for winter and summer expeditions.

❿ Söll

Road map C4. ⛰ 3,500.
Tel 050509-210.

Söll, a small town in the foothills of the Hohe Salve, part of the Wilder Kaiser (Wild Emperor) massif, grew around the **Church of St Peter and St Paul**. Built in 1361 but completely altered in the Baroque style in 1768 by Franz Bock of Kufstein, it contains beautiful vault paintings by Christoph Anton Mayr and, by the same artist, a picture of the Madonna in the main altarpiece. The town has many attractive houses with picturesque façades.

The greatest attraction of Söll, however, is the **Hohe Salve** mountain, rising to 1,828 m (5,997 ft) and visible from every point in the town. Two gondolas provide transport to the summit. There is a small chapel here, and the view over Brixental, the Kitzbühel Alps and the High Tauern Mountains in the distance, is truly majestic.

Söll lies at the centre of a large skiing region, **Skiwelt Wilder Kaiser-Brixental**, in the southern part of Kaisergebirge, which also includes several other attractive resorts, such as the picturesque town of **Scheffau** nearby.

Visitors sunbathing on Hohe Salve, near Söll

⓫ Kufstein

Road map C4. 👥 18,000. 🚃 🚌
Tel (05372) 62207.

The remains of a Stone Age settlement have been found in this health resort and tourist centre on the Bavarian border.
On a rocky hill to the north of the town stands the Feste Kufstein, a mighty fortress with a small barbican and the Emperor's Tower. Today it houses a regional museum and, on the ground floor of the tower, the Heldenorgel (Heroes' Organ), built to commemorate all who were killed in World War I. The late-Gothic **Church of St Vitus** was rebuilt in the 17th century in the Baroque style, but in the 20th century it was partly returned to its original Gothic appearance. Nearby stands the Holy Trinity Chapel, with a beautiful Baroque altar dating from 1765.

Environs
Hechtsee and Stimmersee, two small, scenic lakes west of Kufstein, are excellent for water sports enthusiasts. About 30 km (22 miles) northeast of Kufstein, beyond the Kaisergebirge ridge known as Zahmer Kaiser (Tame Emperor), is **Walchsee**, a beguiling town and lake of the same name, with many fine houses with picturesque façades and a good water sports centre. The road from Kufstein along the Sparchenbach river leads to Stripsenkopf, at 1,807 m (5,929 ft) the highest peak in the Zahmer Kaiser range, with great views of the Kaisergebirge.

⓬ St Johann in Tirol

Road map C4. 👥 9,000. 🚃 🚌
Tel (05352) 63335-0.

St Johann in Tirol is a popular winter sports resort, boasting good downhill runs on the northern slopes of the Kitzbüheler Horn and splendid conditions for cross-country skiing. The town has several Baroque buildings with picturesque elevations, and the walls of the parish house feature the original frescoes from 1480. The first large Baroque church in the area was built in 1728 by Abraham Millauer, on the site of an earlier Gothic structure. Inside **Mariä Himmelfahrtskirche** (church of the Assumption of the Virgin Mary) are magnificent vault paintings by one of the great masters of Baroque art, Simon Benedikt Faistenberger.

⓭ Kitzbühel

Road map C4. 👥 8,500. 🚃 🚌
ℹ️ Hinterstadt 18 (05356) 66660.
🌐 kitzbuehel.com

Once the undisputed winter sports capital of the country, Kitzbühel now has to share its crown with other resorts. The Alpine town is surrounded by several mountain massifs, with scores of well-signposted trails. The best conditions are offered by the Hahnenkamm–Steinbergkogel–Pengelstein group to the southwest, the

A picturesque snow-covered scene in Kitzbühel

Kitzbüheler Horn to the north, the Stuckkogel and the Thurn Pass. This is where the famous Hahnenkammrennen, a downhill skiing race, takes place at the end of January each year.
Kitzbühel is more than a sporting resort; untouched by wartime ravages, it has many historic sights. The **Andreaskirche** was built in 1435 on the site of a Romanesque church and in 1785 it was rebuilt in the Baroque style. Inside are late-Gothic columns and 15th-century traceries and frescoes. There is also an interesting main altarpiece, by Simon Benedikt Faistenberger.
Adjacent to the parish church is **Liebfrauenkirche** (church of Our Lady), with a square tower. The main altar is also by Faistenberger. The 14th-century St Catherine's church in the city centre is now a monument to those killed in the two world wars.

The mighty fortress with the Emperor's Tower in Kufstein

⑭ Zillertaler Alpen

The Zillertal, the valley of the Ziller river, extends from Innau to the Austro-Italian border. Initially a wide upland, beyond Mayrhofen it splits into four narrower valleys that cut into the mountain ranges. Artificial lakes and large dams were built into most of the local rivers to provide a power supply for the entire region. The present popularity of winter sports has contributed to the rapid development of Zillertal. Especially popular with skiers are the Hintertux Glacier runs, the Mayrhofen-Finkenberg trail and the town of Zell am Ziller. The well-marked trails in breathtakingly beautiful countryside lure ramblers here in the summer, and there are many attractive cycling routes.

Zillertaler Alpen
The Zillertaler Alps, a side range of the High Tauern, are steep crystalline mountains. Their highest peak is the Hochfeiler at 3,510 m/ 11,516 ft.

★ Tuxertal
The valley of the Tuxerbach (Tux stream) is picturesque, with many attractive resorts. Tuxer Ferner, the local glacier, offers the best year-round skiing conditions in the entire area.

Key

⚌ Major road

▭ Minor road

- - Cable car, chairlift

— River

☼ Viewpoint

Lanersbach • L6

Tuxertal

▲ 2867

Hintertux

Ginzli

▲ 3231

Zemmtal • 169

▲ 3250

Zamser Grund •

Zemmgrund

▲ 3476

Schlegeis-speicher

▲ 3289

▲ 3478

Schlegeisspeicher
The largest artificial lake in the area is scenically situated at the foot of the Hochfeiler Massif and the Schlegeis glacier.

0 kilometres   5

0 miles   5

★ **Zell am Ziller**
This beautiful fresco (1779) by
Franz A. Zeiller adorns the church
of St Vitus. Another sight to see
here is the old gold mine.

Schwaz

Zell am Ziller

165

• Hippach

Gerlostal

169

Mayrhofen

kenberg

Zillergrund

2700

*Stillupp-
speicher*

Stilluppgrund

▲
3383

▲
3376

▲
3368

Stilluppspeicher
The best views of this lake,
in its pristine natural
environment, are gained
from the top of the dam at
1,130 m (3,707 ft). Nearby
are two waterfalls.

VISITORS' CHECKLIST

Practical Information
Road map C4.
🛈 Zillertal Tourismus
Bundesstrasse 27d, A-6262
Schlitters, (05288) 87187.
email: info@zillertal.at
🌐 **zillertal.at**

Transport
🚆 🚌

Mayrhofen
In this picturesque resort, the most
popular tourist destination in the
Zillertal, the wide valley narrows
and divides into four smaller
Alpine valleys.

Tyrolean Traditional Costumes

The Tyrolean version of Austria's national
costume is not reserved for special
occasions – here many people wear it
every day. The man's *Tracht* consists of
leather shorts (summer) or breeches
(winter) held in place by braces and tied
under the knees, thick socks and a *Loden*
jacket made of thick, woollen cloth, with
bone buttons. To this is added a felt hat
with a distinctive tuft of coarse animal
hair. The woman's *Dirndl* comprises a
puffed-sleeve blouse with a bodice and
a pleated skirt with an apron.

A young couple dressed in typical Tyrolean outfits

Europabrücke, the highest road bridge in Europe

⑮ Brenner

Road map B5.

At an altitude of 1,374 m (4,508 ft), the Brenner Pass is the lowest passage across the Eastern Alps, and as such one of the most easily accessible routes connecting northern Europe with Italy. Separating the Stubai Alps from the Zillertal Alps, the pass was originally used by the Romans as a trade and military route. A highway suitable for carriage traffic was built in 1772, and the first trans-Alpine railway line was opened here in 1867. Today the motorway leading across the wide saddle of the Brenner also boasts the highest and most impressive road bridge in Europe, the Europabrücke, 815 m (2,674 ft) long.

⑯ Stubaital

Road map B4. 🚌 *i* Fulpmes, Bahnstrasse 17 (0501) 881 200. 🅦 **stubai.at**

Travelling on the Brenner motorway from Innsbruck towards Italy you will pass the Stubai Alps to your right, a high ridge massif with few valleys.

The lowest route into the centre of the massif runs along the Stubaital (Stubai Valley), with its busy tourist resorts of Fulpmes and Neustift. The highest peak of the Stubai Alps, Zuckerhütl (Little Sugar Loaf), rises to 3,507 m (11,506 ft). The Stubaital is a very quiet place, particularly when compared with the neighbouring Zillertal, winding its way above a busy motorway. The Stubai glacier provides excellent conditions for all-year skiing and walking.

Fulpmes, a popular tourist centre in the Stubaital

⑰ Ötztal

Road map B4. 🚌 🚋
i Gemeindestrasse 4, Sölden (05720) 05 00. 🅦 **oetztal.com**

Following the course of the Ötztaler Ache, a tributary of the Inn river, is the long valley of Ötztal. At its southern end, near the border with Italy, rise the Ötztal Alps, with many peaks above 3,500 m (11,500 ft); the Wildspitze, at 3,774 m (12,381 ft), is North Tyrol's highest summit.

Nestling within the Ötztal Alps is also the highest parish in Austria, the ski resort of Obergurgl at 1,927 m (6,322 ft). The largest settlement in the lower part of Ötztal is **Oetz**, an old village with attractive, colourful houses. The paintings on the Star Inn date from 1573 and 1615. On a steep slope stands the church of St George and St Nicholas, which retains some original Gothic features, including a vault and portals.

The largest town at the upper end of the Ötztal Valley is **Längenfeld**, where you find the church of St Catherine. It has a 74-m (243-ft) high Gothic tower, a decorative west portal and a Baroque interior.

Ötztal's administrative centre is the old Tyrolean village of **Sölden**. There is good skiing on Tiefenbachferner and superb views from Gaislachkogel and Wilder Mann.

In 1991, a frozen human body was discovered on the Italian side of the Ötztal Alps. Although over 5,000 years old, Ötzi, as he was named, was perfectly preserved by the ice, along with some 70 artifacts.

⑱ Seefeld

Road map B4. 🚋 🚠 3,300.
i Klosterstrasse 43 (05088) 050.

This small town, occupying a large sunny plateau, is one of the most attractive places near Innsbruck. It is a smart resort, with elegant shops along a wide promenade, and boasts a variety of attractions. In the 1964 and 1976 Winter Olympics, Seefeld was the venue for all the Nordic skiing contests,

◀ View of a man-made reservoir at the foot of the Zillertaler Alpen

enhancing the town's prosperity and reputation. The local cross-country skiing trails are the longest in the Alps, measuring some 250 km (155 miles).

At the centre of Seefeld stands the huge 15th-century church of St Oswald while at the western end of the town is a chapel built on the orders of Archduke Leopold V to house a crucifix dating from the early 16th century and said to have miraculous powers. The crucifix stands within the altarpiece of this small, circular building with a Renaissance portal and onion dome.

Visitors to Seefeld can also enjoy a trip to the casino, one of the largest in Austria.

View of Zugspitze from the Ehrwald side

⑲ Ehrwald

Road map B4. 🚌 🚊 🏔 2,600.
ℹ️ Kirchplatz 1 (05673) 20 000-208.
🌐 zugspitzarena.com

Nestling below the western side of Zugspitze (2,965 m/ 9728 ft), the highest peak of the Bavarian Alps, is the resort village of Ehrwald. On the German side of the mountain is the resort of Garmisch-Partenkirchen, the most popular winter sports centre in that area. Several Austrian and German resorts, including Garmisch-Partenkirchen and Ehrwald, have joined up to form one vast skiing area.

The summit of Zugspitze can be reached from both the German and the Austrian sides. From Ehrwald, you take the cable car from the lower station of Ehrwald/ Obermoos. The upper station affords magnificent views. To the south, beyond the mountain ranges

of Kaisergebirge, Karwendelgebirge and Dachstein, you can see the snow-covered peaks of the High Tauern. To the east, there are the Arlberg mountains with Silvretta and Rätikon, with the peaks of the Appenzeller Alpen in between, and the Allgäu mountains in the distance. To the north, Bavaria can be seen.

Clemens Krauss, the founder of the famous Vienna New Year's Day Concerts, lived in Ehrwald and lies buried here.

⑳ Reutte

Road map B4. 🏔 6,000.
ℹ️ Untermarkt 34 (05672) 62336.
🌐 reutte.com

Reutte is the largest town in the Ausserfern district, a remote area that was cut off from the world for a considerable time: it is said that the first car arrived here only in 1947. Reutte can be reached from Innsbruck via the Fern Pass, a route first used in Roman times. In the valley of the Lech river, it is today the main town and trade centre of the region. In medieval times it grew rich on the salt trade, and to this day it has some lovely town houses with oriel windows, open staircases and painted façades. Many of the paintings are by Johann Jakob Zeiller, the best-known

member of an artistic family that settled in Reutte in the 17th and 18th centuries – they once lived at No. 1 Zeiller Platz.

The 15th-century convent church of St Anna features several interesting works of art. In the main altarpiece is a picture of the Madonna with Child and St Anna (c.1515) and two vast figures of St Magnus and St Afra dating from the early 18th century.

The **Heimatmuseum** (regional museum) has a fine collection of paintings by outstanding masters of the Baroque, mainly of the Zeiller family members, as well as exhibits associated with transport and salt mining.

Specimens representative of the local flora can be seen in the **Alpenblumengarten**, an Alpine flower garden on top of the Hahnenkamm, at a height of about 1,700 m (5,577 ft) above sea level.

🏛 Heimatmuseum
Grünes Haus, Untermarkt 25.
Tel (05672) 72304. **Open** May–Oct: 1–5pm Tue–Sat (to 7pm Thu); Dec–Mar: 2–5pm Wed–Sat (to 7pm Thu).

Environs
A short distance east of Reutte is the beautiful, 5-km (3-mile) long **Plansee**, where one of the small pleasure boats can take you on a cruise on the tranquil waters. In winter the entire lake freezes over and becomes one giant ice-skating rink.

Plansee, a tranquil, picturesque lake near Reutte

Warth, a town situated within the most famous winter sports region

㉑ Elbigenalp

Road map A4. ⛰ 850. 🚉
Tel (05634) 621 012.

The Lech river valley, which is parallel to the Inn river valley and snakes between mountain passes, cuts a deep ravine between the Allgäuer Alps and the Lechtal Alps. About halfway between the towns of Reutte and Warth lies Elbigenalp, a small village worth visiting for the local **Nikolauskirche** (church of St Nicholas). Built in the 14th century, the church's oldest surviving parts include the Gothic tower, presbytery and font. It was altered in the Baroque style, and the vault and wall paintings as well as the Stations of the Cross are the work of the artistic Zeiller family, who lived in Reutte.

St Martin's cemetery chapel in Elbigenalp has interesting original Gothic frescoes depicting scenes from the life of St Magdalene and the *Dance of Death* by Anton Falger.

㉒ Lech am Arlberg

Road map A4. ⛰ 1,500. 🚌 🚉
Tel (05583) 2161-0. 🆆 **lech-zuers.at**

This small resort is situated on a large plateau at an altitude of 1,450 m (4,757 ft), not far from the source of the Lech river. Lech is regarded as one of Austria's most beautiful and most elegant mountain resorts. In order to protect the natural environment, some years ago the local authorities drastically limited the available accommodation, thus creating an exclusive

resort. The fame of the resort spread around the world and many celebrities and royals began to spend their winter holidays in Lech, including the late Princess Diana.

The town's development has been closely associated with the construction of the Arlberg and Flexen passes, which made Lech accessible in the winter months. Lifts and cable cars were built, and the vast snowy slopes of the Arlberg began to attract winter sports enthusiasts. Summer, too, can be very pleasant here, and there are many beautiful trails for walking or mountain cycling. Sights to see include the 15th-century Gothic **church of St Nicholas**, with an even older tower. In addition, there are swanky hotels, chic shops, smart cafés and restaurants, which combine to make Lech a tourist magnet for the wealthy.

Lech has joined Zürs, Stuben and St Anton to form a large single skiing region.

㉓ Zürs am Arlberg

Road map A4. ⛰ 130. 🚉
Tel (05583) 2245. 🆆 **lech-zuers.at**

Zürs, a tiny resort some 6 km (4 miles) south of Lech, lies at an altitude of 1,716 m (5,630 ft). Along with neighbouring Lech, Zürs places a great emphasis on

A fabulous scenery of snowy mountain peaks rising above Zürs am Arlberg

For hotels and restaurants in this region see pp298–9 and pp323–4

the protection of the natural environment. As a rule, the few hotels and pensions accept only regular guests in their very limited number of rooms. The exclusive nature of the resort, its elegant cafés, restaurants and a famous discothèque provide truly world-class après-ski entertainment, while the expansive ski slopes and the fairly heavy snowfalls over many months attract dedicated winter sports enthusiasts. Austria's first chair lifts were built in Zürs in 1937 and the first skiing competitions were held here as early as 1906. Lifts and cable cars take you to a number of excellent viewing points.

㉔ Arlberg

See pp260–61.

Ischgl, one of Austria's most attractive skiing resorts

㉕ Ischgl

Road map A5. 🏔 1,550. 🚆
Tel 050990-100. 🌐 ischgl.at

Ischgl, on the Trisanna river at the eastern end of the Silvrettastrasse, is one of the loveliest Austrian resorts. An international ski centre, at an altitude of 1,377 m (4,518 ft), it provides access to 200 km (120 miles) of ski runs and 40 lifts within the Silvretta range on the Austrian–Swiss border. The town is also an ideal starting point for a drive along the Silvrettahochalpenstrasse, a hairpin mountain road, often snow-covered – and therefore closed – from November until

Lünersee, a reservoir lake at the foot of Schesaplana

late May, which connects the Montafon Valley – where Schruns is the best-known resort – and the Ill river with the Trisanna Valley. The road drops by 1,000 m (3,280 ft) over just 15 km (9 miles).

The area around the Silvretta-Stausee, a reservoir on the Bielerhöhe Pass at 2,036 m (6,680 ft), has been made a national park; the ski runs in the Silvretta massif start here. The most beautiful views are to be had from Hohes Rad, 2,934 m (9,626 ft). The high mountain section of Silvrettastrasse ends in Galtür, a lovely village on the Ballunspitze.

㉖ Lünersee

Road map A5. 🚌

Lünersee lies at the foot of the Schesaplana peak (2,965 m/9,728 ft), at an altitude of 1,907 m (6,257 ft). Once this was the largest lake in Eastern Austria, surrounded by rugged mountains criss-crossed with ravines. The dam built here in 1958 raised the water level by 27 m (89 ft), creating an artificial reservoir that now powers Lünersee and Rodund power stations.

㉗ Bludenz

Road map A4. 🏔 14,000. 🚌 🚆
ℹ Werdenbergerstrasse 42 (05552) 63621-970. 🎿 Chocolate Festival (early Jul). 🌐 bludenz.at

Beautifully situated at the confluence of five Alpine valleys, the town of Bludenz is now a

popular resort with excellent skiing areas in its environs. An 10th-century document survives in which Otto I gives the Bishop of Chur a church "in loco Plutenes". During the reign of Friedrich IV the Poor, the town became an administrative centre and power base for the region.

Despite several devastating fires, Bludenz still has some interesting historic sights. The oldest building is **Oberes Tor** (Upper Gate), which houses the local history museum (open in summer). Inside St Lawrence church (1514) are two original altars made from black marble and paintings (1510) showing the Marriage of the Virgin Mary and the Visitation. The seat of the regional authorities is Gayenhofen castle, a medieval building remodelled in Baroque style in 1643.

Today, the town is permeated by chocolate smells from the Suchard factory, producers of the famous confectionery and organizers of an annual chocolate festival.

The octagonal tower of the Laurentiuskirche in Bludenz

㉔ Arlberg

The Arlberg Pass in the Eastern Alps is part of the European watershed between the catchment areas of the North Sea, the Black Sea, the tributaries of the Rhine and the Danube. Arlberg used to be completely cut off from the rest of the country, oriented more towards Germany and Switzerland, until the railway tunnel was built in 1880–84, connecting Vorarlberg with the rest of Austria. The tunnel, at an altitude of 1,310 m (4,298 ft), measures 10,238 m (33,589 ft) in length, and was for many years the longest in Austria. Today, the Arlberg region has some of the country's most exclusive ski resorts.

⑦ **Valluga**
The breathtaking view extending from the summit at 2,809 m (9,216 ft) embraces the Rätikon Mountains, the Montafon Valley as well as the Brenner, Ötztal and Stubai Alps.

⑥ **Flexenpass**
The pass is surrounded by the Rätikon mountain peaks, including Zimbaspitze and Schesaplana. Thanks to a system of avalanche defences, the road across remains passable in winter.

⑤ **Stuben**
This quiet village at the foot of the Albonagrat (2,334 m/ 7,658 ft) has ski runs leading to St Anton. The name ("cosy living room") refers to the cabins from where travellers set off on the mountain trails.

④ **Arlbergtunnel**
The road tunnel underneath the Arlberg Pass, 14 km (9 miles) long, was the longest in the world when it opened in 1978.

① Landeck

Schloss Landeck, built in about 1200 and rebuilt after a fire, has retained its original grand hall with a late-Gothic vault, and a chapel with early 16th-century frescoes. Today, the castle is thet home of the local folk museum.

0 metres   5
0 yards   5

Tips for Drivers

Length of the route: 45 km (28 miles).
Stopping-off points: the hotel by the hospice in St Christoph offers accommodation. There are many restaurants and excellent shops in St Anton am Arlberg.

Key

- ▤ Motorway
- ▤ Suggested route
- ▤ Scenic route
- ═ Other road
- ┈ River, lake
- ▪▪ Tunnel

Innsbruck

E60   A12

97
E60   E60   ①   171
516   180
188   Davos

③ St Christoph

The town's small statue of St Christopher, from the old hospice in St Christoph, was replaced with a new sculpture after fire damage in 1957. The hospice itself is today a luxury hotel. Austria's first regular ski-school was founded in this town in 1901.

② St Anton am Arlberg

The largest tourist resort in Arlberg, St Anton is surrounded by numerous ski trails, and good snow conditions are guaranteed throughout the season.

㉘ Bregenzer Wald

The Bregenzer Wald (Bregenz Forest) occupies the northern part of Vorarlberg and extends along the Bregenzer Ache valley. This region has maintained much of its individual character. Its inhabitants cherish their traditions, and the architecture, the national costumes and the dialect spoken here differ from those found in the rest of the country. Bregenz Forest has many picturesque resorts with excellent facilities for visitors. Apart from Bregenz itself, two larger urban centres have become established on its borders – Dornbirn, and Feldkirch, the "gateway to Austria", with its beautifully preserved old town.

⑥ **Schwarzenberg**
This was the home town of Angelika Kauffmann, a prominent artist of the Neo-Classicist period. Her paintings depicting Christ's apostles and disciples can be seen in the local Holy Trinity church.

Lindau

⑦ **Ammenegg**
From the forecourt of the Sonnblick Inn in Ammenegg, visitors can enjoy lovely views which, on a clear day, extend as far as Lake Constance and the peaks of the Swiss Alps.

Feldkirch

⑧ **Dornbirn**
The largest town in Vorarlberg, this is a centre for the textile industry. The Museum *inatura* houses modern displays on the natural environment and the history of the region.

Angelika Kauffmann

Angelika Kauffmann, a Swiss painter (1741–1807) of idealized portraits in sentimental or Neo-Classical style, was associated with German, English and Italian artistic circles. She left many works in Schwarzenberg, where she had family links. The local church has an altarpiece by her and also a small bust. More works by this celebrated artist can be seen in the Vorarlberger Landesmuseum in Bregenz.

Angelika Kauffmann

⑨ **Rappenlochschlucht**
The road to the Rappenloch gorge runs steeply uphill along the Dornbirner Ache stream, and ends at a reservoir.

⑤ **Bezau**
This picturesque village set among orchards has a lovely church, dating from 1771, and a small but interesting museum devoted to the region's folk art.

④ **Mellau**
A quiet village on the Bregenzer Ache, Mellau is famous for its wooden houses with shingle-clad roofs, characteristically adorned with flowers.

③ **Bregenzer Ache**
The valley of Bregenzer Ache, running from Lechtaler Alpen, is the main axis of the Bregenzer Forest. The river flows between steep rock faces and gentle hills, past pleasant villages, down a long winding gorge, on its way to Bodensee (Lake Constance).

② **Schröcken**
The church in Schröcken, at the foot of the Widderstein (2,533 m/8,310 ft), has a richly decorated interior and beautiful stained-glass windows.

① **Hochtannbergpass**
The pass between Schröcken and Warth winds its scenic way along the upper Bregenzer Ache, and reaches its highest point near Schröcken at 1,679 m (5,508 ft).

Key

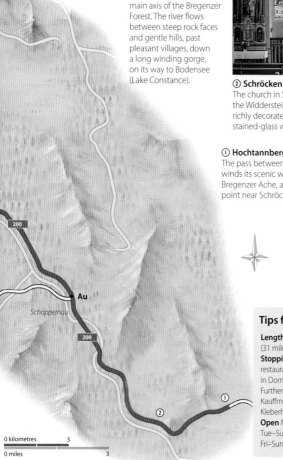

▬▬ Suggested route
▬▬ Scenic road
══ Other road
═══ River, lake

Au
Schoppernau

200

0 kilometres 3
0 miles 3

Tips for Drivers
Length of the route: 50 km (31 miles).
Stopping-off points: there are restaurants and accommodation in Dornbirn, the largest town. Further attractions: Angelika Kauffmann Museum, Brand 34, Kleberhaus. **Tel** (05512) 3570. **Open** May–Oct: 10am–5pm Tue–Sun; Nov–Jan: 2–4pm Fri–Sun.

㉙ Bregenz

The capital of Vorarlberg since 1923, Bregenz is strategically – and attractively – situated on the eastern shore of Bodensee (Lake Constance), at the edge of the Rhine valley and the foot of the Austrian and Swiss Alps. It is a meeting point of four countries: Austria, Germany, Switzerland and the Principality of Liechtenstein. The Romans established the settlement of Brigantium, and later it became the Alemanni town of Brancantia. In 1451 and 1523 Bregenz came under Habsburg rule, and during the Thirty Years' War, it was destroyed by the Swedes. Attractions in Bregenz include walks on the nearby Pfänder massif, and boat trips out on the lake.

Renaissance altarpiece of 1615, in Seekapelle St Georg

View of Bregenz, on the shores of Lake Constance

Exploring Bregenz

Oberstadt (upper town) is the oldest part of Bregenz, with a number of well-preserved historic buildings and the remains of 13th-century fortifications. Innenstadt (inner city) is much newer. It has a theatre and an interesting regional museum. The promenades along Lake Constance, always shrouded in a gentle mist, are worth exploring, as are the grounds of the popular Bregenz summer festivals.

🏛 Vorarlberg Museum

Kornmarktplatz 1. **Tel** (05574) 46 050. **Open** 10am–6pm Tue–Sun (Jul & Aug until 8pm; Thu until 9pm year round). 🅿 🆆 vorarlbergmuseum.at

The Vorarlberg Museum holds collections of prehistoric relics, artifacts dating from the Roman time of the settlement of Brigantium and objects from the days of the Alemanni settlers, all found in Bregenz and its vicinity. A separate department is devoted to

regional handicrafts and customs, old weaponry, coins and medals, as well as regional costumes. One particularly fascinating exhibit is the collection of portable organs. The museum also has an art gallery which holds many beautiful portraits by Angelika Kauffmann (1741–1807), whose family came from Bregenzer Wald *(see p262)*. Other interesting exhibits are early artifacts, Roman and Gothic sculptures and paintings, old altarpieces, and beautiful gold and silver ornaments. The jewels of this museum are the 9th-century stone tablet from Lauterach and the early 16th- century crucifix from the collegiate church in Mehrerau.

🏛 Rathaus

Rathausstrasse 4.
The former granary built in 1686 became the town's chancellery in 1720 and, in 1810, the seat of the town's authorities. It remains the town hall to this day.

🏛 Seekapelle St Georg

Rathausstrasse.
The small chapel of St George, known as the Lakeside Chapel, was built in 1445 and was once lapped by the waters of Lake Constance. Today it is separated from the lake by roads and a railway line and sits just south of the town hall. Between 1690 and 1698, it was moved and rebuilt in the Baroque style by the master bricklayer Kaspar Held. The Renaissance altarpiece from 1615 has been preserved. Depicted at its centre is the Madonna at the foot of the Cross; the side niches show scenes from the Passion.

🏛 Martinsturm

Martinsplatz. **Tel** (05574) 410 1561. **Open** May–Oct: 10am–5pm Tue–Sun.

The Martinsturm, topped with a Baroque dome

The rectangular St Martin's Tower, the symbol of Bregenz, was probably built in the 14th century on earlier Romanesque foundations. Its present look and its staircase date from 1599, while the Baroque cupola was added at a later date. With its Venetian windows and overall muted colour scheme the tower is reminiscent of Moorish architecture. It houses a city archive which presents changing exhibitions.

In the adjacent St Martin's Chapel, beautiful frescoes can be seen, which date back to 1362 and depict Christ in Mandorla with the symbols of the four evangelists and portraits of the chapel founders, members of the Monfort family.

The 17th-century, half-timbered Altes Rathaus

🏛 Altes Rathaus
Oberstadt.

The Old Town Hall, built in 1662 by Michael Kuen, was the seat of the Bregenz municipal authorities until the 19th century. This solid, half-timbered structure stands in the centre of Oberstadt, close to the former town gate, Unteres Tor (Lower Gate). A relief

depicts Epona, the Celtic goddess of agriculture who is shown on horseback, holding a horn of plenty.

🏛 Zisterzienserkloster Mehrerau
Mehrerauerstrasse 66. **Tel** (05574) 71461. **Open** for guided tours for groups only.

To the west of the city centre stands the Zisterzienserkloster Mehrerau, the Cistercian monastery that has been a centre of spiritual and intellectual life since the 11th century.

The church and monastery complex, originally built for the

Benedictines and subsequently taken over by the Cistercians, was remodelled in 1740 in the Baroque style by Franz Anton Beer; the new tower was built using material from the previous Romanesque basilica. It was destroyed in the Napoleonic wars, rebuilt in 1855 and renovated in the 20th century. Inside, two pictures survive with the Stations of the Cross and two late-Gothic statues of the Madonna. The late-Gothic altar in the capitular room dates from 1582.

Adjacent to the reconstructed church and the Romanesque crypt there is now a secondary school, a monastery and a sanatorium.

Bregenz City Centre
① Vorarlberg Museum
② Rathaus
③ Seekapelle St Georg
④ Martinsturm
⑤ Altes Rathaus
⑥ St Gallus
⑦ Festspielhaus

0 metres 250
0 yards 250

⛪ St Gallus
Kirchplatz 3.

Opposite the city centre, on the banks of the Thalbach stream, stands the Stadtpfarrkirche St Gallus (the parish church of St Gallus). According to legend, a previous church on this site had been consecrated by Gallus, an Irish missionary who arrived here in the 7th century. The present church was consecrated in 1318, and the sandstone gate tower in front of it was added in the 15th century. Another tower was added in 1672, and in 1738 the church was altered in the Baroque style, to plans by Franz Anton Beer. At that time the nave was raised and a chapel was added in the transept.

The rather modest interior of the church is typical of Vorarlberg's ecclesiastical style and contrasts sharply with the styles of Tyrol and Bavaria, where Baroque opulence is much more in evidence. The main altarpiece includes statues of the saints Gallus, Peter, Paul and Ulrich, while the side chapel has figures of saints Magnus and Nicholas. St Magnus, an 8th-century Benedictine monk from St Gallen, is the patron saint of the Allgäu, the region between the Tyrol and Vorarlberg; St Nicholas is said to keep a careful watch over the navigation on Bodensee. The beautiful stalls in the presbytery

Decorative detail on the wall of Stadtpfarrkirche St Gallus

are made from walnut wood. They have deep inlays and the backrests are decorated on the outside with the effigies of saints.

🎭 Festspielhaus
Platz der Wiener Symphoniker 1.
Tel (05574) 4130.
w festspielhausbregenz.at

The Festspielgelände (festival grounds) consists of a complex of buildings created specifically for the Bregenz arts festival that has been held every year since 1946, from late July until late August. The festival events feature theatre and opera performances, as well as symphony concerts and fine art exhibitions. Since 1955, the shows have been staged at the Theater am Kornmarkt, a building in the city centre erected in 1838 as a granary and converted into a theatre in 1955. In 1980, a modern festival and congress complex was opened, including show and concert halls, exhibition rooms and a congress centre. The most spectacular of the festival venues, however, is the famous Seebühne, a floating stage extending far onto the lake.

Shows and concerts are staged here and watched by the public on the shore. The summer programme includes opera, operetta, musical and ballet. Behind the festival grounds is the Spielcasino Bregenz.

Gateway of the ruined 10th-century Hohenbregenz fortress

🏰 Hohenbregenz
The Hohenbregenz fortress, whose ruins stand to this day on Gebhardsberg, was built in the 10th century. In 1338, the recorded owner of the castle was Hugo de Montfort.

In 1451, following the death of the last ruler of that line, the castle, together with the town and Bregenz province, were bought by Sigismund of Tyrol.

In 1647, the castle was blown up by the Swedish troops of General Wrangel during the Thirty Years' War, leaving only ruins. The original parts still standing today are the gateway, walls, barbican and a single turret.

In 1723, a chapel devoted to the saints Gebhard and George was built on top of Gebhardsberg and it became a popular pilgrimage site. St Gebhard, a 10th-century Bishop of Constance, was the son of Ulrich of Bregenz, born in Hohenbregenz.

Environs
At the foot of the **Pfänder** (1,065 m/3,494 ft), southeast of the present town, stood the Roman settlement of Brigantium. This area is a favourite destination for walkers; you can also reach the top of the hill by cable car. From this summit, there are magnificent views extending across Bodensee (Lake Constance) and all of Bregenz. Far to the south, the Allgäu Alps can be seen on a clear day, as well as the ice-covered Schesaplana massif, the deep Rhine ravine and the Swiss peaks of Altmann and Säntis.

Seebühne, the floating stage on Lake Constance

⓴ Bodensee

Road map A4. 🚍 🚌 ℹ️ Bodensee-Alpenrhein Tourismus, Bregenz, Römerstrasse 2 (05574) 43 443-0.
🌐 bodensee-vorarlberg.com

Bodensee, or Lake Constance as it is also known, is one of the largest and best-known European lakes. It divides its waters between the three countries surrounding it: Austria, Germany and Switzerland. Austria actually only claims a very small part of it: the total area of the lake is 538.5 sq km (208 sq miles), of which only 38 sq km (14.7 sq miles) is Austrian. Bodensee is 74 km (44 miles) long, and as such the largest lake in the Alps. Once the lake was much larger, but with time deposits carried by the Rhine have reduced its size. The Rhine flows into the lake in a broad delta, wholly in Austrian territory. Having passed through the entire length of Bodensee, it emerges in a waterfall as a turbulent mountain river near Schaffhausen, in Switzerland. The countryside around the lake benefits from a pleasant, moderate climate. Even before World War II, Bodensee was considered to be one of Europe's most polluted lakes, just as the Rhine was one of the dirtiest rivers. However, for several years now it has met all the standards set for environmental protection.

Today, Bodensee forms not so much a border as a link between the countries that lie on its shores. For Austria it is a highly convenient transport route to western Europe, while for the inhabitants of the surrounding towns and villages, as well as for the visitors that arrive here from the neighbouring countries in great numbers every summer, it provides excellent facilities for water sports and relaxation.

The mountains around the town of Bregenz extend right up to the water, creating a picturesque setting for the countless artistic events that take place here, such as the Bregenz Spring and the internationally acclaimed Bregenz Festival. Many performances take place on the famous Seebühne or floating stage.

A number of interesting towns line the shores of Bodensee, including Lindau, Konstanz with its flower island of Mainau, and Friedrichshafen on the German side, which can be reached by ferry or pleasure craft sailing from Bregenz.

17th-century lace in the Stickereimuseum in Lustenau

⓴ Lustenau

Road map A4. 🔼 22,000. 🚍 🚌 ℹ️ Rathausstrasse 1 (05577) 81810.

A fairly large town, Lustenau lies 5 km (3 miles) north of the mouth of the Rhine as it joins Bodensee, on the border with Switzerland. It is famous for its beautiful embroidery and lace-making, popular throughout Austria.

It was at Lustenau that the Romans under the leadership of Emperor Constantine II defeated the Alemanni tribes who had risen up against the empire. The earliest historic records date from 887, when the settlement belonged to the Carolingians. Until 1806, it was a free territory within the empire. In 1814, after the Congress of Vienna, Lustenau came under Austrian rule.

The **Museum Rhein-Schauen** documents the history of the local people and the Rhine. It is also home to the Rheinbähnle, a narrow-gauge train line that takes passengers along the shores of the Rhine to the outmost point of the Rhine delta in Lake Constance, or to an old depot and quarry where materials for the Rhine dams were once taken. A little electric engine pulls the passenger cars and, on occasion, a steam engine takes its place.

🏛 **Museum Rhein-Schauen**
Höchsterstrasse 4. **Tel** (05577) 20 539.
Open 1–5:30pm Wed, Fri–Sun.
Rheinbähnle: 3pm Fri–Sun from the museum. 🌐 rheinschauen.at

Serene blue waters of Bodensee also known as Lake Constance

CARINTHIA & EAST TYROL

Carinthia and East Tyrol, Austria's two southernmost regions, are bordered by Slovenia and Italy in the south, and Styria and Salzburger Land to the east and north. Between them they have many attractions, including the Carinthian lakes and the Hohe Tauern National Park. East Tyrol is separate from the rest of Tyrol, and has closer transport and cultural links with Carinthia.

The earliest inhabitants of what is now Kärnten (Carinthia) were the Celtic Carnuni. In the 1st century AD it was part of the Roman province of Noricum, and in the 6th century was overrun by the Slav tribe of the Carantani, from whom it probably took its name. Although Carinthia belonged to the Habsburgs from 1335, a Slav national minority has survived in the area to this day. After World War I the newly formed state of Yugoslavia tried to annex part of Carinthia from the defeated Austro-Hungarian Empire, but a plebiscite kept the region with Austria. The beauty of its landscape and its pleasant, Mediterranean climate attract many foreign visitors to Carinthia, and numerous Austrians also have second homes here. The most scenic route in the Austrian Alps, the Grossglockner Hochalpenstrasse, separates Carinthia from the East Tyrol, passing through Salzburger Land. Carinthia's two main towns are its capital Klagenfurt, and Villach.

After World War I, the southern part of Tyrol (Südtirol) became an autonomous province of Italy. Thus, geographically isolated from other parts of the Tyrol, East Tyrol (Osttirol) grew closer to its Carinthian neighbour than it was to the Tyrolean administration in Innsbruck. The entire province is surrounded by high mountain ranges and much of it is home to the Hohe Tauern National Park. The administrative centre of East Tyrol is Lienz.

A giant relief model of the province of Carinthia in the Schillerpark pavilion in Villach (see p278)

◄ Impressive view from the 2,572 m (8,438 ft) high Edelweissspitze, Hohe Tauern National Park

Exploring Carinthia and East Tyrol

High mountain peaks that descend right down to expansive lakes make these southernmost regions of Austria a paradise for visitors. Excellent on-shore facilities attract water sports enthusiasts, while the mountain glaciers enable committed skiers to enjoy the slopes even in summer. The loveliest parts of the region are the scenic route of Grossglockner Hochalpenstrasse and the Hohe Tauern National Park. While Carinthia is a lake district, East Tyrol is an inaccessible region of high mountains. In winter, cars need to be properly equipped, and not all roads are passable.

The Hohe Tauern National Park, one of the great attractions of the region

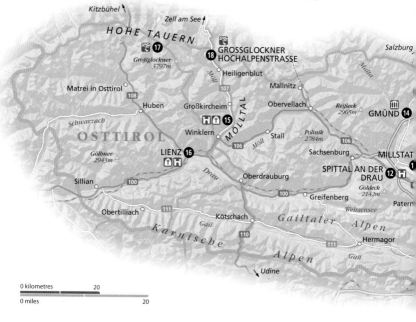

A horse-drawn coach, a Roman relief on Maria Saal Wallfahrtskirche

Key

▬▬ Motorway

▬ Major road

▭▭ Minor road

— Scenic route

-▪- Main railway

— Minor railway

▬▬ International border

▭▭ Province border

△ Summit

Getting There

Villach, in Carinthia, is one of Austria's most important road transport hubs. The southern motorway which comes from Vienna passes through Villach and Klagenfurt, Carinthia's capital, which also has a small passenger airport. The easiest way to reach Lienz, in East Tyrol, is via Carinthia. Road and railway tunnels through the mountain ranges provide convenient transport links.

A church in Gratschach, at the foot of Landskron

The marvellous library in the abbey of St Paul im Lavanttal

Sights at a Glance

1. St Paul im Lavanttal
2. Völkermarkt
3. *Klagenfurt pp274–7*
4. Maria Saal
5. Hochosterwitz
6. Magdalensberg
7. St Veit an der Glan
8. Gurk
9. Friesach
11. Villach
12. Spittal an der Drau
13. Millstatt
14. Gmünd
15. Mölltal
16. Lienz
17. *Hohe Tauern National Park pp282–3*

Excursions

10. Around Wörthersee
18. Grossglockner Hochalpenstrasse

Late 15th-century fresco in the abbey church, St Paul im Lavanttal

❶ St Paul im Lavanttal

Road map E5. 🏔 3,400. 🚌 🚉
ℹ Platz St Blasien 1 (04357) 201722.

On the banks of the Lavant river stands one of the largest churches in Austria, the **Benedictine Abbey of St Paul**. Within the abbey complex is a well-preserved Romanesque church. The apse is decorated with reliefs showing the Adoration of the Magi and the enthroned Christ. Frescoes behind the main altar depict the founders of the abbey and various saints.

The abbey museum also houses many magnificent works of art, including early chasubles, an 11th-century cross-shape reliquary that once belonged to Queen Adelaide, and an art collection with paintings by Peter Paul Rubens and Martin Johann Schmidt, and superb woodcuts by Albrecht Dürer and Rembrandt.

🏛 **Benedictine Abbey of St Paul**
Hauptstrasse 1. **Tel** (04357) 2019-10.
Open May–Oct: 10am–5pm daily.
🛇 🏛 🅿

❷ Völkermarkt

Road map E5. 🏔 11,000. 🚌
ℹ Hauptplatz 1 (04232) 257147.

This town lies on the banks of a reservoir created by damming the Drau river, 25 km (16 miles) east of the Carinthian capital,

Klagenfurt. It grew up around the bridge across the Drau and the 12th-century church of St Rupert, whose Romanesque tower still rises above the town.

The **Kirche St Magdalena** (church of Mary Magdalene), built in 1240 and altered in the 15th century, has a lovely late-Romanesque west portal. Its interior is late-Gothic, with some earlier features, such as the 14th-century frescoes next to the entrance. In one of the side chapels and in the presbytery, details of late-Gothic frescoes can be seen.

In Völkermarkt's Hauptplatz stands a former ducal palace, now the seat of the local authorities, and an arcaded late-Gothic town hall.

The Romanesque portal of Kirche St Magdalena in Völkermarkt

❸ Klagenfurt

See pp274–7.

❹ Maria Saal

Road map E5. 🏔 3,800. 🚌 🚉
ℹ Am Platzl 7 (04223) 2214.

The first church was erected at Maria Saal in the 8th century, and a secondary Christianization was conducted from here, which is why it became known as the cradle of Carinthia. The pilgrimage church, built in 1430–56, has a stone statue of the Virgin Mary in the high altar from 1420. On the outer walls of the church are two remarkable Roman reliefs, one depicting the cart of Death, the other showing Achilles pulling the body of Hector behind the chariot. The relief on the south wall, showing the Coronation of the Virgin Mary, is the work of Hans Valkenauer.

Opposite the church is a late-Gothic octagonal mortuary and the cemetery chapel. It has beautiful 15th-century vault frescoes with the family tree of Jesus, as well as a late-Gothic altar with scenes from the life of St Mary and an altar of St George slaying the dragon. The Sachsen-Kapelle (Saxon Chapel) is devoted to St Modestus, who founded the church and whose tombstone has survived to this day.

Archaeological excavations near Maria Saal, at the site of the Roman town of Virunum, the capital of Noricum, have yielded relics including the Bronze-Age carved stone throne of the Princes of Carinthia (see p42).

❺ Hochosterwitz

Road map E5. **Tel** (04213) 34597.
Open Apr, Oct: 10am–5pm;
May–Sep: 9am–6pm. 🚲 🎫
🌐 burg-hochosterwitz.com

The fortress of Hochosterwitz, one of the symbols of Carinthia, perches on a rock 160 m (525 ft) high and is clearly visible from afar. Although the origins of the castle can be traced back to Roman times, it was built in the 16th century by Domenico dell'Allio.

The present fortress is the result of Renaissance remodelling of earlier Romanesque and Gothic structures. A fief from the mid-16th century, it later became the property of the Khevenhüller family, who own it to this day. Both fortress and fortifications are open to visitors; the access road runs in a loop between the old walls, passing through 14 gates. There is also a local museum.

The turreted fortress of Hochosterwitz is said to have inspired Walt Disney's animated version of *Snow White*.

The slopes of Magdalensberg, site of fascinating archaeological finds

❻ Magdalensberg

Road map E5. 🏔 3,300. 𝒊 Deinsdorf 10, Pischeldorf (04224) 2213.

On top of Magdalene Hill, rising 1,056 m (3,465 ft) from the Glan valley, are the remains of a town believed to be ancient Noricum, dating from the late-Celtic and early-Roman periods. Numerous finds, fragments of statues and the remains of old altars testify to the overlapping nature of Celtic and Roman cultures, with some later Christian additions. Below the summit are the scant remains of a Roman temple and

secular buildings dating from the 1st century AD. In spring and summer, the finds can be viewed in the open-air archaeological park and in the museum.

There is a small church on top of Magdalensberg, with a three-headed stone statue in the nave. This, as well as the hilltop location of the church, indicate the pagan, Celtic origins of the area.

❼ St Veit an der Glan

Road map E5. 🏔 12,500. 🚌 🚉
𝒊 Hauptplatz 23 (0664) 88736032.

From 1174 to 1518, St Veit an der Glan was the seat of the dukes of Spanheim, who ruled Carinthia during the Middle Ages; it then lost its position to Klagenfurt.

Many historic buildings are preserved in the old town around Hauptplatz, including the beautifully decorated **Rathaus** (town hall) of 1468, altered in the Baroque style. It has a lovely 16th-century arcaded courtyard. The 12th- century **Pfarrkirche St Veit** (parish church of St Vitus) contains stone carvings from various periods; the altars are made in the Baroque style.

The most recent symbol of St Veit is the unusual Kunsthotel Fuchspalast, a modern hotel built in 1998 to designs by the outstanding artist, Ernst Fuchs. It is themed around the signs of the zodiac. Also worth a visit is Museum St Veit, which covers the history of the local railways.

Baroque stuccowork on the Rathaus façade, St Veit an der Glan

❽ Gurk

Road map E5. 🏔 1,300. 🚌 𝒊 Dr. Schnerichstrasse 12 (04266) 812527.

Gurk, the former ecclesiastical capital of Carinthia, is dominated by a cathedral church, built in 1140–1200 by Bishop Roman and one of the most outstanding achievements of Austrian Romanesque architecture. The Gothic vestibule is adorned by stained-glass windows (1340) and Gothic frescoes. The original main portal and door have carved and painted Romanesque medallions. Inside it is a startling combination of Romanesque and Gothic, with net vaulting and a Baroque main altar. The striking crypt is supported by 100 columns. The cathedral houses the **Diözesanmuseum**, which exhibits Austria's largest collection of church furnishings as well as many early sacred art objects.

🏛 **Diözesanmuseum**
Domplatz 11. **Tel** (04266) 8236.
Open May–Oct: 10am– 6pm daily. 📷 at 3pm daily Jul & Aug.

The medieval fortress of Hochosterwitz, one of the symbols of Carinthia

❸ Klagenfurt: Street-by-Street

Situated at the eastern end of Wörthersee, the warmest lake in Austria, Klagenfurt, the attractive provincial capital of Carinthia, is an important trade centre and transport hub founded in the 12th century. In 1544, it was almost entirely destroyed by fire and had to be rebuilt. Reconstruction was undertaken mainly by Italian architects and it is highly reminiscent of Italian towns in style. In the 16th century, Klagenfurt was the centre of the Counter-Reformation. During the Baroque period it was extended and partially rebuilt, although most of its historic buildings date from an earlier era. Its historic centre is the district around Alter Platz (Old Square).

Stadtpfarrkirche St Egid
This Baroque church was built on the site of an earlier church destroyed by an earthquake in 1692. Its spire rises to 91 m (299 ft).

URSULINENGASSE

HERRENGASSE

HEILIGEN GEIST PLATZ

WIESBADENER STRASSE

PARADEISERGASSE

Heiligengeistkirche
The church of the Holy Spirit, built in 1355 and altered in 1660, features a beautiful altarpiece by Lorenzo Glaber and an interesting Baroque pulpit.

The square is the site of a modern bus station.

★ Landhaus
The 16th-century Landhaus boasts a lovely galleried inner courtyard and a magnificent heraldic hall with ceiling paintings by Josef Ferdinand Fromiller.

Key

— Suggested route

```
0 metres        75
0 yards         75
```

For hotels and restaurants in this region see p299 and p325

Altes Rathaus
One of the most attractive sights is the galleried courtyard of the 17th-century former town hall. Once known as Welzer Palace, now as Rosenberg Palace, it was the first seat of the Klagenfurt town authorities.

Bamberger Haus

VISITORS' CHECKLIST

Practical Information
Road map E5.
🚹 85,000. 🚻 Rathaus, Neuer Platz 1 (0463) 5372271.
🗓 Benediktiner Market (every day). Pfarrplatz, for organic produce (Fri). 🎪 Klagenfurter Stadtfest (end Aug).
W klagenfurt.at

Transport
✈ Annabichl.
🚌 🚎

Dragon Fountain
In Neuer Platz (New Square) is a fountain with the mythical Lindwurm dragon, created by Ulrich Vogelsang in 1593; a town symbol, it has found its way into the Klagenfurt coat of arms.

KRAMERGASSE

ALTER PLATZ

BURGGASSE

NEUER PLATZ

PARADEISERGASSE

Viktringerhof

Gasthaus Zum goldenen Brunnen

8.-MAI-STRASSE

10.-OKTOBER-STRASSE

LIDMANSKY GASSE

KARFREIT STRASSE

★ Dom St Peter und Paul
The Cathedral of St Peter and St Paul, originally built as a Protestant church, was taken over and altered by the Jesuits in 1604, and in 1727 it was completely rebuilt after a major fire. The high altar (1752) is the work of Daniel Gran.

Market in the historic Old Town of Klagenfurt

Exploring Klagenfurt

Klagenfurt lies south of the Glan river, 30 km (19 miles) from the Slovenian and 60 km (37 miles) from the Italian borders. Its Old Town, laid out on a rectangular grid, extends between Hauptplatz, Alter Platz and Neuer Platz, 4 km (2 miles) from Wörthersee. The road to the lake runs through Europapark and the Minimundus exhibition.

🏛 Landhaus

Landhaus. **Tel** (0463) 577570.
Open 9am–4pm Mon–Fri, 9am–2pm Sat. **Closed** Mon Nov–Mar. 🎨 📷 📹

The Landhaus, the present seat of the Carinthian provincial government, stands on the western side of Alter Platz. Commissioned by the Carinthian

The attractive, galleried courtyard of the Landhaus

estates, it was built in 1574 on the site of a former ducal palace to designs by Antonio Verda of Lugano and Franz Freymann. The resulting structure is Klagenfurt's most important secular building and a Renaissance gem, with two symmetrically spaced spires, beyond which is an open two-storey, galleried courtyard. The domes crowning the two towers and the decorated elevation date from 1740.

The most beautiful room in the Landhaus, the Wappensaal (heraldic hall), dates from the same period. It is almost entirely the work of Josef Ferdinand Fromiller, the foremost Carinthian artist of the day. The walls of the hall display hundreds of Carinthian coats of arms, while the ceiling painting shows the Carinthian nobles paying homage to Charles VI; the flat ceiling is made to look vaulted in this *trompe l'oeil*. The north wing of the Landhaus houses the remains of the armoury.

Many old buildings have survived in the town centre nearby, including the Town Hall with a galleried Renaissance courtyard.

The Trinity Column in Alter Platz, heart of the shopping district, dates from 1680; the crescent and cross were added after the victory over the Turks (1683).

🏛 Neuer Platz

Neuer Platz.

The square is dominated by Lindwurmbrunnen (Dragon Fountain), whose winged beast has become the symbol and crest of the town. The dragon was carved from a single block of stone by Ulrich Vogelsang, in 1593, while the giant who eventually saved the town was added later by Michael Hönel. The unveiling of this monument in 1636 was a great public event.

The Town Hall, formerly the Palace of the Rosenberg family, has been the seat of the municipal authorities since 1918. Built in 1582 and altered in 1650, it has an interesting Renaissance stairway. Originally outside the town walls surrounding Spanheim Castle, it became the centre of the new Renaissance town.

In 1764, Neuer Platz was the site of the first monument to be erected to Maria Theresa in Austria. The square is lined on all sides by many 16th- and 17th-century mansions with beautiful façades.

The pretty 17th-century Old Town Hall in Alter Platz

🏛 Dom St Peter und Paul

Domplatz. **Tel** (0463) 54950.
Open 7am–7pm daily.

Klagenfurt's cathedral was built in 1578 as a Protestant church by Klagenfurt's Mayor, Christoph Windisch. In 1604, the church was taken over by the Jesuits, and was elevated to the rank of cathedral in 1787, when the bishopric was transferred from Gurk to Klagenfurt. In 1723, following a fire, the late-Gothic interior was rebuilt in the Baroque style. The cathedral was badly damaged in World

For hotels and restaurants in this region see p299 and p325

War II, during the 1944 bombing raids, but has been restored to its former splendour. Rich stucco decoration on the walls and ceiling blend elements of various architectural styles into one successful composition. The vault frescoes were painted by Josef Ferdinand Fromiller, while the gallery stucco was the work of Kilian Pittner. Daniel Gran painted the main altarpiece in 1752. The vestry holds the last work by Johann Martin Schmidt.

Statue on the side altar in the Dom

Landesmuseum Kärnten
Museumgasse 2. **Tel** (050536) 30599. **Closed** for refurbishment until 2018.

The collections of the Regional Museum, founded in 1844, illustrate several centuries of history in Carinthia as well as its art, rooted in Celtic and Roman cultures. The floor mosaic of a young Dionysus surrounded by hedonistic satyrs is a beautiful example of Roman art. One of the museum's curiosities is a "dragon's skull" (in fact a rhinoceros), found nearby, which served as a model for the fountain dragon in Neuer Platz. Its discovery gave credence to the legend that a dragon once tormented the town, demanding the sacrifice of animals and humans.

The museum also holds many works of art and handicraft. One of its most interesting exhibits is a carved altar from the St Veit school. In the park in front is a small collection of stones, including some Roman stone statues.

Minimundus
Villacher Strasse 241. **Tel** (0463) 21194. **Open** Mar–Apr: 9am–6pm daily; May, Jun & Sep: 9am–7pm daily; Jul & Aug: 9am–8pm daily (until 11pm Wed).
minimundus.at

Europapark, a large green space west of Klagenfurt, is home to this theme park, with over 170 miniature models of the world's most famous buildings. They are crafted in minute detail to a scale of 1:25, and have been added to since 1959, when a children's charity, *Rettet das Kind*, set up the first architectural miniatures near Wörthersee. All the profits go to the foundation. Among the models from all continents are Rome's St Peter's Basilica, Paris's Eiffel Tower, London's Big Ben, Brussels's Atomium, Agra's Taj Mahal and New York's Statue of Liberty. Not surprisingly, Austria's own historic buildings, such as the Stephansdom in Vienna, are heavily represented. Many other achievements and inventions are also represented by miniature models, for example Austrian watermills, Mississippi paddle steamers and the earliest steam trains.

Environs: The town of Klagenfurt is surrounded by lakes and mountains; the closest is **Wörthersee** *(see pp280–81)*, which gave the Carinthian capital its byname, Rose of the Wörthersee. **Viktring Abbey**, 6 km (4 miles) southwest of Klagenfurt, belonged to the Cistercian monks who arrived in Viktring in 1142. The many castles and palaces in the vicinity testify to the region's prosperity. Sights worth visiting include the fortified castle of **Mageregg** (1590, altered in 1841), surrounded by a zoological park for local animals. The lovely 12th-century **Schloss Hallegg**, which has preserved its old turret, was remodelled in the 16th century and turned into a Renaissance residence with two inner courtyards.

Stained-glass window in the Cistercian Abbey in Viktring

Models of Salzburg Cathedral and Ort Castle, Minimundus

❾ Friesach

Road map E5. 🏔 5,000. 🚌 🚆
ℹ️ Fürstenhofplatz 1 (04268) 2213-40.

Friesach is Carinthia's oldest town, with a history going back to 860, when the nearby fortress of **Petersberg** was founded. Traces of the town's glorious past have survived to this day, including a moated town wall, 820 m (2,690 ft) long, and several castle towers. Of the fortress itself, only the six-storey keep on Petersberg survives. In the former chapel room, on the fourth floor, the remains of 12th-century frescoes can be seen.

Adjacent to the fortress is **Peterskirche** (church of St Peter), which has a Gothic altar (1525) with a Romanesque statue of the Madonna (c.1200). The **Dominikanerkloster** (Dominican abbey) from 1217 holds a 14th-century Madonna, a wooden crucifix (1300) and other medieval artifacts. The church of St Blaise, built by the Teutonic Knights in 1213 on the ruins of an earlier church, has some original 12th-century frescoes.

❿ Around Wörthersee

See pp280–81.

⓫ Villach

Road map E5. 🏔 60,000. 🚌 🚆
ℹ️ Bahnhofstrasse 3 (04242) 205 2900.

Carinthia's second largest town is an important tourist centre, health resort and transport hub. The earliest archaeological finds testifying to the

region's colonization date from Celtic times. It has a small old town. **Stadtpfarrkirche St Jakob** (parish church of St Jacob) was built after a powerful earthquake in 1348, and later rebuilt. Its most notable features are the Renaissance chapels of the Görz-Dietrichstein and the Khevenhüller families and the 95-m (312-ft) high tower. The **Municipal Museum** (open May–Oct) in a 16th-century building at No. 38 Widmanngasse, covers regional history, archaeology and art. In **Schillerpark** you can see an astonishing 3D-map of Carinthia, at a scale of 1:10,000.

Environs: Lovely 14th-century frescoes and a late-Gothic altar (c.1520) can be seen in the church of **Maria Gail**, 3 km (2 miles) southeast of Villach.

⓬ Spittal an der Drau

Road map D5. 🏔 16,000. 🚌 🚆
ℹ️ Schloss Porcia, Burgplatz 1 (04762) 5650220.

The town of Spittal is dominated by the Goldeck peak (2,142 m/ 7,028 ft). The history of the town began in the 12th century, when Count Ortenburg founded a church and a *Spittal* or hospice on this site. The town owes its Renaissance character to the vast 16th-century **Schloss Porcia**, which is also known as Salamanca Palace after its builder, the Spanish nobleman Gabriel of

Schloss Porcia's galleries, Spittal an der Drau

Salamanca. The Porcia family, who owned the palace from 1662 until 1918, added to its decor while preserving the original architecture based on Spanish Renaissance palaces. Its most beautiful aspect is the galleried inner courtyard; be sure to have a close look at the rich decorations of its individual storeys. The well-preserved palace now houses a museum of folk art on the two top floors.

Environs: On a hill near the village of St Peter in Holz, 5 km (3 miles) northwest of Spittal an der Drau, stand the ruins of an Early Christian church and the **Römermuseum Teurnia** (open May–Oct). The hill was settled first by Celts, then by Romans, and the museum exhibits many small items, scripts and coins.

⓭ Millstatt

Road map D5. 🏔 3,400. 🚌 ℹ️
Rathaus, Marktplatz 8 (04766) 2023.

The greatest attraction in Millstatt, on the northern shore of Millstätter See, is a **Benedictine Abbey** dating from 1070. From then until 1469 it was run by the Hirsau Benedictines; later the monastery and church passed into the hands of the Order of the Knights of St George, and from 1598 until 1773 it was owned by the Jesuits. The most beautiful part of the abbey is its Renaissance

The former thermal bath complex in Villach

courtyard surrounded by two-storey arcades. This was built in the 16th century, when the abbey was run by the Order of St George. The monastery is linked with the church by a 12th-century cloister whose pillars, decorated by medieval carvers, display a grotesque world of animals, plants and faces. Even older, dating back to the Carolingian period, are the magical ornaments on the old buildings, possibly representing some pagan spells. An eye-catching feature inside the church is the Romanesque portal, made by master craftsman Rudger in 1170. In the side chapels are the red marble tombs of the Order's Grand Masters. Also worth seeing is a fresco from 1519, depicting the Last Judgement.

Courtyard of the Benedictine Abbey in Millstatt

⑭ Gmünd

Road map D5. 🏔 2,600. 🚌
ℹ️ Hauptplatz 20 (04732) 221514.

In the 12th century, the Archbishops of Salzburg who ruled Gmünd began to encircle the town with mighty fortifications, many of which survive to this day, including old gate turrets and bastions. Two castles tower over the town: the older one, **Altes Schloss**, was destroyed by a fire in 1886, but was restored and is now used as a cultural centre. It was commissioned in 1506 by Archbishop Leonhard von Keutschach. The **Neues Schloss** (New Castle) was built in 1651–4 by Count Christoph von Lodron. Today

An alley in Gmünd, famous for its former Porsche factory

the former castle keep houses a school and a concert hall.

The Austrian-born designer Ferdinand Porsche worked in Gmünd in 1944–50, and 52 of the classic "365" models were hand-made locally. The most famous models and construction frames are displayed in the **Porsche Museum**.

🏛 **Porsche Museum**
Gmünd. **Tel** (04732) 2471.
Open 15 May–15 Oct: 9am–6pm, 16 Oct–14 May: 10am–4pm.
🌐 porschemuseum.at.

⑮ Mölltal

Road map D5. 🚌 🚆

The Möll river, a tributary of the Drau and overshadowed by Grosses Reisseck peak, runs along the Mölltal, a valley whose upper reaches form a natural extension of the magnificent road known as Grossglockner Hochalpenstrasse. The river meanders scenically between the high mountain peaks. The road along the valley, starting in Winklern, is an important transit route between Carinthia at one end and Lienz and the Dolomites at the other, winding its way between old mills, waterfalls and huts.

The parish of **Grosskirchheim** was once a major mining district, and the 16th-century **Schloss Grosskirchheim** now houses an interesting mining museum.

In **Döllach** you can see the interesting late-Gothic church

of St Andrew, and in **Sagritz** the originally late-Gothic church of St George. **Schloss Falkenstein**, near Obervellach, has an unusual tower with a wooden top.

⑯ Lienz

Road map D5. 🏔 12,000. 🚌 🚆
ℹ️ Europaplatz 1 (050212) 400.

The town has been the capital of East Tyrol since 1919 but its origins date back to the Middle Ages. The **Stadtpfarrkirche St Andrä** (parish church of St Andrew), a triple-nave Gothic basilica, was built in the 15th century; western sections include parts of an earlier Romanesque church. Today, following many alterations, the church is predominantly Baroque in style. Inside are a fresco by Josef Adam von Mölk and a high altar by Franz Engel. The **Franziskanerkirche** (Franciscan church), built around 1350, features original 15th-century frescoes and a Gothic Pietà standing by a side altar.

High above the town sits **Schloss Bruck**, the seat of the Görz Counts, built between the 13th and 16th centuries. The castle has a tall Romanesque turret; its main body contains a Romanesque chapel with 13th- and 15th-century frescoes. Today it also houses a regional museum with Gothic and Baroque artifacts and paintings by the local Tyrolean artist Albin Egger-Lienz (1868–1926).

The Romanesque tower of Schloss Bruck in Lienz

⑩ Around Wörthersee

Wörthersee is the warmest lake in Austria; in summer, the temperature of its waters reaches 24–28°C. Numerous resorts are lined along its shores; the largest of these is the modern, brash town of Velden, with its casino. Krumpendorf and the exclusive resort of Pörtschach lie on the easily accessible northern shore; quiet Reifnitz is on the southern shore. Not far from Wörthersee are other, smaller lakes, including Ossiacher See, in a scenic mountain setting. To the south, the Carinthian lake district extends along the Slovenian border, surrounded by the snowy peaks of the enchanting Karawanken Alps.

① Ossiach

The former Benedictine Abbey in Ossiach and its church were built in the 11th-century and altered in the early-Baroque style. The oldest monastery in Carinthia, it was burned down by Turkish invaders and is now a hotel.

② Schloss Landskron

Not much remains of the original medieval castle, but the ruins are never-theless impressive. Today, the bird of prey show, held on the slopes of the castle hill, and "Monkey Mountain" are the greatest attractions nearby.

0 kilometres   4
0 miles   4

Bodensdorf

94   L49

Spittal am der Drau

②

83   A2   E66

Villach   Drawa   83

A11   E61   ③

③ Rosegg

This small village between Wörthersee and Faaker See has a beautiful 19th-century landscaped wildlife park, attempting to recreate a natural habitat for its resident animals and birds.

Tarvisio   Faaker See

Jesenice ↓

④ Schloss Velden

The well-known, swanky resort on the shores of Wörthersee boasts an early-Baroque castle, originally built by the Khevenhüller family, which featured as setting for a popular Austrian TV series. It is now an elegant hotel.

Tips for Drivers

Length of route: 45 km (28 miles).
Stopping-off points: There are several resorts around the lake offering restaurants and hotels; Velden is the largest resort.
Further attractions: Wildpark in Rosegg. **Tel** (04274) 52357. **Open** Apr–Oct.

⑤ Maria Wörth
On a promontory that extends far into the lake stands a 12th-century church built on earlier foundations and featuring original 11th-century Romanesque frescoes.

⑥ Wörthersee
Wörthersee is Austria's warmest lake and its shores have become known as the Austrian Riviera. Entertainment here ranges from relaxation to swimming and all sorts of water sports.

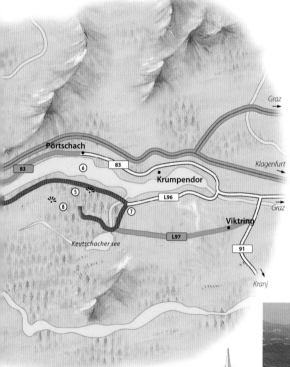

⑦ Reifnitz
Established as early as 1195, this was once one of the mightiest castles in Carinthia. All that remains today are the main body and the castle keep.

Key

- ▬▬▬ Motorway
- ▬▬▬ Suggested route
- ▬▬▬ Scenic route
- ▬▬▬ Other road
- ∙∙∙∙∙ River, lake
- ✸ Viewpoint

⑧ Pyramidenkogel
From the top of the hill Pyramidenkogel, above the lake, there are stunning vistas of the entire area, including Wörthersee itself, with the Karawanken Alps to the south, and several beautiful neighbouring lakes.

⑰ Hohe Tauern National Park

The beautiful area around Austria's highest peak, the Grossglockner, is a national park. The unique landscape, flora and fauna of the region, the Hohe Tauern, is jointly protected by the provincial governments of Salzburger Land, Tyrol and Carinthia. The Hohe Tauern has more than 300 peaks rising above 3,000 m (9,850 ft) and several glaciers – the Pasterze is the longest and most spectacular. This whole national park area is protected by law and visitors are asked to keep to the marked trails. On its edges are many popular tourist resorts such as Bad Gastein, Kaprun, Zell am See and East Tyrol's capital, Lienz.

Artificial Lakes
One of the great attractions of the Hohe Tauern is its many picturesque reservoirs, gathering the crystal-clear meltwaters from the glaciers high above each spring.

★ Pasterze Glacier
The largest glacier in the Eastern Alps is 10 km (6 miles) long and covers an area of 19.5 sq km (7.6 sq miles). Its far end can be reached by stairs carved into the ice or by cable car.

★ Grossglockner
Austria's highest peak (3,797 m/12,457 ft) towers at the border between Carinthia and East Tyrol, a crucifix marking the summit.

Grossglockner
3797

3368

3564

3401

Traunee

3331

2548

3247

3797

Key

━━ Major road

━━ Minor road

···· Cable car

–·– Provincial border

━━ River

✳ Viewpoint

Edelweissspitze

Edelweissspitze, 2,572 m/ 8,438 ft high, is the central peak of the Fusch-Rauriser range. There are amazing views from the viewing tower at the summit.

VISITORS' CHECKLIST

Practical Information
Road map D4.
[i] Nationalpark Hohe Tauern, A-9971 Matrei in Osttirol, Kirchplatz 2 (04875) 5112-0.
[w] hohetauern.com

Alpine Flora

An impressive range of Alpine plantlife, such as this aromatic Alpine tansy (Tanacetum) can be seen in the park at different altitudes.

Zell am see
↑

erleiten

▲ 2924

▲ **Edelweissspitze**
2572

▲ 2588

▲ 3006

▲ 3103

Schareck
2604

107

Heiligenblut

↓ *Lienz*

Cable Car to Schareck

Schareck peak (2,606 m/8,550 ft) in the Goldberggruppe (Gold Mountains) can be reached by cable car, with one change en route. Schareck is an excellent starting point for excursions into the upper mountains.

Alpine Ibex

This protected species inhabits the upper regions of the Alps. It is easiest to see them in the Ferleiten Reserve *(see p284)*.

0 kilometres   2
0 miles   2

⑱ Grossglockner Hochalpenstrasse

Traversing the Hohe Tauern National Park is the Grossglockner High Alpine Road, regarded as one of the world's most beautiful mountain routes. Completed in 1935, the road was built along the old mountain passes between Bruck in Salzburger Land and Heiligenblut in Carinthia. Measuring 47.8 km (29.7 miles) long, it forms part of a north–south route from Bavaria to Italy. Branching off the main road are two trails leading to viewpoints. The highest point of the route is Hochtor, at 2,505 m (8,218 ft), the lowest is Bruck, at 755 m (2,477 ft). With the 1.5 km (1 mile) rise in altitude, the flora also changes.

⑤ Hochtor
The Hochtor (High Gate) is the highest point along the Grossglockner Hochalpenstrasse. Here the road runs through a tunnel measuring 2.3 km (1.5 miles) in length.

⑥ Fuscher Törl
The road winds its way above steep ravines, offering splendid views on both sides of this ridge to the Goldberggruppe (Gold Mountains).

⑦ Viewing Tower on Edelweissspitze
The tower built on top of Edelweissspitze (2,572 m/8,438 ft) affords fantastic views of the Grossglockner to the west and the Goldberggruppe to the east.

⑧ Alpine Naturschau Museum
Situated at an altitude of 2,260 m (7,415 ft) is a small museum of the local flora, fauna and ecology, offering free admission to visitors. In Ferleiten, to the north, is an Alpine animal reserve.

Key

▬▬ Suggested route

══ Other road

- - - Cable car

⋯⋯ River, lake

• ▬ Provincial border

❋ Viewpoint

④ Schareck

The Schareck peak, part of the Goldberg massif, was once mined for gold. From here visitors can see the Schildberg peak and the looming Grossglockner massif to the west, as well as the superb high-altitude ski slopes.

Zell am See

Ferleiten

Piffkar

107

8

⑦

⑥

⑤

④

① **107**

Lienz

Tips for Drivers

Length of the route: 40 km (25 miles).

Stopping-off points: You can stay at one of the mountain hostels, and many restaurants also offer accommodation.

Additional information: The route is a toll road, open to cars only from May to November.

③ Observatory

The Swarovski Tower, built in 1998 above Franz-Josefs-Höhe, enables visitors to view the magnificent Alpine landscape using the latest optical equipment.

0 kilometres 2
0 miles 2

① Heiligenblut

The church in Heiligenblut was built in the 15th century by monks from Admont. Inside is a beautiful altar from the workshop of Michael Pacher, and a richly carved tabernacle said to house a phial of Christ's blood.

② Franz- Josefs-Höhe

Along the Gletscherstrasse (Glacier Road) is a viewing terrace at 2,369 m (7,772 ft), giving fabulous views of both Grossglockner and the Pasterze Glacier.

TRAVELLERS' NEEDS

WHERE TO STAY

Austria has a highly developed tourist infrastructure, making it extremely easy to find accommodation to suit one's personal preference. There are numerous hotels and pensions, offering varied standards and services at a range of prices. One can also find friendly private lodgings and good campsites. Most hotels enjoy great locations or are well connected to the city centre. The rooms are mostly well furnished and comfortable, and the staff kind and courteous. Away from towns, where transport is not always readily available, hotel staff may even offer to pick up travellers without cars from railway or coach stations. A list of recommended hotels is given on pages 292–9.

A hotel complex in Kampl, in a typically scenic location

The Range of Hotels

Hotels and pensions are awarded between one and five stars, as in other countries, with the number of stars depending on the facilities offered by the hotel. However, small hotels and pensions often have a more inviting atmosphere despite fewer overall facilities.

The choice of hotel is usually determined by what one intends to do while visiting Austria. Visitors who are mainly interested in sightseeing and are likely to be constantly on the move may prefer to stay in modest private lodges or pensions. Winter sports enthusiasts need to look for hotels that offer the appropriate facilities. Alternatively, for peace and quiet, or personal health and wellbeing, visitors can choose from numerous, well-equipped spa hotels. Whatever the plan, there is always a perfect accommodation option available here.

How to Book

As in other countries, hotel accommodation can be booked directly by phone, email or through a website. Most local tourist offices can help with reservations, and will also advise on the kind of specialist accommodation options available in their area.

It is generally advisable to book in advance, particularly for the summer months, Christmas and Easter.

International and Austrian Chain Hotels

In addition to well-known and popular hotel chains, such as **Mercure** and **Hilton**, the **50plus Hotels**, which mostly offer spa facilities and access to various health treatments, are also worth considering. The largest clusters of such hotels are to be found in the vicinity of Salzburg and in the Vorarlberg province. Other hotel chains include Romantik-Hotels, Grand Hotel, Marriott, Bristol, Austria Trend, Hotel-Post, Renaissance and Ibis. Chain hotels tend to have dependably high standards and good service.

A majestic hotel set in the mountains of Bad Gastein

Hotels in Historic Buildings

Visitors looking for something special beyond the usual hotel experience should consider a stay at one of the many medieval castles that have been converted into hotels. Often the name *Schlosshotel* is used to indicate that an establishment is a hotel within a palace. Some excellent examples of such converted fortresses or palace hotels are

The impressive grand lobby of the Imperial Hotel, Vienna (*see p294*)

◀ Café in the Cupola Hall of the Kunsthistorisches Museum, Vienna

Schloss Hotel Dürnstein (see p295) in the Wachau region, the lakeside Schloss Freisitz Roith (see p296) in Gmunden and Schloss Mönchstein (see p298) in Salzburg. Each of these offers up-to-date accommodation facilities in luxurious surroundings. All of them are richly furnished and some even exude the romantic atmosphere of a bygone era. Health-spa resort Schloss Fuschl (see p297), for example, is a set in a sumptuous former palace near Salzburg.

Prices at such historic establishments are often higher than those demanded by other well-known hotels. Information about accommodation in converted palaces can be obtained from local tourist offices, which have all the relevant brochures, catalogues and booking details, as well as on the **Schlosshotels und Herrenhäuser** website.

The cosy, candle-lit interior of the Hotel Weismayr in Bad Gastein (see p297)

Hotel Prices

The price of hotel accommodation is dictated not only by the category of the hotel, but also by its location and the local events at the time. Differences may be significant, even within the same category. Accommo-

Sign of the Golden Eagle in Innsbruck

dation in Vienna, Salzburg and Graz is often expensive, and many hotels and pensions situated in prime locations are overpriced. It is possible to cut costs by staying outside the main town centres; in Vienna, for example, one can expect to pay approximately a fifth less for a room in an establishment just outside the Ringstrasse, and less further afield. Staying in provincial towns tends to be somewhat cheaper, though these still cover a wide range of prices.

Accommodation will be less expensive for visits outside the main tourist season. For example, visiting a resort specializing in winter sports during the summer

months is cheaper. In the cities, it is also possible to negotiate discounted room rates for weekend visits or longer stays.

Hidden Extras

When booking a room, check in advance if any additional charges, such as Kurtaxe (health spa tax) or for cleaning on departure, will be levied. Generally, prices are inclusive of taxes such as Mehrwertsteuer (VAT), but occasionally these are separate. Breakfast is included in all but

A charming rustic pension in the mountainous region of Lech

the five-star hotels. Other extras to watch out for are charges for off-road parking, especially in the larger cities, unfavourable exchange rates and high costs for making phone calls. For full-board accommodation in a pension, you will need to take the additional cost for lunch and dinner drinks into account, and also allow for a small tip.

Pensions and Gasthöfe

Pensions are widespread and popular in Austria. Less formal than a hotel, they are typically run by a family and usually provide modest accommodation, breakfast and a pleasant ambience – guests often meet the owners, usually friendly and willing to help with travel plans. Most rooms have an en-suite bathroom, some have telephone, TV and a balcony as well. In smaller towns and villages, the owners often invite their guests to social evenings with music, dancing or a barbecue.

A Gasthof is a traditional inn with a restaurant on the ground floor and rooms to rent above. A wide range of establishments are covered under this category, from small, inexpensive, family-run hotels with modestly equipped rooms, to exquisitely restored country inns offering the most luxurious accommodation.

Traditional chalet-style country hotel surrounded by towering peaks

Inexpensive Accommodation

Relatively inexpensive accommodation can often be found in private homes. In attractive tourist areas, it is common for owners of larger villas and private houses to rent rooms to visitors. Vacancies are generally indicated by the sign *Fremdenzimmer* or *Zimmer frei* (rooms available). The standard of furnishing varies; some have en-suite rooms, others come with shared bathrooms. Breakfast may or may not be included in the room price.

There are plenty of back-packer-friendly hostels and *Jugendherbergen* (youth hostels) throughout Austria. Many of them offer double rooms and family rooms as well as simple bunk beds in dorms. Most have high standards, and some are located in old castles, beautiful villas or other historic buildings. Further details are available from **Österreichischer Jugendherbergsverband (ÖJHV)**.

Farm Stays

In rural Austria, most holiday accommodation takes the form of rooms in working *Bauernhöfe* (farms), offering high service standards in traditional and rustic surroundings. Some provide self-catering facilities, in others meals are provided by the farmer, on a similar basis as in pensions, offering *Zimmer mit Frühstück* (bed and breakfast), *Halbpension* (half-board) or *Vollpension* (full-board). The number of rooms available in a *Bauernhof*, and the prices charged, vary but the rooms are of a perfectly acceptable standard. For children from towns and cities it is an ideal opportunity to observe the daily workings of a farm and to have contact with farm animals. There may also be the opportunity to go horse-riding, or hire a bike, boat or fishing tackle, so that a full programme of outdoor activities can be enjoyed by the whole family.

Information on *Bauernhof* holidays with pictures, detailed descriptions and price lists can be obtained from tourist offices. In many provinces such tourist centres also send out free brochures to interested holidaymakers.

Mountain Hostels and Shelters

Mountain hostels and shelters can be found along all the major walking trails. In Vienna, a picturesque hut stands on the banks of the old Danube at 155 m (509 ft); however it is reserved exclusively for groups. Lower Austria has a large number of hostels, some at relatively low altitudes. Travellers can find numerous huts or shelters in the high Alps. These usually have rooms for two or three and sometimes more on a sharing basis; people sleep on simple mattresses. Higher in the mountains and in more remote regions, the huts are basic. If you're planning to hike for several days, book huts through the **Österreichischer Alpenverein (ÖAV)** well in advance. Hostels can provide information on the local hiking trails, current climbing conditions and the weather forecasts.

Depending on the popularity of an area and the season, hostels will be open either all year round or only during the summer months, usually until the end of September or October. Some open only at the weekend, even in summer, or by appointment. Some hostels are closed one day in the week, on the *Ruhetag* (rest day). The ÖAV or the local tourist bureau will be able to advise on timings.

Camping

Travelling with a camping trailer, camper van or just a tent is popular in Austria, and there are dedicated campsites in all the larger towns and popular resorts. Generally of a high standard, sites are equipped with washrooms and kitchens, and they allow caravan owners to exchange gas bottles and use

A caravan site on the shores of Ossiacher See in Carinthia

A mountain hostel near Schöpfl, in the Vienna Woods

washing machines, dishwashers and ironing rooms. Some sites have fixed caravans for hire, and almost all have a play-ground for children. A few sites are also adapted for the needs of differently abled people. The average price is typically €20–40 per day for two people sharing; *Kurtaxe* (health resort tax) may also be charged by some, and the use of showers and electricity may cost extra. Check the **Österreichischer Camping Club** website for further information on campsites.

Travelling with Children

A lot of hotels and pensions in Austria specifically offer facilities for children, with play areas, toys and child-minding services available to guests. Many of these hotels advertise themselves as *Baby und Kinderhotels* (Baby and Child Hotels) in their promotional literature. Local tourist offices will have details on where the nearest ones are.

Some pensions, particularly those aimed at families with children, organize special activities to keep young people engaged. These might include all sorts of sports activities, ranging from skiing, skating and tobog-ganing to horse riding, tennis, canoeing, swimming and cycling.

Recommended Hotels

The lodging options featured in this guide have been selected across a wide price range for their excellent facilities and unique value. They are all representative of their context, be it bustling Vienna, fairytale Salzburg or the placid mountain resorts of the Tyrol. The hotels are listed by area and then by price. They cover a diverse array of accommodation, from simple **pensions** to stunning **boutique** options. There are **family-friendly** guesthouses for those who seek a homely atmosphere and **luxury** hotels that offer all the comfort one needs. Alternatively, one may opt for **spa** hotels to unwind in style or **contemporary** hotels for all the modern comforts. For those looking to get a taste of the traditional there are always **country** guesthouses. The places highlighted as DK Choice are the very best of the pack, chosen for being outstanding in some way. They may be set in historically important buildings, stand in beautiful surroundings, have particularly eco-friendly policies or may just be incredibly charming.

DIRECTORY

Information on Accommodation & Reservations

Austrian Tourism Board
Margaretenstrasse 1, Vienna.
Tel 00800 400 200 00 (free from EU and UK).
W austriatourism.com

Carinthia Information
Völkermarkter Ring 21–23, Klagenfurt.
Tel (0463) 30 00.
W carinthia.at

Lower Austria Information
Niederösterreich Ring 2, Haus C, St Pölten.
Tel (02742) 9000-9000.
W lower-austria.info

Styria Information
St Peter-Hauptstrasse 243, Graz. **Tel** (0316) 4003-0.
W steiermark.com

Tyrol Information
Maria-Theresien-Strasse 55, Innsbruck.
Tel (0512) 72720.
W tyrol.com

Upper Austria Information
Freistädtstrasse 119, Linz.
Tel (0732) 221 022.
W oberoesterreich.at

Vienna Information
Albertinaplatz, Vienna.
Tel (01) 24 555.
W wien.info

Hotel Chains

50plus Hotels
W 50plushotels.at

Hilton
W hilton.com

Mercure
W mercure.com

Hotels in Historic Buildings

Schlosshotels und Herrenhäuser
Austrasse 7, Oberalm.
Tel (06245) 90123.
W schlosshotels.co.at

Youth Hostels

Österreichischer Jugendherbergs-verband (ÖJHV)
Zelinkagasse 12, Vienna.
Tel (01) 533 53 53.
W oejhv.or.at

Mountain Hostels and Shelters

Österreichischer Alpenverein (ÖAV)
Olympiastrsse 37, Innsbruck.
Tel (0512) 59 547-0.
W alpenverein.at

Camping

Österreichischer Camping Club
Schubertring 1–3, Vienna.
Tel (01) 713 61 51.
W campingclub.at

Where to Stay

Vienna

Inner City

Domizil €
Pension Map 2 C4
Schulerstrasse 14, 1010
Tel *(01) 513 31 99*
W hoteldomizil.at
Clean, contemporary rooms in a
great central location close to all
the main historic sights. There's a
generous breakfast buffet of cold
meats, cheeses, pastries and fruit.

Graben Hotel €
Boutique Map 2 B4
Dorotheergasse 3, 1010
Tel *(01) 512 15 31-0*
W kremslehnerhotels.at
Although a bit on the small
side, the rooms in this quaint
hotel are comfortable and well
cared for. The location, right by
Stephansdom, couldn't be better.

Hotel Am Parkring €
Contemporary Map 3 D4
Parkring 12, 1015
Tel *(01) 514 80-0*
W schick-hotels.com
With stunning views that take in
the city's major landmarks, this
hotel boasts very good service
and modern, comfortably
furnished rooms.

Hotel Capricorno €
Contemporary Map 3 D3
Schwedenplatz 3–4, 1010
Tel *(01) 533 31 04-0*
W schick-hotels.com
A buzzing metropolitan hotel
located close to the city's best
nightlife venues. It offers single,
double and family rooms, with
hearty breakfasts for late risers.

Pension Nossek €
Pension Map 2 B4
Graben 17, 1010
Tel *(01) 533 70 41-0*
W pension-nossek.at
Charming, family-run pension set
in a historic building that was
occupied by Mozart for several
months in 1781. The rooms are
decorated with chintzy floral prints.

**Best Western Plus Hotel
Das Tigra** €€
Contemporary Map 2 B3
Tiefer Graben 14–20, 1010
Tel *(01) 533 96 41-0*
W hotel-tigra.at
The bright, modern rooms and
helpful staff at this hotel attract
both tourists and business exe-
cutives alike. Excellent facilities
and a convenient central location.

DK Choice

Hollmann Beletage €€
Boutique Map 2 C3
Köllnerhofgasse 6, 1010
Tel *(01) 961 196-0*
W hollmann-beletage.at
With its sleek tangerine and
granite decor and 25 spacious
rooms boasting an array of
luxury amenities and thoughtful
details, this quirky hotel is a real
find. Mammoth breakfasts,
friendly staff and a sauna are
just some of the many perks
of staying here. The hotel also
has a pretty courtyard – the
perfect place to enjoy an afternoon tea laid on by the hosts.

Hotel Am Stephansplatz €€
Contemporary Map 2 C4
Stephansplatz 9, 1010
Tel *(01) 534 05-0*
W hotelamstephansplatz.at
Staff go out of their way to ensure
you enjoy your time at this chic
design hotel. Request a room on
one of the upper floors for the
great views of Stephansdom and
minimal noise.

**Imperial Riding School
Renaissance Vienna** €€
Historic Map 3 E5
Ungargasse 60, 1030
Tel *(01) 711 75-0*
W marriott.co.uk
This former military riding school,
built in 1850, has been sensitively
converted into a hotel with first-
class facilities. The opulent rooms
hark back to the building's history
but boast all the usual mod cons.

A cosy library with stylish furnishings at
Hollmann Beletage

K&K Palais €€
Contemporary Map 2 C3
Rudolfsplatz 11, 1010
Tel *(01) 533 13 53*
W kkhotels.com
This handsome imperial building
has a stylish interior with
66 contemporary guest rooms
and a bistro decorated in
subdued tones.

Kaiserin Elisabeth €€
Luxury Map 2 C4
Weihburggasse 3, 1010
Tel *(01) 515 26-0*
W kaiserinelisabeth.at
An elegant hotel set in a
historic building dating back to
the 14th century. Beautifully
appointed rooms, friendly staff
and an exceptional location right
in the historic centre.

König von Ungarn €€
Luxury Map 2 C4
Schulerstrasse 10, 1010
Tel *(01) 515 84-0*
W kvu.at
Founded in 1746, this hotel has
welcomed heads of state, artists
and other luminaries. Some
rooms are decorated in a classic
style inspired by the history of
the building and some in a
contemporary style with an array
of state-of-the-art gadgets.

Radisson Blu Style Hotel €€
Boutique Map 2 B4
Herrengasse 12,1010
Tel *(01) 227 80-0*
W radissonblu.com
A first-rate boutique hotel with a
great range of amenities. Chic,
contemporary rooms with plenty
of space and large bathrooms.
The breakfast buffet is excellent.

**Schlosshotel Römischer
Kaiser** €€
Luxury Map 2 C5
Annagasse 16, 1010
Tel *(01) 512 77 51-0*
W bestwestern.at/roemischerkaiser
Set in a Baroque palace dating
back to 1684, this sumptuous
hotel retains much of its former
splendour. Rooms are decked out
with Baroque-style furnishings,
chandeliers and antiques, and
have all the modern amenities
you'd expect of a first-rate hotel.

DO & CO Hotel Vienna
Contemporary   €€€
  Map 2 C4
Stephansplatz 12, 1010
Tel *(01) 241 88*
w doco.com
This top luxury hotel offers discerning travellers beautifully designed rooms with a range of extra-special high-tech touches, such as iPad docks and safes that can accommodate laptops.

Palais Coburg
Luxury   €€€
  Map 3 D5
Coburgbastei 4, 1010
Tel *(01) 518 18-200*
w palais-coburg.com
Steeped in six centuries of history, this refined hotel is set in a majestic former palace. Enjoy beautifully appointed guest rooms, impeccable service and world-class facilities.

Palais Hansen Kempinski Vienna
Luxury   €€€
  Map 2 B2
Schottenring 24, 1010
Tel *(01) 236 100-0*
w kempinski.com
Elegant contemporary rooms and suites in a grand hotel originally built for the World Exhibition in 1873. Fantastic central location and state-of-the-art facilities.

North of Mariahilfer Strasse

Altstadt Vienna
Contemporary   €
  Map 1 B5
Kirchengasse 41, 1070
Tel *(01) 522 66 66*
w altstadt.at
A stylish boutique hotel combining period features with contemporary furnishings. Opt for a room on the mezzanine level with pretty stucco-work on the ceilings.

Harmonie
Contemporary   €
  Map 2 A1
Harmoniegasse 5–7, 1090
Tel *(01) 317 66 04*
w bestwestern-ce.com
Located in one of the trendiest parts of town, this well-designed hotel is known for its extensive complimentary breakfast buffet, which includes cooked items and good quality organic produce.

Hotel Alpha
Contemporary   €
  Map 1 C3
Buchfeldgasse 8, 1080
Tel *(01) 403 52 91*
w austria-hotels.at/hotel-alpha/index.html
A no-frills hotel with clean, comfortable rooms in a quiet but central location. Helpful staff.

Hotel-Pension Museum
Pension   €
  Map 1 C4
Museumstrasse 3, 1070
Tel *(01) 523 44 26*
w hotelmuseum.at
A charming hotel in a historic building in the heart of the city. Ask for a room with a view as some of the rooms at the back can be on the small side. The communal areas, decorated with period-style furniture, are stunning.

Hotel Rathaus Wine & Design
Boutique   €€
  Map 1 B3
Lange Gasse 13, 1080
Tel *(01) 400 11 22*
w hotel-rathaus-wien.at
An unusual hotel with a wine theme that extends to the decor, artworks and (of course) the bar. Guests can enjoy wine tastings at the hotel and regular excursions to vineyards.

The Levante Parliament
Boutique   €€
  Map 1 C4
Auerspergstrasse 9, 1080
Tel *(01) 228 28-0*
w thelevante.com
Bold modern decor pervades at this hotel. The communal areas are especially eye-catching, and include a bar made of glass and a courtyard with clever lighting.

Sans Souci
Luxury   €€€
  Map 1 C5
Burggasse 2, 1070
Tel *(01) 522 25 20*
w sanssouci-wien.com
A trendy hotel with chic, contemporary furnishings and original art dotted throughout the communal areas. There's an exceptionally large swimming pool.

South of the Ring

Hotel Beethoven
Contemporary   €
  Map 4 B1
Papagenogasse 6, 1060
Tel *(01) 587 44 82-0*
w hotel-beethoven.at
Enchanting hotel owned by the Ludwig family, who sponsor many cultural institutions. Guests may find themselves invited to sip champagne and enjoy a free art show or concert in the lobby. Small but comfortable rooms.

Hotel Daniel Vienna
Contemporary   €
  Map 5 F4
Landstrasser Gürtel 5, 1030
Tel *(01) 901 31-0*
w hoteldaniel.com
Chic hotel with quirky rooms and an in-house bakery that emits the seductive smell of freshly baked bread in the morning. Vespa hire is available to all guests.

Hotel Beethoven, perfect accommodation for culture lovers

Hotel am Konzerthaus
Boutique   €
  Map 5 E1
Am Heumarkt 35–37, 1030
Tel *(01) 716 16-0*
w mgallery.com/Vienna
A well-run hotel in a convenient central location. The rooms have pretty Klimt-inspired furnishings and a range of modern amenities.

Hotel Kaiserhof Wien
Historic   €€
  Map 4 C2
Frankenberggasse 10, 1040
Tel *(01) 505 17 01*
w kaiserhof-wien.at
This historical property dates back to the early 1900s. Among the elegant period features is the original lift. Enjoy afternoon tea in the refined Kaiserhof bar.

Le Meridien Vienna
Design   €€
  Map 2 B5
Opernring 13, 1010
Tel *(01) 588 90-0*
w lemeridienvienna.com
This hip hotel appeals to the young, cultured and well-off with contemporary art, scooter rental, a champagne bar and special "art experience" suites.

Lindner Hotel Am Belvedere
Contemporary   €€
  Map 5 F2
Rennweg 12, 1030
Tel *(01) 794 77-0*
w lindner.de
Popular with business travellers, this hotel has comfortable, modern rooms. The excellent facilities include a spa and sauna.

Bristol
Luxury   €€€
  Map 5 D1
Kärntner Ring 1, 1010
Tel *(01) 515 16-0*
w bristolvienna.com
Opulent, grand and imposing, the five-star Hotel Bristol is steeped in history and rich in antiques. It's also home to one of the city's best restaurants *(see p314)*.

For more information on types of hotels see p291

Hotel Sacher €€€
Luxury Map 2 B5
Philharmonikerstrasse 4, 1010
Tel *(01) 514 56-0*
W sacher.com
Mix with the city's elite at this
landmark hotel, which was
founded by the son of the
inventor of *Sachertorte*. Today,
it offers some of the most
sumptuous accommodation
in Vienna. Every aspect of the
hotel oozes luxury, and it's best
suited to those who can forget
about cost.

Imperial €€€
Luxury Map 2 B5
Kärntner Ring 16, 1015
Tel *(01) 501 10-0*
W imperialvienna.com
Opulent accommodation in a
former palace built in 1863 as the
Vienna residence of the Prince of
Württemberg. Transformed into a
hotel in 1873, this place is now a
byword for luxury, with personal
butlers serving the suites.

DK Choice

The Ring €€€
Boutique Map 2 B5
Kärntner Ring 8, 1010
Tel *(01) 22 122*
W theringhotel.com
Set in a historic building, this
relaxing boutique hotel has an
elegant interior that blends old-
world charm with contemporary
design and modern comforts.
Expect ultra-efficient staff who
go the extra mile. Guests dine
on top-notch cuisine at Eight
(see p313) and enjoy fantastic
views of the skyline while being
pampered in the spa.

Further Afield

A&O Wien Stadthalle €
Hostel
Lerchenfelder Gürtel 9–11, 1160
Tel *(01) 493 04 80-3900*
W aohostels.com
Great value accommodation in
this clean, stylish hostel. There
are some wonderfully quirky
communal areas, including a
stylish bar in a vaulted cellar and
a book-lined reading corner.

Das Capri €
Contemporary Map 3 E3
Praterstrasse 44–46, 1020
Tel *(01) 214 84 04*
W dascapri.at
A comfortable hotel with a range
of well-appointed rooms, suites
and apartments. Appeals to a mix
of weekenders and business
travellers on longer trips.

Flemings Deluxe Hotel €
Contemporary
Josefstädter Strasse 10–12, 1080
Tel *(01) 205 99-0*
W flemings-hotels.com
This hotel is blessed with high-
tech gadgets and plenty of class.
Nothing is too much trouble for
the professional staff.

Hostel Ruthensteiner €
Hostel
Robert Hamerlinggasse 24, A-1150
Tel *(01) 893 42 02*
W hostelruthensteiner.com
Opened in 1968, this friendly,
laid-back place remains a firm
favourite with backpackers and
makes a great choice for families.
Rentable iPads and DVDs.

Hotel Bellevue €
Historic
Althanstrasse 5, 1090
Tel *800 9733 4226 (within the EU)*
W bellevue-hotel-vienna.com
This hotel focuses on business
travellers, with meeting and
conference facilities available.
Room furnishings vary from
dated to more modern.

DK Choice

Hotel Boltzmann €
Boutique
Boltzmanngasse 8, 1090
Tel *(01) 354 50-0*
W hotelboltzmann.at
Named after the Viennese
physicist Ludwig Boltzmann, this
family-run hotel has spacious,
well-cared-for rooms. In summer,
enjoy a hearty breakfast buffet in
the peaceful courtyard garden.
The friendly staff are eager to
ensure your visit is as pleasant
as possible. Book ahead.

Tastefully decorated, comfortable room
at the Ring

Hotel Korotan €
Contemporary
Albertgasse 48, 1080
Tel *(01) 403 41 93*
W korotan.com
This ultra-modern glass-fronted
hotel offers good views of the
city. The rooms are comfortable
and decorated in a trendy
monochrome colour scheme,
with big, bold modern artworks
imparting splashes of colour.

Hotel Mozart €
Family
Julius-Tandler-Platz 4, 1090
Tel *(01) 317 15 37*
W hotelmozart-vienna.at
This family-run hotel has a great
location for those keen to explore
the city's bike trails. Bike storage is
available along with information
and maps on the Danube trails.
Solar power heats the water for
the hotel's bathrooms.

Hotel Stefanie €
Historic
Taborstrasse 12, 1020
Tel *(01) 211 50*
W schick-hotels.com
Pleasant, modern rooms in an
excellent four-star hotel with
over four centuries of history.
The family of the current owners,
who take pride in offering good
old-fashioned service, purchased
the hotel in 1880.

Landhaus Fuhrgassl-Huber €
Family
*Rathstrasse 24, Neustift am
Walde, 1190*
Tel *(01) 440 30 33*
W landhaus-fuhrgassl-huber.at
Overlooking vineyards on
Vienna's outskirts, this lovely
country house is a relaxing base
from which to explore the city.
Designed by a former stage
designer at the Vienna Opera
House, it has country-style
parlours and pretty leafy patios.

DK Choice

Boutiquehotel Stadthalle €€
Boutique
Hackengasse 20, 1150
Tel *(01) 982 42 72*
W hotelstadthalle.at
First-time guests are delighted
by the many pleasing extras
offered by this contemporary
family-run eco-hotel, including
flowers, candles and DVD
players. The courtyard garden is
an oasis of calm and in June the
lavender roof blooms. Staff
harvest and dry the lavender,
using it in the hotel's lotions,
potions, soaps and oils.

Lower Austria and Burgenland

DÜRNSTEIN: Schloss Hotel Dürnstein €€
Luxury **Road map** F3
Dürnstein 2, A-3601
Tel *(02711) 212*
W schloss.at
This dreamy castle is the ultimate romantic address, with four-poster beds, silver-service dining and indoor and outdoor pools.

EGGENBURG: Stadthotel Eggenburg €
Pension **Road map** F2
Kremserstrasse 8, A-3730
Tel *(02984) 35 31*
W oppitz.at
This family-run hotel is located in the centre of medieval Eggenburg. It offers quiet, comfortable rooms decorated in a traditional style with modern amenities.

EISENSTADT: Hotel Ohr €
Family **Road map** G3
Ruterstrasse 51, A-7000
Tel *(02682) 62 46-0*
W hotel-ohr.at
A friendly hotel some distance from the centre, with elegant, modern rooms and an excellent breakfast buffet. Horse-riding excursions are on offer.

GÖSING: Alpenhotel Gösing €
Spa **Road map** F3
Gösing an der Mariazellerbahn 4, A-3221
Tel *(02728) 217*
W goesing.at
This large rural chalet in the foothills of the Alps offers splendid views of the peak of Östcher. The rustically decorated rooms have original wooden beams.

LOIPERSDORF: Pension Krainz €
Family **Road map** G4
Henndorf-Therme 1, A-8282
Tel *(03329) 46 611*
W krainz-loipersdorf.at
Set in a quiet countryside location, near the large thermal spa centre of Loipersdorf, this family-oriented hotel offers bright, spacious rooms. It is popular with golfers as it's close to the Loipersdorf Thermal Golf Course.

MAUERBACH: Berghotel Tubingerkogel €
Contemporary **Road map** F3
Tulbingerkogel 1, A-3001
Tel *(02273) 73 91*
W tulbingerkogel.at
Every room at this fine hotel boasts floor-to-ceiling windows with forest views. There's an infinity lap pool and sauna, and

Lobby and bistro-bar at the Hotel Metropol in St Pölten

walking and cycling trails run nearby. The fine restaurant has a 1,200-bottle wine cellar.

NEUSIEDL AM SEE: Hotel Wende €€
Family **Road map** G3
Seestrasse 40, A-7100
Tel *(02167) 81 11*
W hotel-wende.at
Set in beautiful countryside, this child-friendly hotel offers an indoor pool, extensive grounds and guest rooms with balconies.

RETZ: Althof Retz €€
Family **Road map** F2
Althofgasse 14, A-2070
Tel *(02942) 37 11*
W althof.at
This country lodge is in an idyllic location surrounded by vineyards. The rooms are basic, but the staff are extremely helpful and the restaurant is excellent.

RUST: Hotel Sifkovits €
Pension **Road map** G3
Am Seekanal 8, A-7071
Tel *(02685) 276*
W sifkovits.at
A lovely little hotel in the perfect spot for exploring Rust. There's a good organic breakfast buffet and a pretty garden with sun loungers.

ST PÖLTEN: Hotel Metropol €
Contemporary **Road map** F3
Schillerplatz 1, A-2680
Tel *(02742) 7070-0*
W hotel-metropol.at
This centrally located business hotel offers well-equipped rooms and a decent buffet breakfast.

SEMMERING: Belvedere €
Family **Road map** F4
Hochstrasse 6, A-2680
Tel *(02664) 22 70*
W belvedere-semmering.at
A pretty, traditional-style hotel with bags of character, spacious, comfortable rooms, and superb pool and spa facilities.

WEISSENKIRCHEN/WACHAU: Donauwirt €
Traditional **Road map** F3
Wachaustrasse 47, A-3610
Tel *(02715) 22 47*
W donauwirt.at
This cheerfully decorated family-run hotel is set right on the edge of the Danube, and offers wonderful views, an exceptional restaurant and a convenient location close to the railway station.

ZWETTL: Schwarz-Alm €
Family **Road map** F2
Almweg 1, A-3910
Tel *(02822) 53173-0*
W schwarzalm.at
A pretty country hotel surrounded by a large alpine forest, with a wellness centre on site and a wide range of hiking and biking activities right on the doorstep.

Styria

BAD AUSSEE: Hotel Erzherzog Johann €€
Spa **Road map** D4
Kurhausplatz 62, A-8990
Tel *(03622) 525 07-0*
W erzherzogjohann.at
A modern hotel with comfortable, spacious rooms and spectacular views of the Alps. The fabulous spa and attentive staff ensure a thoroughly relaxing stay.

BAD BLUMAU: Rogner-Bad Blumau €€€
Spa **Road map** F4
Bad Blumau 100, A-8283
Tel *(03383) 5100 - 0*
W blumau.com
Designed by eccentric artist Friedensreich Hundertwasser, this spa hotel looks like something from a fantasy novel. The building is made up of irregular undulating forms, with a maze of tunnels and pools and brightly coloured mosaics.

For more information on types of hotels *see p291*

BAD GLEICHENBERG:
Hotel Stenitzer €€
Spa Road map F5
Schulstrasse 51, A-8344
Tel *(03159) 22 50*
W hotel-stenitzer.com
An elegantly furnished four-star
hotel with extensive spa facilities
and pretty formal gardens.

BAD RADKERSBURG:
Thermenhotel
Radkersburger Hof €€
Spa Road map F5
Thermenstrasse 22, A-8490
Tel *(03476) 3560-0*
W radkersburgerhof.at
Comfortable four-star spa resort
with water fitness classes, group
sports, and a range of therapies,
pools and saunas.

FOHNSDORF: Hotel Schloss
Gabelhofen €€
Luxury Road map E4
Schlossgasse 54, A-8753
Tel *(03573) 55 55-0*
W gabelhofen.at
Splendidly atmospheric castle
hotel with beautifully decorated
rooms, some of which are in the
castle towers.

DK Choice

GRAZ: Augarten €
Boutique Road map F4
Schönaugasse 53, A-8010
Tel *(0316) 20 80-0*
W augartenhotel.at
A trendy, minimalist design
hotel featuring modern
bespoke furnishings and a
wealth of contemporary art
from the private collection of
the hotel's owner, Helmut
Marko. The building, designed
by Günther Domenig,
combines curving surfaces and
sheets of glass to provide a
feeling of light and space.

Light-filled modern room at the boutique
design-hotel Augarten in Graz

Key to Price Guide *see p292*

GRAZ:
Hotel Erzherzog Johann €
Historic Road map F4
Sackstrasse 3–5, A-8010
Tel *(0316) 811 616*
W erzherzog-johann.com
This charming hotel first acted
as an inn in the 16th century.
All the rooms are richly furnished
with antiques.

GRAZ: Hotel Zum Dom €
Boutique Road map F4
Bürgergasse 14, A-8010
Tel *(0316) 82 480-0*
W domhotel.co.at
A unique boutique hotel set in a
historic building. The stylish
rooms combine modern luxuries
with period features.

KAPFENBERG: Bohlerstern €
Contemporary Road map F4
Friedrich-Böhler-Strasse 13, A-8605
Tel *(03862) 206 375*
W boehlerstern.at
The classical exterior belies the
modern design of the serviceable
rooms. Good on-site restaurant.

MARIAZELL: Hotel Drei Hasen €
Pension Road map F4
Wienerstrasse 11, A-8630
Tel *(03882) 24 10*
W dreihasen.at
This friendly guesthouse with
simple, comfortable rooms is
in a great location for skiers,
right at the foot of the cable
car. Excellent on-site restaurant.

MARIAZELL:
Hotel Schwarzer Adler €
Pension Road map F4
Hauptplatz 1, A-8630
Tel *(03882) 28 63-0*
W hotelschwarzeradler.at
Traditional and cheerfully painted
hotel with comfortable rooms
right in the town centre. A great
place for those hiking or skiing
in the area.

RAMSAU:
Alpengasthof Peter Rosegger €
Traditional Road map D4
Ramsau 233, A-8972
Tel *(03687) 81 223-0*
W alpengasthof-peter-rosegger.at
Comfortable rooms with natural
pine furniture and stunning views
of the Dachstein mountains.
There's also a reading room and
a pretty garden.

RAMSAU-KULM: Almfrieden €
Family Road map D4
Leiten 47, A-8972
Tel *(03687) 81 753*
W almfrieden.at
Child-friendly resort hotel with
a playground and a range of
beautifully decorated rooms.

SCHLADMING: Posthotel €€
Pension Road map D4
Hauptplatz 10, A-8970
Tel *(03687) 22 571*
W posthotel-schladming.at
This attractive 400-year old inn
has a superb restaurant and small
but well-appointed rooms. The
staff are exceptionally friendly
and helpful.

TURRACHER HÖHE:
Schlosshotel Seewirt €€
Family Road map D4
Turracher Höhe 33, A-8864
Tel *(04275) 82 34*
W schlosshotel-seewirt.com
This cosy 19th-century
guesthouse with original timber
features offers a range of facilities,
including a good-sized indoor
pool and a sauna.

Upper Austria

BAD GOISERN/ST AGATHA:
Landhotel Agathawirt €
Pension Road map D4
St Agatha 10, A-4822
Tel *(06135) 83 41*
W agathawirt.at
Built in 1517, this historic hotel
offers basic but comfortable rooms
in an atmospheric setting. Relax
in the garden in summer or by a
wood-burning stove in winter.

BAD ISCHL: Goldenes Schiff €
Contemporary Road map D4
Adalbert-Stifter-Kai 3, A-4820
Tel *(06132) 24 241*
W goldenes-schiff.at
This attractive four-star hotel has
been an inn since the 17th century.
Rooms are modern and spacious,
and the breakfast is excellent.

BAD LEONFELDEN:
Kurhotel Bad Leonfelden €€
Spa Road map E3
Spielau 8, A-4190
Tel *(07213) 63 63*
W daskurhotel.at
An excellent four-star hotel in a
resort with a long spa history.
Therapies include massage, mud
baths and beauty treatments.
Friendly and hospitable staff.

GMUNDEN:
Schloss Freisitz Roith €€
Luxury Road map D3
Traunsteinerstrasse 87, A-4810
Tel *(07612) 649 05*
W freisitzroith.at
A castle-hotel dating back to the
16th century with magnificent
views of the lake. Some rooms
are a little spartan, but the
service is excellent and the
scenic setting is hard to beat.

HALLSTATT:
Seehotel Grüner Baum €
Pension Road map D4
Marktplatz 104, A-4830
Tel *(06134) 8263-0*
☑ gruenerbaum.cc
This lakeside hotel dates from at least 1700, and its splendid façade dominates Hallstatt's quaint marketplace. The charming rooms are furnished with both modern and antique items.

LINZ: Arcotel Nike €
Contemporary Road map E3
Untere Donaulände 9, A-4020
Tel *(0732) 76 26-0*
☑ arcotelhotels.com/Nike
This high-rise is close to the Danube and offers great views. Most rooms follow a red-and-white colour scheme.

LINZ: Austria Trend
Hotel Schillerpark €
Contemporary Road map E3
Rainerstrasse 2–4, A-4020
Tel *(0732) 695-0*
☑ austria-trend.at
This cube-like glass and steel building offers functional, well-appointed modern rooms. There's also a good on-site restaurant and several bars.

MONDSEE:
Seegasthof-Hotel Lackner €€
Contemporary Road map D3
Mondseestrasse 1, A-5310
Tel *(06232) 23 59-0*
☑ seehotel-lackner.at
A family-owned inn with spectacular views and a first-rate restaurant. Well-designed spacious rooms with balconies overlooking the lake, and warm, friendly staff.

ST GEORGEN IM ATTERGAU:
Attergauhof €
Pension Road map D3
Attergaustrasse 41, A-4880
Tel *(07667) 64 06*
☑ attergauhof.at
A friendly, family-run hotel. Some of the rooms are a little dated, but they are all clean and comfortable. A good bar serves local beers on tap. Request a room on the upper floors as the bar can get noisy in the evenings.

ST WOLFGANG:
Landhaus zu Appesbach €€
Luxury Road map D4
Au 18, A-5360
Tel *(06138) 22 09*
☑ appesbach.com
This former private mansion has been converted into an exclusive hotel with beautiful rooms and apartments. Grandest is the Windsor Suite, where the Duke of Windsor once stayed.

DK Choice
ST WOLFGANG:
Weisses Rössl €€€
Luxury Road map D4
Markt 74, A-5360
Tel *(06138) 23 06*
☑ weissesroessl.at
This famous lakeside hotel, celebrated in an operetta by Ralph Benatzky and Robert Stolz, embodies traditional Austrian style and hospitality. Consisting of several historic houses clustered together, it offers a range of elegant, romantic rooms, many with 17th-century wooden ceilings. Excellent facilities, including an outdoor swimming pool with spectacular views over the lake.

SCHÄRDING: Stiegenwirt €
Pension Road map D3
Schlossgasse 2–6, A-4780
Tel *(07712) 30 70-0*
☑ stiegenwirt-schaerding.at
Set in a pretty Baroque building, this hotel has been owned by the same family since 1910 and offers large, comfortable rooms. Excellent regional cuisine is served in the hotel restaurant.

TRAUNKIRCHEN:
Symposionhotel Post €€
Contemporary Road map D3
Ortsplatz 5, A-4801
Tel *(07617) 23 07*
☑ hotel-post-traunkirchen.at
Comfortable, modern four-star hotel on the shores of the Traunsee. Room overlooking the lake also take in the peaks of Johannesberg – a stunning view.

Salzburger Land

BAD GASTEIN:
Hotel Weismayr €€
Spa Road map D4
Kaiser-Franz-Josef-Strasse 6, A-5640
Tel *(06434) 25 94*
☑ weismayr.at
Built at the turn-of-the-19th-century, this grand four-star hotel retains all the glamour of the Austrian *belle-époque* and offers great views of the Gastein valley.

BAD GASTEIN:
Haus Hirt €€€
Spa Road map D4
Kaiserhofstrasse 14, A-5640
Tel *(06434) 27 97-0*
☑ haus-hirt.com
A stylish, contemporary spa resort offering trendy, modern rooms and plenty of pampering in the wellness centre.

High-rise hotel Arcotel Nike, located near the Danube in Linz

EUGENDORF: Holznerwirt €
Pension Road map D3
Dorf 4, A-5301
Tel *(06225) 82 05*
☑ holznerwirt.at
Atmospheric hotel in a traditional chalet. The charming rooms, many of which have four-poster beds, include special touches such as down duvets and Kachelofen-style heating.

FILZMOOS: Tannenhof €
Pension Road map D4
Filzmoos 84, A-5332
Tel *(06453) 82 020*
☑ sieberer-filzmoos.at
A delightful B&B nestled in the mountains, Tannenhof is perfect for families on hiking or skiing holidays. Friendly, hospitable hosts. Apartments also available.

FUSCHL: Seewinkel €€
Resort Road map D4
Seestrasse 31, A-5330
Tel *(06226) 83 44*
☑ seewinkel.com
This picturesque hotel offers a splendid panorama over the Fuschlsee. Facilities include a private bathing beach, sailing and windsurfing facilities, and a small spa and sauna.

FUSCHL: Schloss Fuschl €€€
Luxury Road map D4
Schloss Strasse 19, Hof bei Salzburg, A-5322
Tel *(06229) 22 530*
☑ schlossfuschlsalzburg.com
This stately hotel set in a 15th-century castle overlooks the lake and has spa facilities and a nine-hole golf course. Refined, elegant rooms both in the main castle and in lakeside cottages.

Charming hotel complex of Berghof, next to the Hintertux Glacier, Hintertux

KLEINARL: Viehof
Family   Road map D4
Viehofstrasse 15, A-5603
Tel *(06418) 240*
W pension-viehhof.at
Traditional chalet-style guesthouse with pine furnishings, family apartments, and a children's playroom. Very convenient for hiking and skiing.

SAALBACH: Hotel Bauer   €€
Contemporary   Road map C4
Oberdorf 232, A-5753
Tel *(06541) 62 13-0*
W hotel-bauer.at
Located a stone's throw from the lifts and ski slopes, this hotel has well-appointed rooms and a superb restaurant.

ST GILGEN: Parkhotel
Billroth   €€
Contemporary   Road map D4
Billrothstrasse 2, A-5340
Tel *(06227) 22 17*
W billroth.at
This calm lakeside retreat is a perfect base for long walks around the edge of Wolfgangsee. The comfortable rooms, many of which overlook the lake, are only surpassed in grandeur by the opulent dining and social areas.

SALZBURG: Berglandhotel   €
Pension   Road map D3
Rupertgasse 15, A-5020
Tel *(0662) 872 318*
W berglandhotel.at
About a ten-minute walk from the Old Town, this efficiently run family-owned hotel offers neat rooms at reasonable prices.

SALZBURG: Auersperg   €€
Boutique   Road map D3
Auerspergstrasse 61, A-5020
Tel *(0662) 889 440*
W hotel-salzburg.net
With sleek contemporary decor, a soothing garden setting

and organic food at breakfast time, this place is ideal for a weekend away.

SALZBURG: Goldener
Hirsch   €€€
Luxury   Road map D3
Getreidegasse 37, A-5020
Tel *(0662) 80 840*
W goldenerhirsch.com
Set in a 15th-century building, this charming hotel is decked out with pretty hand-crafted furnishings and antiques that complement the historic surrounds. It also boasts a truly exceptional restaurant.

SALZBURG:
Hotel Sacher Salzburg   €€€
Luxury   Road map D3
Schwarzstrasse 5–7, A-5020
Tel *(0662) 889 770*
W sacher.com
A turn-of-the-19th-century hotel that offers traditional luxuries such as marble bathrooms, richly furnished rooms and the famous *Sachertorte* chocolate cake in the hotel café.

SALZBURG:
Schloss Mönchstein   €€€
Luxury   Road map D3
Mönchsberg 26, A-5020
Tel *(0662) 848 555-0*
W monchstein.at
An enchanting hotel set in a 14th-century castle with its own park. It offers unparalleled views of the city and high standards of comfort and service.

STROBL: Bergrose   €
Spa   Road map D4
Weissenbach 162, A-5350
Tel *(06137) 54 31*
W bergrose.at
A family-run hotel surrounded by mountains and meadows. The rooms are spotlessly clean and beautifully decked out in vintage fabric and wooden furniture. The spa facilities are in keeping with the hotel's serene, relaxing atmosphere.

Tyrol and Vorarlberg

AU: Hotel Rössle   €€
Traditional   Road map A4
Lisse 90, A-6883
Tel *(05515) 22 16*
W roessle-au.at
This traditional village hotel offers spacious rooms with balconies and panoramic mountain views. Guests can hire mountain bikes from the hotel lobby to explore the area. There is also an excellent spa for the less adventurous.

BEZAU: Gasthof Sonne   €
Family   Road map A4
Kriechere 66, A-6870
Tel *(05514) 22 62*
W diesonnigen.at
An immaculately presented traditional *Gasthof*. Rooms offer either private balconies or panoramic views of the lake. Very friendly staff and an excellent spread at breakfast.

BREGENZ: Weisses Kreuz   €€
Luxury   Road map A4
Römerstrasse 5, A-6900
Tel *(05574) 49 88-0*
W hotelweisseskreuz.at
Guests can expect exceptional service at this hotel, which combines over 100 years of hospitality with glamorous rooms featuring exposed beams, ornate cornices and a wide range of modern facilities.

FONTANELLA/FASCHINA:
Fascina   €€
Family   Road map A4
Faschina 55, A-6733
Tel *(05510) 224*
W hotel-faschina.at
A comfortable mountain retreat featuring wood-panelled interiors and a fully equipped spa. The on-site restaurant serves excellent food.

FULPMES: Waldhof   €€
Family   Road map B4
Gröbenweg 19, A-6166
Tel *(05225) 62 175*
W waldhof-stubaital.at
This charming mountain hideaway with traditional Tyrolean decor offers a wide range of luxurious amenities. The comfortable rooms offer panoramic views of the Stubai Alps.

HINTERTUX: Berghof   €€
Luxury   Road map C4
Hintertux 754, A-6293
Tel *(05287) 85 85*
W berghof.at
This luxurious modern hotel is right next to the Hintertux Glacier, which offers skiing almost all year round. Excellent facilities, impeccable service and a good hotel restaurant.

INNSBRUCK: Goldener Adler   €€
Historic   Road map B4
Herzog-Friedrich-Strasse 6, 6020
Tel *(0512) 571 111-0*
W goldeneradler.com
An elegant 14th-century inn in the heart of the Old Town, boasting European royalty and Mozart among its former guests. The rooms offer panoramic views of the city and the mountains beyond.

INNSBRUCK:
Schlosshotel Igls €€€
Luxury **Road map** B4
Viller Steig 2, A-6080
Tel *(0512) 377 217*
w schloss-igls.com
Guests are treated like royalty at this luxurious and discreet mountain castle. Rooms are beautifully appointed and boast superb views of the surrounding Alps.

KIRCHBERG: Sportalm €€
Contemporary **Road map** C4
Brandseitweg 26–28, A-6365
Tel *(05357) 27 78*
w hotel-sportalm.at
Amid the rolling foothills of the Kitzbühel Alps, this hotel offers spa facilities and sleek, modern rooms that pay homage to traditional Tyrolean style.

KITZBÜHEL: Kitzhof €€
Luxury **Road map** C4
Schwarzseestrasse 8–10, A-6370
Tel *(05356) 63 211-0*
w hotel-kitzhof.com
A pretty resort hotel with swish designer rooms, a full range of spa and wellness facilities, and breathtaking mountain views. Staff are very professional and helpful.

KITZBÜHEL: Goldener Greif €€€
Luxury **Road map** C4
Schulgasse 3/Hinterstadt 24, A-6370
Tel *(05356) 64 311*
w hotel-goldener-greif.at
This hotel dates from the 13th century and has a pretty flower-covered façade. Rooms have beautiful wood-panelled interiors and ceiling frescoes.

LERMOOS: Mohr €€€
Spa **Road map** B4
Innsbruckerstrasse 40, A-6631
Tel *(05673) 23 62*
w mohr-life-resort.at
Built entirely with traditional materials, this bold, contemporary building frequently stars in design magazines. The ultra stylish rooms are decked out with iconic design pieces and free-standing bath tubs. Choose from a full range of spa-resort facilities.

MAYRHOFEN/FINKENBERG:
Sporthotel Stock €€€
Spa **Road map** C4
Dorf 142, A-6292
Tel *(05285) 67 75*
w ssl.sporthotel-stock.com
A destination resort hotel with romantic rooms, indoor and outdoor pools, wellness facilities and numerous sports activities. The food in the hotel restaurant is excellent.

DK Choice

OBERLECH: Montana €€€
Luxury **Road map** A4
Oberlech 279, A-6764
Tel *(05583) 24 60-0*
w montanaoberlech.at
A hotel of top-notch ski pedigree, owned by the family of former world ski champion Patrick Ortlieb. Located on the edge of the piste, it is ideal for skiers in search of a luxury base. Everything is beautifully designed and well thought through, keeping the needs of the skier in mind. Baby-sitting and a children's ski school.

Carinthia and East Tyrol

BAD BLEIBERG:
Der Bleibergerhof €€
Spa **Road map** D5
Drei Lärchen 150, A-9530
Tel *(04244) 22 05*
w falkensteiner.com
This spa hotel offers thermal waters, modern design and state-of-the-art facilities including indoor and outdoor pools and numerous saunas.

BODENSDORF: Stofflwirt €
Family **Road map** E5
Deutschberg 6, A-9551
Tel *(04243) 69 20*
w stofflwirt.at
An attractive hotel that combines traditional materials with modern style. Guests can enjoy the garden, mountain views and spa facilities.

KLAGENFURT: Palais Porcia €€
Boutique **Road map** E5
Neuer Platz 13, A-9020
Tel *(0463) 511 590-0*
w palais-porcia.at
An elegant hotel set in a historical palace with opulently decorated

Roaring log fire at the luxurious Schlosshotel Igls, Innsbruck

rooms, plush carpets and a wide range of modern amenities. Truly exceptional service.

LIENZ: Traube €€
Spa **Road map** D5
Hauptplatz 14, A-9900
Tel *(04852) 64 444*
w hoteltraube.at
An elegant and romantic hotel boasting wonderful views of the Alps and beautifully furnished rooms, some with antiques.

MILLSTATT: Hotel Seevilla €€
Luxury **Road map** D5
Seestrasse 68, A-9872
Tel *(04766) 21 02*
w see-villa.eu
A pretty spa hotel decked out in traditional style and set amid well-tended grounds. Very warm and hospitable hosts.

OSSIACH:
Strandgasthof Seewirt €
Pension **Road map** E5
Ossiach 2, A-9570
Tel *(04243) 22 68*
w seewirt-ossiach.at
A charming guesthouse with a lovely garden located on the shores of Ossiacher See. Perfect for lakeside strolls, boating and fishing.

DK Choice

PORTSCHACH: Schloss Leonstain €€
Boutique **Road map** E5
Leonstainerstrasse 1, A-9210
Tel *(04272) 28 16*
w leonstain.at
Brahms was enchanted enough to write a violin concerto here, such was the effect of this atmospheric property. Built in 1492, Schloss Leonstain offers the perfect balance between old-world charm and contemporary facilities.

VELDEN:
Casino Hotel Velden €€
Luxury **Road map** E5
Am Corso 10, A-9220
Tel *(04274) 51 233*
w casino-hotel.at
Beautifully designed rooms in a classic Wörthersee hotel, with a casino and private beach.

VILLACH: Holiday Inn €€
Boutique **Road map** E5
Uropaplatz 1–2, A-9500
Tel *(04242) 22 522-0*
w hi-villach.at
This is a hotel of genuine flair and individuality, offering a range of pretty rooms with enormous bathrooms. Great service.

For more information on types of hotels *see p291*

WHERE TO EAT AND DRINK

Austrian cooking forms one of the classic European schools of cuisine, incorporating many elements such as *Wiener Schnitzel* that have become standard across the continent. Traditional Austrian fare such as breaded chicken, boiled beef and *Gulasch* soup are served in almost all establishments. Freshwater fish is a feature of Austria's many lakes and rivers, while hearty dumplings and noodle dishes are common in the south and west. Larger cities are also home to Italian, Greek, Turkish and Chinese restaurants.

The restaurants listed on pages 310–25 have been selected from the best on offer, across all price ranges. They are organized by region and price. The phrasebook on page 380 will help you order a meal although most restaurants will have English menus.

Display of pastries and rolls at the charming Café Mozart *(see p310)*

What to Eat and When

For breakfast Austrians tend to eat a roll or two with butter and jam, accompanied by coffee. Most hotels offer a self-service buffet breakfast and it is generally served throughout the day. Even small bakeries usually have a few tables for sitting and enjoying a breakfast pastry.

Most restaurants serve lunch from noon to 2 or 3pm. Many offer a *Tagesmenü* (fixed-price menu of the day), or a *Tagesteller* (dish of the day), as one of the best-priced options. This is usually displayed on a blackboard outside the restaurant.

In Austrian homes, dinner is eaten early, at about 6pm. In restaurants, however, food is generally served throughout the evening. Beer, wine, fruit juice or water are normally drunk with the meal, and stronger drinks, such as one of the locally produced fruit brandies, may be served as a *digestif*. Some establishments serve food throughout the day.

Opening Hours

A few small grocery stores, bakeries and coffee houses open as early as 7am in the morning, but most open between 8am and 10am.

Restaurants are usually open from around 11am to 10pm, although many establishments take a break after lunch (around 3pm) and then reopen at around 6pm for dinner. Rural restaurants often serve as meeting points for the locals and may remain open until the early hours, although the kitchen may close much earlier. Many places close for the *Ruhetag* (off day set aside for rest), and may also be closed on public holidays. At a country inn it may be difficult to order a meal after 9pm.

Types of Restaurants and Snack Bars

A wide range of restaurants, bars and snack bars offer modest or grand meals at any time of day. There are a large number of luxurious restaurants, often located within the luxury hotels, which offer first-class international menus prepared by top chefs.

A *Wirtshaus* is a country inn and a *Gasthaus* is a slightly more sophisticated restaurant – both typically concentrate on local cuisine. A *Beisl* is something like a local pub serving drinks alongside hot meals. Many classic cafés in Vienna and Salzburg also serve good food, but you should watch the prices, as they can be higher than in a restaurant or *Gasthaus*.

One typically Austrian culinary establishment is the *Heuriger*, a simple, often seasonal wine bar in the wine-growing villages, with light meals at low prices. Here, wine is served at your table in a glass mug, and food is to be taken from a buffet. If fir branches are displayed outside it means the the *Heuriger* is open and serving the fresh home-pressed vintage.

Tables set in front of a typical *Wirtshaus* inn in Lech

Elegant interiors of a charming *Gasthaus* in St Christoph

In cities, pubs and bars often have quite extensive menus of sandwiches, burgers and other hot food. One Austrian classic snack that should be tried at least once is the hot sausage, traditionally served at an *Imbissstube* (snack bar) or a *Würstelstand* (sausage stand). These joints usually offer a variety of sausages and frankfurters, served with bread and mustard or sometimes freshly grated horseradish.

Reservations

In general it is wise to make a reservation if you wish to eat in a particular restaurant, especially if any kind of entertainment is on offer or if the restaurant is in a popular location. During the high season and in busy tourist areas it is often essential to book ahead. Even a simple *Gasthof* or *Beisl* may have a faithful local clientele and you may be disappointed if you wander in and expect to find a free table. If you are going to a *Heuriger* in a group, again, you will need to book a table in advance.

Prices and Tips

It is difficult to generalize about prices. Lunch at an average restaurant should cost about €15–25 per person. For an evening meal you need to allow two or three times that price, or more if drinks

are included. Most of the self-service establishments usually charge by the size of the plate.

In the more expensive restaurants, the bill may also include *Gedeck*, the cover charge, or a cover charge may be levied for the bread served at the table.

Although a service charge is almost always included in the bill, you are expected to leave an additional sum of up to 10 per cent for service.

Credit cards are accepted in most luxury and hotel-restaurants, but the majority of rural establishments and snack bars accept only cash.

Children and Vegetarians

Some restaurants offer smaller servings for children and light eaters, but these may be only marginally less expensive than the regular portions – it might be cheaper to buy a regular meal to share if you have more than one child. Many restaurants, however, do have a special children's menu with the usual favourites such as burgers and french fries.

Austrians are avid meat-eaters, but most popular restaurants in the main tourist areas also offer a range of vegetarian dishes. Delicious pasta, mixed vegetables or a *Salatplatte* (mixed salad)

with bread or *Salzstangerl* (salt sticks) are popular. Many places, such as the *Heurigen*, offer buffets with a wide selection of vegetarian dishes to choose from.

Recommended Restaurants

The restaurants featured in this guidebook have been selected for their good value, food, location and atmosphere. A wide range of establishments have been included which are representative of their setting. Each one stands out and has earned a noteworthy reputation.

The listings cover a vast variety of eateries, from the simple *Heuriger* wine tavern to the family-run *Gasthaus*, historic Viennese cafés and smart gourmet restaurants. Particular attention is devoted to regional specialities, from the freshwater fish of the Neusiedler See to the sumptuous sweets of Salzburg.

Those establishments labelled DK Choice are places that have been highlighted in recognition of an exceptional feature – celebrity chef, exquisite food, inviting ambience or simply great value. Most of these eateries are quite popular among locals and visitors, so be sure to make reservations well in advance to avoid waiting.

A *Heuriger* awaiting its guests, in the vicinity of Mörbisch

The Flavours of Austria: Savoury Dishes

Austrian cuisine is a direct legacy of the country's imperial past, when culinary traditions from many parts of Europe influenced Viennese cooks. As a result, it is far more varied and flavoursome than most people realize. There are Italian and Adriatic influences, Polish- and Hungarian- inspired dishes, and even a rich seam of Balkan flavours running through much of the Austrian kitchen repertoire. *Schnitzel*, for example, may have come to Austria via Milan, which was once under Austrian control, while *Gulasch* is the Austrian version of a Hungarian dish that became popular in Vienna in the 19th century.

Chanterelle mushrooms

Cheese stall at a local Austrian farmers' market

Meat, Poultry & Dairy

Beef is narrowly ahead of pork as the nation's favourite meat. Austrian cattle farmers have a long and proud heritage of producing fine beef, which is used in many dishes, such as paprika-rich *Gulasch*. That most famous of Austrian dishes, *Wiener Schnitzel*, is traditionally made with veal. Pork is used primarily to make hams and sausages. The classic Austrian way with pork is to cure it, smoke it and leave it to mature for months in the clean air of the high Alpine pastures. The result is called *Speck*. Lean *Speck* is similar to Italian *prosciutto*, though with a distinctive smoky tang, while fattier cuts are more like *pancetta* or streaky bacon.

Bratwurst, made with beef, pork and veal, are Austria's preferred sausages, but other types such as *Frankfurters* are also common. Chicken is almost always served breaded, but *Grillhendl* is a whole chicken roasted over an open fire, or on a spit. Duck *(Ente)* is often served with sweet sauces, but sometimes with

Frankfurters   Bierwurst   Bratwurst   Frankfurters   Lean Speck   Speck

Selection of typical Austrian cured pork, sausages and salami

Austrian Dishes and Specialities

While most classic Austrian dishes (especially those originating in Vienna) are found all over the country, there are some regional differences. *Knödel* are more popular in the east, as are carp, game and pork, while beef and lamb appear more often the further west (and higher up the mountains) you travel. Beef is essential for *Tafelspitz*, often called the national dish. *Speck* is used to make *Speck Knödel*, small, dense dumplings, but the one part of the pig that Austrians do love to eat uncured is the knuckle, called *Stelze*, roasted and served chopped with heaps of sauerkraut. *Fischgröstl* is a mix of fish and seafood, fried together with onion, potato and mince (usually leftovers). It is rarely found on menus, but you may be lucky enough to try it in an Austrian home.

Paprika

Tafelspitz is silverside of beef, boiled with root vegetables and served thickly sliced with gherkins and sauerkraut.

Spectacular array of vegetables on display in a Viennese market

sour accompaniments such as pickled red cabbage. Roast goose (Gänsebraten) is also popular, as are goose livers. The milk of Austrian dairy cows, grazed on sweet Alpine pastures, produces some excellent artisan cheeses, such as fruity Wälder.

Fish

While not great seafood lovers, Austrians have developed a number of their own fish dishes. Trout (Forelle) is the most popular fish, usually served grilled with boiled potatoes. Herring (Hering) is pickled and eaten as an appetizer. Heringsschmaus, a smoked herring and apple salad, is hugely popular at Easter. Carp (Karpfen) is a favourite Christmas dish, but is eaten all year, as is plaice (Scholle or Goldbutt), which is often served with a rich vegetable-based sauce.

Vegetables

Vegetables in Austria are of the highest quality and so, while imported produce is available all year round, seasonality is still important to Austrians. That is truest of all for the nation's favourite vegetable, asparagus (Spargel).

Bunches of pale spears of Austrian spargel (asparagus)

Only local produce is used, and so is found on menus only during the harvesting season, which runs from the end of April to early July. Austrians use asparagus in every way imaginable at this time of year. Wild mushrooms are another seasonal prize, especially chanterelles (Eierschwammerl).

Potatoes (Erdäpfel) feature widely, sometimes in the form of Knödel (dumplings, which may be savoury or sweet). Cabbage (Kohl) is popular: the white variety is often pickled (Sauerkraut) and red (Rotkraut) served with venison and game dishes.

SAVOURY SNACKS

Liptauer: Goat's or sheep's milk cheese is mixed with paprika, caraway seeds, capers, mustard, chives and onions to create this paste, a staple of Austrian wine bars.

Maroni: Roast chestnuts are a winter treat; the aroma of them, toasting over a brazier on a snowy day, is somehow quintessentially Vienna.

Saure Blunzen: Blood sausage is marinated in vinegar and thinly sliced and served with brown bread. A popular "beer snack".

Schmaltzbrot: Brown bread spread thickly with beef or pork dripping, and eaten with onions and pickles.

Wiener Schnitzel should classically be veal, breaded and fried. In Austria it is never served with sauce.

Rindsgulasch is the beef version of Hungarian goulash, a rich stew flavoured with paprika and caraway.

Forelle Blau, literally "blue trout", is made by poaching an unscaled fish in stock, which gives it a blueish hue.

The Flavours of Austria: Cakes and Pastries

Few cities in the world can rival Vienna's devotion to all things sweet. The Viennese enjoy cakes mid-morning or afternoon, and set aside time for between-meal snacks. The finest *Torten* (gâteaux), pastries and cakes tend to be found in *Konditoreien*. Traditional Viennese desserts can be found in all good restaurants, and are typically rich. From the classic Viennese *Apfelstrudel* to *Gugelhupf* from the Tirol, Austrian desserts carry a regional influence. In Vienna, pastries take pride of place while, to the west, the Italian influence is strong and cakes, ice creams and meringues are preferred.

Poppy seeds

Relaxing over coffee and cake in an elegant Viennese café

Cakes

The Austrian tradition of cake-baking goes back centuries, with competition fierce between towns and cities to produce the finest. Even in small villages, bakeries would try to outdo each other with their sweet creations. Almost every Austrian city now has its trademark cake, with its citizens quick to boast that theirs is the best. The most famous Austrian cake is a Viennese creation, the *Sachertorte*, a rich chocolate cake invented by chef Franz Sacher for Chancellor Metternich in 1832. The signature dish of many an Austrian chef, it should be the first cake the visitor tries – with so much choice on offer, it will be difficult to decide on the second. While the Viennese rave about *Sachertorte*, over in Linz the locals insist their own *Linzertorte* – an almond based cake usually topped with raspberries – is superior. The people of Linz also say that the *Linzertorte* is older, dating back – legend has it – to the 17th century. Around the Hungarian border, they are proud of their *Dobostorte*,

Stollen   Sachertorte   Dobostorte   Esterházytorte
Linzertorte
Some of the many mouthwatering Austrian cakes available

Viennese Desserts

Hazelnuts

From *Topfentascherl* (curd cheese envelopes) to *Kastaniereis* (chestnut purée), Vienna's dessert cuisine uses rich and varied ingredients. Fruits such as plums and apples fill featherlight dumplings, pancakes, fritters and strudels, and although *Mehlspeisen* (puddings) translates literally as "dishes with flour", ground hazelnuts or almonds can be used in its place. Nuts play a key role, especially hazels and pine nuts, the latter often featuring in *Apfelstrudel*. More unusual desserts include sweet "pasta" served with poppyseeds to create *Mohnnudeln*, and *Böhmische Omeletten* (Bohemian omelettes) served with whipped cream and prune sauce. Conversely, *Palatschinken* may also be a savoury snack.

Mohr im Hemd, a hazelnut and chocolate pudding, is served with chocolate sauce and whipped cream.

Display of traditional pastries and cakes in a *Konditorei*

named after the Budapest chef who created it in the 19th century. Its layers of biscuit and chocolate butter cream are topped with a caramel glaze. From Salzburg, the cake of choice is baked meringue, known as *Salzburger Nockerl*, or Salzburg Soufflé. *Esterházytorte* also features meringue, layered with a rich hazelnut cream. Stollen is a marzipan-filled fruit cake originally from Germany and now an integral part of an Austrian Christmas. Regional or not, you'll now find all these classic cakes in Vienna and across the country.

Pastries

In the perfect global village, a place on the main street would always be reserved for an Austrian pastry and coffee shop. That the French collective name for sweet pastry is *Viennoiserie* underlines the noble Viennese tradition of sweet baking. Austrian legend has it that the nation's café habit began when the Turks left all their coffee behind as they abandoned Vienna after the failed siege of 1529. The *Kipfel*, a light, crescent-shaped pastry (which later became famous as the croissant) also dates from the

Entrance to one of the world-famous Mozart chocolate shops

time of the Turkish siege, its shape being based on the crescent moon in the Ottoman flag. While such symbolism is often lost today, the importance of the café in Austrian society is not. Modern-day Austrians view cafés as extensions of their home, and spend hours reading, chatting and even watching television in them. Treats on offer in cafés will generally include a classic *Apfelstrudel*, *Cremeschnitte* (slices of puff pastry filled with custard and glazed with strawberry fondant), and *Punschkrapferl*, a calorie-packed, pink-fondant-topped pastry laced with rum.

MOZARTKUGEL

Fine chocolates, presented in colourfully decorated boxes carrying the portrait of Mozart, are probably the quintessential Austrian souvenir. Known in Austria as *Mozartkugel*, the chocolates originated in Salzburg, where Mozart lived while composing *Cosi fan Tutti*, the opera in which he worships chocolate. In 1890, master confectioner Paul Fürst made the first Mozart chocolates by forming small balls of marzipan which he coated in a praline cream and then dipped in warm chocolate. Viennese confectioners soon adopted the technique and even today producers vie with one another as to whose *Mozartkugel* are the best and most authentic.

Apfelstrudel rolls paper-thin pastry with apple, sultanas, cinnamon and sometimes pine nuts or poppyseeds.

Palatschinken are fat, fluffy crêpes that may be filled with fruit or jam, or served with vanilla or chocolate sauce.

Topfenknödel are light curd cheese dumplings rolled in breadcrumbs, fried and served with fruit compôte.

Cafés and Bars in Vienna

The café has been an ingrained part of Viennese life for centuries, and there are plenty of traditional cafés found throughout the city. The majority of the popular cafés are found in central Vienna, where they are best seen as architectural ambassadors from the days of the Habsburg monarchy. But Vienna is not all about history and tradition: many sleek cafés and bars have opened up, adding a new dimension to a city that not long ago was still in a post-World War II slumber; yet now it is a vibrant European Union capital.

The spacious Café Central with its fine Neo-Gothic vaulted ceiling

The Viennese Café

It may be an exaggeration to call Vienna's cafés the heart of the city, but they are certainly one of its lifelines. Following the Turkish invasions of the 16th and 17th centuries, cafés in Vienna have been important meeting places, and have traced the history of this remarkable city. In Vienna's oldest café, **Café Frauenhuber**, Mozart himself once performed; in **Café Central**, once a gathering spot for intellectuals, Leon Trotsky made some revolutionary plans for Russia; Sigmund Freud often took therapy breaks at the traditionally elegant **Café Landtmann**, and the Bohemian-esque **Café Bräunerhof** provided inspiration for renowned writer Thomas Bernhardt.

Café Culture

One of the best advantages of Vienna's cafés is that you can linger at your table for several hours by ordering just one cup of coffee. You can also read local and international newspapers and magazines, provided free of charge, and depending on the establishment, enjoy a host of other offerings. At **Café Prückel**, for example, the bridge tables are set up, while **Café Sperl** is ideal for billiard playing. And literary readings are a favourite at the 200-year-old **Café Dommayer**.

Architecture- and design-gazing is highly important, too. **Café Museum**, built in 1899, shows off the talent of Art Nouveau functionalist Adolf Loos. The **Kleines Café** (*Kleines* meaning "little") is a wonder with its nearly Lilliputian proportions. And the splendidly painted Neo-Gothic vaulting is the main feature of Café Central.

At Cafe Prückel diners can enjoy a game of bridge with their coffee

Types of Coffee

In most of Vienna's finer cafés, a tuxedoed waiter will serve your coffee, along with a glass of water, on a silver metal tray. But ordering coffee in the first place may be no easy task, as there are at least 20 different types to choose from. Some variations are:

Kleiner Brauner: small coffee with milk

Grosser Brauner: large coffee with milk

Kleiner Schwarzer: small espresso

Grosser Schwarzer: double espresso

Melange: light Grosser Brauner with steamed milk

Mokka: strong black coffee

Kapuziner: black coffee with frothed milk

Franziskaner: lighter version of the Kapuziner

Milchkaffee: half coffee, half milk

Verlängerter: espresso with a dash of hot water

Einspänner: large glass of Mokka with whipped cream on top and sometimes sprinkled with cocoa

Eiskaffee: cold, black, with vanilla ice cream and topped with whipped cream

Coffee is elegantly served on a silver tray with a glass of water

What to Eat

Café fare can range from sausages to soups to cakes and pastries. Lunch at **Café Landtmann** and the mirror-laden **Café Schwarzenberg** can include traditional *Wiener Schnitzel*, while **Demel**, formerly the confectioners to the Habsburg Court, offers fancy salads and an array of tantalizing sweets. **Café Diglas** never runs out of over-sized portions of strudels and cream cakes, while **Café Hawelka** is famous for its *Buchteln* (jam-filled buns) served late into the evening.

The elegant interior of the sophisticated Blaue Bar

Vienna's Bars

Vienna has an exciting bar scene, with several modern bars, serving as buzzing alternatives to the more traditional establishments. Fabulous views of the Stephansdom, plus fine mixed drinks, can be had at the rooftop **Skybar** on the pedestrian Kärntnerstrasse. Cocktails, including tasty martinis, are served just down the street

at the sophisticated **Loos Bar**. For sumptuous elegance there is nothing like the **Blaue Bar** inside the venerable Hotel Sacher. For a taste of old-fashioned 1950s nightclub glamour, **Eden Bar** is the place to go.

Austrian Wines in Vienna

Today, Austria produces some of the finest wines in the world, from whites such as Grüner Veltliner and Riesling from the Wachau and Kamptal regions, to reds including Blaufränkisch from Mittelburgenland and Zweigelt from Neusiedlersee, and luscious dessert wines (in styles such as Eiswein and Trockenbeerenauslese) from around the towns of Illmitz and Rust.

Vienna, a wine-growing area in its own right, produces excellent Gemischte Satz, a traditional dry white varietal blend. Most bars in Vienna

feature Austrian wines. **Weinbar Coburg** in Palais Coburg offers a fine range by the glass as does **Wein & Co**, which has several branches around the city.

Austrian Beers

An array of beers are produced in Austria, with the light-bodied Märzen as the most common. There is also Weissbier (wheat beer), and even the alcohol-free beer, Null Komma Josef, which is made by Vienna's Ottakringer brewery. Also produced from this brewery are the soft Gold Fassl brand, plus a pilsner and an unfiltered Zwickl beer.

The cosy, vaulted-ceiling **Bierhof** serves these and other fine Austrian beers. Most order either a Seidl (0.3 litre glass) or the half-litre Krügel, but there is also the tiny 0.2 litre Pfiff, which is a must served with the single-face sandwiches at **Trzesniewski**.

What to Drink in Austria

Austria is a source of excellent wine and good rich beers. Austrian wine is mainly white, though there are excellent local red wines. The wine is drunk before it has finished maturing: *Most*, available from late summer, is the product of the first fermentation of the grapes. In early autumn, this is followed by *Sturm*, a gently fizzing, low-alcohol drink produced by the next stage of grape fermentation. Finally, the *Heuriger*, new-vintage wine, is served. Sweet *Eiswein* is made from grapes left on the vines until the first frosts. Some first-class brandies are also produced – fruit brandies and *Schnaps* are typical drinks.

Vineyards beyond the villages north and west of Vienna, producing *Heuriger* wines

Chardonnay from Styria and sparkling wine from Lower Austria

Austrian Wines

The most popular wine in Austria is Grüner Veltliner (*see below*); a grape variety that also makes an excellent *Eiswein*. Other varietal wines include superb dry Rieslings, especially from the Wachau, and rich Weissburgunders (Pinot Blanc), Chardonnays and Traminers. Red wines tend to be soft and lush – robust reds come from the Blaufränkisch and Zweigelt grapes.

Riesling from the Wachau can be light or full-bodied in style.

Producer's name

Grape variety

Vintage

Producer's address

Level of ripeness

Alcohol content

Style (dry)

Quantity

Grüner Veltliner is a fresh, fruity white grape. It makes a dry wine that is widely available.

St Laurent is a soft red wine from the Neusiedler See region; it is rich and stylish.

Blaufränkisch is a quality red wine – the best is produced in Burgenland.

Krügel or 0.5-litre tankard

Seidl or standard 0.3 litre measure

Krügel or 0.5-litre of pale beer

Pfiff, the smallest measure of beer, a 0.2-litre glass

Kaiser is a light beer

Weizengold wheat beer

Gösser Spezial, a rich beer

Austrian Beers

Good malty beers have been produced in Austria for more than 150 years. The most popular beers are made by the Gösser brewery in Styria – light *Gösser Gold*, stronger *Gösser Spezial* and dark, sweet *Gösser Stiftsbräu*. One of the oldest breweries, based in Schwechat, Lower Austria, produces a variety of pale beers and a slimming beer (so it is claimed) – *Adam Schlank & Rank*. In Vienna, beer from the local brewery in the Ottakring district, the pale sweet *Gold Fassl*, is popular although Bavarian-style wheat beers such as *Weizengold* are also available. The most popular alcohol-free beer in Austria is *Null Komma Josef*.

Bierhof beer mat advertising a pub in the Haarhof.

Null Komma Josef, (Nought Point Joseph), an alcohol-free beer.

Other Austrian Drinks

Austria offers a good range of non-alcoholic fruit juices such as *Himbeersaft* (raspberry juice) or *Johannisbeersaft* (blackcurrant juice). *Almdudler* (Alpine pasture yodler), a herbal lemonade, is also a speciality. Fruit is the basis of many types of schnaps (sometimes called *Brand*). This powerful eau-de-vie is distilled from berries such as juniper or fruits such as apricots *(Marillen)* and quince *(Quitten)*. It is worth paying the extra to sample the schnaps from specialists. Mixer drinks are popular: they include *Radler* (cyclist), a beer with lemonade. An innkeeper is said to have invented this drink on a hot day when, almost out of beer, he served it to thirsty cyclists.

Apricot schnaps

Wiener Rathauskeller, a popular beer-drinkers' haunt

Where to Eat and Drink

Vienna

Inner City

Beaulieu   €
Mediterranean   **Map** 2 B3
Herrengasse 14, 1010
Tel *(01) 532 11 03*
The seafood risotto with saffron
is a popular draw at Beaulieu.
Or go for a plate of delectable
Austrian cheese and breads,
paired with local wines.

Café Bräunerhof   €
Café   **Map** 2 B4
Stallburggasse 2, A-1010
Tel *(01) 512 38 93*
A lovely red-fronted café offering
standard Viennese delicacies.
The fascinating clientele of
intellectuals and academics
at the café more than bolsters
its appeal.

Café Frauenhuber   €
Classic Austrian   **Map** 2 C5
Himmelpfortgasse 6, A-1010
Tel *(01) 512 53 53*
Come here for simple, old-
fashioned Viennese cooking in
a venue that found fame as the
setting of Mozart's last public
performance in 1791.

Café Hawelka   €
Café   **Map** 2 B4
Dorotheergasse 6, 1010
Tel *(01) 512 82 30*
Family-run eatery and a meeting
point for post-war writers and
critics, this place won fame for
its desserts, especially *Buchteln*
(Austrian sweet roll).

Café Prueckel   €
Café   **Map** 3 D4
Stubenring 24, A-1010
Tel *(01) 512 61 15*
A much-loved Viennese café,
with 50s style decor, offering
excellent coffee, meals and
pastries. Cool, arty crowd.

Gasthaus Pöschl   €
Gasthaus   **Map** 2 C5
Weihburggasse 17, 1010
Tel *(01) 513 52 88*
Sit down with a crisp chicken
Schnitzel with parmesan potatoes
and a glass of Austrian beer in
this laidback restaurant.

Gasthaus Reinthaler   €
Gasthaus   **Map** 2 B4
Gluckgasse 5, 1020
Tel *(01) 512 33 66*   **Closed** *Sat & Sun*
Locals flock to this friendly
Gasthaus for delicious Viennese
lunches such as cabbage rolls
followed by apricot dumplings.

Konditorei Gerstner   €
Classic Austrian   **Map** 2 B5
Kärntner Strasse 13–15, 1010
Tel *(01) 512 49 630*
One of the city's greatest pastry
makers and chocolatiers,
Gerstner is a favourite with tour
groups. Indulge in heavenly
macaroons, delectable cupcakes
or scrumptious poppy seed pie.

Oberlaa   €
Patisserie   **Map** 2 B4
Neuer Markt 16, 1010
Tel *(01) 513 29 36-0*
A treasure trove for the sweet-
toothed, this lovely patisserie

dishes out gorgeous cakes and
fruit-topped pastries. Try the
Apfelstrudel. Outdoor seating area.

Restaurant Figlmüller   €
Classic Austrian   **Map** 2 C4
Wollzeile 5, 1010
Tel *(01) 512 61 77*
This tiny, classy restaurant calls
itself the home of *Schnitzel* and
has been serving up huge plates
of Austrian standards for over a
century. Wine only to drink and
no pastries on offer.

TokoRi   €
Japanese   **Map** 2 C3
Salztorgasse 4, 1010
Tel *(01) 532 77 77*
Contemporary restaurant serving
sizzling hot plates of spicy noodles,
tempura prawns and large trays
of sushi to share.

Trzesniewski   €
Café   **Map** 2 B4
Dorotheergasse 1, 1230
Tel *(01) 512 32 91*   **Closed** *Sun*
Follow your nose to find this really
popular bakery. Trzesniewski
offers a superb range of local
breads, yummy pastries, muffins,
delicious bagels and cakes.

Café Central   €€
Café   **Map** 2 B3
Herrengasse 14, 1010
Tel *(01) 533 37 24* or *61*
Once a gathering point for lumin-
aries in art, literature, politics and
science, this café serves a top-
notch two-course lunch.

Café Demel   €€
Café   **Map** 2 B4
Kohlmarkt 14, 1010
Tel *(01) 535 17 17-0*
Oozing with style, this place
is blessed with finesse and
grandeur. Come here to sample
glorious cakes, scones, sweets
and pastries.

Café Hofburg   €€
Café   **Map** 2 B4
Hofburg-Innerer Burghof, 1010
Tel *(01) 24 100-400*
This grand café, next to the Sisi
Museum, is a great stop-off point
for coffee, snacks or lunch after a
visit to the Imperial palace. Classical
piano music every afternoon.

Convivial atmosphere at the popular Café Mozart *(see p311)*

Café Mozart €€
Café Map 2 B5
Albertinaplatz 2, 1010
Tel *(01) 24 100*
An excellent €12.50 set lunch menu means this café can be packed. In 1947, Graham Greene worked on the screenplay of *The Third Man* here. Great service.

Café Sacher €€
Classic Austrian Map 2 B5
Philharmonikerstrasse 4, 1010
Tel *(01) 51 456 661*
One of the city's swankiest addresses is also the authentic home of the *Sachertorte*. A great place to enjoy exquisite coffee and watch people.

Griechenbeisl €€
Classic Austrian Map 3 D3
Fleischmarkt 11, A-1010
Tel *(01) 533 19 77*
Enjoy a *Schnitzel* meal and a few drinks in Vienna's oldest inn. Excellent beef fillet and a long wine list. Framed images of such figures as Beethoven and Schubert nod their approval sagely.

DK Choice

Ilona Stüberl €€
Classic Austrian Map 2 B4
Bräunerstrasse 2, 1010
Tel *(01) 533 90 29*
Founded in 1957, this family-run Austro-Hungarian restaurant is a well-respected part of Vienna's culinary scene. A menu in eight languages covers veal, pork, fish, beef and vegetarian dishes. The restaurant also serves salads, pastas, soups and a few hearty desserts. The waiters are amateur historians, well versed in the 1867 unification history of Austria and Hungary under Emperor Franz Josef.

Charming outdoor seating at Oberlaa, a patisserie and confectionery *(see p310)*

The opulent dining area at Café Sacher

Landtmann Café €€
Café Map 2 A3
Universitätsring 4, 1010
Tel *(01) 24 100–100*
Sigmund Freud, Marlene Dietrich, Paul McCartney and other legendary figures have graced this elegant café since 1873.

Lebenbauer €€
Vegetarian Map 2 A3
Teinfaltstrasse 3, 1010
Tel *(01) 533 55 56* **Closed** *Sat & Sun*
This upmarket vegetarian restaurant boasts a creative, meat-free menu. Recipes use mainly organic produce and are cooked without fat, eggs or flour. Do not miss the pumpkin risotto.

Ofenloch €€
Classic Austrian Map 2 B3
Kurrentgasse 8, 1010
Tel *(01) 533 88 44* **Closed** *Sun*
Traditional menu with all the usual soups, potato dumplings and *Schnitzel*. The service is a cut above the rest.

Oswald & Kalb €€
Classic Austrian Map 2 C4
Bäckerstrasse 14, 1010
Tel *(01) 512 13 71*
Owned by arty patrons, this exciting eatery is set within a vaulted medieval house. Offers some unusual home-made breads and herb-infused oils.

Palmenhaus €€
European Map 2 B5
Burggarten 1, 1010
Tel *(01) 533 10 33*
One of Vienna's plushest venues with a menu to match. Opt for a carpe diem breakfast – fresh pineapple, honeycracker, rye bread and jam, and a goat's cheese omelette.

Plachutta €€
Classic Austrian Map 3 D4
Wollzeile 38, 1010
Tel *(01) 512 15 77*
The Plachutta Wollzeile plays host to numerous Austrian soap

stars and other celebrities. Savour Viennese dishes such as the famous *Tafelspitz* (boiled beef).

Regina Margherita €€
Italian Map 2 B4
Wallnerstrasse 4, 1010
Tel *(01) 533 08 12*
Bite into handmade pizzas, yummy pastas, grilled meats and fish alongside some regional Neapolitan dishes.

Restaurant Kanzleramt €€
Classic Austrian Map 2 B4
Schauflergasse 6, 1010
Tel *(01) 533 13 09* **Closed** *Sun*
Grab a glass of good Austrian wine or fresh local draft beer while choosing from a wide range of specialities such as pork steak with cream sauce.

Sapori Restaurant €€
Mediterranean Map 2 B4
Herrengasse 12, 1010
Tel *(01) 227 80-0* **Closed** *Sat & Sun*
Tasty, modern takes on delicious Mediterranean fare. The beetroot and anchovy salad with dijon mustard and braised lemon chicken are truly delicious.

Le Siècle €€
Mediterranean Map 3 D5
Parkring 16, 1010
Tel *(01) 515 17 34 40*
Serving a delectable array of international dishes, this award-winning restaurant is renowned for decadent dining. Le Siècle serves everything from caviar and suckling pig to herb-rubbed roasted lamb and Chateaubriand.

Teahouse Haas & Haas €€
International Map 2 C4
Stephansplatz 4, 1010
Tel *(01) 512 26 66*
A 25-year-old institution, this friendly teahouse is known for its inviting courtyard. It expertly delivers a wide selection of Germanic dishes for brunch, lunch and afternoon tea.

For more information on types of restaurants *see p301*

Tian €€
Vegetarian **Map** 2 C5
Himmelpfortgasse 23, 1010
Tel *(01) 890 46 65* **Closed** *Sun*
This vegetarian diner is a
meatless gem in the city's
carnivorous dining scene.
All dishes make use of produce
grown in the restaurant's own
organic garden.

Trattoria Martinelli €€
Mediterranean **Map** 2 B3
Freyung 3/Palais Harrach, 1010
Tel *(01) 533 67 21*
This beautiful courtyard restaurant in a historic Baroque palace
with high arched ceilings offers
wonderful food and flawless
service. The steak is unbeatable.

DK Choice

Vestibül €€
Classic Austrian **Map** 2 A3
Universitätsring 2, 1010
Tel *(01) 532 49 99* **Closed** *Sun*
This accolade-winning kitchen
specializes in seasonal dishes
with everything made from
scratch, be it home-made
stock or elderberry juice.
Great food, reliable service
and a superb location just a
stone's throw from Vienna's
fine cultural venues.

Walter Bauer €€
Classic Austrian **Map** 3 D4
Sonnenfelsgasse 17, 1010
Tel *(01) 512-98 71* **Closed** *Sat
& Sun*
Exuding old Viennese charm, this
first-class restaurant is famed for
its modern interpretation of local
culinary classics. The smoked eel
and venison dishes are a delight
to the tastebuds.

Wrenkh Wiener Kochsalon €€
Modern Viennese **Map** 2 C3
Bauernmarkt 10, 1010
Tel *(01) 533 15 26* **Closed** *Sun*
The simple menu here lays an
emphasis on regional food and
healthy vegetarian dishes. Try the
mango and quinoa salad.

Fabios €€€
Mediterannean **Map** 2 B4
Tuchlauben 4–6, 1010
Tel *(01) 532 22 22* **Closed** *Sun*
Stunning architecture and dramatic
use of glass and orange-tinted
lighting at this restaurant. The
food is outstanding – try the
venison with sage gnocchi.

Kervansaray Hummerber €€€
Seafood **Map** 2 C5
Mahlerstrasse 9, 1010
Tel *(01) 512 88 43* **Closed** *Sun*
Revel in a seafood menu that
ranks among Vienna's finest and
features succulent Norwegian
lobster and salmon caviar.

Zum Schwarzen Kameel €€€
Classic Austrian **Map** 2 B3
Bognergasse 5, 1010
Tel *(01) 533 81 25 11* **Closed** *Sun*
Step inside this century-old
Jugendstil building and be wowed
by an 800-strong wine list. Choose
from dozens of cheeses on a first-
class menu. The wild boar with
red wine is particularly good.

North of Mariahilfer Strasse

Café Bellaria €
Café **Map** 2 A5
Bellariastrasse 6, 1010
Tel *(01) 523-53-20*
For superb coffee and blissful
piano music, visit this typical

Café in the magnificent Cupola Hall of
the Kunsthistorisches Museum *(see p313)*

Viennese café where the owner
runs operetta and *Lieder*
evenings. The menu offers
traditional Austrian food and the
service is charming.

Café Eiles €
Café **Map** 1 B4
Josefstädter Strasse 2, 1080
Tel *(01) 405 34 10*
This local café with high ceilings
remains a favourite haunt of
playwrights and stage actors.
Enjoy great food in an
unassuming setting – faded
black-and-white photographs
chronicle a fascinating past.

Café Europa €
Classic Austrian **Map** 4 A1
Zollergasse 8, 1070
Tel *(01) 526 33 83*
Excellent breakfast served for
16 hours a day. The late-night
Wiener Schnitzel is delicious and
a life-saver for those still hungry
in the evenings.

Café Leopold €
Mediterannean **Map** 2 A5
Museumsplatz 1, 1070
Tel *523 67 32* **Closed** *Tue & Wed*
Traditional Viennese café that
serves innovative dishes. Try the
asparagus rocket salad or the
green chilli chicken wrap.

Café Schottenring €
Classic Austrian **Map** 2 B2
Schottenring 19, 1010
Tel *(01) 315 33 43*
This coffee house first threw open
its doors 130 years ago. Order a
melange (an Austrian speciality
coffee with steamed milk) rather
than a *caffe latte* to avoid the
waiter's disappointment.

Spacious dining room of the Vestibül with marble pillars and arches

Key to Price Guide *see p310*

Centimetere II
Classic Austrian €
Map 1 C5
Stiftgasse 4, 1070
Tel *(01) 470 060 642*
Meat eaters will love gorging on the monster-sized ribs served here, and choosing between the numerous sausage varieties, giant burgers and succulent slabs of steak.

Pizzeria-Osteria Da Giovanni
Italian €
Map 1 C5
Sigmundsgasse 14, 1070
Tel *(01) 523 77 78*
Cosy Italian joint where one can choose from bruschetta, soups, salads, pastas, pizza and calzone. Delicious Italian desserts.

Schnitzelwirt
Classic Viennese €
Neubaugasse 52, 1070
Tel *(01) 523 37 71*
This friendly place serves *Schnitzel* in just about every way imaginable. Large servings and traditional decor.

Amerlingbeisl
Classic Austrian €€
Map 1 C5
Stiftgasse 8, 1070
Tel *(01) 526-16 60*
Experiment with the speciality cocktails and daily specials on the tiny seasonal menu – the pasta with smoked salmon and white wine cream is particularly good. Lovely shaded courtyard.

Café & Restaurant, Kunsthistorisches Museum
Classic Austrian €€
Map 2 B4
Burgring 5, 1010
Tel *(0) 50 876 10 01*
Fine dining in the Cupola Hall of the Kunsthistorisches Museum. Beautiful, opulent and grand, the hall provides an idyllic setting for a Sunday brunch or a romantic supper.

La Delizia
Italian €€
Map 1 A3
Florianigasse 19, 1080
Tel *(01) 406 37 02*
The pizzas at this authentic, cosy Italian place may be considered among the best in the city, but it's worth trying to find room for the rest of the delicious Neapolitan cuisine served here.

Österreicher im MAK
Classic Austrian €€
Map 3 D4
Stubenring 5, 1010
Tel *(01) 714 01 21*
Although the restaurant at the Austrian Museum of Applied Arts offers an excellent set lunch menu, it is the elaborate Sunday brunch spread that really pulls in the crowds here.

Pretty interiors at Café Sperl, one of the finest coffee houses in Vienna

Restaurant Braubräu
Classic Austrian €€
Map 4 A1
Mariahilfestrasse 47, 1060
Tel *(01) 941 23 32* **Closed** *Sun & hols*
The fun decor of this diner belies the serious regard it holds for its food – try the breaded cheese with plum compote or venison ragout with potato dumplings.

Schnattl
European €€
Map 1 B3
Lange Gasse 40, 1080
Tel *(01) 405 34 00* **Closed** *Sat & Sun*
Discerning gastronomes come here for the extensive three-course or nine-course tasting menu depending on their appetite. Outdoor dining available.

Ulrich
Classic Austrian €€
Map 1 B5
Sankt-Ulrichs-Platz 1, 1070
Tel *(01) 96 12 782*
Across from the Baroque church of St Ulrich and perfect for a leisurely brunch, this hip, lively place serves up generous plates of omelettes, eggs and *Schnitzel* until late. Superb desserts.

Zu ebener Erde und erster Stock
Classic Austrian €€
Map 1 C5
Burggasse 13, 1070
Tel *(01) 523 62 54* **Closed** *Sat & Sun*
Charming Viennese café offering the whole range of experiences: from candlelit dinners to set-price meals of classics such as *Schnitzel* and potato dumplings.

South of the Ring

Café Museum
Classic Austrian €
Map 4 C1
Operngasse 7–Karlsplatz, 1010
Tel *(01) 24 100-620*
Lovely 1800s café that hosted famous artists such as Gustav Klimt and Egon Schiele. Enjoy good Austrian food and evening piano music on weekends.

Salm Bräu
Classic Austrian €
Map 5 E1
Rennweg 8, 1030
Tel *(01) 799 59 92*
A very popular eatery with colour-washed walls and good atmosphere. Come here to sample smoked venison and garlic bread and dumpling-topped brown beer soup. The daily specials are good value.

Café Schwarzenberg
Café €€
Map 2 C5
Kärntner Ring 17, 1010
Tel *(01) 512 89 98*
Discover dozens of tea varieties here together with great coffee. The glass-fronted cabinet is full of tempting sugar-frosted buns, shiny *Torten* and scrumptious fruit pies. This café offers considerable value.

Café Sperl
Classic Austrian €€
Map 4 B1
Gumpendorferstrasse 11, 1060
Tel *(01) 586 41 58*
An ideal place to visit for a simple Austrian breakfast of ham, eggs and freshly baked breads. Café Sperl also serves lip-smacking lunches, snacks and dinners from dumpling soups and rabbit stews to a mile-long menu of different cream-topped coffees.

Opus
Classic Austrian €€
Map 5 D1
Kärntner Ring 16, 1010
Tel *(01) 501 10 389*
The Opus Restaurant is located in the grand luxury Hotel Imperial, where Austrian monarchs gaze down from gilt frames. Guests are treated like royalty in the plush yet understated dining room and the tables are laden with crystal. An imperial indulgence to savour.

> **DK Choice**
>
> ### Restaurant at Eight
> **Classic Austrian** €€
> **Map** 5 D1
> *Kärntner Ring 8, 1010*
> **Tel** *(01) 221 22 38 30*
> This slick eatery has a dual personality – light, airy and bustling by day, and then lively, vibrant and moody by night. As the home of the city's youngest head chef, Daniel Kraft, the restaurant has been deluged by accolades. Today, this innovative culinary wizard continues to perform his magic, transforming heavy Austrian classics into chic, beautifully presented, bite-sized morsels bursting with flavour. Absolutely flawless service.

For more information on types of restaurants *see p301*

Anna Sacher
€€€
Classic Austrian **Map** 2 B5
Philharmonikerstrasse 4, 1010
Tel *(01) 51 456 840* **Closed** *Mon*
One of Vienna's best-loved
high-end traditional dining
venues. Try the exquisite
Angus beef or the lobster
salad. Good selection of wines
and impeccable service.

DK Choice

Restaurant Bristol €€€
Classic Austrian **Map** 2 B5
Kärntner Ring 1, 1010
Tel *(01) 515 16 553*
Enjoy some of the finest food
in Vienna at this highly regarded
restaurant where menu highlights run from pumpkin soup
and venison *Gulasch* to
delicately smoked fish. Revel in
finely-honed service born out
of a lengthy gourmet tradition.
The setting is grand, so dress up
to the nines for a culinary treat.

Steirereck
€€€
Classic Austrian **Map** 3 D5
Am Heumarkt 2A/Stadtpark, 1030
Tel *(01) 713 31 68* **Closed** *Sat & Sun*
Steirereck's offers an incredible
seven-course tasting menu –
a luxurious feast of seafood,
poultry and game with such
unusual ingredients as
nasturtium root and goat's liver,
accompanied by honey, rye and
lavender bread.

Further Afield

Café Cuadro
€
Café
Margaretenstrasse 77, 1050
Tel *(01) 544 75 50*
Chrome, beech and opaque glass
lends this café a Scandinavian
feel by day. The place gets filled
up quickly after dark. Great for
burgers and cocktails.

Café Dialog
€
Café
Renweg 43, 1030
Tel *(01) 544 75 50*
Eat and drink while reading the
newspapers along with locals at
this authentic coffee house,
where umpteen coffee refills
are offered. Liquor is served
20 hours a day.

Café Dommayer
€
Café
Dommayergasse 1, 1130
Tel *(01) 877 546 50*
Revel in the classic decor of this
stylish café and relax with a
steaming cup of *melange* (a
café au lait or *caffe latte*) on a
comfortable red couch under
crystal chandeliers.

Café Goldegg
€
European
Argentinierstrasse 49, 1040
Tel *(01) 505 91 62*
This fine Viennese café has
leather chairs and a pool table
where gentlemen's etiquette
applies. Brass beer pumps are
polished to perfection.

Café-Restaurant Dunkelbunt
€
Classic Austrian
Weissgerberlände 14, 1030
Tel *(01) 715 26 89*
A tranquil gourmet oasis, with
beautiful gardens filled with
plants and blooms. This place
makes use of organic, fresh
produce wherever possible,
and the vegetarian meals are
much acclaimed.

Café Ritter
€
Café
Ottakringer Strasse 117, 1160
Tel *(01) 486 12 53*
Choose from a range of
breakfasts as well as snacks,
lunches, afternoon teas and dinner.
Special dishes include a delectable
grilled bream with spinach.

Dellago
€
Italian
Payergasse 10, 1160
Tel *(01) 95 747 95*
This lovely Italian eatery offers
excellent breakfasts that draw
crowds with fresh fruit, big jugs
of juice, coffee and baskets of
freshly baked Viennese breads
and pastries. For lunch, try the
salmon fettuccine.

Das Moped
€
Modern Austrian
Salmgasse 23, 1030
Tel *(01) 966 11 44* **Closed** *Sat & Sun*
Furnished with mid-century
modern pieces, this modish bar
serves decent Viennese food with
a modern twist. A hip, fun place
to linger over a drink.

Rasouli
€
Mediterranean
Payergasse 12, 1160
Tel *(01) 403 13 47* **Closed** *Mon*
Arrive early for a breakfast of
feta cheese omelette or pancake
stacks, or opt for a lunch of
sausages with chickpeas. The
chicken couscous is heavenly.

Rote Rübe
€
Vegetarian
Zieglergasse 37, 1070
Tel *(01) 507 9138 60* **Closed** *Mon;
Sun from Nov–Apr*
An art café with a distinct white-
and-red decor, Rote Rube boasts
a completely meat-free menu.
Crêpes and frittatas fuse Greek
flavours with local produce.

Strandcafé
€
Classic Austrian
Florian-Berndl Gasse 20, 1220
Tel *(01) 203 67 47*
Popular Viennese waterfront food
joint. Choose a table out on the
deck or in the boat's cabin for a
menu of pork, steak, fish and pasta.

Tewa
€
International
Naschmarkt 672
Tel *(01) 676 847 74 12 11* **Closed** *Sun*
Fresh and exciting food at this
trendy restaurant. Try honey
toasts for breakfast and wash
them down with mango lassi.
The lunchtime wraps and soups
are great.

Vegetasia
€
Vegetarian
Ungargasse 57, 1030
Tel *(01) 713 83 32*
This place serves an amazing
all-you-can-eat lunchtime buffet –
a utopia for hungry vegetarians
in Vienna. Other meal options
include lentil soups, olive breads,
tofu stir-fry and aubergine stew.

Pretty façade of the Restaurant Cobenzl *(see p315)*, known for its spectacular views

Elegant interiors of the Restaurant Bristol

Wetter   €
Italian
Payergasse 13, 1160
Tel *(01) 406 07 75*
Former launderette transformed into a busy little eatery. Visit for wholesome northwestern Italian dishes and Ligurian wines.

Xu's Cooking   €
Vegetarian
Kaiserstrasse 45, 1070
Tel *(01) 523 10 91*
Nutrition is taken very seriously at Xu's where vegetarian dishes are rich in proteins, vitamins and minerals and free from glutamate. Try the popular warm buffet – excellent value for money.

An-Do Fisch   €€
Seafood
Brunnenmarkt Stand, 1160
Tel *(01) 308 75 76* **Closed** *Sun & hols*
This lively restaurant with an open kitchen is one of the few in the city specializing in fish. It is also one of the best.

DK Choice

Café Noir   €€
International
Goldschlagstraße 172, 1140
Tel *(01) 932 567 825* **Closed** *Mon & Sun*
Connect with food in an exciting new way by dining on the "dark side of the spoon". Come to Café Noir for a sensual and tantalizing exploration of cuisine in which the taste, texture and aromas of dishes are relished in complete darkness to achieve a heightened state of enjoyment.

Café Weimar   €€
Classic Austrian
Währinger Str 68, 1090
Tel *(01) 317 12 06*
Set on an attractive corner plot, this peculiarly shaped building is one of the last Viennese classic coffee houses run in traditional style. Visit for coffee, pastries, cakes, snacks or *Schnitzel* meals.

Flatschers Restaurant & Bar   €€
Steakhouse
Kaiserstrasse 113–115, 1070
Tel *(01) 523 42 68*
Popular steak house where smoked meats, beef tartar, chilli steak wrap and deconstructed burgers with umpteen toppings wow a loyal clientele. Do not miss the signature dish – Argentine fillet.

Le Loft   €€
International
Praterstrasse 1, 1020
Tel *(01) 906 160*
Impressive decor plus dazzling views across the lights of the city, ensures a great atmosphere to go with the excellent French-Austrian menu. Incredible selection of wines.

Colourful and vibrant dining area at Motto

Motto   €€
Classic Austrian
Schönbrunnerstrasse 30, 1050
Tel *(01) 587 06 72*
One of Austria's premier gay-friendly restaurants, this place offers an eclectic menu that includes sushi, Thai-inspired curries, salmon ragout and salads.

Restaurant Cobenzl   €€
Classic Austrian
Am Cobenzl 94, 1190
Tel *(01) 320 51 20*
This historic eatery is in the bright yellow Schloss Cobenzl, where Mozart lived for a time in 1781 and enjoyed the splendid views. The old-fashioned menu features the Viennese delicacy of boiled beef fillet with mustard and herbs.

DK Choice

Saint Charles Alimentary   €€
Vegetarian
Gumpendorferstrasse 33, 1060
Tel *650 97 00 350* **Closed** *Sun*
Located in a pharmacy with medicine jars, pill bottles and apothecary gear lining the walls, this quirky eatery focuses on wellness cuisine. The restaurant uses herbs, plants, nuts and seeds with healing properties. Try an aromatic wild root soup or spelt with roast pumpkin and walnuts for a meal that is truly healthy. Book ahead; there are only eight seats.

Servitenwirt   €€
Classic Austrian
Servitengasse 7, 1090
Tel *(01) 315 23 87*
The outdoor seating at wooden slatted benches and tables is popular once spring arrives – so arrive early for lunch here. The menu changes daily, but is the usual Viennese fare.

For more information on types of restaurants *see p301*

Guests enjoying the Dining Room, perfect for private dining *(see p316)*

The Dining Room €€€
Mediterranean
Maygasse 31, 1130
Tel *(01)* 804 85 86   **Closed** *Tue, Thu, Sat & Sun*
This little restaurant is ideal for diners who prefer intimate gastronomic experiences. The food is exquisite; the service impeccable.

Mraz und Sohn €€€
European
Wallensteinstrasse 59, 1200
Tel *(01)* 330 45 94   **Closed** *Sat & Sun*
A creative kitchen serving beautifully seasoned saddle of lamb with barley, celery and capers as well as a nine-course menu with a wine pairing.

Neuer Wind €€€
Pan-Asian
Hoher Markt 12, 1010
Tel *(01)* 319 02 42 **Closed** *Sun & Mon*
Renowned Asian chef Kim Kocht leads the way at this sleek, contemporary restaurant. Tables are booked weeks in advance for Kocht's signature "surprise dinner".

Lower Austria & Burgenland

AMSTETTEN: Stadtbrauhof €
Classic Austrian   **Map** E3
Hauptplatz 14, A-3300
Tel *(07472)* 628 00
Cheerful bar and restaurant serving standard wok-fried dishes, steaks and daily specials. Wash it all down with locally brewed beer. It's a popular place with a young crowd.

BADEN: Primavera €€
Gourmet   **Map** G3
Weiburgstrasse 3, A-2500
Tel *(02252)* 855 51   **Closed** *mid-Jul– mid-Aug; Sun–Tue*
Award-winning gourmet restaurant rated by both Michelin and

Gault Millau. This place offers a haute cuisine take on the European range of beef and lamb.

BADEN: Rauhenstein €€
International   **Map** G3
Weiburgstrasse 11, A-2500
Tel *(02252)* 412 51 0   **Closed** *Sun*
Rauhenstein is the in-house restaurant of the magnificent Sauerhof hotel. Choose from an extensive selection of beef and pork mains or try the salmon fillet.

DÜRNSTEIN: Loibnerhof €€
Regional   **Map** F3
Unterloiben 7, A-3601
Tel *(02732)* 828 90   **Closed** *Mon & Tue*
Family-run restaurant set in a 17th-century house; offers superb regional dishes, yummy desserts and excellent wines.

**DÜRNSTEIN:
Schloss Dürnstein** €€€
International   **Map** F3
Schloss Dürnstein, A-3601
Tel *(02711)* 212   **Closed** *Nov–Mar*
It is difficult to imagine a place more scenic than the terrace of this castle restaurant overlooking the blue Danube. Impeccable service and international cuisine.

GAADEN: Meierei Gaaden €
Classic Austrian   **Map** F3
Anningerstrasse 5, A-2531
Tel *(02237)* 81 43   **Closed** *Mon–Thu*
Light meals feature on the menu at this popular coffee house and *jausenstation* (snack bar). Enjoy sausages and delicious strudels on the sunny terrace.

GÖTTELSBRUNN: Jungwirt €
Wine Tavern   **Map** G3
Landstrasse 36, A-2464
Tel *(02162)* 89 43   **Closed** *Mon, Tue & Wed*
Outstanding example of the new generation of wine taverns in

lower Austria, with its own vineyard and vintages. The rustic high-ceilinged dining room has a warming central fireplace, and the cuisine is imaginatively presented. Try the boiled beef or the veal.

**GÖTTELSBRUNN:
Bittermann Vinarium** €€
Wine Tavern   **Map** G3
Abt-Bruno-Heinrich-Platz 1, A-2464
Tel *(02162)* 811 55   **Closed** *Mon & Tue*
Smart wine bar that deals in all the popular local vintages and offers innovative cuisine. Ideal place to sample local delicacies.

**GRAFENEGG:
Schlosstaverne Grafenegg** €€
International   **Map** F3
Grafenegg 12, A-3485
Tel *(02735)* 26 160 **Closed** *Dec–Mar; Mon & Tue*
A mix of international and Austrian cuisine with excellent presentation and service. Just sitting in the castle dining room is a treat. When the weather is fine, dine on the patio.

**HALBTURN:
Wieser Knappenstöckl** €€
Classic Austrian   **Map** G3
Im Schloss, 7131
Tel *(02172)* 823 90   **Closed** *Mon*
Sample fine Austrian cuisine in a historic castle dining room. The emphasis is on locally sourced ingredients, organically reared cattle and seasonal game.

**HINTERBRÜHL BEI MODLING:
Hexensitz** €€
Regional   **Map** G3
Johannesstrasse 35, A-2371
Tel *(02236)* 229 37   **Closed** *Mon & Tue*
The best of Austrian country cuisine prepared and served by devoted staff in a simple single-storey building.

**KLOSTERNEUBURG:
Poseidon** €
Greek   **Map** G3
Kierlingerstrasse 47a, A-3400
Tel *(02243)* 336 43
Popular Greek restaurant with authentic fare, which you can follow with a glass of retsina or a shot of ouzo. Great decor with big garden-facing windows.

KLOSTERNEUBURG: Redinger €
Wine Tavern   **Map** G3
Agnesstrasse 23, A-3400
Tel *(02243)* 379 21
A typical *Heuriger* or wine tavern offering the best of local wines and a good choice of regional food. Friendly service.

KREMS: Kloster Und €€
International Map F3
Undstrasse 6, A-3500
Tel *(02732) 747 45* **Closed** *Sun & Mon*
Atmospheric dining inside the walls of a historic 17th-century monastery, with lovely courtyard seating, a wide-ranging international menu and an extensive wine list.

KRUMBACH: Triad €€
Gourmet Map G4
Ödhöfen 25, Bad Schönau, A-2851
Tel *(02646) 83 17* **Closed** *Mon & Tue*
Lovely rustic-style restaurant set in an old stable, serving superb quality modern Austrian cuisine. Ecological and locally sourced ingredients are a priority at this restaurant.

LANGENLOIS:
Heurigenhof Bründlmayer €€
Wine Tavern Map F3
Walterstrasse 14, A-3550
Tel *(02734) 28 83* **Closed** *Mon & Tue*
Upmarket *Heuriger* serving the best of the local Grüner Veltliner and Riesling, accompanied either by cold cuts or gourmet dishes featuring game and fish. Lovely courtyard seating.

MARIA TAFERL: Donauterrasse €
Classic Austrian Map F3
Maria Taferl 24, A-3672
Tel *(07413) 63 55*
This restaurant of the Krone & Kaiserhof hotel has an outdoor terrace offering magnificent views over the Danube. The menu is mainstream Austrian with a few international touches.

Simple and understated decor at Heurigenhof Bründlmayer, Langenlois

Impressive Baroque dining space at Nikolaihof Wachau, Mautern

DK Choice

MAUTERN:
Nikolaihof Wachau €€
Wine Tavern Map F3
Nikolaigasse 3, A-3512
Tel *(02732) 829 01* **Closed** *Dec–Apr; Sun, Mon & Tue*
This historic wine estate with Baroque dining rooms and a historic garden serves delicious local food. The smoked ox-tongue, boiled beef and *saumaise* (a regional meatloaf speciality) are exceptionally well made. The owners use local organic ingredients wherever possible.

MAYERLING: Hanner €€€
Fusion Map F3
Mayerling 1, A-2534
Tel *(02258) 23 78*
This restaurant, set within a hotel and sports complex, offers an individual take on Austrian and international fusion, with some exciting local food and exotic spice combinations.

MICHELBACH:
Landgasthof Schwarzwallner €€
Regional Map F3
Untergoin 6, A-3074
Tel *(02744) 82 41* **Closed** *Tue & Wed*
Home-style food in a farm house where guests can dine in the garden in summer or conservatory in winter. Local specialities include *blunzl* (fried black pudding).

MÖDLING: Babenbergerhof €€
Classic Austrian Map G3
Babenbergergasse 6, A-2340
Tel *(02236) 222 46*
Restaurant, café and bistro attached to the upmarket Hotel Babenbergerhof, where the emphasis is on natural ingredients. It's a great place to try out Austrian classics. The fried goose liver is particularly good.

NECKENMARKT: Zur Traube €
Classic Austrian Map G4
Herrengasse 42, A-7311
Tel *(02610) 422 56*
Lamb, local beef and game feature on the menu at this convivial family restaurant. A garden with picnic tables is available for the summers.

NEUSIEDL AM SEE:
Landgasthaus am Nyikospark €€
Gourmet Map G3
Untere Hauptstrasse 59, A-7100
Tel *(02167) 402 22* **Closed** *Mon & Tue*
Regional gourmet cooking in a contemporary ambience. Enjoy a modern twist on classic dishes such as *tafelspitz* and freshwater fish. Fine service.

NEUSIEDL AM SEE:
Mole West €€
Gourmet Map G3
Seegelände 9, A-7100
Tel *(02167) 202 05* **Closed** *Jan–Mar, Mon, Tue & Wed*
A stunning restaurant on the timber-decked lakeshore with glass-fronted dining rooms overooking the water.

PODERSDORF: Dankbarkeit €
Wine Tavern Map G3
Hauptstrasse 39, A-7141
Tel *(02177) 22 23* **Closed** *April–Nov: Wed & Thu; Jan–Mar: Mon, Tue, Wed & Thu*
A country restaurant with its own vineyards, and a menu featuring locally sourced fish, lamb and goose. The summer garden is a perfect setting for a relaxed meal.

PÖTTSCHING: Der Reisinger €€
Regional Map G3
Hauptstrasse 83, A-7033
Tel *(02631) 22 12* **Closed** *Mon–Thu*
Stylish local restaurant offering good value regional cooking with a haute-cuisine flair. The Sunday brunches are very popular.

For more information on types of restaurants *see p301*

PURBACH: Kloster am Spitz €€
International   **Map** G3
Waldsiedlung 2, A-7083
Tel *(02683) 55 19*   **Closed** *Mon, Tue & Wed*
Part of a complex that includes a restaurant, vineyard and hotel, the Kloster offers a classy menu, with dishes planned according to the best seasonal ingredients.

RITZING: Horvath €€
Regional   **Map** G4
Lange Zeile 92, A-7323
Tel *(02619) 672 29*   **Closed** *Mon & Tue*
Cottage-style country restaurant with a large outdoor terrace. Serves seasonal game, lamb, vegetables from its own gardens and mouthwatering desserts.

RUST:
Mooslechners Rusterhof €€
Seafood   **Map** G3
Rathausplatz 18, A-7071
Tel *(02685) 607 93*   **Closed** *Wed & Thu*
Country restaurant and hotel that serves freshwater fish from the Neusiedler See, and regional delicacies such as the popular, and fiery paprika-fuelled fish soup.

SCHÜTZEN AM GEBIRGE:
Taubenkobel €€€
Gourmet   **Map** G3
Hauptstrasse 31–33, A-7081
Tel *(02684) 22 97*   **Closed** *Mon & Tue*
This place, inspired by local ingredients, presents haute cuisine with flair and imagination. The menu changes according to the best seasonal ingredients available. The house wines are first rate.

Styria

BAD RADKERSBURG:
Romantik Hotel im Park €€
International   **Map** F5
Kurhausstrasse 5, A-8490
Tel *(03476) 25 710*
Lavish spa hotel offering top-quality Austrian food in the gourmet restaurant, and light bites in the poolside bar. There is also a restaurant serving Mediterranean food.

BAD WALTERSDORF:
Safenhof €€€
Gourmet   **Map** F4
Hauptstrasse 78, A-8271
Tel *(03333) 22 390*   **Closed** *Mon*
Feast on locally sourced beef, duck and game at this highly rated, popular restaurant that mixes the best of Austrian tradition with international inventiveness.

DEUTSCHLANDSBERG:
Alpengasthof Koralpenblick €
Regional   **Map** F5
Rostock 15, Trahütten, A-8530
Tel *(03461) 210*
Lovely guesthouse with a cosy restaurant that serves superb Styrian beef, local game, mountain trout and home-baked bread.

ETMISSL: Hubinger €€
Regional   **Map** F4
Etmissl 25, A-8622
Tel *(03861) 81 14*   **Closed** *Mon & Tue, except hols*
Set in an ancient house in the foothills of the Hochschwab. The menu here features home-grown vegetables, naturally reared cattle and local game.

FISCHBACH: Zum Forsthaus €€€
Gourmet   **Map** F4
Fischbach 2, A-8654
Tel *(03170) 201*   **Closed** *Mon & Tue*
Award-winning restaurant within a wood-panelled 17th-century house. Come here to experience the best of local cuisine. Creative cooking with a light touch.

GAMLITZ: Jaglhof €€
Wine tavern   **Map** F5
Sernau 25, A-8462
Tel *(03454) 66 75*   **Closed** *Jan & Feb*
Right in the heart of wine country, this hotel-restaurant boasts contemporary design and has a scenic terrace to woo diners when the weather is right. Choose from a great selection of wines.

GAMLITZ: Sattlhof €€€
Gourmet   **Map** F5
Sernau 2a, A-8462
Tel *(03453) 44 54*   **Closed** *Dec–Feb; Sun & Mon*
Styrian restaurant offering an imaginative take on locally reared meats and home-grown vegetables. A huge list of local wines accompanies the food.

GRAZ: Frankowitsch €
Café   **Map** F4
Stempfergasse 2/4, A-8010
Tel *(0316) 822 212*   **Closed** *Sun*
Downtown patisserie with a popular pavement terrace. Serves deli sandwiches, pastries and typically extravagant Austrian cakes. Good service.

GRAZ: Der Steirer €
Regional   **Map** F4
Belgiergasse 1, A-8010
Tel *(0316) 703 654*
Sample traditional Austrian dishes and Styrian tapas with local wines by the glass. Try the fried chicken. The traditional Sunday roast meal is a treat.

GRAZ: Thomawirt €
International   **Map** F4
Leonhardstrasse 40, A-8010
Tel *(0316) 328 637*
Bare-brick bar-restaurant serving Austrian, fusion and vegetarian food to a young, professional crowd. Frequent live music and DJs in the evenings.

GRAZ: Anna €€
Gourmet   **Map** F4
Sackstrasse 3–5, A-8010
Tel *(0676) 969 11 44*
Spectacular atrium restaurant built into the courtyard of the Erzherzog Johann hotel. Serves classic Austrian cuisine with a Mediterranean twist.

Bright and tasteful interiors at Bruno, Graz

GRAZ: Bruno
International   €€   Map F4
Sackstrasse 27, A-8010
Tel *(0316) 829 109*   **Closed** *Sun*
A centrally located café-restaurant with pleasant outdoor seating and a predominantly Mediterranean menu. Try the risotto with pumpkin and brie cheese. Good selection of international wines.

GRAZ: Häuserl im Wald
Classic Austrian   €€   Map F4
Roseggerweg 105, A-8044
Tel *(0316) 391 1650*
Come here for classic Austrian dishes at reasonable prices. There is a playground and petting zoo on the grounds to keep kids happy.

GRAZ: Landhauskeller
Classic Austrian   €€   Map F4
Schmiedegasse 9, A-8010
Tel *(0316) 830 276*   **Closed** *Sun*
This long-established restaurant is highly rated for its classic Austrian *Schnitzel* and boiled beef dishes. Choose from a wide range of inexpensive set lunches.

GRAZ: Magnolia
International   €€€   Map F4
Schönaugasse 53, A-8010
Tel *(0316) 823 835* **Closed** *Sat & Sun*
Located in the Augarten design hotel, Magnolia has an outstanding reputation for contemporary creative cooking. They also serve inexpensive business lunches.

GRÖBMING:
Landhaus das Georg
Seafood   €€   Map E4
Kulmweg 555, A-8962
Tel *(03685) 227 40*
Modern family hotel with a restaurant offering a good choice of local Styrian fare and Adriatic

seafood. Besides the usual meat dishes, this place also has a good vegetarian selection. Fine service.

GRUNDLSEE: Alpengasthof Max Schraml
Classic Austrian   €   Map E4
Bräuhof 14, 8993
Tel *(03622) 86 42*
This popular *Gasthof*, serving a wide range of Austrian staples, has amazing views from its terrace over Grundlsee and the Tote Gebirge (Dead Mountains). The wood-panelled interior is warm and inviting. Book ahead.

GRUNDLSEE: Fischkalter
Seafood   €€   Map E4
Mosern 19, A-8993
Tel *(0676) 960 59 83*   **Closed** *Thu*
Relish delicious fish soup, mountain trout and freshly caught Grundlsee fish in this charming wood-panelled lakeside house.

HART BEI GRAZ: Hirschenwirt
Regional   €€   Map F4
Rupertistrasse 115, A-8075
Tel *(0316) 465 600*   **Closed** *Sun & Mon*
Popular with Graz residents for its mix of traditional Austrian cooking and Styrian specialities. Enjoy the hearty meals on a summer garden. Dogs are permitted in the restaurant.

HOHENTAUERN: Passhöhe
Gourmet   €€   Map E4
Hohentauern 110, A-8785
Tel *(03618) 219*
This family-run hotel-restaurant has a loyal clientele and is renowned for combining local Styrian cuisine with Mediterranean influences. Well-chosen list of Austrian wines.

Stylish seating at the highly-rated restaurant, Magnolia in Graz

KITZECK: Kirchenwirt
Regional   €€   Map F5
Steinriegel 52, A-8442
Tel *(03456) 22 25*   **Closed** *Dec–mid Mar; Sun, Mon & Tue*
Cottage-style restaurant set among some of Europe's highest vineyards. Sample organic Styrian fare with seasonal delicacies such as asparagus and pumpkins.

LEBRING/LEIBNITZ: Gollner
International   €€   Map F5
Grazerstrasse 36, Lebring-St Margarethen, A-8403
Tel *(03182) 25 21*   **Closed** *Thu*
A smart family-friendly hotel-restaurant that dishes out classic Austrian and international dishes. It has a lovely garden for outdoor dining.

MARIAZELL: Brauhaus Mariazell
Classic Austrian   €   Map F4
Wienerstrasse 5, A-8630
Tel *(03882) 25 23* **Closed** *Mon & Tue*
This restaurant serves local, organic products, accompanied by palatable light and dark Girrer beers brewed on the premises.

MURAU: Hotel Gasthof Lercher
Classic Austrian   €€   Map E4
Schwarzenbergstrasse 10, A-8850
Tel *(03532) 24 31*
Modernized 18th-century establishment in the village centre. The menu focuses on Styrian beef dishes and fresh trout from the local rivers.

PISTORF: Zur Hube
Gourmet   €€   Map F5
Sausal 51, A-8443
Tel *(03457) 32 71*
Creative cuisine in a rustic location, with the Austrian-Central European menu changing according to season. Reservations should be made in advance.

Subtle lighting and romantic interiors at Landhauskeller in Graz

For more information on types of restaurants *see p301*

RAMSAU AM DACHSTEIN:
Pehab-Kirchenwirt €
Classic Austrian   Map D4
Ramsau 62, A-8972
Tel *(03687) 817 32*
Family-run establishment
with farmhouse style decor
offering classic Austrian cuisine.
The emphasis is on seasonally
fresh produce. Also has
a popular beer cellar.

ST SEBASTIAN/MARIAZELL:
Lurgbauer €€
Regional   Map F4
Lurg 1, A-3224
Tel *(03882) 37 18*   **Closed** *Mon &*
Tue May–Oct; Mon–Thu Nov–Apr
Home-raised beef is the star
item on the menu of this unique
farm-restaurant. Boiled beef
or steak are the standard mains,
followed by home-grown
vegetables. Excellent service.

DK Choice

TURNAU: Steirereck €€
Regional   Map F4
Pogusch 21, A-8625
Tel *(03863) 20 00*   **Closed** *Mon–*
Wed
Located in a gorgeous
ensemble of farm buildings
deep in rural Styria, Steirereck
is renowned throughout the
country for turning the natural
bounty of rural Austria into
haute cuisine. Expect free-range
fowl, locally sourced meats and
freshwater fish, all prepared with
an inventive edge. Steirereck
also offers a good choice of
vegetarian dishes, and some
irresistible traditional desserts.
There is a summer garden
and terrace.

Upper Austria

AIGEN-SCHLAGL:
Bärnsteinhof €€
Regional   Map E2
Marktplatz 12, A-4160
Tel *(07281) 62 45*   **Closed** *Wed*
Family-run hotel-restaurant
with a country house ambience.
Offers a blend of Viennese and
rustic Austrian cuisine. Plenty of
vegetarian options as well.

ATTERSEE:
Seegasthof Oberndorfer €€
Seafood   Map D3
Hauptstrasse 18, A-4864
Tel *(07666) 78 640*   **Closed** *Jan*
Freshwater fish and classic
Austrian *Schnitzel*-type dishes
are the order of the day at this
lakeside hotel-restaurant with
a wonderful terrace.

BAD GOISERN: Agathawirt €
Classic Austrian   Map D3
St Agatha 10, A-4822
Tel *(06135) 83 41*
A 16th-century hotel-restaurant
with an atmospheric dining
room, the Agathawirt focuses
on fresh ingredients and a
seasonally changing menu
of local meat and poultry.

BAD ISCHL: Café Zauner €
Café   Map D4
Pfarrgasse 7, A-4820
Tel *(06132) 233 10-20*
In the cake-baking business
since 1832, Zauner is Bad Ischl's
must-visit location for anyone
with a sweet tooth. Study the
display cabinet brimming
with treats before taking a seat
among the chandeliers and
house plants.

EFERDING:
Landgasthof Dieplinger €
Seafood   Map E3
Brandstatt 4, A-4070
Tel *(07272) 23 24*   **Closed** *Thu*
A lovely countryside inn serving
organically raised beef and
lamb with fresh local vegetables.
The house schnapps is particularly
good. Great range of fish dishes.

GMUNDEN:
Schloss Freisitz Roith €€
Gourmet   Map D3
Traunsteinstrasse 87, A-4810
Tel *(07612) 649 05*   **Closed** *Wed*
A lakeside castle-restaurant hailed
for its quality cuisine, Freisitz is a
great place to enjoy freshwater
fish and game. Good wine list.

GRIESKIRCHEN: Waldschänke €€
Regional   Map D3
Kickendorf 15, A-4710
Tel *(07248) 623 08*   **Closed** *Mon*
& Tue
With a seasonally changing menu
overseen by a creative team, this
is a great place to sample rustic,
well-prepared Austrian fare.

KEFERMARKT: Schlossbrauerei €
Classic Austrian   Map E3
Weinberg 2, 4292
Tel *(07947) 71 11*   **Closed** *Mon*
Enjoy beer brewed on the
premises and hearty Austrian
veal and poultry dishes at this
enjoyable castle-restaurant.

LINZ: Brandl €
Café   Map E3
Bismarckstrasse 6, A-4020
Tel *(0732) 773 635-2*   **Closed** *Sun*
This long-standing Linz
bakery also has a sit-down
section where you can munch
your way through a dizzying

Delightful and cosy interiors of Café Zauner in Bad Ischl

range of crusty-bread sandwiches, crisp croissants and brioches.

LINZ: Klosterhof €
Classic Austrian **Map** E3
Landstrasse 30, A-4020
Tel *(0732) 773 373*
Solid Austrian cuisine from sausages to *Gulasch* soup to *Schnitzel* served in a beer-hall restaurant that offers the full range of Stiegl beers.

LINZ: Bombay Palace €€
Indian **Map** E3
Goethestrasse 34, A-4020
Tel *(0732) 658 605* **Closed** *Mon*
This centrally located Indian restaurant makes good use of its tandoor oven and has a longer than usual list of vegetarian options as well. Respectable wine list.

LINZ: Cook €€
Fusion **Map** E3
Klammstrasse 1, A-4020
Tel *(0732) 781 305* **Closed** *Sat & Sun*
Wok-fried salmon and curried herring are on offer at this inventive Scandinavian-Asian restaurant. Good service and an impeccable dining experience guaranteed.

MONDSEE: Jausenstation Holzingerbauer €
Classic Austrian **Map** D3
Oberburgau 12, A-5310
Tel *(06232) 38 41* **Closed** *Wed, Sat & Sun*
Walk into this traditional wooden-bench *Gasthof* and sample wine, schnapps, cheese-and-sausage cold cuts, home-baked bread and simple Austrian dishes. Outdoor seating under fruit trees.

Diners enjoying a meal at Austria's first Scandinavian-Asian restaurant, Cook, Linz

NUSSDORF AM ATTERSEE: Hotel Aichinger €€
Regional **Map** D3
Am Anger 1, A-4865
Tel *(07666) 80 07*
A hotel-restaurant set in a former brewery offering a wide-ranging menu of Austrian and Mediterranean flavours, with locally raised meat and poultry being the highlights.

SCHÄRDING: Stiegenwirt €
Classic Austrian **Map** D3
Schlossgasse 2–6, A-4780
Tel *(07712) 30 70* **Closed** *Thu; Jan–Apr*
A family-run guesthouse and restaurant in a Baroque square, featuring classic Austrian dishes such as *Wiener Schnitzel*, boiled beef and duck.

ST FLORIAN: Landgasthof zur Kanne €
Regional **Map** E3
Marktplatz 7, A-4490
Tel *(07224) 42 88* **Closed** *Mon*
Tucked away in a quiet spot on a cobbled street, this former bakery serves classic Austrian dishes with several vegetarian choices and seasonal game options.

Outdoor tables at the lakeside restaurant, Joseph's in St Wolfgang

ST WOLFGANG: Joseph's €€
Gourmet **Map** D4
Markt 17, A-5360
Tel *(06138) 204 60* **Closed** *Mon*
An intimate restaurant with a gorgeous lakeside terrace, serving local fish and meat prepared in a creative, modern fusion spirit. Five-and seven-course tasting menus available.

STEYR: Wirtshaus Knapp am Eck €
Classic Austrian **Map** E3
Wehrgrabengasse 15, A-4400
Tel *(07252) 762 69* **Closed** *Sun & Mon*
The menu here features typical Austrian meat and game dishes presented in modern style in a contemporary-rustic interior. The summer garden is one of Steyr's nicest. Great value for money.

STEYR: Mader €€
Classic Austrian **Map** E3
Stadtplatz 36, A-4400
Tel *(07252) 533 58* **Closed** *hols*
Austrian staples are handled with flair at this restaurant that is part of a historic city hotel. Guests can choose from a range of dining areas, including an atmospheric vaulted wine cellar.

TRAUNKIRCHEN: Symposionhotel Post €€
International **Map** D3
Ortsplatz 5, A-4801
Tel *(07617) 23 07*
This classy restaurant set in a traditional coaching inn offers the best of Austrian cuisine and local lake fish. The menu changes according to what is fresh and seasonal.

WEYREGG AM ATTERSEE: Kaisergasthof €€
Seafood **Map** D3
Weyreggerstrasse 75, A-4852
Tel *(07664) 22 02*
A former imperial post station, this lovely restaurant delivers a blend of Austrian fare and Adriatic seafood. Local freshwater fish and game specialities also offered.

DK Choice

MONDSEE: Seehotel Lackner €€
Seafood **Map** D3
Mondseestrasse 1, A-5310
Tel *(06232) 23 59*
This seaside hotel-restaurant on the Mondsee is a wonderful spot for outdoor eating in the summer. There is a lakeside terrace, which has its own barbecue grill and offers fantastic mountain views. The inventive Austrian-French cuisine makes use of the best local ingredients with lamb, venison and freshwater fish featuring prominently on the menu. Kitchen supremo Martin Lackner is a sommelier as well as a chef, ensuring a well-chosen cellar.

For more information on types of restaurants *see p301*

Salzburger Land

ANIF: Schlosswirt zu Anif €€
Classic Austrian **Map** D4
Salzachtalbunesstrasse 7, A-5081
Tel *(06246) 721 75* **Closed** *Mon & Tue Sep–mid-Jul*
A 17th-century house with a shady summer garden, this traditional restaurant serves Austrian classics such as *Schnitzel* with seasonal game dishes.

BERGHEIM: Gmachl €€
International **Map** D3
Dorfstrasse 35, A-5101
Tel *(0662) 452 124-0*
This hotel-restaurant and spa has five dining rooms, each with a slightly different menu. The emphasis is on Mediterranean cuisine. Great for vegetarians too.

FILZMOOS:
Hubertus Johanna Maier €€€
Gourmet **Map** D4
Am Dorfplatz 1, A-5532
Tel *(06453) 82 04*
Renowned gourmet destination serving contemporary Austrian- and French-influenced cuisine. The restaurant also dishes up seasonal game and local trout.

FUSCHL AM SEE: Brunnwirt €€
Regional **Map** D3
Wolfgangseestrasse 11, A-5330
Tel *(06226) 82 36*
Picture-perfect 15th-century farmhouse in an idyllic lakeside setting. Come here to sample Salzburg cuisine cooked with locally sourced ingredients.

FUSCHL AM SEE: Schlick €€
Seafood **Map** D3
Seestrasse 12, A-5330
Tel *(06226) 82 37*
Lakeside hotel-restaurant, Schlick is a good place to sample Austrian freshwater fish. Large summer garden for outdoor dining.

GOLDEGG AM SEE: Hecht €€€
Gourmet **Map** D4
Hofmark 8, A-5622
Tel *(06415) 81 37-0*
Expect top-quality cooking at this hotel-restaurant. Old-fashioned cuts such as calf sweetbreads and brains are given a modern twist here.

GOLLING AN DER SALZACH:
Döllerer's
Geniesserrestaurant €€€
Gourmet **Map** D4
Markt 56, A-5440
Tel *(06244) 42 20* **Closed** *Sun & Mon*
Highly regarded gourmet restaurant that elevates local fare into the realm of haute cuisine.

Popular dishes include lamb and beef bred on Alpine pastures as well as local trout.

HALLWANG/SALZBURG:
Pfefferschiff €€€
Gourmet **Map** D3
Söllheim 3, A-5300
Tel *(0662) 661 242* **Closed** *Sun & Mon*
One of Austria's most celebrated restaurants, the "Pepper Ship" serves Austrian and international cuisine in an elegant dining room with an antique ceramic oven.

KAPRUN: Zur Mühle €
Regional **Map** D4
Nikolaus-Gassner-Strasse 62, A-5710
Tel *(06547) 82 54*
This hotel-and-camp ground restaurant serves up the standard Salzburger fare, including plenty of meat and dumplings, in a farmhouse-style dining room.

MAISHOFEN:
Schloss Kammer €€
Regional **Map** D4
Kammererstrasse 22, A-5751
Tel *(06542) 68202-0*
Relaxed dining in the wood-panelled rooms of a historic castle. Local specialities, Austrian classics and game are the main culinary attractions here.

MITTERSILL:
Meilinger Taverne €€
Regional **Map** C4
Stadtplatz 10, 5730
Tel *(06562) 42 26*
Housed in an 18th-century build-ing, the Meilinger Taverne is a lively local meeting place, thanks to its emphasis on typically Austrian dishes at reasonable prices.

Signature chocolate *torte* at Hotel Sacher Salzburg (*see p323*)

SALZBURG: Bärenwirt €
Classic Austrian **Map** D3
Müllner Hauptstrasse 8, A-5020
Tel *(0662) 422 404*
An unpretentious and welcoming restaurant popular with the locals and always reliable for inexpensive staples such as *Gulasch*, *Schnitzel* and fried chicken.

SALZBURG: Paulstub'n €
Classic Austrian **Map** D3
Herrengasse 16, A-5020
Tel *(0662) 843 220* **Closed** *Sun & Mon*
This rustic den is something of a mecca for inexpensive Austrian fare, handling everything from cheese-and-sausage platters to lavish boiled-beef feasts.

SALZBURG: Pescheria Backi €
Seafood **Map** D3
Franz-Josef-Strasse 16b, A-5020
Tel *(0662) 879 778* **Closed** *Sun*
A snug old-fashioned restaurant set in a shed-like setting, Backi is an eatery truly dedicated to fresh fish. Good selection of fruity Slovenian wines.

SALZBURG: Zum
Hirschenwirt €
Regional **Map** D3
St-Julien-Strasse 21–23, A-5020
Tel *(0662) 872 581* **Closed** *Sun*
An intimate and traditional restaurant that concentrates on the region's rustic cuisine, prepared and served with finesse.

SALZBURG: Alt Salzburg €€
Classic Austrian **Map** D3
Burgerspitalgasse 2, A 5020
Tel *(0662) 841 476*
A popular and atmospheric restaurant with a reputation for quality Salzburg food at reasonable prices. Three dining areas, including one carved out of rock.

SALZBURG: Braurestaurant
IMLAUER €€
Classic Austrian **Map** D3
Rainerstrasse 14, A-5020
Tel *(0662) 877 694*
A laid-back restaurant near the train station with a lovely beer garden and bar. This place has long been favoured for its traditional Austrian dishes and locally brewed Stiegl beer.

SALZBURG: Hölle €€
Classic Austrian **Map** D3
Dr-Adolf-Altmann-Strasse 2, A-5020
Tel *(0662) 820 760-0*
Popular and attractive hotel-restaurant with three beautiful wood-panelled dining areas serving Austrian cuisine with plenty of fowl and game.

Homely and Intimate setting at Zum Hirschenwirt, Salzburg *(see p322)*

SALZBURG: Hotel Sacher Salzburg €€
Café **Map** D3
Schwarzstrasse 5-7, A-5020
Tel *(0662) 889 770*
The café of the Sacher claims to be the home of the famous chocolate *Torte, (see p304)* and serves many other irresistible cakes and pastries.

SALZBURG: Triangel €€
Classic Austrian **Map** D3
Wiener Philharmonikergasse 7, A-5020
Tel *(0662) 842 229* **Closed** *Sun & Mon*
The full range of classic Austrian culinary repertoire is served here with contemporary pizazz, in a modern bistro setting. The daily specials are worth trying.

SALZBURG: Esszimmer €€€
Gourmet **Map** D3
Müllner Hauptstrasse 33, A-5020
Tel *(0662) 870 899* **Closed** *Sun & Mon*
Exquisite modern-European cuisine in a soothingly furnished restaurant with atmospheric lighting. The three-course lunch menu is very affordable.

WERFEN: Obauer €€
Gourmet **Map** D4
Markt 46, A-5450
Tel *(06468) 521 20*
An award-winning restaurant renowned for inventive and stylish variations of Austrian and European classics, backed up by a broad selection of wines.

ZELL AM SEE: Steinerwirt 1493 €€
Classic Austrian **Map** D4
Dreifaltigkeitsgasse 2, A-5700
Tel *(06542) 725 02*
At this charming 15th-century guesthouse Austrian classics are prepared with attention to detail. Most of the traditional features of this place have been preserved.

Tyrol and Vorarlberg

BEZAU: Post €€
Gourmet **Map** A4
Brugg 35, A-6870
Tel *(05514) 22 07-0* **Closed** *Tue, Wed & Thu*
Indulge the senses at this gourmet restaurant in Hotel Post. The restaurant dishes out local lamb and the beef is served with the freshest ingredients available.

BRAZ BEI BLUDENZ: Rössle €€
Classic Austrian **Map** A4
Albergstrasse 61, A-6751
Tel *(05552) 281 050* **Closed** *Mon & Tue*
Charming village guesthouse with low-ceilinged dining room. The menu features regional Bregenzerwald specialities and set-piece Austrian mains such as boiled beef and *Schnitzel*.

BRAZ BEI BLUDENZ: Traube €€
Classic Austrian **Map** A4
Klostertalerstrasse 12, A-6751
Tel *(05552) 281 03*
A golf-resort hotel with very traditional wood-panelled dining rooms serving Vorarlberg specialities and Austrian classics.

BREGENZ: Gebhardsberg €€
International **Map** A4
Gebhardsberg 1, A-6900
Tel *(05574) 425 15*
Stately castle-restaurant with great views overlooking Bregenz. Try the Vorarlberg beef, local fish and suckling pig.

BREGENZ: Stadtgasthaus €€
Gourmet **Map** A4
Römerstrasse 5, 6900
Tel *(05574) 4988-0* **Closed** *Sat & Sun*
Traditional Austrian dishes are given a contemporary twist in the formal dining room of the Weissen Kreuz Best Western.

DORNBIRN: Hirschen €€
Regional **Map** A4
Haselstauderstrasse 31, A-6850
Tel *(05572) 263 63* **Closed** *Sun*
Quaint guesthouse with contemporary furnishings. Hirschen offers good-value meals with a choice of local specialities and Austrian standards.

DORNBIRN: Rickatschwende €€
Classic Austrian **Map** A4
Dornbirn, A-6850
Tel *(05572) 253 50-408* **Closed** *Mon*
Modern dining room in a spa hotel serving Austrian classics such as *Schnitzel*, boiled beef and freshwater fish, plus a selection of vegetarian options.

EBBS: Gourmethotel Unterwirt €€€
Gourmet **Map** C4
Wildbichlerstrasse 38, A-6341
Tel *(05373) 422 88* **Closed** *Tue*
Lovingly restored 15th-century inn with vaulted ceilings, offering a range of excellent regional and international dishes – all prepared with great skill.

EICHENBERG/BODENSEE: Schönblick €€
Regional **Map** A4
Dorf 6, 6911
Tel *(05574) 459 65* **Closed** *Mon*
Beautiful chalet-style building offering a well-chosen mixture of traditional Austrian staples and local specialities. Well-stocked wine and cheese cellar.

ELLMAU: Der Bär €€
Gourmet **Map** C4
Kirchbichl 9, 6352
Tel *(05358) 23 95*
This Alpine hotel-restaurant presents a wonderful blend of Tyrolean tradition and contemporary European cooking style. The dining rooms mix modern and folk design themes perfectly.

For more information on types of restaurants *see p301*

ELLMAU: Kaiserhof €€
Gourmet   Map C4
Harmstätt 8, A-6452
Tel *(05358) 20 22*   **Closed** *Sun*
Austrian gourmet cuisine at its
best in a hotel-restaurant that
places a strong emphasis on
local organic ingredients.

FELDKIRCH: Gutwinski €€
Regional   Map A4
Rosengasse 4–6, A-6680
Tel *(05522) 721 75*   **Closed** *Sun
& Mon*
The chef here uses regional ingre-
dients for his exquisitely light
creations based on traditional
dishes. In the summer eat in the
courtyard beneath lime trees.

HIPPACH: Sieghard €€
Regional   Map C4
Johann-Sponring-Strasse 83, A-6283
Tel *(05282) 33 09*   **Closed** *Mon*
An attractive eatery with a
growing reputation for its rustic
cuisine. A balanced menu of
locally raised meats, fowl and
freshwater fish.

INNSBRUCK: Der Bierwert €€
Classic Austrian   Map B4
Bichlweg 2, A-6020
Tel *(0512) 342 143*   **Closed** *Sun*
This traditional restaurant is
located in a chalet-style
guesthouse. The bright dining
room is panelled in pine and has
a menu that changes with the
season, offering asparagus in
spring and game in autumn.

DK Choice

INNSBRUCK: Chez Nico €€
Vegetarian   Map B4
*Maria-Theresien-Strasse 49,
A-6020*
Tel *(0650) 451 06 24*   **Closed** *Sun*
Chez Nico projects itself not only
as a restaurant but an "arts-
workshop" where the aesthetics
of dining experience and the
quality of food are equally
satisfying. Here, vegetarian cuisine
is accorded a haute-cuisine
approach by chef Nicolas Curtil.
The menu changes according
to what is fresh. Opt for the
lunchtime menu or the seven-
course evening gourmet menu.

INNSBRUCK: Goldener Adler €€
Regional   Map B4
Herzog-Friedrich-Strasse 6, A-6020
Tel *(0512) 571 11 10*
Located in one of the oldest inns
in Europe, the Golden Eagle serves
traditional Austrian *Schnitzel*,
poultry and game dishes in
rooms where Mozart is believed
to have eaten.

INNSBRUCK:
Schwarzer Adler €€
Classic Austrian   Map B4
Kaiserjägerstrasse 2, A-6020
Tel *(0512) 587 109*
Locally sourced meat and
fish is elegantly presented
and served in a variety of
different rooms at this rooftop
terrace restaurant. Great views
and excellent service.

ISCHGL: Trofana Royal €€€
Gourmet   Map A5
Dorfstrasse 95, A-6561
Tel *(05444) 600*
Fine dining in a five-star hotel,
with traditional Tyrolean fare.
The restaurant features period
panelled walls and a brick-
vaulted wine cellar.

KELCHSAU: Fuchswirt €€
Regional   Map C4
Oberdorf 11, A-6361
Tel *(05335) 406 30*   **Closed** *Tue*
A traditional timber chalet
in an Alpine village offering
Tyrolean dishes as well as
standard Central-European fare.
There is a playground for kids
outside and a large summer
garden dining area.

KIRCHBERG: Rosengarten €€€
Gourmet   Map C4
Aschauerstrasse 46, A-6365
Tel *(05357) 42 01*   **Closed** *Tue & Wed*
Dine in smart and elegant
surroundings at the Rosengarten.
Creative modern-European
cuisine with a pronounced
Mediterranean slant – the menu
changes according to season.

Sleek and sophisticated decor at
Rosengarten in Kirchberg

KITZBÜHEL: Tennerhof €€€
Gourmet   Map C4
Griesenauweg 26, A-6370
Tel *(05356) 631 81*   **Closed** *Mon
& Tue*
Classic Austrian fare meets
European haute cuisine in the
elegant dining room of this
highly acclaimed gourmet
restaurant. Expect good food
and impeccable service.

LANDECK: Schrofenstein €€
International   Map B4
Malserstrasse 31, A-6500
Tel *(05442) 623 95*
Historic hotel-restaurant with a
nice blend of Austrian dishes.
Features locally sourced veal and
pork, as well as Mediterranean-
influenced meals.

LECH: Gasthof Post €€€
Gourmet   Map A4
Dorf 11, A-6764
Tel *(05583) 220 60*
Traditional ski-resort with several
dining areas. This place has been
rated by both Michelin and
GaultMilau. Come here to enjoy
Austrian classics and try the *kalbs
beuscherl* (veal offal dish).

OBERGURGL: Hohe Mut Alm €€
Classic Austrian   Map B5
Obergurgl, A-64556
Tel *(05256) 6396 32*   **Closed** *Oct
& Apr*
Tyrolean regional specialities,
Austrian classics and a few
Mediterranean dishes served
with real panache in this
charming Alpine restaurant.

SÖLL: Söllerstuben €
International   Map C4
Dorf 120, A-6306
Tel *(05333) 53 60*
A welcoming place in the middle
of Söll village offering a broad
range of food, from Austrian
Schnitzel to Italian pizza and pasta.

ST CHRISTOPH AM ARLBERG:
Hospiz Alm €€€
Gourmet   Map A4
St Christoph, A-6580
Tel *(05446) 36 25*
Arguably the oldest mountain
restaurant in the world, this high-
altitude establishment is famous
for its superbly stocked wine
cellar and stunning location.

STUMM: Landgasthof Linde €€
Regional   Map C4
Dorf 2, A-6275
Tel *(05283) 22 77*
One of the best places in the
Zillertal to sample regional
Tyrolean fare prepared and
served with contemporary flair.
Lovely garden dining area.

Carinthia and East Tyrol

BAD BLEIBERG: Der Bleibergerhof €€
Regional   Map D5
Drei Lärchen 150, A-9530
Tel *(04244) 22 05*
Swish restaurant in a chic spa hotel serving locally sourced, bio-natural dishes, with a good range of vegetarian options.

FELD AM SEE: Lindenhof €€€
Gourmet   Map D5
Kirchenplatz 2, A-9544
Tel *(04246) 22 74*
Lakeside hotel-restaurant offering an eclectic mix of Carinthian and Mediterranean cuisine, with emphasis on light and wholesome ingredients.

HERMAGOR: Barenwirt €
Regional   Map D5
Hauptstrasse 17, 3400
Tel *(04282) 20 52*
Small-town guesthouse with rustic interiors, serving excellent Carinthian cheese dumplings, fresh vegetables from the garden and seasonal game.

KLAGENFURT: Felsenkeller €
Classic Austrian   Map E5
Feldkirchner Strasse 141, A-9020
Tel *(0463) 420 130*   **Closed** *Sun*
A tunnel-like bar-restaurant burrowed into a small cliff, offering hearty Austrian meat and poultry dishes accompanied by locally brewed Schleppe beer.

KLAGENFURT: Pumpe – Gasthaus zum Grossglockner €
Classic Austrian   Map E5
Lidmanskygasse 2, A-9020
Tel *(0463) 571 96*   **Closed** *Sun*
Popular local tavern with wood-panelled interiors serving inexpensive local dishes. The *Gulasch* is legendary. Great service.

DK Choice

KLAGENFURT: Zum Augustin €
Regional   Map E5
Pfarrhofgasse 2, A-9020
Tel *(0463) 513 992*   **Closed** *Sun*
A speciality beer hall and restaurant, Zum Augustin is the ideal place to sample traditional Carinthian fare such as *Kärntner Nudeln* (ravioli-like parcels stuffed with cheese or potato) or boiled beef. The young crowd keeps the atmosphere upbeat. The Landhaushof room at the back is more formal.

Seating at the well-reviewed Parkhotel Tristachersee in Lienz

KLAGENFURT: Dolce Vita €€
International   Map E5
Heuplatz 2, A-9020
Tel *(0463) 554 99*   **Closed** *Sat & Sun*
Creative cuisine in contemporary bistro surroundings with an emphasis on Mediterranean cuisine and seafood.

KRUMPENDORF: Hudelist €€
International   Map E5
Wieningerallee 12, A-9201
Tel *(04229) 26 81*
This attractive family inn has a wide menu that incorporates a range of Carinthian and Finnish-Scandinavian dishes.

LIENZ: Gasthof Goldener Fisch €
Seafood   Map D5
Kärntner Strasse 9, A-9900
Tel *(04852) 621 32*
This 15th-century guesthouse serves fresh trout and pikeperch. In the summer, enjoy a barbecue in the garden with live music.

LIENZ: Parkhotel Tristachersee €€
Seafood   Map D5
Am Tristachersee 1, 9900
Tel *(04852) 676 66*
On the edge of lake Tristachersee, this eatery offers tranquility, a touch of romance and superb freshwater fish. Large outdoor terrace.

MATREI: Rauter €€€
Gourmet   Map C5
Rauterplatz 3, A-9971
Tel *(04875) 66 11*
Cosy hotel-restaurant in an idyllic setting. The menu focuses on local trout, goose and game. The wine cellar is very well stocked.

MILLSTATT: Hotel See-Villa €€
Seafood   Map D5
Seestrasse 68, A 9872
Tel *(04766) 21 02*
A fortified house right by the water, with a lakeside garden

makes this the perfect spot for dining. Sample the freshwater fish and Carinthian staples, or simply enjoy strudel and coffee.

PÖRTSCHACH: Leon €€
Gourmet   Map E5
Leonstainerstrasse 1, A-9210
Tel *(04272) 28 16*
Occupying the colonnaded courtyard of the Schloss Leonstain Hotel, this restaurant prepares Carinthian dishes with haute-cuisine flair and imagination.

PÖRTSCHACH: La Terrasse €€€
Gourmet   Map E5
Töschling 1, A-9210
Tel *(04272) 23 77*
Located in the Schloss Seefels luxury hotel, the award-winning La Terrasse offers fine Austrian-international cuisine and superb lakeside views.

RADENTHEIN: Die Gartenrast €
Classic Austrian   Map D5
Gartenrastrasse 9, A-9545
Tel *(04246) 20 17*
Charming farmhouse inn famous for its locally reared breaded chicken, although there is other seasonal produce on offer too. Good value for money.

SPITTAL/DRAU: Edlingerwirt €
Classic Austrian   Map D5
Villacherstrasse 88, A-9800
Tel *(04762) 51 50*   **Closed** *Mon & Tue*
A largely local clientele come here to enjoy regional cooking that relies heavily on Carinthian-sourced produce and lots of local game.

VELDEN: Landhaus Kutsche €€
Regional   Map E5
Göriacherstrasse 2, 9220
Tel *(04274) 29 46*   **Closed** *Wed*
Traditional Carinthian fare in rustic, yet elegant surroundings. Special emphasis on local beef and good service.

VELDEN: Goritschniggs €€€
International   Map E5
Seecorso 6, 9220
Tel *(04274) 24 75*
Highly regarded steak house run by a family of butchers. Quality steaks in the evening, superb value buffet lunch during the day.

VILLACH: Caldarium €€
International   Map E5
Hausergasse 27, A-9500
Tel *(0664) 213 91 31*   **Closed** *Sat & Sun*
A quiet out-of-town spot near the Leonharder See offering pizzas, seafood and Mediterranean fare. Definite value for money.

For more information on types of restaurants see p301

SHOPPING IN AUSTRIA

Until quite recently, shops in Austria kept to strict opening and even stricter closing hours. Around lunchtime or after 6pm for example, no self-respecting Austrian would dream of doing any shopping, even in Vienna. The *Wochenende* (weekend) was even more sacrosanct – at many shops it started on Friday evening. Today though, opening hours have become liberalized, and now it is much more common for shops to stay open at lunchtime and for longer in the evenings. Markets, ranging from international fairs to street and flea markets, are widely popular with visitors, and there is an excellent range of goods to buy. Check out traditional crafts and clothes, speciality foods and drinks, as well as exquisite ceramics and glassware.

Opening Hours

Shops usually open at 8:30 or 9am and close at 6pm or later. Supermarkets open from 8am to 7pm, and until 5pm on Saturdays. The Mercur and Billa supermarkets are open late on Fridays, until 7:30pm, and Billa branches at Vienna's Nordbahnhof railway station and at the airport open seven days a week.

Smaller shops still close at lunchtime for an hour or so. In provincial towns opening hours may vary from those in Vienna and be more suited to the local needs.

Markets and Fairs

Markets and fairs are a firm part of tradition in Austria. The country hosts many international fairs, where anything from household items and construction machinery to modern jewellery or Austrian folk art, wines and spirits are exhibited. For holiday-makers there are countless charming street markets, which are often held

Shop window, displaying typical souvenirs in Innsbruck

in the main square of small villages. On Friday and Saturday mornings, some streets close to traffic and fill with market stalls offering produce straight from the farm, including fruit, vegetables, flowers, meat products and freshly baked goods. The market is often surrounded by historic buildings, allowing you to combine shopping and sightseeing.

The Naschmarkt near Karlsplatz in Vienna is the biggest street market in Austria, and besides food and clothes, there is also a flea market on Saturdays. The dates and venues for other flea markets or antiques fairs are published in the daily papers.

VAT Refunds

Except for citizens of other EU countries, visitors to Austria are entitled to reclaim *Mehrwertsteuer* (abbreviated as MwSt), the equivalent of VAT, on their purchases. The rate is 20 per cent on industrial goods and 10 per cent on food products. You need to tell the vendor that you are buying the goods for export. Larger department stores will be able to provide you with the appropriate form; alternatively, you can get it from customs. Fill in the form and present it together with the receipt when you leave Austria. You may be asked to show the goods, which must still be in their original packaging, unopened and unused. If the money is not refunded at the border, you can apply for it by writing to Global Blue, P.O. Box 363, 810 00 Bratislava, Slovenia (tel +421 232 111 111) and have it sent by post or transferred to your bank account.

End-of-Season Sales

Twice a year, the shopping scene is enlivened by seasonal price reductions; the

Wine shop in a private vineyard in Mörbisch

A typical market selling a wide range of goods in Deutschlandsberg

Winterschlussverkauf (winter sales) start in the last week of January, and the *Sommerschlussverkauf* (summer sales) at the end of July. This is a good time to buy clothes, sports equipment and shoes. Look for much reduced skis, an anorak or a warm coat; or you could find a lovely dress or a lightweight suit at half its original price or less. Occasionally a shop will sell all its stock at the same price in order to make room for new collections.

Billa supermarket logo

Different rules apply to electronic goods, for which price reductions are governed by supply and demand. Large department stores tend to reduce some prices in late autumn, particularly on electrical goods, but this depends on individual establishments.

There is no fixed season for food price reductions, which may occur at any time. If you are looking for a bargain, keep an eye out for the promotional leaflets issued by most large supermarkets.

Ceramics and Crystal Glass

Austria is famous for its beautiful porcelain from the Augarten factory, based in the Viennese park, where Johann Strauss once played his waltzes. The decorations on vases, jugs, boxes and tableware reflect the artistic trends of past centuries, from Baroque through Neo-Classical and Biedermeier right up to the present day. Porcelain goods can be purchased in the shop in Graben or from the factory, which is open to visitors. Also worth buying is the attractive hand-painted pottery from Gmunden, with colourful Biedermeier-style flowers, dots and other ornamentation.

Glassware – including superb chandeliers and delicate tableware – tends to be highly original, although expensive. Many people also collect imaginative crystal ornaments such as dogs and cats made by Swarovski.

Crafts and Folk Art

Hand-embroidered items, such as tablecloths, are also in great demand. The true works of art in this field are ladies' evening purses, miniature pictures and even jewellery, embroidered in *petit point* with 300 to 2,500 stitches per sq cm (2,000 to 16,000 stitches per sq inch). This work, carried out with the aid of a magnifying glass, is so exhausting that it can be done only for a maximum of three hours a day.

Folk costumes are another popular purchase. They vary in the detail, but the woman's *Dirndl* always consists of a skirt with an apron, a waistcoat and a white, often embroidered blouse, while the man's *Tracht* includes short or calf-length leather trousers and a distinctively cut felt jacket. All this is topped by a jaunty hat adorned with feathers or goats' beard.

Alcoholic Drinks

Most supermarkets stock a good selection of Austrian wines, but if you head to one of the vineyards you can try before you buy. Visit one of the many vineyards in the Wachau Valley or among the hills of Burgenland, and you can sample the wine, and even buy direct. One of the stronger drinks would also be a good souvenir – try *Weinbrand* (cognac), *Slivovitz* (plum brandy), *Obstler* (fruit brandy) or *Marillenbrand* (apricot brandy).

Speciality Foods

The most popular purchases from the food counter are Austrian chocolates in their many guises. You can buy good-quality confectionery at most supermarkets; popular chains include Billa, Merkur, Interspar, Eurospar, Zielpunkt and Hofer, with the latter charging the lowest prices. There are also smaller food stores, especially in the large cities, but these are generally more expensive.

Sweets and confectionery in front of a shop in Salzburg

What to Buy in Austria

The range of souvenirs worth buying in Austria is vast, ranging from the unashamedly kitsch to the exquisite and delicate. The most typical purchases are chocolates and all kinds of alcoholic drinks which are often attractively packaged. Quality purchases include Tyrolean costumes and warm winter coats made of loden as well as attractive porcelain or glassware made in Austria, including the stunning Swarovski crystal chandeliers.

Sissi Figurines
The Austrian people's love for "Sissi", Emperor Franz Joseph's unhappy wife, knows no bounds. It is evident to this day from the many statuettes of the Empress Elisabeth, on sale all over the country.

Souvenirs

In a country as reliant on tourism as Austria, the souvenir industry naturally plays an important role, with market stalls, shops and motorway service stations all offering an enormous selection of Andenken (souvenirs) designed to help you remember your stay in one of Austria's provinces – and hopefully make you come back for more.

Glass Snowstorms
Glass snowstorms with swirling snowflakes may be considered as kitsch by some, yet they remain very popular with tourists, and children are particularly keen on them. Inside, you can see any number of famous Austrian landmarks such as the Big Wheel in the Prater, a symbol of Vienna.

Wanderhut
The Tyrolean "walker's hat" is popular with mountain walkers. In winter it protects against the cold; in summer it provides shade from the sun, which can be surprisingly fierce in the mountains.

Augarten Figurines
An attractive souvenir from the Augarten porcelain makers are the delicate, hand-finished porcelain figurines of the famous white Lipizzaner stallions and riders from the Spanish Riding School in Vienna.

Bells
In the autumn, the cattle of Tyrol and Vorarlberg are driven down from the Alm, the summer mountain pastures, and the bells around their necks have always fascinated visitors. The bells come in all shapes and sizes, often highly decorated. They make, of course, a great souvenir.

Saddles
One of the more unusual gifts you can find are intricately made miniature horses with tack and saddles, often copies of items seen in the collections of armouries and arsenals.

Handicrafts and Folk Art
Austria is deservedly proud of its local crafts traditions. In specialist shops or markets you can find delicate embroidery and lacework or great wood carvings, such as this mask.

Ceramics

Austria is famous for its traditional and modern ceramics. Whether you choose a fine porcelain figure from Augarten or a hand-painted, ornamental faience from Gmunden, they will add elegance to your home. Many factories also produce less costly items, such as busts of the famous.

Modern Ceramics
This curiously shaped tea service, produced at the Provincial College for Ceramics at Stoob, would make a great addition to any tea-time table.

Bust of Mozart
Mozart memorabilia such as this bust are sold all over Salzburg, a city devoted to marketing the memory of Wolfgang Amadeus Mozart.

Dinner Service
Attractive ceramic tableware, such as this colourful dinner service from Klagenfurt, would make a welcome present to bring home or a useful and practical addition to your own household collection.

Confectionery

Austrian confectioners, of whom many were suppliers to the Imperial Court, look back with pride on centuries of tradition. The Sachertorte *has a particularly distinguished history, but there are numerous other specialities worth bringing back for friends and family – if you can bear to share.*

Mozartkugeln
This speciality chocolate from Salzburg, produced in various shapes and wrapped in silver foil, always bears the portrait of the famous composer.

Gingerbread
Gingerbread hearts are decorated with a variety of mostly romantic messages and intricate patterns in coloured icing. This one says "Because I love you".

Christmas decorations in a confectionery shop window

Alcoholic Drinks

Many Austrian wines have come a long way and are now highly regarded by connoisseurs. The country produces some excellent white dry and dessert wines, as well as the heavier Rieslings. Among the reds, Styrian Schilcher and Blaufränkisch from Burgenland can both compete with Italian and Spanish wines. Austria also produces other alcoholic beverages, including fruit brandies and liqueurs.

Glass tankards, an excellent present for beer lovers

Wine
Specially sealed and bottled at the vineyard where it is produced, a bottle of Austrian wine makes an unusual but welcome present.

Beer
Although they are little known abroad, Austria produces some very fine beers. Try some of the local brands and take home a few bottles – you won't easily find them elsewhere.

ENTERTAINMENT IN AUSTRIA

Witty, fun loving and charming, the Austrians manage to defy pretty much every cliché of what it means to be Germanic. Their sense of *Gemütlichkeit*, or good times, comes alive in the music, festivals, cafés and bars that pulse across the country. *The Sound of Music* may now be one of its most renowned attractions, but you are sure to find more than a few of your favourite things in Austria. From a lederhosen-lined folk dance in an old-world village, to extreme sports on mountain tops, to a classical music concert beneath the stars, it's a variety show of amusements. Against the setting of breathtaking lakes and mountains, an array of entertainment choices await, both formal and informal. Inevitably, excellent regional cuisine, wine and the ubiquitous beer are also part of the experience.

Mozart's opera *Apollo Et Hyacinthus*, performed at the Salzburg Festival

Information Sources

Austria is an information-friendly destination. Each province, city and indeed nearly every village of any size boasts a full-service tourist bureau at the ready for walk-in and online information. Here you can find events calendars and background information on anything and everything taking place in the way of music, theatre, festivals and holiday events. Posters announcing current events from concerts to exhibitions are widely displayed in town squares and café windows. The events listing magazine **Falter** is widely available across the country.

For personalized tours, Austria's superb network of professionally accredited English-speaking tour guides, **austriaguides**, is highly recommended. Before travelling, be sure to look at www.austria. info, the website of the **Austrian National Tourist Office**. The website is packed with useful information including listings of free events and suggestions for saving money.

Booking Tickets

All the big music festivals offer online booking for seats. Some of them, like the Salzburg Festival, sell out months in advance. It is also possible to buy tickets, sometimes last minute, from ticket agencies.

Money-saving discount cards are available for sightseeing and public transport in all the major cities, including Innsbruck, Linz, Salzburg and Vienna. For a small price, these cards offer significant discounts, or in some cases completely free access to public transport, sightseeing, shopping, dining, and museums. The cards can be purchased upon arrival at your destination, and if you are planning to travel around a lot and take in many of the sights, they can prove to be very economical.

Free Events

While particular museum and gallery exhibits may charge an entrance fee, access to most churches, markets and galleries in Austria is free of charge, offering a wealth of great architecture, art and history at no cost whatsoever. Attending an organ recital or choir-led mass at one of the country's many Baroque cathedrals is an unforgettable experience. Many churches also offer complimentary guided tours; a small tip for the guide at the end of the tour is customary.

Facilities for the Disabled

Most large concert halls and theatres have reserved areas for wheelchairs and seats for people with mobility problems. These must be reserved in advance when booking. Many music and theatre venues also provide help for those with hearing difficulties. Be sure to make your needs very clear when booking tickets.

You will find information on barrier-free access on the Austria National Tourist Office

Guided tour of Salzburg Cathedral with its fine Baroque architecture

website, as well as on each of the **regional tourism authority websites**. For more information on facilities and information for disabled travellers see pp344–5.

Religious Celebrations

A predominantly Catholic country, Austrian religious celebrations are pageants of colour which everyone can join in. Starting at the end of November through to Christmas Day, Christmas markets spring up in towns and cities, offering handicrafts, seasonal foods, mulled wine and heaps of atmosphere. On 5 or 6 December, you may see St Nikolaus wandering the streets accompanied by a scary devil figure, Krampus, who threatens to beat naughty children. Austria's biggest Krampus festival is held in Schladming, Styria, each November.

Fasching is the Austrian version of Carnival, and is a let-loose party that takes place just before Lent with masked balls and socially sanctioned outrageousness.

At Easter, real eggs are hand-painted and hung on plants or twigs called *Palmskatzerln*. At Palm Sunday processions, children carry tall sticks decorated with streamers and pretzels.

Traditional Music and Dance

When your neighbour lives on the next mountaintop, communicating is a challenge – hence the rise of yodelling as an art form. The melodic throat singing relies on echo and yips and yells, which are impressive performed solo, and mesmerising when sung *en masse*.

Traditional folk celebrations often include the Schuhplattler, a lively Austro-Bavarian men's dance with plenty of stamping and clapping.

The Ländler, an adaptation of which was performed in *The Sound of Music*, is danced by couples amid much clapping and spinning. The Polka and, ever the pride of Vienna, the Waltz, are classic dances

Local brass band playing at an Austrian beer festival

performed both professionally and at private celebrations.

Salzburg Festival

Each summer, since 1920, the weaving cobblestone streets of Salzburg swell with the thousands attending the **Salzburg Festival**. No less than 220,000 spectators arrive to enjoy the 170 performances of classical music, opera and drama.

The main festival halls are located in a prime location in the old town. From Shakespeare and Molière, to Mozart and Beethoven, the Salzburg Festival represents the *non plus ultra* of high culture in Austria. Booking ahead is imperative, and that includes accommodation.

Casinos

A dozen casinos across the country, from Bad Gastein to Vienna, offer an assortment

of games of chances – from traditional roulette, blackjack and baccara – to modern day Texas Hold 'em. The minimum age for entrance is 18 years. Blackjack, poker, even slot machine tournaments are held regularly. The elegant and atmospheric architecture in **Bad Gastein** and **Baden** add a distinctly James Bond element to the thrill.

Nightlife

Austrian nightlife does not start and stop in Vienna by any means. The provincial capitals certainly hold their own in the party department. There is a wide choice of relaxed pubs, trendy bars, discos and nightclubs that stay open till 4am. For world-class clubbing, DJs Kruder & Dorfmeister have put Austrian electronic music on the map.

Linz boasts some 80 night spots open until well after midnight; its "Bermuda Triangle" bars stay open until the small hours. University towns like Innsbruck and Graz have a young vibrant feel.

In the countryside there is action, especially in summer, at the discos and bars round Austria's lakes. All the best late nights culminate in a snack at a Würstlstand, where the party crowd congregate alongside late-night truck drivers.

Viennese Christmas Market, capturing the essence of Christmas spirit

Beer garden and restaurant by St Wolfgang Lake, Wolfgangsee

Beer Gardens & Cafés

Café culture is its own form of entertainment and the Austrians are rightfully proud of theirs. People watching, reading newspapers mounted on traditional wooden sticks and chatting are the norm – all accompanied by strong coffee and tasty cakes.

Kaffee und Kuchen hour falls between lunch and dinner, and goes nicely with a visit to the *Heurige* (taverns where young, "early" wine is served).

Drinkers sit comfortably out in the open under trees drinking a glass of wine or a *G'spritzn*, a mixture of wine and soda water. As a point of etiquette, when toasting Austrians always look each other directly in the eyes; those failing to do so risk seven years of bad sex or bad weather – take your pick.

Cattle decorated with flowers and bells for the Almabtrieb

Festivals

From spring to autumn, hundreds of festivals celebrate food, wine and the harvest up and down the country. Austrians are proud of their traditional farming methods, and its resulting quality organic products.

Winemakers of Lower Austria's **Wine Route** offer local wine, food and culture at various regional wine festivals throughout the summer, with live music, exhibitions, children's programmes and wine tastings. Similarly, a variety of summer festivals are devoted to an assortment of pumpkins, cheeses, hams, chocolate, even a **dumpling festival**, Knödelfest, in St Johann in Tirol, where the world's longest dumpling table takes centre stage. The Gail Valley hosts a **Speck festival** in June and a **cheese festival** in September.

Among the most charming of the autumn traditions are the annual **herding festivals**, or Almabtrieb, where the animals from the high-Alpine, where they graze free all summer, are brought down to the village to spend the winter in barns. The animals are paraded through the villages festooned with flowers and bells. In Styria, the famous **Lipizzaner Horse Procession** brings down the horses from their mountain pastures in this way to the delight of onlookers.

Not to be outdone by the animals, humans as performance art are the focus of the **World**

Body Painting Festival at Poertschach. Also, Europe's largest **Harley Meeting at Faaker See** attracts its fair share of tattooed bodies as well.

Spectator Sports

As national interests go, skiing and snow boarding take bronze, silver and gold in the hearts of Austrians. Don't let the possibility that you're not actually taking part stop you from getting in on the excitement. The season kicks off with the **Ski World Cup Opening** race at Sölden in late October, which attracts thousands of enthusiasts.

The most famous ski race in the world is held in Kitzbühel each January, the **Hahnenkamm**, a weekend of street parties and music. More than 10,000 people come to the major ski season-ending bash at Ischgl for the **Top of the Mountain** concert. In past years, the free April outdoor concert has featured Elton John, Tina Turner, Sting, Lionel Richie, Jon Bon Jovi, Alanis Morisette, Bob Dylan and Enrique Iglesias.

While it definitely plays second fiddle to skiing, football is still a popular sport. As host of UEFA EURO 2008 the cities of Vienna, Klagenfurt, Salzburg and Innsbruck all have welcoming stadiums and the opportunity to watch a professional match should not be missed. The Ernst Happel Stadion in Vienna is home to Austria's national team.

Ski contestant at Kitzbühel, the most famous ski race in the world

Spas

Part entertainment, part just what the doctor ordered, spa holidays are more than a mere indulgence, and have the added bonus of being regarded as a necessity to good health. Austria's more than 100 mineral spas have a long tradition of healing all manner of complaints from rheumatism to respiratory illness. **Bad Gastein**'s water contains Radon, a gas whose powerful properties require that patients produce a doctor's certificate before participating. Others offer full regimes of medical supervision, tailored fitness programmes, and of course the more run of the mill massage and beauty treatments.

Rogner Bad Blumau spa, designed by Friedensreich Hundertwasser

The clean, cool lines of the post-modern **Alpen Parks Resort** in Maria Alm is a stylish venue for classic sports massage. In Leogang's **Krallerhof Wellness Hotel** a full menu of cool and warm, wet and dry saunas and pools bubble and simmer.

Many of the most lovely wellness hotels are located in the mountains, like the five-star splendour of the spa at **Hospiz** in St Christoph.

High-tech, architecturally ambitious waterworlds are sprouting up across the country: the post-modern minimalism of Langenfeld **Aqua Dome**, two thermal slopeside baths at **Römerbad** and **St Kathrein-Therme** in Carinthia and the spectacular **Felsentherme** in the Gastein Valley. The dreamscape of Friedensreich Hundertwasser's **Rogner Bad Blumau** thermal spa resort is unforgettable.

DIRECTORY

Information Sources

austriaguides
🔲 austriaguides.at

Austrian National Tourist Office
🔲 austria.info

Falter
🔲 falter.at

Booking Tickets

oeticket.com
Tel (01) 1 96 0 96.
🔲 oeticket.com

ticketonline.at
Tel (01) 188 0 88.
🔲 ticketonline.at

Vienna Classic
Tel (01) 1 982 13 51.
🔲 viennaclassic.com

Vienna Ticket Office
🔲 viennaticketoffice.com

Facilities for the Disabled

Regional Tourism Authority Websites:
Styria
🔲 steiermark.com/fueralle
Tirol
🔲 handicap.tirol.at
Upper Austria
🔲 barrierefreies-oberoesterreich.at

Salzburg Festival

Salzburg Festival
Tel (0662) 8045 500.
🔲 salzburgerfestspiele.at

Casinos

Baden Casino
🔲 casinos.at

Bad Gastein Casino
🔲 badgastein.casinos.at

Festivals

Cheese Festival
Tel (04715) 8516.
🔲 kaese-festival.at

Dumpling Festival
Tel (05352) 633350.
🔲 knoedelfest.at

Harley Meeting at Faaker See
🔲 europeanbikeweek.com

Herding Festivals
🔲 austria.info

Lipizzaner Horse Procession
🔲 austria.info

Speck Festival
Tel (0650) 428 2000.
🔲 speckfest.at

Wine Route
🔲 weinstrassen.at

World Body Painting Festival
🔲 bodypainting-festival.com

Spectator Sports

Hahnenkamm
🔲 kitzbuehel.com

Ski World Cup Opening
🔲 skiweltcup.soelden.com

Top of the Mountain
🔲 ischgl.com

Spas

Alpen Parks Resort
Am Gemeindeplatz 2, 5761, Maria Alm.
Tel (06584) 2100.
🔲 alpenparks.at/resortmariaalm

Aqua Dome Spa
Tel (05253) 6400.
🔲 aqua-dome.at

Bad Gastein
Tel (06432) 33930.
🔲 gastein.com

Felsentherme
Tel (06434) 22230.
🔲 felsentherme.com

Hospiz
Tel (05446) 2611.
🔲 arlberghospiz.at

Krallerhof Wellness Hotel
Tel (06583) 82460.
🔲 krallerhof.com

Rogner Bad Blumau
Tel (03383) 5100 - 9449.
🔲 blumau.com

Römerbad
Tel (04240) 8212.
🔲 badkleinkirchheim.at/en/roemerbad-thermal-spa/

St Kathrein-Therme
Tel (04240) 8282301.
🔲 vondenpistenindiethermen.com

Live Music and Concerts

It's true: the hills are alive with the sound of music. However, there is much more to be enjoyed musically in this tuneful land than the Rogers and Hammerstein song with angel-voiced siblings. Dozens of annual classical music festivals attract the world's premier artists and musicians to stunning venues where the music was often originally performed. Whether in Mozart's Innsbruck or Haydn's Eisenstadt, the settings are as spectacular as the melodies. Also, it is possible to leap out of the cradle of classical music and straight into a leather-lined folk evening, a vibrant electronic music scene or club DJs who are famous across Europe, such as DJ Ötzi. Music programmes vary each year but each of the following summer festivals is an annual extravaganza of sound.

Opera and Operetta

Though Vienna's reputation for opera is renowned, the rest of the country's operatic contribution is not to be forgotten. There is no better example of a perfect harmony of space and sound than the **Bregenz Festival**. Its dramatic 20 m (66 ft) stage floats atop the dark waters of Lake Constance and past audiences have enjoyed the strains of Puccini's *Tosca* and Verdi's *The Troubador*. As well as the headline performance, other musical works are performed in the Festival Hall.

Also on a floating stage, the **Mörbisch Festival on the Lake** celebrated its 50th anniversary of operetta in the open air with *Vienna Blood* by Johann Strauss in 2007.

In Upper Austria, opera lovers flock in large numbers to Bad Ischl, the former summer hunting retreat of Emperor Franz Josef, for the **Lehar Festival**. Also nearby is the extraordinary Roman quarry of St Margarethen – the backdrop for the **Burgenland Opera Festival** with productions like Verdi's *Nabucco*.

The **Tiroler Festspiele Erl** is held in the lowlands of the Tyrol every July. Founded by the conductor Gustav Kuhn, the festival features a mix of opera and chamber music.

Lighter fare is also on the menu for those new to opera. The **Steyr Music Festival** highlights the musical *Les Misérables* and the reform opera *Orpheus and Eurydike*.

Classical Concerts and Festivals

The concert halls of Austria are the mainstay of classical music in the country, and you will find concerts in both small towns and the grand provincial capitals. Perhaps most famous is the **Salzburg Festival** *(see p331)* the internationally recognized festival celebrating classical music, opera and drama. Every summer thousands come from around the world to listen to the world's greatest plays and music.

The main *Festspielhaus* (festival hall) has been impressively refurbished. Lesser known is the **Salzburg Whitsun Festival**, which offers delightful opera buffa pieces. In 2007, the Salzburg Whitsun Festival began a co-operation with the celebrated conductor Riccardo Muti, which lasted until 2011. The festival takes place on a yearly basis.

The **Haydn Festival** in Eisenstadt each September is a high point of the concert season calendar. The works of Joseph Haydn are performed against the works of other composers to show contrast in programmes expertly selected by artistic director Dr Walter Reicher.

In 2009, Burgenland commemorated the 200th anniversary of Hadyn's death with many musical events. In September a splendid series of concerts dedicated to the works of Johannes Brahms takes place in Styria, home

to the Brahms Museum and the **International Brahms Festival**. Many festivals guarantee a feast for the ears and eyes. **Allegro Vivo**, Lower Austria's most traditional music festival, opens its doors every summer to thousands of music lovers who revel in the beautiful castles and Baroque abbeys, which form the backdrop for the events. Matinees at Schloss Esterházy offer a wonderful chance to experience the music of Haydn in the very rooms where the composer himself worked and where many of his compositions were first performed. In Radstadt's Renaissance palace of Höch near Flachau, **Paul-Hofhaimer Days** offers early music and new sounds. Past festivals have provided a mixed bag of the oratories, varying from *The Four Seasons* by Haydn to *King David* by Honecker. Since 1978, the **Innsbruck Festival of Ancient Music** has delighted concert-goers with its grand halls and diverse programmes.

In addition to mixing music with grand architecture, other pleasing combinations are on offer. **Schloss Grafenegg** music festival, the brain child of top contemporary pianist Rudolf Buchbinder, combines tastings from Austria's top vineyards with musical programmes. Similarly, the **Brucknerfest Linz** features a dynamic combination of classical music and modern media art.

The rural charm of the Bregenzerwald region goes well with the music of Schubert and his contemporaries.

The annual **Schubertiade** in Schwarzenberg boasts some 70 events including chamber concerts, song evenings, readings and master classes. More than 70,000 fans also come for the Schubertiade; the little sister to this is Steyr's Schubert Festival, offering a smaller cross-section of Schubert and his contemporaries.

For lovers of something a little edgier, Nikolaus Harnoncourt's Styrian festival of classical music, **Styriarte**, is probably the most avant-garde Austria has to offer outside Vienna. "A connoisseur's choice" is the description often heard.

Rock, Pop, Jazz and Alternative

It is outdoor rock surrounded by outdoor rocks at the mountain-ringed city of Salzburg's massive outdoor **Frequency Festival**. The annual Salzburg outdoor music fest means 3 days, 3 stages and 40 bands worth of hard rock. It's a full camping experience, with showers and earplugs available. Previous headliners have included The Kaiser Chiefs. Graz buzzes during **Springsix**, Austria's largest festival for electronic art and music. International electronic acts, DJs and visual artists transform the city into a massive party zone.

Blues and boogie are the vibe at the **Kitzbühel Summer Concerts** on five stages across this pretty medieval mountain resort town. A few dozen peaks over in Montafon, the cultural **Montafon Summer** festival comprises some 20 events including concerts ranging from opera to jazz to classical music, as well as children's entertainment. The best of the international jazz scene meets at the **Jazz Fest in Saalfelden** amid the excellent acoustics of the Congress Center main stage, plus "short cuts" at the Kunsthaus Nexus, and free concerts in the town square.

The **Ramsau Festival** stages a pick and mix of culture. Previous years have welcomed the Vienna State Opera Ballet, choreographed by Renato Zanella; the Bratislava Symphonic Orchestra, conducted by Mario Kosik; the L'Orfeo Baroque Orchestra, with light installations by Stefan Knor; Austria's best accordion player Otto Lechner and many others.

Of course, no discussion of Austrian popular music is complete without mention of **Hansi Hinterseer**, former World Cup ski racer turned aging pop idol. He plays venues across Austria year round, with the stamina one expects of a ski racer.

Folk Music

You'll find many folk music concerts in Austrian towns and villages throughout the year. Of the annual ones, St Anton's **Folk Music Time** is a favourite. The charming mountain town's pedestrian zone provides the perfect setting for authentic Alpine music, attracting traditionally costumed ensembles from Austria, South Tirol, Bavaria and Switzerland.

The Sound of Music

It has been more than 40 years since actor Julie Andrews put Salzburg on the (modern) musical map. The Von Trapp odyssey has become an industry in Salzburg, yet most Austrians have never heard of it. **Sound of Music** tours (of which there are many every day in Salzburg) take in all the big backdrops, and a musical dinner theatre plays all the favourites live.

DIRECTORY

Opera and Operetta

Bregenz Festival
Tel (05574) 4076.
w bregenzerfestspiele.com

Burgenland Opera Festival
Tel (02680) 42042.
w ofs.at

Lehar Festival
Tel 43 6132 23839.
w leharfestival.at

Mörbisch Festival on the Lake
Tel (02682) 662 100.
w seefestspiele-moerbisch.at

Steyr Music Festival
Tel (07252) 53229-0.
w musikfestivalsteyr.at

Tiroler Festspiele Erl
Tel (05373) 81000.
w tiroler-festspiele.at

Classical Concerts and Festivals

Allegro Vivo
Tel (02982) 4319.
w allegro-vivo.at

Brucknerfest Linz
Tel (0732) 775 230.
w brucknerhaus.at

Haydn Festival
Haydn & Esterházy.
Tel (02682) 61866.
w esterhazy.at
w haydnfestival.at

Innsbruck Festival of Ancient Music
Tel 01 88088.
w altemusik.at

International Brahms Festival
Tel (03852) 3434.
w brahmsmuseum.at

Paul-Hofhaimer Days
Tel (06452) 7150.
w radstadt.com

Salzburg Festival
Tel (0662) 8045 500.
w salzburger festspiele.at

Salzburg Whitsun Festival
Tel (0662) 8045 500.
w salzburger-festspiele.at

Schloss Grafenegg
Tel (02735) 5500.
w grafenegg.com

Schubertiade
Tel (05576) 72091.
w schubertiade.at

Styriarte
Tel (0316) 825 000.
w styriarte.com

Rock, Pop, Jazz and Alternative

Frequency Festival
w frequency.at

Hansi Hinterseer
w hansi-hinterseer.at

Jazz Fest in Saalfelden
Tel (06582) 70660.
w jazzsaalfelden.com

Kitzbühel Summer Concerts
Tel (05356) 777.
w kitzbuehel.com

Montafon Summer
Tel (05556) 722530.
w montafon.at

Ramsau Festival
Tel (03687) 81833.
w ramsau.com

Springsix
w springsix.at

Folk Music

Folk Music Time
Tel (05446) 22690.
w stantonamarlberg.com

The Sound of Music

Sound of Music
Tel (0662) 889870.
w salzburg.info

OUTDOOR ACTIVITIES

Austria is an ideal country for sports enthusiasts all year round. For winter sports you can find some 22,000 perfect pistes for downhill skiing and 16,000 km (10,000 miles) of dedicated trails for cross-country skiing in the Alps as well as some 14,000 km (9,000 miles) of walking trails, which are cleared of snow so that you can admire the stunning mountain scenery unimpeded. The countless lakes are perfectly suited for water skiing, sailing and wind surfing, and of course for swimming in summer, while the Tyrolean Alps are a paradise for rock climbers and mountaineers. Throughout Austria there are also superb facilities for more unusual sports, such as glacier climbing, snowshoe walking, rafting, canoeing, bungee jumping or paragliding.

Skiing

The main sport in the Alps is, of course, skiing. Visitors have a choice from skiing on the gentlest family slopes to braving rough runs down the steep slopes of the high Alps, from staying in the deep, fresh snow of the nursery slopes to venturing onto extremely difficult "black" downhill runs. Even nighttime skiing is possible, since some of the runs are illuminated at night.

The best areas for skiing are in Upper and Lower Austria and in Styria. Around Innsbruck, one of Austria's largest winter sports areas, year-round skiing is possible, for example in the Stubaital, Glungezer, Axamer Lizum and Mutterer Alm.

The Salzburg region has some 860 km (530 miles) of ski trails and 270 ski lifts, and resorts such as Filzmoos and Kleinarl regularly host many famous skiing contests. The permanent glaciers, such as those in the Ötztal Alps, welcome skiers all year round. Most Austrian winter sports centres sell passes which give access to all the local ski facilities. If you wish to experience the thrill of skiing down the route that has been used in the World Cup since 1972, go to the Planai slopes in the Styrian resort of Schladming.

The Baroque monastery in Stams in Tyrol has a skiing college whose graduates include several international champions. Those who are more interested in the high life among Europe's aristocracy and in the pleasures of *après-ski*, should make for the pistes in Lech and Zürs am Arlberg, in Voralberg, and in Kitzbühel, in Tyrol.

Langlauf, nordic or cross-country skiing, is also well catered for in Austria, with numerous attractive routes, called *Loipe*. Almost all cross-country routes also have sprint sections, where you can try out your steps.

A skier studying an information board in the mountains

Snowboarding

Snowboarding is one of the most popular winter activities in Austria after skiing. The sport arrived in Europe from the United States and was originally no more than a teenage craze. It has long since turned serious – Austria was one of the first countries to hold contests in the discipline, and the annual event in Seefeld, Tyrol, has become a meeting ground for the world's snowboarding elite. Austrians won many medals in the last two Olympic Winter Games, both in the parallel slalom and the half pipe (something between a ski piste and a bobsleigh run), and one of the first snowboarding champions, Stefan Gimpl, enjoys great popularity in his country.

Tyrol is the snowboarder's paradise and it used to be the home of the International Snowboarding Federation. Young people from all over the world come here to participate in the Powder Turns, in Kaprun or Saalbach-Hinterglemm.

Downhill skiing – Austria's most popular sport

Sleighs and Toboggans

As well as skiing, almost all Austrian winter sports centres have facilities for bobsleigh and toboggan rides. Resorts such as Ischgl, in western Tyrol, are famous for their excellent tobogganing facilities. There are also several summer sleigh runs, for example in northern Tyrol. Sleigh hire costs between €3 and €5 per day. In some places it is possible to carry your sleigh up the hill on the mountain lift, but you cannot carry it down again – you have to ride it along the track.

If you're not too keen on racing down the mountain, you can enjoy the romantic and more leisurely pursuit of admiring the countryside while being transported in a horse-drawn sleigh, for €12 to €15 per person. The hire of a whole carriage costs between €40 and €70.

Mountaineering

Wherever there are mountains you will always find rock climbers and mountaineers. In Austria, the largest organization for climbers is the **Österreichischer Alpenverein**. It has more than 190 regional divisions all over Austria, with its headquarters in Vienna. Besides selling maps, books and guides, the association also runs a library and hires out equipment, it maintains mountain hostels and walking trails, organizes skiing courses and runs a school of

Ramblers on one of the many mountain trails in summer

mountaineering. Members of the Alpenverein enjoy many discounts, for example on accommodation in mountain huts. There is also a meteorological phoneline, giving information about current and expected weather conditions, including any avalanche warnings, which allows rock climbers to make the appropriate arrangements for their expedition.

Walking

Rambles on the mountain trails are a popular activity, enjoyed by Austrians and visitors alike. The Rosengartenschlucht, a ravine northwest of Imst whose sides reach 100 m (328 ft) in height, is a particularly attractive walk; you walk along the valley of the Ötz River and get to see the Stuibenfall, Tyrol's tallest waterfall, created by a fallen rock. Many rambling trails can also be found in the region of Eben im Pongau. In Kleinarl, one of the attractions are the *Fackelwanderungen*, nighttime walk with torches. In the Salzkammergut, a lift takes visitors to the top of the Grünberg or Feuerkogel mountains, where many long tourist trails grant walkers views of the fairy-tale landscape of the Alpine lakes.

There are walking trails all over the country, and they are all clearly signposted and marked on tree trunks by black-and-white signs. As with the ski runs, the level of difficulty is indicated by a colour. Local tourist offices have detailed maps of the area. And, if you don't trust your map-reading

skills, you can always hire a mountain guide or join a rambling group.

Cycling

On the flat, bicycles are an ideal and inexpensive way of getting around. In the mountains, cycling becomes more of an endurance test. Nonetheless, mountain-biking is popular and every holiday resort and most hotels offer bikes for hire. St Johann, in the highest part of the Alps, plays host to various international cycling races. In June and September, cyclists meet in East Tyrol to compete in an arduous race around the Lienz Dolomites. Less ambitious cyclists choose the scenic *Radwege* along rivers such as the Danube or Drau. In Vienna, despite heavy car traffic, cyclists can be seen everywhere. In towns and suburbs, many cycle routes have been marked; you can see them on maps available in any bookshop.

Mountaineering – a sport for the brave and determined

Visitors on a winter mountain biking expedition

Yachting marina in Mörbisch

Water Sports

Snow is not the only element attracting sports enthusiasts to Austria – an abundance of rivers and lakes offer much to the summer visitor, whether it's in the form of relaxation or active holidays. The lovely lakes in the Salzkammergut, especially, are worth exploring.

Austrian lakes come in all shapes and sizes, but most are suitable for swimming and sailing. The largest and most famous are Bodensee (Lake Constance) and Neusiedler See. The latter, easily accessible from Vienna, is a 40-km (25-mile) long lake on the Hungarian border, and the venue every weekend for an Olympic-standard regatta. There are sailing and windsurfing schools on many Austrian lakes, and on the larger ones waterskiing and paraskiing are also on offer.

Scuba-diving is also possible at certain times of the year and in designated areas of some lakes, particularly in the Salzkammergut.

Many mountain rivers, particularly those in the western part of Austria, flow through narrow ravines and tumble down in numerous waterfalls – thus creating endless thrills for canoeists and competitors in the annual white-water rafting contests. An especially popular rafting event takes place along a gorge, the Imsterschlucht.

Even in Vienna you can enjoy watersports – along the Old Danube many places hire out water skis, rowing or sailing boats, without the need to prove any special expertise.

Lastly, the lakes and rivers are perfect for fishing. Local tourist offices will be able to advise you on where the best spots are, and sell you a licence.

Horse Riding

Horse riding, while not as popular as skiing, also has many followers. Lower Austria has a number of studs which offer a variety of riding holidays. Some hotels, too, own their own horses or have an arrangement with a local riding centre which allows guests to use its facilities. In many resorts, riding lessons can also be booked in indoor arenas, which is especially useful during bad weather or in the winter months.

Even if your visit only takes you to Vienna, you still don't have to forego the pleasures of horse riding – the Prater funfair, once the favourite riding course of the Empress Elisabeth, is open to this day to lovers of the sport.

Horse riding is one of the more costly activities, but it is not exorbitant; in the Tyrol, for example, one hour's riding in winter costs about €15 per person – about the same as you would have to pay for hiring a tennis court.

Hang-gliding – a spectacular sport, enjoyed in Stubaital

Tennis

Indoor tennis courts, which are also open in winter, can be found in any of the larger resorts and in many hotels; outdoor courts are available in most cities. They are less common in the mountain resorts which specialize in other sports. Prices vary; in Styria the cost of hiring a court for one hour is around €13–17 during the day, or €18–19 in the evening.

Extreme Sports

So-called extreme sports, such as rafting, canyoning, speed-boat racing, paragliding, hang gliding, bungee jumping or free climbing, are all well represented in Austria. New companies open every day, offering equipment hire and organized events to tempt the adventurous who are seeking an adrenaline kick.

Horse riding along the shores of Neusiedler See

DIRECTORY

Skiing, Snowboarding, Tobogganing

Dachstein Gletscherbahn
Coburgstrasse 52,
8970 Schladming.
Tel (03687) 22042.
W planai.at

Zell am See/ Kaprun Information
Bruckner Bundesstrasse 1a, 5700 Zell am See.
Tel (06542) 770.
W zellamsee-kaprun.com

Österreichischer Bob- und Skeletonverband
Haus des Sports,
Stadionstrasse 1, 6020 Innsbruck.
Tel (0512) 20 02 50.
W bobskeleton.at

Tourismus-gemeinschaft Mölltaler Gletscher
9831 Flattach 99.
Tel (04785) 615.
W flattach.at

Tourismusverband Ötztal Arena
Gemeindestrasse 4,
6450 Sölden.
Tel 057 200.
W oetztal.com

Tourismusverband Pitztal
Unterdorf 18,
A-6473 Wenns im Pitztal.
Tel (05414) 869 99.
W pitztal.com

Tourismusverband Stubai Tirol
Stubaitalhaus, Dorf 3,
6167 Neustift, Tirol.
Tel (0501) 8810.
W stubai.at

Tourismusverband Tux
Lanersbach 401. 6293 Tux.
Tel (05287) 8506.
W tux.at

Mountaineering

Österreichischer Alpenverein
Olympiastrasse 37, 6010 Innsbruck.
Tel (0512) 595 47.
W alpenverein.at

Österreichischer Touristenklub
Bäckerstrasse 16, 1010 Vienna.
Tel (01) 51 23 844.
W oetk.at

Verband Alpiner Vereine Österreichs
Bäckerstrasse 16, 1010 Vienna.
Tel (01) 512 54 88.
W vavoe.at

Walking

Europa-Wanderhotels
Stresweg 8, 9773 Irschen.
Tel (04710) 2780.
W wanderhotels.com

Cycling

Mountain Bike Holidays
Saalfeldnerstrasse 14,
5751 Maishofen.
Tel (06542) 80 480-22.
W bike-holidays.com

Radtouren in Österreich
Freistädterstrasse 119,
4041 Linz.
Tel (0732) 221022.
W radtouren.at

Water Sports

Austrian Water Ski Federation
Schottenring 17/3/6,
A-1010 Vienna.
Tel 00151 4624.
W oewsv.at

Österreichischer Segelverband
Seestrasse 17b,
A-7100 Neusiedl am See.
Tel (02167) 40243-0.
W segelverband.at

Horse Riding

Reiten in Österreich Reitarena Austria
Urzenweg 14
A-4121 Altenfelden.
Tel (0664) 424 8036.
W tiscover.com

Urlaub am Bauernhof
Gabelsbergerstrasse 19, 5020 Salzburg.
Tel (0662) 88 02 02.
W farmholidays

Extreme Sports

Action Club Zillertal
Hauptstrasse 458,
6290 Mayrhofen.
Tel (05285) 62977.
W actionclub-zillertal.at

Adventure Club Tuxertal
Lanersbach 376,
A-6293 Tux.
Tel (05287) 87287 or (0676) 307 0000.
W natursport.at

Aktiv-Zentrum
Neugut 43,
6882 Schnepfau.
Tel 0676 7837878.
W aktiv-zentrum.at

AOS Adventures
Friedau 1a, 8940 Liezen.
Tel (03612) 253 43.
W rafting.at

Austria-Adventure Sportagentur Raab
Mairenben 30, 4452 Ternberg.
Tel (0664) 503 13 72.
W austria-adventure.at

Ballonhotel Thaller
Hofkirchen 51,
8224 Kaindorf.
Tel (03334) 2262.
W ballonhotel.at

Club Aktiv Mölltal
Flattach 25, 9831 Flattach.
Tel (04785) 410.
W cam.at

Club Montée Adventure Center
Wolfgangseestrasse 26,
5322 Hof bei Salzburg.
Tel (06228) 30008.
W montee.com

Feelfree
Platzleweg 5, 6430 Ötz.
Tel (05252) 60350.
W feelfree.at

Flugschule Salzkammergut
Flachbergweg 46, 4810 Gmunden.
Tel (07612) 730 33.
W paragleiten.net

Freelife
8923 Palfau 102.
Tel (07230) 79160.
W freelife.at

Jauntal Bungy & Event GmbH
Eis 81, 9113 Ruden.
Tel (04234) 222.
W bungy.at

Kormoran (Canyoning)
Neue Siedlung 19,
3125 Absdorf.
Tel (02786) 30065.
W kormoran.at

Outdoor Leadership
Steinach 4, 4822 Bad Goisern.
Tel (06135) 6058.
W outdoor-leadership.com

Österreichischer Aero Club
Prinz Eugen-Strasse 12,
1040 Vienna.
Tel (01) 505 10 28.
W aeroclub.at

Perschlingtal Ballooning
Weisching 70,
3071 Böheimkirchen.
Tel (0664) 400 8491.
W perschlingtal ballooning.at

Salzburg Adventures
Mehr Abenteuer für Salzburg, Halberstätten 21, 5201 Seekirchen.
Tel (0680) 326 6767.
W salzburgadventures.com

SURVIVAL GUIDE

PRACTICAL INFORMATION

Austria is a fantastic holiday destination, for both winter and summer. It features numerous attractions, from well-equipped Alpine skiing centres to quaint and charming villages, from fascinating historic sights in the towns to the superb collections of its museums – there is something on offer for every taste and budget. Visitors will have no problems finding suitable accommodation, interesting restaurants or enjoyable cultural events, and the tourist offices in most towns and villages will be only too pleased to furnish you with all the information you require. Alternatively, you can find useful details on the Internet. Many larger towns and all major sights post helpful hints and fascinating facts on their own websites.

Visitors crowding around a cable car station in Ischgl

When to Visit

There is no such thing as a low season in Austria – the tourist season continues virtually all year round. Most hotels divide the year into two main parts: spring–summer (1 May–30 Sep) and autumn–winter (1 Oct–30 Apr). The winter season peaks at Christmas and again from the end of January to the beginning of March. Only small hotels and pensions far from winter sports facilities close for the winter. Ski enthusiasts can enjoy the Alps from Christmas until Easter, while walkers are best advised to visit in the spring, when there is a breeze in the air and the mountain slopes display a rich tapestry of colourful flowers.

The peak of the summer season is between June and August, and this period coincides with the greatest number of cultural events, festivals and village fairs all over the country. At any time of year you will be able to discover and explore new sides of this multi-faceted country.

Immigration and Visa Formalities

Nationals from most European and many overseas countries do not need a visa to enter Austria. You will need a national identity card or, in the case of Britain which does not have an identity card, a valid passport. Citizens of EU countries can stay as long as they like. Visitors from the US, Canada, Australia or New Zealand are welcome for up to three months, or longer with a visa obtained from the Austrian Embassy or Consulate in their home country before the first date of entry.

Dogs and cats require a current rabies vaccination certificate; motorists need a green card as proof of third-party insurance.

Customs Regulations

Nationals of EU countries, including Britain and Ireland, may take home unlimited quantities of duty-paid alcoholic drinks and tobacco goods as long as these are intended for their own consumption, and it can be proven that the goods are not intended for resale.

Citizens of the US and Canada are limited to a maximum of 200 cigarettes (or 50 cigars) and one litre of spirits (or 2¼ litres of wine or 3 litres of beer). Regulations for residents of Australia and New Zealand vary slightly from these guidelines.

If you are in doubt, consult the customs offices in your own country before you travel to Austria.

Up-to-date information and details on what may be brought into Austria can be found on the Internet at www.bmf.gv.at and in the *Zollinfo* brochure, available at the border.

A useful orientation board and map of the local area in Zell am See

◄ A skier at the Kuhtai Ski Resort near Innsbruck

Embassies and Consulates

The Embassies for all countries, including the UK, are based in Vienna. Some larger cities have consulates where you can turn for help *(see p344)*.

Tourist Information

There are many local tourist offices all over Austria, offering useful advice to visitors on accommodation, restaurants, excursions and cultural events *(see p291)*. Offices are signposted with the white letter "i" against a green background. Every province also has its own tourist information centre, where you can turn for help. Most of the local tourist offices offer their services free and hand out free leaflets, maps and information booklets.

You can plan your trip in advance by getting in touch with travel agencies or the representatives of **Österreich Werbung** (the Austrian National Tourist Office) directly. For cheaper accommodation and information about youth hostels or pop concerts, the multilingual team at **Jugendinformation Wien** will provide assistance.

Sign of a pension in Lofer

Opening Hours

This guide provides the opening times for each individual sight you may want to visit. Most businesses start work at around 8am and close at about 4pm. On Fridays, many close early and, even if they do not, it may be hard to get anything done. Most shops are open from Monday to Friday, 8am to 6pm (sometimes 7:30pm) and on Saturdays from 8am mostly until 5pm (in larger cities). Shops also close on Sundays and public holidays, and in the countryside some close on Wednesday afternoons.

Banks in many towns are open from 8am until 3pm (5:30pm on Thursdays); smaller branches close at lunchtime. All banks remain closed on Saturdays, but you can change money at the airport, the main railway stations or in bureaux de change, or use an automatic teller machine.

Museums and Historic Monuments

The national list of palaces, castles and ruins comprises a staggering 2,000 sights, and this does not even include Austria's countless churches, monasteries or abbeys. Vienna alone has more than 60 museums, and Styria over 200; of these only 58 are state-owned; the remainder belong to associations, churches, companies or private individuals. Opening hours vary and depend on the local tourist seasons. Generally speaking, museums are open from 10am until 4pm or 7pm. Once a week they stay open longer, some until 9pm or even midnight. Some museums close for one day in the week, usually on a Monday.

A group of sightseers admiring historic buildings in Innsbruck

Signposts help visitors find the way to the Alpine huts

Check times, special events and arrangements for guided tours locally. For groups of 10 people or more it is often possible to arrange the time of their visit in advance – and you may be eligible for a group discount. At the end of a guided tour it is customary to leave a small tip.

Admission Prices

Museum entrance fees can vary from €2 to €8. Admission to historic houses costs about €10–15. Children up to the age of 6 (in some museums, up to the age of 7) are admitted free, and 6–15 year-olds pay half price, as do senior citizens (60 and over). There are also reductions for students. Some museums offer family tickets (admitting for example two adults and three children); a few allow free admission on a particular day in the week.

An adult cinema ticket costs around €7–10. Some cinemas sell tickets at lower prices at the beginning of the week.

For theatre tickets you will need to set aside €30–40 or more; musicals cost upwards of €40. Concert tickets start at around €14. The three-day *Wien-Karte* entitles you to unlimited use of all public transport facilities for 72 hours as well as reduced admission to some museums, and discounts in selected shops and restaurants.

A range of foreign-language newspapers and magazines on street stands

Information for Disabled Visitors

Austria is better prepared to receive disabled visitors than most other countries, and many trams and buses can accommodate wheelchairs. At train stations, ask about lifts when you get your ticket. Facilities vary at underground stations, so it is best to check first. In some regions the facilities are fairly basic, but concessions on tickets are available for disabled visitors.

Special parking spaces are set aside for disabled drivers and are clearly marked as such; if your car displays the appropriate sticker, parking is also free of charge.

Most of the main sights have access ramps. Contact the museums in advance so they can organize help with wheelchairs if needed.

Some of the larger 5-star hotels have special facilities for disabled guests, including extra-wide showers that allow easy wheelchair access. Just a few restaurants have access ramps for wheelchairs.

For a directory of accessible travel services check the website of Europe-wide organization **Pantou**. There is also information on barrier-free travel on the Austria National Tourist Office website, as well as on each of the regional tourism authority websites. The website of rail operator **Österreichische Bundesbahn** has information in English on barrier-free rail travel.

Travelling with Children

Many hotels offer a free stay or reduced rates for children under the age of 12 who share a room with their parents. Children up to the age of 15 pay half fare on public transport; on Sundays, public holidays and during the summer vacations they travel for free. They are also entitled to reduced admission when visiting museums and historic sights. The large supermarkets and also chemists have a department with essential items for babies as do the Drogeriemarkt and Bipa Stores.

Senior Travellers

Austrians are extremely respectful of older people. Senior travellers are often given priority seating on public transport and many theatres, cinemas, attractions and museums offer generous discounts to travellers with senior ID.

Information for Students

Students holding an international student card and a valid college ID are entitled to discounts on railways and municipal public transport, as well as reduced admission to cinemas, museums and sports events. They will also be offered accommodation in a *Jugendherberge* (youth hostel) at a lower price. Up-to-date information on accommodation in student dormitories and youth hostels can be obtained from any tourist office.

Religion

Austria is a predominantly Catholic country – as is apparent from the large number of Catholic churches; Protestants make up just 5 per cent of the population. There is also a fair-sized immigrant population from various national backgrounds and following various religious faiths; probably the largest group among them are Muslims. In Vienna, there is a sizeable Jewish community, which has its own synagogues. Cemeteries are communal.

Information board on a building in Innsbruck

Language

Although all Austrians officially speak German, in reality they speak "Austrian". While this variety of Low German does not differ from High German as markedly as Swiss German, its pronunciation and even some rules of grammar and vocabulary may make it seem like a different language.

Added to this are several Austrian dialects, which differ from province to province. Austrians are the first to admit that it would be impossible to learn them all in their countless regional varieties. For instance, visitors who know a little German find *Tirolerisch*, the dialect spoken in Tyrol, completely incomprehensible.

You will have few problems making yourself understood in English, especially in the larger cities and main tourist centres. English is also spoken by most young people who learn it at elementary school.

Etiquette

Peace and quiet are highly valued by Austrians who live outside the cities. They are friendly and easy-going people who tend to keep up their traditions, especially in the mountainous regions. Austrians, especially the older generation, tend to be very courteous, and they expect the same from visitors.

When asked for directions, Austrians will always do their best to help. The Austrians like polite formalities, though hand-kissing is no longer the norm. It is the exception to go on to first-name terms immediately. Forms of address such as Herr Doktor and Herr Ober (head waiter) can be used liberally.

It is worth knowing a few phrases, too, such as, when meeting someone, *Wie geht es Ihnen?*, to enquire after their health. In the morning, *Guten Morgen* is the standard greeting, at lunchtime *Mahlzeit*, later in the day *Guten Tag*. Everywhere and at any time *Grüss Gott* is used, literally "greet the Lord".

Tourist information for students and young travellers

Responsible Tourism

Austria is one of the world's leading destinations for sustainable tourism. About 70 per cent of energy is generated from renewable sources and about 60 per cent of all waste is recycled. In Vienna, recycling bins are located throughout the city and there are numerous organic restaurants, food shops and even clothes stores that promote sustainable fashion.

The *Österreichisches Umweltzeichen* (Austrian Eco-Label) is a seal of approval awarded to hotels and restaurants that meet high environmental and waste-reduction standards. Hotel Stadthalle, near to Westbahnhof station, was the first hotel in Vienna to be awarded the *European Ecolabel* for its green credentials. This innovative hotel uses solar panels to heat up water and collects rain water to flush its toilets.

Electrical Adaptors

The voltage in Austria is 220V AC. Plugs have two small round pins. It is a good idea to buy a multi-adaptor before coming to Austria, as they are not easy to find here. Some of the more expensive hotels may offer guest adaptors, but usually only for use with electric shavers.

Time

Austria uses Central European Time (GMT plus one hour). Clocks move forward one hour on the last Sunday in March and back on the last Sunday in October.

DIRECTORY

Embassies & Consulates

Australia
Mattiellistrasse 2–4, 1040 Vienna.
Tel (01) 506 740.
W austria.embassy.gov.au

Canada
Laurenzerberg 2, 1010 Vienna.
Tel (01) 531 383 000.
W kanada.at

Ireland
Rotenturmstrasse 16–18, 1010 Vienna.
Tel (01) 715 42 46.
W embassyofireland.at

New Zealand
Mattiellistrasse 2-4/3, A-1040 Vienna.
Tel (01) 505 3021.
W nzembassy.com

United Kingdom
Jauresgasse 12, 1030 Vienna. **Tel** (01) 716130.
W british-embassy.net

United States of America
Boltzmanngasse 16, 1090 Vienna. **Tel** (01) 31339-0.
W usembassy.at

Tourist Offices

Wiener Tourismusverband
Albertinaplatz & Maysedergasse, 1010 Vienna. **Tel** (01) 24555. W wien.info

WienXtra-Jugend-Info
Babenbergerstrasse 1, 1040 Vienna.
Tel (01) 400084-100.
W jugendinfowien.at

Österreich Werbung – Austrian Holiday Information
Margaretenstrasse 1, 1040 Vienna. **Tel** 00800 400 20 000 (toll free).
W austria.info
W austriatourism.com

Tourist Offices Abroad

London
Austrian Holiday Service
Tel 00800 400 20 000 (toll free). W austria.info

New York
Email travel@austria.info
W austria.info/us

Sydney
36 Carrington Street, 1st floor, Sydney, NSW 2000.
Tel (02) 9299 3621.
W austria.info.au

Information for Disabled Visitors

Österreichische Bundesbahn
W oebb.at/en/Planning_your_trip/Barrier-free_travelling/index.jsp

Pantou
W pantou.org

Personal Security and Health

Austria is one of Europe's safest countries. Tourists are unlikely to encounter any violence (though there has been an increase in petty crimes such as pickpocketing in busy tourist areas) and the police and emergency services are easy to contact. Pharmacists are respected and their advice is often sought by locals. A visit to the pharmacy, unless the problem is serious, is probably the easiest choice if you are feeling unwell. Above all, this is a peaceful country, a land of historic sights, works of art, and beautiful, stunning scenery.

Typical SOS sign seen on a regular U-Bahn platform

DIRECTORY

Emergency Telephone Numbers

Ambulance
Tel 144.

Emergency Medical Assistance
Tel 141. Can be consulted evenings, nights, Saturdays, Sundays and public holidays.

Fire Service
Tel 122.

Flying Ambulance Service
Tel 401 44-0.

Mobile Telephone Emergency Line
Tel 112.

Police
Tel 133.

Roadside Assistance
Tel 120.

Police

In Vienna, in the provincial capitals, and in all the larger towns, public order is maintained by the *Polizei*. The police also run lost property departments (*Fundbüro*), which can be found in any district police station. In the provinces, policing is carried out by the *Gendarmerie*.

Personal Security and Property

There are few places in Austria to steer clear of, even at night. However, it is as well to be careful. Avoid areas around stations at night and pay extra attention at funfairs

or large gatherings. Don't become an easy target for thieves: never leave items visible in a car; carry money and documents safely. Women should avoid placing bags on the floor in cafés, bars and restaurants.

In case of a theft, report it without delay to the nearest *Polizeiwache* (police station). If you lose traveller's cheques, seek help at the nearest bank, which will stop them. Credit and debit card thefts should be reported immediately to your credit card company or bank. Contact your consulate if you lose your passport, or if it is stolen.

Lost Property

Go to the nearest police station in the first instance. If they do not succeed in restoring your property within seven days, then try the lost property bureau (*Fundbüro*). For property lost on railways or the Schnellbahn, go to the Westbahnhof in Vienna and enquire in person.

Accidents and Emergencies

Britain has a reciprocal arrangement with Austria whereby emergency hospital treatment is free if you have a British passport. Visits to doctors, dentists or outpatient departments are also free of charge, but getting free treatment can involve a lot of bureaucracy. Britons should be sure to get a European Health Insurance Card, available from post offices or the Internet, before travelling. It is also a good idea to take out full health insurance.

Visitors from other countries should establish what is required to cover their medical treatment either with their home embassy or with their medical insurance company.

If you are ill, it is best to go to a clinic at a state hospital. In Vienna, the main hospital (and the largest in Europe) is the **Allgemeines Krankenhaus** (General Hospital) in the ninth district. People without insurance or money

Police motorcycle

Policeman

Fire engine

Police car

Ambulance

to pay for medical services are cared for at the **Krankenhaus der Barmherzigen Brüder** (Brothers of Mercy Hospital), which also runs a free emergency dental clinic. In a medical emergency, call an ambulance (Rettungsdienst).

Health Precautions

Tick-Borne Encephalitis is a possible danger wherever there are deciduous trees in Austria. Only a tiny proportion of ticks carry the disease, which may cause brain damage and in some cases lead to death. Most Austrians and foreign residents are inoculated against it. Inoculation is done in several stages, but is not usually recommended for holiday-makers. The risk of infection is minimal, but to be on the safe side, if you are bitten, do not remove the tick but go to an outpatients department.

Pharmacies

If it is not an emergency, it is best to go to an Apotheke

Façade of a typical *Apotheke* (pharmacy) in Vienna

(pharmacy) for advice on medicines and treatment. Pharmacies display a red "A" sign and operate a night rota system. Any closed pharmacies will display the address of the nearest one open, and the **Pharmacy Information Line** also has details of some which are open.

Apart from medicines, pharmacies also sell some herbal remedies. *Reformhäuser* specialize in such products and natural healthcare.

Policewoman   Fireman

Banking and Currency

Austrian banking services are very accessible. Money-changing machines (ATMs) can be found in all the major cities, and most shops, hotels and restaurants accept credit cards, although some still only take cash. You can take up to the equivalent of €10,000 cash into or out of the country without declaring it. The largest Austrian banks, including Bank Austria Creditanstalt, BAWAG and Raiffeisenbank, have branches in most of the provincial cities.

Money Exchange

The best place to change money is at a bank. Bank Austria and Erste Bank charge 3 per cent commission or a minimum handling fee of €5.50. Although you can use travel agents and hotels, the banks give you a better rate and charge less commission. Railway station *Wechselstuben* (bureaux de change) charge 4 per cent on the exchanged sum. Exchanging a larger amount of money at one time can save on commission. You can also exchange pounds sterling for euros at an automatic money-changing machine.

Most banks are open from 8:30am to 12:30pm and from 1:30pm to 3pm Monday to Friday (to 5:30pm on Thursdays). A few, such as the main Creditanstalt bank in Vienna, Bank Austria and some banks in the provincial capitals as well as those in the busier tourist resorts or close to railway stations and airports, have extended opening hours.

Credit Cards

The banks operate a large network of ATMs, many of which take foreign credit cards with PIN codes. This facility will be clearly stated on the front of the machine – just look for the logo of your card. Instructions are often given in English and other languages. Be aware money drawn out using a credit card often incurs a considerable fee.

At most hotels, shops and restaurants you can pay by credit or debit card, although some do not take all cards. It is best to always carry some cash on you. Some establishments also set a minimum sum that can be paid for by credit card. Make sure you report lost or stolen cards to your own or nearest Austrian bank without delay.

Traveller's Cheques

Traveller's cheques are best avoided as very few banks now change them and they are unheard of in shops. As there is a wide network of ATMs across the country, either cash, a debit card or a widely accepated credit card is a preferable option.

DIRECTORY

Bureaux de Change (Wechselstuben)

Vienna
Airport. **Open** 5am–11:15pm daily.
Erste Bank: Rauhensteingasse 1.
UniCredit Bank Austria: Stephansplatz 7a.

Graz
Bank Austria Creditanstalt AG: Herrengasse 15.
BAWAG PSK Filiale und Post: Europaplatz 4, Objekt 1.

Innsbruck
BAWAG PSK Filiale und Post: Südtirolerplatz 10–12.

Melk
BAWAG PSK: Wiener Strasse 85 (in the post office).

Salzburg
Airport, Terminal 1.
Österreichische Verkehrskreditbank AG: Main station, Südtiroler Platz.
Salzburger Sparkasse: Bundesstrasse 95.

Automatic Money-Changing Machines

Vienna
Kärntner Strasse 23.
Kärntner Strasse 51.
Graben 21.
Operngasse 2.
Tegetthoffstrasse 1.
Schottenring 1. Stephansplatz 2.

Feldkirch
Sparkassenplatz 1.

Krems
Obere Landstrasse 19.

Kufstein
Georg-Pirmoser-Strasse 2.
Oberer Stadtplatz 1.

Salzburg
Getreidegasse 1.

St Wolfgang
Markt 106.

Velden
Am Korso.

A Bankomat automatic money-dispensing machine

Currency conversion machine that accepts foreign banknotes

The Euro

The Euro (€) is the common currency of the European Union. It went into general circulation on 1 January 2002, initially for 12 participating countries. Austria was one of those 12 countries taking the Euro in 2002, with the Austrian schilling phased out in the same year.

EU members using the Euro as sole official currency are known as the Eurozone. Several EU members have opted out of joining this common currency. Euro notes are identical throughout the Eurozone countries, each one including designs of fictional architectural structures and monuments. The coins, however, have one side identical (the value side), and one side with an image unique to each country.

Bank Notes

Euro bank notes have seven denominations. The grey €5 note is the smallest, followed by the pink €10 note, blue €20 note, orange €50 note, green €100 note, yellow €200 note and purple €500 note. All notes show the stars of the European Union and architectural motifs.

€5 note

€10 note

€20 note

€50 note

€100 note

€200 note

€500 note

€2 coin

€1 coin

50 cents

20 cents

10 cents

Coins

The euro has eight coin denominations: €1 and €2; 50 cents, 20 cents, 10 cents, 5 cents, 2 cents and 1 cent. The €2 and €1 coins are both silver and gold in colour. The 50-, 20- and 10-cent coins are gold. The 5-, 2- and 1-cent coins are bronze.

5 cents

2 cents

1 cent

Media and Communications

Austria has a highly developed and efficient telephone system. Public telephone boxes are still widely available in Austria, in spite of the popularity of mobile phones. They are very easy to operate, but they can be expensive for international calls. If you plan to make a lot of calls, it may be cheaper to purchase a local SIM card from one of the country's many mobile operators.

Dedicated Internet cafés are far less widespread than they used to be, thanks to the growing presence of Wi-Fi, which can be found in most cafés as well as many public spaces, and is usually free. The Austrian postal system, run by Österreichische Post, is similarly highly efficient. Newspapers and magazines, both hard copy and online, are readily available – many, particularly in Vienna, have excellent listings sections.

International and Local Telephone Calls

Public telephone boxes (Telefonzelle) are easy to find, while payphones can also be found in some post offices. Coin-operated telephones accept 10-, 20- and 50- cent as well as 1- and 2-euro coins – the minimum charge for a local call is 30 cents. Note, however, that there is often a high minimum connection charge for international calls, so it's best to ensure that you have plenty of change to hand. More convenient are phonecards (Telefonwertkarte), which may be purchased at post offices, Telekom Austria shops and tobacconists; cards currently cost €3.60 or €6.90. Most phones carry instructions in English and other languages.

The cheap-rate calling time for international calls from Austria is between 6pm and 8am and at weekends; for domestic calls, it is between 8pm and 6am, and weekends. Be warned that calling from a hotel can be prohibitively expensive.

T-Mobile logo

Mobile Phones

Austria has a number of mobile operators, the main ones being **A1**, **BOB**, **Tele.Ring** and **T-Mobile**. Roaming rates vary widely depending on agreements between your service provider and the local Austrian provider. Some operators offer special deals for travelling in EU countries, though recent EU-wide regulations have seen roaming costs come down considerably. Conversely, roaming can be very expensive if your provider is outside the EU. It is always best to check with your service provider before leaving if you plan to make a lot of calls.

If you do intend to make numerous calls, consider buying a prepaid SIM card, which typically costs around €15 and includes around €10 credit; you then use top-up vouchers (from around €5), which can be purchased from phone shops and tobacconists. Note, though, that your phone will probably need to be unlocked. If you want to buy a handset, expect to pay around €30. Austrian mobile phone numbers begin with 0650 (or higher) up to 0699. 0800 numbers are free while 0810, 0820 and 0900 numbers all incur a charge.

Internet

Vienna has a smattering of dedicated Internet cafés, but, as elsewhere, these are a dying breed as just about every café or coffeehouse now has Wi-Fi – which you are free to use yourself, just so long as you make a purchase. Where you do find an Internet café, expect to pay around €3–6 per hour. Increasingly, many public areas in the bigger towns and cities offer free Wi-Fi; in Vienna, for example, there are hotspots all over the city, as well as the train and subway stations – a full list of these is available at **freewave.at**. Many tourist offices offer Wi-Fi and/or a terminal, though you may need a password from the staff. Otherwise, nearly all hotels (and many hostels) have Wi-Fi, and often a terminal for guests to use.

Emergency phone sign

Coin-operated phone

Sign for cardphone

Reaching the Right Number

- The international dialling code for Austria is +43. When calling from abroad, omit the initial 0 from the area code.
- For directory enquiries, dial 118877, 118899 or 118811.
- Railway timetable information: 05 17 17.
- Road conditions and snowfall: 0800 400 12 400.
- Central Post Office Information (Zentrale Postauskunft): (0810) 010 100.
- To ring home from Austria, dial the appropriate country code, followed by the number.
- Omit the 0 from the local area code.
- For the **UK** dial 0044.
- For the **Irish Republic** dial 00353.
- For the **USA** dial 001.
- For **Australia** dial 0061.
- For **New Zealand** dial 0064.

Postal Services

Österreichische Post, Austria's postal service, is as efficient as you might expect. Postboxes are yellow, and those with a red band are emptied on weekends and public holidays, as well as weekdays. Stamps (Briefmarken) can be bought from post offices (which also have vending machines), as well as tobacconists (Tabak Trafiken). Postal rates for postcards and light envelopes are 55 cents within Austria, 65 cents within Europe, and €1.40 for the rest of the world. To send a parcel, registered letter or express package, you need to fill in a form, which is available at the post office. You can collect correspondence marked Postlagernd (poste restante), but you will need proof of identity.

A typical signboard indicating a Post office

Most post offices in Vienna and larger towns and cities are open Monday to Friday 8am–6pm, while some (such as those at train stations) stay open until 8 or 10pm. Post offices in smaller resorts are likely to close between noon and 2pm, or may even only be open in the mornings. Larger branches are also open on Saturdays between 8am–10pm.

Yellow post- or mailbox used for sending letters

Newspapers and Magazines

Quite a few newsagents and kiosks in Vienna and other major towns and cities stock English-language newspapers, sometimes on the day of publication – typically the Guardian International, Financial Times, USA Today and the International Herald Tribune. In addition, you'll find weekly news magazines such as Time and Newsweek. Online newspapers include Austria Today, though its full content is only available via subscription. Austria's most well regarded broadsheet – and one of the oldest still-published newspapers in the world – is Wiener Zeitung, while other reputable dailies include the right-of-centre Die Presse, and the left-leaning Der Standard; the tabloid brigade, meanwhile, is led by Kronen Zeitung. In Vienna, the best read is Der Falter, which also has weekly listings. Well worth consulting is the excellent Vienna In Your Pocket, a fun online magazine with comprehensive, irreverent, and up-to-date information and listings on the city.

Television and Radio

ORF, the state service broadcaster, offers two channels, ORF1 and ORF2, while the main commercial channels are ATV and TW1. Inevitably, German channels like SAT1 and RTL are prominent on Austrian TV. The majority of hotels have satellite or cable TV, providing the ubiquitous English-language channels CNN and BBC World News, and occasionally one or two others. The main public radio stations are O1

A kiosk in Vienna selling a range of international newspapers

for news and culture (97.7FM), O3 for popular music (103.9FM) and FM4, which offers a more alternative musical slant. Radio Austria International (ROI) presents Austria-related news in various languages. BBC World Service frequencies and listings can be found on their website bbc.co.uk/worldservice.

DIRECTORY

Mobile Phones

A1
W a1.net

BOB
W bob.at

Tel.Ring
W telering.at

T-Mobile
W t-mobile.at

Internet

W freewave.at
W wien.info

Postal Services

Central Post Office
Fleischmarkt 19
Tel 57 76 77 10 10

Couriers

DHL
Tel 82 055 05 05
W dhl.at

FedEx
Tel 80 012 38 00
W fedex.at

TNT
Tel 57 700 77
W tnt.at

TRAVEL INFORMATION

As a popular tourist destination, Austria is well served by both air and rail. The major cities – Vienna, Linz, Graz, Innsbruck, Salzburg and Klagenfurt – have international airports and there are direct flights from all main European cities as well as from the USA, Canada, Japan and Australia. Vienna is a key transit point between West and East, and about eight million passengers a year pass through its Schwechat airport. There are good rail and coach links, too, but from Britain this involves a long journey, often overnight, and is not significantly cheaper than air travel. The motorway network linking Austria and the rest of Europe is extensive, and the roads are clearly signposted and well maintained.

Check-in counters at the international airport in Vienna

Air Travel

There are several flights a day between London's Heathrow and Vienna's Schwechat Airport, which are operated by **British Airways** and by Austria's national airline **Austrian Airways**. Austrian Airways also serves Innsbruck from London Heathrow and Vienna from Manchester. Of the "low-cost" airlines **Ryanair** tends to be good value for money and flies from London Stansted to Graz, Klagenfurt, Linz, Bratislava and Salzburg, with connections from Glasgow and Dublin; and **Flybe** flies from Birmingham and London Gatwick to Salzburg.

If you wish to fly from the United States, there are direct flights with Austria Airlines and **United Airlines** from both New York City and Chicago. There are also direct flights from Toronto with Austrian Airlines and **Air Canada**.

Thanks to its central location **Vienna International Airport** (Flughafen Wien-Schwechat) is a major European transit airport, meaning that all the major airlines have offices here. The airport is located 19 km (12 miles) from Vienna's city centre, and is easily accessible by train or bus. A modern airport, Schwechat is very easy and quick to use.

Bus transfer information board

Domestic Flights

Domestic flights within Austria are operated by **Tyrolean Airways**, part of the Austrian Airlines Group. There are daily flights from Vienna to Graz, Klagenfurt, Innsbruck, Salzburg and Linz. Air travel in Austria is expensive and, with extra time needed for checking in, the journey to and from the airport and for retrieving your luggage, it is not the fastest and best way of getting to another destination in Austria.

Special Deals

It is not necessary to pay full price for a scheduled ticket. There are good deals if you shop around the discount agencies and the Internet. You can usually get APEX tickets if you book at least two weeks in advance and if you can travel at days other than the weekend. Charters are available at very competitive rates. Weekend package offers, including the price of two nights at a good hotel, can be excellent value, sometimes costing less than the economy-ticket price. In addition, budget airlines often have special extra-low deals.

Frequent travellers with British Airways or Austrian Airlines enjoy many privileges if they join the respective frequent fliers' programmes, which may include priority for upgrades to business class. Such programmes also often award points for car hire from major companies such as Avis, Europcar, Hertz or Sixt, as well as overnight stays at major hotel chains such as the Hilton, Holiday Inn or Marriot.

Travellers with special needs, for example those with mobility issues, should notify the airlines of their requirements. Children up to and including the age of two travel free (or at 10 per cent of the price). Children aged three years and over pay the same price for flights as adults on all airlines.

The modern building of Schwechat International Airport near Vienna

Austrian Airports and Transfers

Many business travellers to Vienna never leave the airport: opposite the terminal building is the five-star luxury hotel Astron, and next to it the vast World Trade Centre, where many companies have their head offices. Vienna's airport has all the facilities that a traveller might need: information desks, service desks, shops, automatic money-exchange machines, bureaux de change and banks (though the rates for exchanging money at the airport are less favourable than elsewhere).

The taxi journey from the airport to the centre of Vienna costs around €35. Flughafentaxi Neudeck also has vans available in its fleet.

Alternatively, you can hire a car at the airport, from companies such as **Avis**, Budget, Europcar, **Hertz** or Thrifty. All you need when hiring a vehicle is a driver's licence, a passport and a credit card for the deposit.

The CAT (City Airport Train: www.cityairporttrain.com) leaves every half hour and takes you to Wien-Mitte Station. The journey time is 16 minutes and the fare (one way) is around €11. Buses go to Schwedenplatz and Westbahnhof. They depart every 25 minutes and the 30-minute journey costs about €8 one way.

The cheapest means of transport into the city is the suburban railway line, the *Schnellbahn*, which operates a half-hourly service.

Salzburg Airport, which is at No. 95 Innsbrucker Bundesstrasse, is situated extremely close to the town centre, a mere 4 km (2 miles) to the west. It can be reached by bus or taxi.

Innsbruck Airport is also located near the town centre (4 km/ 2 miles) and the transfer by taxi or bus "F" takes 10–15 minutes. Buses from Klagenfurt Airport run every 30 minutes and take approximately 15 minutes to reach the centre of town.

Logo of Austrian Airlines

DIRECTORY

Airport Information

Vienna International Airport
Tel (01) 7007-22233.
🆆 viennaairport.com

Airlines

Air Canada
Tel 1888 247 2262 in Canada; 069 27115 111 in Austria.
🆆 aircanada.com

Austrian Airlines
Marxergasse, at corner of Invalidenstrasse 1030 Vienna.
Tel (05176) 61000. 🆆 aua.com

British Airways
Tel (0845) 7733377 in UK; (01) 7956 7567 in Austria.
🆆 britishairways.com

Flybe
Reservations for UK passengers:
Tel 0371 700 2000 in UK; 01392 683 152. 🆆 flybe.com

Ryanair
Tel From Ireland: (0818) 303030. From the UK: (0871) 246 0000.
🆆 ryanair.com

Tyrolean Airways
Tel (0)5 1766 1000.
🆆 tyrolean.at

United Airlines
Tel 1800 864 8331 in US.
🆆 united.com

Car Hire

Avis
Tel (01) 587 6241 or 7007 32700.
🆆 avis.at

Hertz City
Tel (01) 512 8677 or 7007 32661.
🆆 hertz.at

Shopping centre inside Vienna's Schwechat International Airport

Travelling by Train

Situated in the heart of Europe, with Vienna as its main railway hub, Austria has excellent rail links with every important centre on the Continent, and there is a good network of lines within the country itself. The trains are comfortable, clean and safe; they run frequently and regularly. Punctuality is one of the main benefits – the old adage that you can set your watch by an Austrian train is largely true, although a few minutes' delay can occur. Unfortunately railway tickets are expensive. The largest railway line is the ÖBB – Österreichische Bundesbahnen, the Austrian Federal Railway Lines, and there are also 12 smaller, private railway lines.

Vienna's Franz-Josefs-Bahnhof, the terminal for trains from the north

Trains

Österreichische Bundesbahnen – ÖBB – runs several types of services. The modern EuroCity trains (marked with the letters EC) cover long-distance routes in record time. Night passengers travel on the EuroNight (EN) or CityNight-Line, with sleeping cars and couchettes. Comfortable InterCity (IC) and SuperCity trains connect major towns and tourist resorts. Every seat on the InterCity Express has a radio with headphones installed, and the first-class carriages are equipped with videos as well as power points for laptop computers. Domestic lines are also served by the D-Züge (D), long-distance trains running every day, at greater or lesser speed. More recently, the local routes have acquired modern, double-decker City Shuttle

Bundesbahn logo

trains. Motorists can also travel by rail with their cars from Vienna, Graz, Feldkirch and Villach. It costs €98 to transport a car from Vienna to Feldkirch.

Seat Reservations

In Austria, it is not compulsory to reserve a seat, even on express or international routes. It is entirely up to you, though trains can become busy, particularly during the peak tourist season in summer or when there is snow. Reservations can be made at the ticket offices of any of the larger stations, at the ÖBB Reiseservicecenter or online at www.oebb.at. The computerized system allows staff to check which seats are still available on any given train. Reserved seats are marked on the door of each compartment; you should take note of your carriage number when you are boarding, and again at the compartment door. Seat reservations are included in the price of first-class tickets.

Railway Stations

The German word for a railway station is *Bahnhof*, and the main railway station is *Hauptbahnhof*. The capital city of each province has a *Hauptbahnhof*, Vienna has two. Railway stations are sometimes sited away from the city centre. They have bureaux de change, luggage deposits and information desks, with English-speaking staff. If there is no ticket office, you can buy a ticket from the machine on the platform.

Arriving from Britain

The most direct form of rail travel to Austria from Britain is by Eurostar from London to either Paris or Brussels. From Paris you can take a German sleeper train to Munich and connect there for travel on to Graz, Innsbruck, Klagenfurt, Salzburg or Vienna. From Brussels, take a Thalys train to Cologne then travel on to either Linz or Vienna on a CityNight-Line overnight sleeper. For further details visit www.seat61.com/Austria.htm. The travel agency (Reisebüro) at Westbahnhof is open from 8am to 7pm on weekdays and 8am to 1pm on Saturdays; staff will be able to provide information

Railway line passing through Zell am See, Salzburg

as well as help with the booking of hotel rooms or other accommodation.

The main train station in Vienna, Hauptbahnhof Wien, is located on Südtirolerplatz and officially opened in 2014. It serves all international routes and is connected to line U1 on the underground.

Many trains from Germany, as well as some domestic services, terminate at Westbahnhof in the western part of the city. Some of these trains will be rerouted to Hauptbahnhof Wien over the next few years, but many will continue to serve Westbahnhof. You can access this train station from the U-Bahn underground lines U3 and U6. Trains from the north arrive at Franz-Josefs-Bahnhof; this is served by the Schnellbahn and the cross-city tram "D", which takes you to the Ringstrasse in the centre.

The Schnellbahn, Vienna's suburban train line

A railway viaduct near the small town of Mattersburg

Tickets

Railway tickets are not cheap. A second-class ticket from Vienna to Salzburg, 300 km (190 miles) away, costs around €50 and this price is not influenced by the speed of the train. Prices are not calculated by the time it takes to reach your destination but according to the class of travel. Up to two children under six years, accompanied by an adult, travel for free. Each additional child, and children aged 6–15 years, pay half price.

Ticket offices can be found in all larger railway stations. They also sell tickets for international routes. You can book a ticket on the phone with ÖBB Reiseservicecenter (05 17 17) or online. International tickets, with only a few exceptions, are valid for two months; domestic tickets, for journeys over 100 km (62 miles), are valid for one month.

There are many types of tickets, such as group, family and tourist travel, with or without

concessions. When buying a ticket, seek advice at the ticket office of the Reiseservicecenter as to which is best for you.

Young people up to the age of 26 years may travel at a lower cost at certain times and on some types of trains. Further information may be obtained from a ticket office, the ÖBB Reiseservicecenter or via the Internet (www.oebb.at). If you are in possession of a credit card or *Vorteilscard* (advantage card) you may have your ticket printed straight away. It is then valid in conjunction with proof of age and identity.

A large number of different *Vorteilscards* are available at low prices, giving reductions on rail travel – Classic gives a 45 per cent reduction on all Austrian ÖBB trains and the majority of private lines, and 25 per cent off of fares for international lines, for one year. There is a family version (*Vorteilscard Familie*), one for young people up to the age of 26 (*Vorteils-card<26*) and one for those over 61 years (*Vorteilscard Senior*). When buying these cards, you will need to have with you proof of identity and a recent photograph. Alternatively, holders of a *Vorteilscard* can buy tickets on the phone, via text message or through the Internet on the Österreichische Bundesbahnen website (www.oebb.at).

Railway Network Map

Key

— Main railway routes

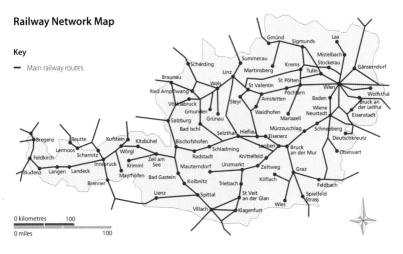

Travelling by Car

Travelling by car on Austrian roads can be a real pleasure. The road surfaces are in good condition and Austrians tend to comply with the traffic laws. Even in crowded cities, the traffic is relatively calm – you are forbidden to sound your horn other than to warn others of a danger. Routes are generally well signposted, but even so the motorists should carry an accurate map of the area. Motorways are marked with the letter A (for *Autobahn*) or E (for European motorway route); in addition, there are fast-traffic roads and a network of secondary roads that often pass through very scenic regions.

The spectacular Grossglockner Hochalpenstrasse *(see pp284–5)*

Driving in Austria

Visitors arriving by car can make use of any of a number of border crossings, although there are no border checks; Austria is within the Schengen Area (26 European countries that have abolished border controls) and surrounded by other Schengen states.

A toll is charged on the motorways and some other fast-traffic roads (in urban areas as well as the countryside). It is collected via a pre-paid disc, known as *Autobahnpickerl*, which can be bought at border crossing points, and from kiosks and petrol stations in Austria. The stickers, valid for 10 days, two months or one year, currently cost €8.70, €25.30 or €84.40 respectively. A 10-day sticker is valid from 9am on the day of issue until midnight of the ninth day thereafter. Stick the sticker to the top left corner of your car windscreen. The sticker does not entitle the driver to use any private pay-roads, of which fortunately there are very few; usually

such roads are situated at high altitudes. You will also be asked to pay a separate charge for going across Alpine passes and through tunnels.

What to Take

Visitors travelling by car in Austria need to carry a valid passport and driver's licence as well as their vehicle's registration document and green card (insurance policy). The vehicle must have a plaque showing the country of registration, and it must also be equipped with a first-aid

box and a red warning triangle. In winter, it is obligatory to have winter tyres and snow chains, which are essential for driving on the mountain roads.

Roads and Signposts

Motorways *(Autobahnen)* and the slip roads leading to them are signposted with white lettering on blue boards; on maps, motorways are shown as yellow lines between two thinner lines. An inn near a turning is indicated by a short sign with black lettering on white background.

Fernstrassen (long-distance roads) or *Bundesstrassen* (federal roads) are marked in red, and *Landstrassen* (country roads) in yellow. On the road, traffic signs are black-and-white. The written ones you may need to know are: *Stau* – traffic jam, *Schnee* – snow, *Umleitung* – diversion, and *Baustelle* – road works. All the remaining road signs follow the European standard.

Road Traffic Regulations

In Austria, motorists drive on the right-hand side of the road. The speed limit on motorways is 130 km/h (81 mph), and on other roads 100 km/h (62 mph). In towns and built-up areas the limit is 50 km/h (31 mph), but only 30 km/h (19 mph) in Graz. Lorries, caravans and cars with trailers are restricted to 100 km/h (62 mph) on motorways. While not everyone follows the prescribed speed limits, Austrian police carry out checks with infra-red guns and can fine you on the spot. Drivers and passengers are obliged to wear

A toll station at the entrance to a pay-road in the mountains

seatbelts at all times. Children up to the age of 15, or until they reach a height of 1.5 m (5 ft), are not allowed to travel in the front seat, unless the car is equipped with a special child restraint.

Driving in Towns

Finding a place in which to park is not easy, especially in the centre of the larger towns; it is often best to use a multi-storey car park which is indicated by the word *Parkhaus*. *Frei* means that parking spaces are available.

Cars left in a controlled parking zone, indicated by blue lines on the road, must display a parking ticket or be parked validly near a meter (see below for how to buy a parking ticket from a meter). In most parts of Vienna parking is restricted to resident permit holders. Visitors may park for up to 2 hours, if they display a parking card (from newsagents).

It is never worth leaving your car in a prohibited area – a traffic warden will arrive immediately, impose a fine and arrange for your car to be towed away. Retrieving an impounded car is a lengthy, costly and difficult procedure.

Schneekettenpflicht Angertal in 500 m

Sign informing motorists of the need to fit wheel-chains

Car Hire

Major car hire firms, such as Autohansa, Avis, Denzel, Europcar, Hartl, Hertz and Trendcar, all have offices in Austria. Car hire is more

A road hugging the edge of the Seidewinktal valley

expensive at the airport, but it is the only place where you will be able to hire a car late at night or at weekends.

To hire a car you must be 19 or over, and for some car companies the age limit is 25; you must also hold a valid passport and a driver's licence as well as a credit card or charge card from an approved company. (A charge card can sometimes be obtained from selected tourist offices, inside or outside Austria.)

A car may be hired for any duration and dropped off at any agreed point, to be collected by the hire company. Not all destinations, however, have suitable drop-off points. Cars may be taken outside Austria to approved EU countries. You may also take hired cars to some, but not to all Eastern Europe countries, with special permission from the hiring company.

Arriving by Coach

Eurolines runs coaches from London Victoria to Wien Mitte. This is also the terminal station for routes to major European cities such as Bratislava, Budapest, Zurich, Paris, Brussels, Milan and Copenhagen, plus domestic routes from eastern Austria.

Coaches are equipped to the European standard and tickets may be cheaper than rail travel, but the journey from the UK is long and fares are not particularly cheap. Often, budget airlines offer a more convenient way to travel at a comparable cost (see p352).

Travelling by Coach

The entire country is served by an excellent coach network, allowing you to reach almost any destination including some remote places not connected to the rail network. Prices are similar to those charged for rail travel.

Hitchhiking

It is not always easy to get a lift in Austria; few drivers are willing to take hitchhikers. If you decide to thumb a lift, the best point to wait is by the exit road from a town. Young people waiting there often carry cardboard notices stating their desired destination. As anywhere, women travelling alone should take extra care. In some provinces, children below the age of 16 are forbidden to hitchhike.

Parking meters
In many towns you will have to obtain a ticket from a parking meter to park your car. Display it on the windscreen.

Date and time display

Coin slot

"Cancel" button

"Confirm" button

Credit card slot

Ticket collection slot

Push-buttons for entering the price of the ticket

Getting Around Towns

Finding your way around an unfamiliar town, even with a map, is often difficult. One-way traffic systems, pedestrianized areas and parking restrictions are all designed to keep car traffic out. Walking is the easiest and most enjoyable way to get around the compact city centres, where most of the historic sights are to be found. Austrian towns generally have a well-developed public transport system, including buses and, in most cities, trams. Vienna also has an underground network (metro) – the quickest way to reach any destination. In some cities, travel cards give you unlimited travel on all local transport facilities for a specified number of days.

Walking

Pedestrians have priority, even on roads – but you should never rely on this. Try to use subways or crossings where there are signals, especially when crossing wide roads with fast-moving traffic. Visitors from the UK and Australia need to remember that motorists drive on the right. Do not cross a road when the red signal shows even if there is no traffic – you may be spot-fined for jay walking. Watch out also for cyclists who share the pavement with pedestrians.

In larger cities, guided walking tours are available during the summer months, which will take you past all the sights. Exploring themes such as the Baroque, or Vienna 1900, they are available in English and other languages. For information contact the local tourist offices.

Tourists strolling through a mountain village

Bicycles

Cycle routes usually run on the pavement and are clearly marked with lines and arrows. Pedestrians need to take extra care not to stray into the cycling area. Where there is no cycle route, cyclists join the road traffic and are obliged to adhere to all normal traffic rules. There are special posts on pavements and in public squares for parking and securing bicycles.

In Vienna, bike paths take you around the Ringstrasse and past many of the sights. Bikes may also be hired from some stations, at a discount if you have a train ticket.

One of the most scenic long-distance cycling routes is the *Radweg* (cycle track) along the Danube river.

Taxis

You can recognize a taxi by the TAXI sign on the roof. They are usually saloon cars, often Mercedes. If a taxi is for hire, the sign will be illuminated. In the centre of a city it is easier to get a taxi at one of the taxi ranks, rather than hailing it in the street. Taxi ranks can be found near railway stations and large hotels. Alternatively, you can book a taxi by phone. In the rush hour it may be faster to travel by underground or by tram. All taxis have meters and charges are calculated per kilometre travelled.

Additional charges are made for more than one passenger, luggage, late night and week-end journeys. In Vienna, a taxi to the airport will cost about €35. It is usual to tip 10 per cent of the fare, rounding up the fare to the nearest euro.

Buses

Many city centres are served by hopper buses, while larger buses take visitors to the inner suburbs. Municipal bus lines are often extensions of tram lines. This is signalled by a letter in the number of the bus, thus bus No. 46A extends the route of tram No. 46, making it easy to find the correct line.

Trams

Along with buses and the underground, trams are the most convenient form of transport in the cities. It is easy to track your progress as each stop is announced

A typical bicycle sharing station

The vital Vienna tramway network or Strassbahn

by a pre-recorded voice and all carriages display the route map, indicating the stops.

The doors are released by pressing a button. Make sure you press the button to signal your intention to get out – trams or buses may continue without stopping if no one is waiting at the station.

Tickets

Tickets can be bought at newsagents, in blocks of five or ten, or in suburban railway stations where blocks of two or four are also available. In Vienna you can also purchase tickets at the subway stations. You should always buy a ticket before travelling, since it is not always possible to buy one from the driver or the ticket machine inside the vehicle. Having boarded the bus, tram or train you need to stamp your ticket at the start of your journey; you will not need to stamp it again if you change to a different line or different mode of transport.

The tickets are valid for travel on all forms of transport within a town, within varying time limits. Besides single tickets, visitors can also opt to buy a 24-hour, 48-hour and 72-hour pass, a *Streifenkarte* (strip of tickets) valid for three or eight days, a *Wochenkarte* valid for one week, a *Monatskarte,* valid for one month, or a *Jahreskarte,* which permits you to travel for one year.

The rules of public transport vary between the provinces in Austria. The tourist offices and hotels in the area will be able to advise you on local regulations.

Making a Journey by Underground

1 To determine which line to take, travellers should look for their destination on a U-Bahn map. The five lines are distinguished by colour and number (U1, U2, U3, U4 & U5). Simply trace the line to your destination, making a note of where you need to change lines. Connections to other forms of transport are also shown.

2 Tickets can be bought from a newsagent, ticket vending machines or ticket offices. To get to the trains, insert your ticket into the ticket-stamping machine in the direction of the arrow. Wait for the ping indicating that it is validated, and pass through the barrier. Follow the signs (with the number and colour of the line) to your platform.

3 Once you are on the platform, check the direction and destination of the train on an electronic destination indicator.

4 Stops along the line are shown on a plan. A red arrow in the corner shows the direction in which the train enters the station.

5 At your destination follow the *Ausgang* signs to reach street level.

6 At stations with more than one exit, use the map of the city to check which street or square you will come out at.

Pull handle to open door

The door opens out to the side

Sign showing stops on line 3 of the U-Bahn, including the connecting stops

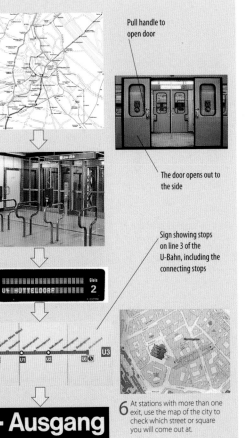

General Index

St Pauler Kultursommer 37
St Pölten 12, **136–7**
  hotels 295
  map 137
St. Sebastian, restaurants 320
St Stephen's Cathedral (Vienna)
  see Stephansdom
St Stephen's Day 39
St Veit an der Glan **273**
St Wolfgang 193, **209**, 210
  hotels 297
  restaurants 321
Saints
  see also Cathedrals; Churches;
  Saints by name
Salamanca, Gabriel of 278
Sales, end-of-season 326–7
Salt mines 184, 208, 213, 215
  Bad Dürrnberg 229
  Hallein 228–9
  Salzwelten (Hallstatt) 212
Salzach Valley 237
Salzatal tour **186–7**
Salzburg 14, 32, 215, **218–27**
  festivals 36–9
  Frequency Festival 335
  history 41
  hotels 298
  maps 219, 220–21
  restaurants 322–3
  Salzburg Festival 37, **225**, 331,
  333, 334, 335
  Salzburg Whitsun Festival 36,
  334, 335
Salzburg Museum **222**
Salzburger Land **215–37**
  hotels 297–8
  map 216–17
  restaurants 322–3
Salzkammergut 161, 192, **213**
Salzkammergut Lakes **210–211**
Salzwelten (Hallstatt) 212
Samsonumzug Tamsweg 37
Schafberg **209**
Schallaburg **148**
Schallenberg, Leopold 144
Schärding **201**
  hotels 297
Schareck 283, 285
Schattberg 236
Schatzkammer (Vienna) 12
Schäufelein, Hans 249
Scheffau 229, 250
Schemerl von Leytenbach,
  Joseph 97
Schesaplana 259, 260
Schiele, Egon 33, 74, 245
  Egon-Schiele-Museum (Tulln)
  13, 138
  Kneeling Female Nude 87
  Leopold Museum (Vienna) 86
Schiffsprozession (Wörther See) 37
Schikaneder, Emanuel 97
Schiller, Friedrich 94

Schillerpark (Villach) 269, 278
Schladming 182
  hotels 296
Schladminger Tauern **182–3**
Schlegeisspeicher 252
Schloss see also Castles; Palaces
Schloss Ambras (Innsbruck) 15, **245**
Schloss Esterházy (Eisenstadt) 12,
  158–9
Schloss Hoff **155**
Schloss Lockenhaus, festivals 37
Schloss Mirabell (Salzburg) 14, 30,
  219
Schloss Riegersburg 13, **174–5**
Schlossalm 234
Schlossberg (Graz) **166**
Schlosshotels 288–9, 291
Schmalhofer, Karl 109
Schmiding **202–3**
Schmidt, Friedrich 80
Schmidt, Johann Georg 61
Schmidt, Johann Martin 277
Schmidt, Martin Johann
  (Kremser) 33, 136, 142, 143,
  148, 195, 203, 224, 272
Schmitz, Bruno 196
Schmitzer, Josef Michael 248
Schneeberg tour **151**
Schneider, Georg 232
Schneider, Romy 232
Schnorr von Carolsfeld, Julius 33
Schönberg, Arnold **28**, 29, 110
Schönbrunn Palace (Vienna) 12,
  114–15
Schönlaterngasse (Vienna) 59
Schrammel, Josef 28
Schratt, Katharina 210
Schröcken 263
Schruns 259
Schubert, Franz **28**, 97, 136, 140
  grave 111
  Schubertiade (Schwarzenberg)
  37, 334, 335
  statue of 101
Schulhof (Vienna) **66**
Schumann, Robert 59
Schuschnigg, Karl 50
Schutzen am Gebirge, restaurants
  318
Schwanenstadt **205**
Schwanthaler, Franz 224
Schwanthaler, Johann Peter the
  Elder 201, 202
Schwanthaler, Thomas 208, 209,
  224
Schwarzenberg 262
  festivals 37
  Schubertiade 334, 335
Schwarzenberg Palace (Vienna) 101
Schwarzenbergplatz (Vienna) **101**
Schwarzenberg, Prince Karl 101
Schwarzenegger, Arnold 22
Schwarzkogler, Rudolf 33
Schwarzkopf 233

Schwaz 30, **248–9**
Schwechat Airport 352, 353
Schwedenplatz (Vienna) **64**
Schwertsik, Kurt 29
Sciassia, Domenico 178, 188
Sebastiansfriedhof (Salzburg) **218**
Secession Building (Vienna) 94,
  96–7
Seckau **187**
Seebühne (Bregenz) 266, 267
Seefeld 15, **256–7**
Seekapelle St Georg (Bregenz) **264**
Seeschloss Ort 211
Seewinkel National Park 12, 157
Seipel, Dr Ignaz 61
Seisenegger, Jakob 32
Seminarkirche (Linz) **196–7**
Semmering 151
  hotels 295
Semper, Gottfried 82, 86, 88
Senior citizens
  admission prices 343
  rail cards 355
Seusenhofer, Konrad 169
Seyss-Inquart, Arthur 50–51
Sforza, Bianca Maria 244
Shopping **326–9**
  ceramics and crystal glass 327
  crafts and folk art 327
  end-of-season sales 326–7
  food and drink 327
  markets and fairs 326
  opening hours 326
  VAT refunds 326
  Vienna **116–17**
  What to Buy in Austria **328–9**
Siccardsburg, August Sicard von
  31, 96
Sigismund, Archduke 244
Sigismund of Luxemburg,
  Emperor 42
Sigismund of Tyrol 266
Signposts 356
Silberbergwerk (Schwaz) 249
Silent Night (Gruber/Mohr) 224,
  228, 233
Silvretta range 259
Simon, Hugo 35
Sindelar, Matthias 35
Sissi see Elisabeth, Empress
Ski Alliance 232
Skiing 34, **336**, 339
  competitions 251, 332, 333
  ski jump competitions 34, 232,
  247
Skiwelt Wilder Kaiser-Brixental
  250
Sleigh and toboggan rides **337**, 339
Snow White (film) 273
Snowboarding **336**, 339
Soccer 35
Social Democratic Party 51
Socialist Party 51
Solari, Antonio 168

Acknowledgments

Dorling Kindersley would like to thank the following people whose contributions and assistance have made the preparation of this book possible.

Consultant

Gerhard Bruschke

Additional Contributors

Helen Harrison, Darrel Joseph, Doug Sager, Leslie Woit

Additional Photography

Maciej Bronarski, Dip. Ing. Walter Hildebrand, Renata and Marek Kosińscy, Piotr Kiedrowski, Ian O'Leary, Peter Wilson, Paweł Wroński

Cartography

An Bundesamt Eich- und Vermessungwesen, Lundesaufnahme (BEV), Uma Bhattacharya, Mohammad Hassan, Jasneet Kaur

DTP

Vinod Harish, Vincent Kurien, Azeem Siddiqui

Reader

Judith Meddick

Fact-Checkers

Martina Bauer, Melanie Nicholson-Hartzell

Proofreader

Emily Hatchwell

Indexer

Helen Peters

Senior Editor

Jacky Jackson/Wordwise Associates Ltd.

Managing Art Editor

Kate Poole/Ian Midson

Publishing Manager

Helen Townsend

Revisions and Relaunch Team

Namrata Adhwaryu, Asad Ali, Subhashree Bharti, Jo Cowen, Conrad Van Dyk, Mariana Evmolpidou, Karen Fitzpatrick, Anna Freiberger, Rhiannon Furbear, Rupanki Kaushik, Juliet Kenny, Sumita Khatwani, Rahul Kumar, Kathryn Lane, Leena Lane, Carly Madden, Hayley Maher, Alison McGill, Sam Merrell, Deepak Mittal, Kate Molan, Rakesh Kumar Pal, Sangita Patel, Marianne Petrou, Marisa Renzullo, Beverly Smart, Sadie Smith, Susana Smith, Rachel Symons, Ajay Verma

Additional Picture Research

Ellen Root

Special Assistance

Wiedza i Życie would like to thank Mr. Roman Skrzypczak of the Austrian Tourist Information Centre for his help in obtaining materials and for facilitating contacts with other Austrian institutions.

The publisher would also like to thank all the people and institutions who allowed photographs belonging to them to be reproduced, as well as granting permission to use photographs from their archives:

Agencja Forum (Krzysztof Wójcik)
Artothek (Susanne Vierthaler and Holger Gehrmann)
Basilika Mariazell, Benediktiner-Superiorat
 (P. Karl Schauer OSB, Superior)
Brahms Museum, Mürzzuschlag
Burgenländisches Landesmuseum, Eisenstadt
 (Julia Raab and Gerard Schlag)
Corbis (Gabriela Ściborska)
Chorherrenstift Klosterneuburg-Stiftsmuseum
 (Mag. Wolfgang Huber)
Die Österreich Werbung, Bildarchiv (Dr. Dietmar
 Jungreithmair)
DK Library
FIS Wintersportmuseum, Mürzzuschlag
 (Mag. Hannes Nothnagl)
Festung Hochensalzburg
Heeresgeschichtliches Museum in Arsenal (Peter Enne)
Kunsthistorisches Museum, Wien (Elisabeth Reicher)
Lurgrotte Peggau
Museum Schloss Greillenstein (Elisabeth Kuefstein)
Museumsverein Schloss Rosenau, Österreichisches
 Freimaurermuseum
Naturpark Grebenzen Büro St. Lambrecht
 (Frater Gerwig Romirer)
Österreichischen Freilichtmuseum, Stübing bei
 Graz (Egbert Pöttler)
Rathaus w St. Pölten (Andrea Jäger)
Salzburger Burgen und Schlösser, Betriebsführung
Stadtmarketing Eisenstadt, Schloss Esterházy
 (Guenter Schumich)
Stift Melk, Kultur and Tourismus (Maria Prüller)
Wien-Tourismus (Waltraud Wolf)
Zefa (Ewa Kozłowska)

Picture Credits

Key: a = above; b = below/bottom; c = centre; f = far; l = left; r = right; t = top.

akg-images: 42ca, 99cr; **Alamy Images:** Pat Behnke 332tl; Caro 214; Cephas Picture Library 68tr; Colinspics 331tc; Denis Cox 22b; Rob Crandall 102bl; Danita Delimont/ Walter Bibikow 333tc; David Noble Photography 305tl; FAN travelstock/Michael Schindel 306cla; imagebroker 12tc, 319bl, 320b; imagebroker/ Christian Handl 303tl; INSADCO Photography/ Martin Bobrovsky 303c; Rainer Jahns 15br; Scott Kemper 160; LOOK Die Bildagentur 286-7; Barry Mason 305cb; mediacolor's 304cla; nagelestock.com 190; Pictures Colour Library 331br; Charles Ridgway 330br; Robert Harding Picture Library Ltd/Richard Nebesky 302cla; Westend 61/ GmbH 21t Hans Huber 332bl; **Arcotel Hotels:** 297tr; **Artothek:** Chr. Brandstätter 33cla; Photobusiness 33tr; Ernst Reinhold 32br; **Augartenhotel art & design:** 296bl; **Austria Trend Hotels & Resorts:** 295tr.
Basilika Mariazell: 188-189 all; **Hotel Beethoven GmbH &**

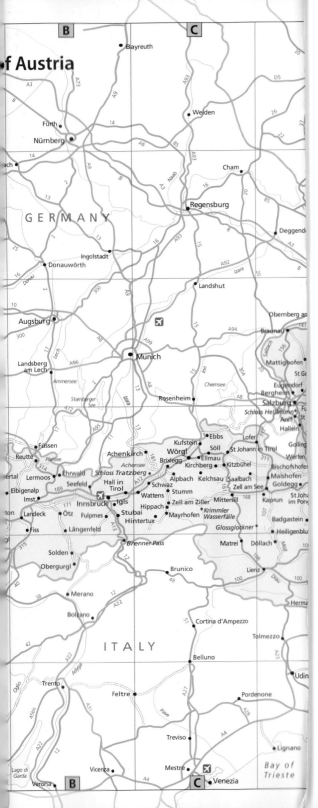

Co KG: 293tr; Hotel Berghof Crystal Spa & Sports: 298tl; Benediktinerstift St. Lambrecht 178tc; Brahms Museum (Mürzzuschlag) 172tc; The Bridgeman Art Library: 83clb; Hotel Bristol: 314bl; Bronarski, Maciej 329cr; Bruno - brasserie.cafe.restaurant: 318bl; Burgenländisches Landesmuseum: (Eisenstadt) 28bl.

Café Pruckel: 306bc; Café Sacher: 311tr; Cook: 321tr; Corbis: 50crb; AFP 51crb, 51tl, 51bc; Archivo Iconografico 44bl, 47crb, 49tl; Bettmann 47tl, 50br; Walter Bibikow/JAI 76; Jonathan Blair 35tl; Corbis Sygma 35br; EJW/ Westend61 128-9; Wolfgang Kaehler 147crb; Bob Krist 225bl, 225br; Massimo Listri 146cra, 246tr; Ali Meyer 33br, 45tc; José F. Poblete 13bc; Leonard de Selva 50tl; James A. Sugar 164cla.

The Dining Room: 313t; Dreamstime.com: Anskuw 2-3; Buurserstraat386 10cl; Chaoss 92; Neacsu Razvan Chirnoaga 56; Julius Kielaitis 206-7; Peter Lovás 352cl, 354bl; Pavle Marjanovic 14tr; Krisztian Miklosy 14bc; Mtdozier23 13tr; Caranica Nicolae 359tl; Grigore Gabriel Petre 52-3; Piotnikov 10bc; Jerard Octav Preisler 267bl; Tomas Sereda 152-3; Tupungato358; Sborisov 1c.

Festung Hohensalzburg (Salzburg): 227cra; Fotolia: badahos 104; Zechal 69bl; Freilichtmuseum Stübing: 171tc, 171br.

Getty Images: AFP/Josch 330cla; DEA/A. DAGLI ORTI 8–9; Werner Dieterich 238; Fly away with your imagination 12br; Roy Jankowski 18, 268; Joe Klamar 332br; Zoran Milich 351tr.

Haus Widdersteinblick: 290tl; Heeresgeschichtliches Museum, Wien: 43cra, 48br, 50bl; Österreichische Galerie 48cla; Heurigenhof Bründlmayer: 317bl; Hollmann Beletage: 292bc; Hotel Sacher, Wien: 307tl, 322bc; Josefstadt Theatre: 85tl; Restaurant Joseph: 321bc. Kiedrowski, Piotr: 329bc; Kosiński, Renata and Marek: 21br, 26cla, 26bl, 27 all; Kunsthistorisches Museum, Wien: 44ca, 44cb, 46crb, 88–91.

Lurgrotte, Peggau: 172tl.

Restaurant Magnolia: 319tr; Museum Schloss Greillenstein: 145tl; Café Restaurant Mozart bei der Oper GsmbH: 310bl; Restaurant Motto: 315bc; Museumsverein Schloss Rosenau, Österreichisches Freimaurermuseum: 145br.

Naturhistorisches Museum: 86tl.

Oberlaa, Neuer Markt: 311bl; Österreich Werbung: 20br; Ascher 23t; Bald 21c; Bartl 55cra, 55ca, 96tl, 119tr, 136cla, 328clb; Bohnacker 166br, 201b, 210tr; Carniel 212tl; W. Daemon 85br; Diejun 42clb, 186cla, 187bl, 328br; Fankhauser 38cr, 253br 337br; H. Graf 71cra; Gruenert 204cla, 237b, 257br; Haider 29b, 48bl, 80br; Haller 49cr; Herzberger 30-1, 118t, 225ca 329clb,

355tc; Hinterndorfer Ch. 150bl; Imprima 138br; Jalain 39bl; Jellasitz 159tl; Jezierzański 144tr, 148tr, 179t, 183cr; Kalmar 81tc, 81br, 112tl, 328cla, 328bl; Kneidinger 23c, 185br, 197tl; Lamm 179bl, 182cl, 182bc, 183br; Landova 203tl; R. Liebing 290br; Mallaun 216cla, 237t, 256bc, 260tr, 261tl, 336b, 337bl; Markowitsch 36cra, 37br, 108tl, 131tl, 183tl, 195tl, 225cla, 245clb, 251tr, 329tc; Mayer 63tr, 250tl; Nechansky 263tl; A. Niederstrasser 250bc; OEW-Bildarchiv 150tc, 328cra; Robert Pfeifer 78bl; Pigneter 194cla, 195cr, 211tl; 186br, 338br; Porizka 197br, 211br, 213bl; Ramstorfer 46bc; Salzburger Burgen/S/B 221tr; Schmeja 329tr; Simoner 28tr, 151bl; Storto 46br 209cl, 257cl; Trumler 28cla, 29c, 29cr, 29tl, 32cla, 40, 41br, 41bc, 43tl, 44cl, 46ca, 47bl, 69crb, 115b, 138c, 145bl, 149cra. 149cl, 149crb, 149bl, 187c, 196bc, 198bl, 199br, 200tl, 200clb, 201tl, 203bl, 210b, 243cr, 244tr, 274br, 277tra. 328tr; W. Weinhaeupl 211cra, 217tr, 229b, 276tl; H. Wiesenhofer 23br, 28cb, 36bl, 37cl, 39cra, 45crb, 142tl, 145cra, 158br, 165tc, 166tl, 166c, 167br, 173t, 187br, 205tr, 258b, 274clb; Winderer 38bl.

Parkhotel Tristachersee: 325tc.

Rathaus (St. Pölten): 136br; Reuters 34bl, 34cr, 35c; The Ring, Vienna's Casual Luxury Hotel: 294bc; Rosengarten: 324bc.

Schloss Igls: 299bc; Schloss - Restaurant Cobenzi: 316tl; Schloss Schönbrunn: 114-5 all; Stift Melk 146cla, 146clb, 147tl, 147bl, 147br; Cafe Speri: 313tc; Superstock: F1 Online 230-1, 254-5; Henry Georgi/Aurora Open 340-1; imagebroker.net 180-1.

T-Mobile Austria GmbH: 350c.

Restaurant Vestibül: 312bl.

Nikolaihof Wachau: 317tr; Wroński, Paweł: 289tr, 326c, 329bl, 329crb, 337tr, 342br, 343c, 348c;

Wintersportmuseum (Mürzzuschlag): 172c; Wien museum: 66bc; Wien-Tourismus 62tr, 63c, 68cla, 68bl; Wirtshaus Zum Hirschenwirt: 323t.

Zefa: DAMM 354; Mathis 239b; Raga 218cla; Rose 26-27c, 185tl; Spichtinger 184tl; Weir 182tr.

Front endpapers: Alamy Images: Caro Lbl; Scot Kemper Rbr; nagelestock.comRtl; Corbis: Walter Bibikow/JAI Ltl; Pascal Deloche/Godong Rtr; Dreamstime.com: Chaoss Lfcl; Neacsu Razvan Lftl; Fotolia: badahos Lbl; Getty Images: Werner Dieterich Lca; Roy Jankowski Lbr.

Map Cover: 4corners: Gräfenhain Günter/SIME

Jacket Front and spine: 4corners: Günter Gräfenhain

All other images © Dorling Kindersley For further information: www.dkimages.com

Phrase Book

In Emergency

Help!	Hilfe!	hilf-er
Stop!	Halt!	hult
Call	Holen Sie	hole'n zee
...a doctor	...einen Arzt	...ine'n artst
...an ambulance	...einen Krankenwagen	...ine'n krank'nvarg'n
...the police	...die Polizei	...dee pol-its-eye
...the fire brigade	...die Feuerwehr	...dee foy-er-vair
Where is a telephone?	Wo finde ich ein Telefon?	voh fin-der ish ine tel-e-fone?
Where is the hospital?	Wo ist das Krankenhaus?	voh ist duss krunk'n-hows?

Communication Essentials

Yes	Ja	yah
No	Nein	nine
Please	Bitte	bitt-er
Thank you	Danke vielmals	dunk-er feel-mahlse
Excuse me	Gestatten	g'shtatt'n
Hello	Grüss Gott	groos got
Goodbye	Auf Wiedersehen	owf veed-er-zay-ern
morning	Vormittag	for-mit-targ
afternoon	Nachmittag	nakh-mit-targ
evening	Abend	ahb'nt
yesterday	gestern	gest'n
today	heute	hoyt-er
tomorrow	morgen	morg'n
here	hier	hear
there	dort	dort
What?	Was?	vuss?
When?	Wann?	vunn?
Where?	Wo/Wohin?	voh/vo-hin?

Useful Phrases & Words

Where is...?	Wo befindet sich...?	voe b'find't zish...?
Where are...?	Wo befinden sich...?	voe b'find'n zish...?
How far is it to...?	Wie weit ist...?	vee vite ist...?
Do you speak English?	Sprechen Sie englisch?	shpresh'n zee eng-glish?
I don't understand	Ich verstehe nicht	ish fair-shtay-er nisht
I'm sorry	Es tut mir leid	es toot meer lyte
big	gross	grohss
small	klein	kline
open	auf/offen	owf/off'n
closed	zu/geschlossen	tsoo/g'shloss'n
left	links	links
right	rechts	reshts
near	in der Nähe	in dair nay-er
far	weit	vyte
up	auf, oben	owf, obe'n
down	ab, unten	up, oont'n
early	früh	froo
late	spät	shpate
entrance	Eingang/Einfahrt	ine-gung/ine-fart
exit	Ausgang/Ausfahrt	ows-gung/ows-fart
toilet	WC/Toilette	vay-say/toy-lett-er

Making a Telephone Call

I'd like to place a long-distance call	Ich möchte ein Ferngespräch machen	ish mer-shter ine fairn-g'shpresh mukh'n
I'd like to call collect	Ich möchte ein Rückgespräch machen	ish mer-shter ine rook-g'shpresh mukh'n
local call	Ortsgespräch	orts-g'shpresh
Can I leave a message?	Kann ich etwas ausrichten?	kunn ish ett-vuss ows-rikht'n?

Staying in a Hotel

Do you have a vacant room?	Haben Sie ein Zimmer frei?	harb'n zee ine tsimm-er fry?
double room	ein Doppelzimmer	ine dopp'l-tsimm-er
twin room	ein Doppelzimmer	ine dopp'l-tsimm-er
single room	ein Einzelzimmer	ine ine-ts'l-tsimm-er
with a bath/shower	mit Bad/Dusche	mitt bart/doosh-er
key	Schlüssel	shlooss'l
I have a reservation	Ich habe ein Zimmer reserviert	ish harb-er ine tsimm-er rezz-er-veert

Sightseeing

bus	der Bus	dair booss
tram	die Strassenbahn	dee stra-sen-barn
train	der Zug	dair tsoog
art gallery	Galerie	gall-er-ee
bus station	Busbahnhof	booss-barn-hofe
bus (tram) stop	die Haltestelle	dee hal-te-shtel-er
castle	Schloss, Burg	shloss, boorg
palace	Schloss, Palais	shloss, pall-ay
post office	das Postamt	dee pohs-taamt
cathedral	Dom	dome
church	Kirche	keersh-er
garden	Garten, Park	gart'n, park
museum	Museum	moo-zay-oom
information (office)	Information	in-for-mut-see-on

Shopping

How much does this cost?	Wieviel kostet das?	vee-feel kost't duss?
I would like...	Ich hätte gern...	ish hett-er gairn...
Do you have...?	Haben Sie...?	harb'n zee...?
expensive	teuer	toy-er
cheap	billig	bill-igg
bank	Bank	bunk
book shop	Buchladen	bookh-lard'n
chemist/pharmacy	Apotheke	App-o-tay-ker
hairdresser	Friseur/Frisör	freezz-er/freezz-er
market	Markt	markt
newsagent	Tabak Trafik	tab-ack tra-feek
travel agent	Reisebüro	rye-zer-boo-roe

Eating Out

Have you got a table for... people?	Haben Sie einen Tisch für... Personen?	harb'n zee ine'n tish foor... pair-sohn'n?
The bill please	Zahlen, bitte	tsarl'n bitt-er
I am a vegetarian	Ich bin Vegetarier	ish bin vegg-er-tah-ree-er
Waitress/waiter	Fräulein/Herr Ober	froy-line/hair oh-bare
menu	die Speisekarte	dee shpize-er-kart-er
wine list	Weinkarte	vine-kart-er
breakfast	Frühstück	froo-shtook
lunch	Mittagessen	mit-targ-ess'n
dinner	Abendessen	arb'nt-ess'n

Menu Decoder

Ei	eye	egg
Eis	ice	ice cream
Fisch	fish	fish
Fleisch	flysh	meat
Garnelen	gar-nayl'n	prawns
gebacken	g'buck'n	baked/fried
gebraten	g'brart'n	roast
gekocht	g'kokht	boiled
Gemüse	g'mooz-er	vegetables
vom Grill	fom grill	grilled
Hendl/Hahn/Huhn	hend'l/harn/hoon	chicken
Kaffee	kaf-fay	coffee
Kartoffel/Erdäpfel	kar-toff'l/air-dupf'l	potatoes
Käse	kayz-er	cheese
Knödel	k'nerd'l	dumpling
Lamm	lumm	lamb
Meeresfrüchte	mair-erz-froosh-ter	seafood
Milch	milhk	milk
Mineralwasser	minn-er-arl-vuss-er	mineral water
Obst	ohbst	fresh fruit
Pfeffer	pfeff-er	pepper
Pommes frites	pomm-fritt	chips
Reis	rice	rice
Rind	rint	beef
Rostbraten	rohst-brart'n	steak
Rotwein	roht-vine	red wine
Salz	zults	salt
Schinken/Speck	shink'n/shpeck	ham
Schlag	shlahgg	cream
Schokolade	shock-o-lard-er	chocolate
Schwein	shvine	pork
Tee	tay	tea
Wasser	vuss-er	water
Weisswein	vyce-vine	white wine
Wurst	voorst	sausage (fresh)
Zucker	tsook-er	sugar

Road Map

Key

— Motorway
— Major road
=== Minor road
— International border
✈ Airport

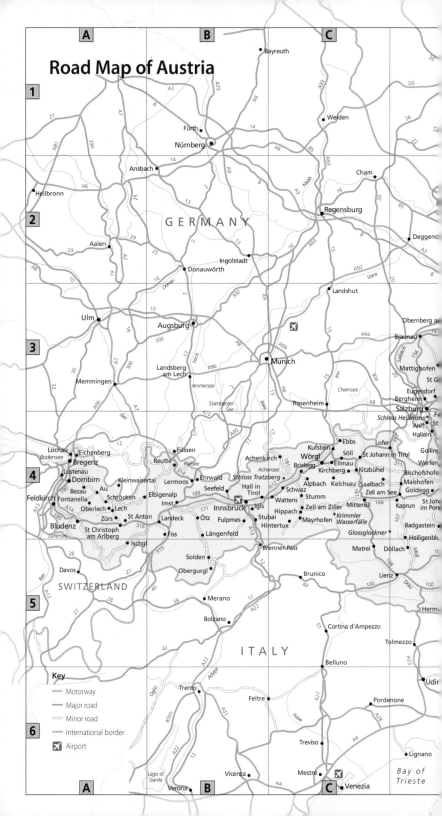

Road Map of Austria

Co KG: 293tr; Hotel Berghof Crystal Spa & Sports: 298tl; Benediktinerstift St. Lambrecht 178c; Brahms Museum (Mürzzuschlag) 172c; The Bridgeman Art Library: 83clb; Hotel Bristol: 314bl; Bronarski, Maciej 329cr; Bruno-brasserie.cafe.restaurant: 318bl; Burgenländisches Landesmuseum: (Eisenstadt) 28bl.

Café Pruckel: 306bc; Café Sacher: 311tr; Cook: 321tr; Corbis: 50crb; AFP 51crb, 51tl, 51bc; Archivo Iconografico 44bl, 47crb, 49tl; Bettmann 47tl, 50br; Walter Bibikow/JAI 76; Jonathan Blair 35tl; Corbis Sygma 35br; EJW/Westend61 128-9; Wolfgang Kaehler 147crb; Bob Krist 225bl, 225br; Massimo Listri 146tr, 246tr; Ali Meyer 33br, 45tc; José F. Poblete 13bc; Leonard de Selva 50tl; James A. Sugar 164cla.

The Dining Room: 313t; Dreamstime.com: Anskuw 2-3; Buurserstraat386 10cl; Chaoss 92; Neacsu Razvan Chirnoaga 56; Julius Kielaitis 206-7; Peter Lovás 352cl, 354bl; Pavle Marjanovic 14tr; Krisztian Miklosy 14bc; Mtdozier23 13tr; Caranica Nicolae 359tl; Grigore Gabriel Petre 52-3; Piotnikov 10bc; Jerard Octav Preisler 267bl; Tomas Sereda 152-3; Tupungato358; Sborisov 1c.

Festung Hohensalzburg (Salzburg): 227cra; Fotolia: badahos 104; Zechal 69bl; Freilichtmuseum Stübing: 171tc, 171br.

Getty Images: AFP/Josch 330cla; DEA/A. DAGLI ORTI 8–9; Werner Dieterich 238; Fly away with your imagination 12br; Roy Jankowski 18, 268; Joe Klamar 332br; Zoran Milich 351tr.

Haus Widdersteinblick: 290tl; Heeresgeschichtliches Museum, Wien: 43cr, 48br, 50bl; Österreichische Galerie 48cla; Heurigenhof Bründlmayer: 317bl; Hollmann Beletage: 292bc; Hotel Sacher, Wien: 307tl, 322bc.

Josefstadt Theatre: 85tl; Restaurant Joseph: 321bc.

Kiedrowski, Piotr: 329bc; Kosińscy, Renata and Marek: 21br, 26cla, 26bl, 27 all; Kunsthistorisches Museum, Wien: 44ca, 44cb, 46crb, 88–91.

Lurgrotte, Peggau: 172tl.

Restaurant Magnolia: 319tr; Museum Schloss Greillenstein: 145tl; Cafe Restaurant Mozart bei der Oper GsmbH: 310bl; Restaurant Motto: 315bc; Museumsverein Schloss Rosenau, Österreichisches Freimaurermuseum: 145br.

Naturhistorisches Museum: 86tl.

Oberlaa, Neuer Markt: 311bl; Österreich Werbung: 20br; Ascher 23t; Bald 21c; Bartl 55cra, 55ca, 96tl, 119tr, 136cla, 328clb; Bohnacker 166br, 201b, 210tr; Carniel 212tl; W. Daemon 85br; Diejun 42clb, 186cla, 187bl, 328br; Fankhauser 38cr, 253br 337br; H. Graf 71cra; Gruenert 204cla, 237b, 257br; Haider 29b, 48bl, 80br; Haller 49cr; Herzberger 30-1, 118t, 225ca 329clb,

355tc; Hinterndorfer Ch. 150bl; Imprima 138br; Jalain 39bl; Jellasitz 159tl; Jezierzański 144tr, 148tr, 179t, 183cr; Kalmar 81tc, 81br, 112tl, 328cla, 328bl; Kneidinger 23c, 185br, 197tl; Lamm 179bl, 182cl, 182bc, 183br; Landova 203tl; R. Liebing 290br; Mallaun 216cla, 237t, 256bc, 260tr, 261tl, 336b, 337bl; Markowitsch 36cra, 37br, 108tl, 131tl, 183tl, 195tl, 225cla, 245clb, 251tr, 329tc; Mayer 63tr, 250tl; Nechansky 263tl; A. Niederstrasser 250bc; OEW-Bildarchiv 150tc, 328cra; Robert Pfeifer 78bl; Pigneter 194cla, 195cr, 211tl; 186br, 338br; Porizka 197br, 211br, 213bl; Ramstorfer 46bc; Salzburger Burgen/S/B 221tr; Schmeja 329tr; Simoner 28tr, 151bl; Storto 46br 209cl, 257cl; Trumler 28cla, 29c, 29cr, 29tl, 32cla, 40, 41br, 41bc, 43tl, 44cl, 46ca, 47bl, 69crb, 115b, 138c, 145bl, 149cra. 149cl, 149crb, 149bl, 187tc, 196bc, 198bl, 199br, 200tl, 200clb, 201tl, 203bl, 210b, 243cr, 244tr, 274br, 277tra. 328tr; W. Weinhaeupl 211cra, 217tr, 229b, 276tl; H. Wiesenhofer 23br, 28cb, 36bl, 37cl, 39cra, 45crb, 142tl, 149cla, 158br, 165tc, 166tl, 166c, 167br, 173t, 187br, 205tr, 258b, 274clb; Winderer 38bl.

Parkhotel Tristachersee: 325tc.

Rathaus (St. Pölten): 136br; Reuters 34bl, 34cr, 35c; The Ring, Vienna's Casual Luxury Hotel: 294bc; Rosengarten: 324bc.

Schloss Igls: 299bc; Schloss - Restaurant Cobenzi: 316tl; Schloss Schönbrunn: 114-5 all; Stift Melk 146cla, 146clb, 147tl, 147bl, 147br; Cafe Speri: 313tc; Superstock: F1 Online 230-1, 254-5; Henry Georgi/Aurora Open 340-1; imagebroker.net 180-1.

T-Mobile Austria GmbH: 350c.

Restaurant Vestibül: 312bl.

Nikolaihof Wachau: 317tr; Wroński, Paweł: 289tr, 326c, 329bl, 329crb, 337tr, 342br, 343c, 348c; Wintersportmuseum (Mürzzuschlag): 172c; Wien museum: 66bc; Wien-Tourismus 62tr, 63c, 68cla, 68bl; Wirtshaus Zum Hirschenwirt: 323t.

Zefa: DAMM 354; Mathis 239b; Raga 218cla; Rose 26-27c, 185tl; Spichtinger 184tl; Weir 182tr.

Front endpapers: Alamy Images: Caro Lbl; Scot Kemper Rbr; nagelestock.comRtl; Corbis: Walter Bibikow/JAI Ltl; Pascal Deloche/Godong Rtr; Dreamstime.com: Chaoss Lfcl; Neacsu Razvan Lftl; Fotolia: badahos Lbl; Getty Images: Werner Dieterich Lca; Roy Jankowski Lbr.

Map Cover: 4corners: Gräfenhain Günter/SIME

Jacket Front and spine: 4corners: Günter Gräfenhain

All other images © Dorling Kindersley For further information: www.dkimages.com

Dorling Kindersley Special Editions

Dorling Kindersley books can be purchased in bulk quantities at discounted prices for use in promotions or as premiums. We are also able to offer special editions and personalized jackets, corporate imprints, and excerpts from all of our books, tailored specifically to meet your own needs.

To find out more, please contact:
in the United States specialsales@dk.com
in the UK travelguides@uk.dk.com
in Canada specialmarkets@dk.com
in Australia penguincorporatesales@penguinrandomhouse.com.au

Phrase Book

In Emergency

Help!	Hilfe!	hilf-er
Stop!	Halt!	hult
Call	Holen Sie	hole'n zee
…a doctor	…einen Arzt	…ine'n artst
…an ambulance	…einen Krankenwagen	…ine'n krank'nvarg'n
…the police	…die Polizei	…dee pol-its-eye
…the fire brigade	…die Feuerwehr	…voh foy-er-vair
Where is a telephone?	Wo finde ich ein Telefon?	voh fin-der ish ine tel-e-fone?
Where is the hospital?	Wo ist das Krankenhaus?	voh ist duss krunk'n-hows?

Communication Essentials

Yes	Ja	yah
No	Nein	nine
Please	Bitte	bitt-er
Thank you	Danke vielmals	dunk-er feel-malse
Excuse me	Gestatten	g'shtatt'n
Hello	Grüss Gott	groos got
Goodbye	Auf Wiedersehen	owf veed-er-zay-ern
morning	Vormittag	for-mit-targ
afternoon	Nachmittag	nakh-mit-targ
evening	Abend	ah'bnt
yesterday	gestern	gest'n
today	heute	hoyt-er
tomorrow	morgen	morg'n
here	hier	hear
there	dort	dort
What?	Was?	vuss?
When?	Wann?	vunn?
Where?	Wo/Wohin?	voh/vo-hin?

Useful Phrases & Words

Where is…?	Wo befindet sich…?	voe b'find't zish…?
Where are…?	Wo befinden sich…?	voe b'find'n zish…?
How far is it to…?	Wie weit ist…?	vee vite ist…?
Do you speak English?	Sprechen Sie englisch?	shpresh'n zee eng-glish?
I don't understand	Ich verstehe nicht	ish fair-shtay-er nisht
I'm sorry	Es tut mir leid	es toot meer lyte
big	gross	grohss
small	klein	kline
open	auf/offen	owf/off'n
closed	zu/geschlossen	tsoo/g'shloss'n
left	links	links
right	rechts	reshts
near	in der Nähe	in dair nay-er
far	weit	vyte
up	auf, oben	owf, obe'n
down	ab, unten	up, oont'n
early	früh	froo
late	spät	shpate
entrance	Eingang/Einfahrt	ine-gung/ine-fart
exit	Ausgang/Ausfahrt	ows-gung/ows-fart
toilet	WC/Toilette	vay-say/toy-lett-er

Making a Telephone Call

I'd like to place a long-distance call	Ich möchte ein Ferngespräch machen	ish mer-shter ine fairn-g'shpresh mukh'n
I'd like to call collect	Ich möchte ein Rückgespräch machen	ish mer-shter ine rook-g'shpresh mukh'n
local call	Ortsgespräch	orts-g'shpresh
Can I leave a message?	Kann ich etwas ausrichten?	kunn ish ett-vuss ows-rikht'n

Staying in a Hotel

Do you have a vacant room?	Haben Sie ein Zimmer frei?	harb'n zee ine tsimm-er fry?
double room	ein Doppelzimmer	ine dopp'l-tsimm-er
twin room	ein Doppelzimmer	ine dopp'l-tsimm-er
single room	ein Einzelzimmer	ine ine-ts'l-tsimm-er
with a bath/shower	mit Bad/Dusche	mitt bart/doosh-er
key	Schlüssel	shlooss'l
I have a reservation	Ich habe ein Zimmer reserviert	ish harb-er ine tsimm-er rezz-er-veert

Sightseeing

bus	der Bus	dair booss
tram	die Strassenbahn	dee stra-sen-barn
train	der Zug	dair tsoog
art gallery	Galerie	gall-er-ee
bus station	Busbahnhof	booss-barn-hofe
bus (tram) stop	die Haltestelle	dee hal-te-shtel-er
castle	Schloss, Burg	shloss, boorg
palace	Schloss, Palais	shloss, pall-ay
post office	das Postamt	dee pohs-taamt
cathedral	Dom	dome
church	Kirche	keersh-er
garden	Garten, Park	gart'n, park
museum	Museum	moo-zay-oom
information (office)	Information	in-for-mut-see-on

Shopping

How much does this cost?	Wieviel kostet das?	vee-feel kost't duss?
I would like…	Ich hätte gern…	ish hett-er gairn…
Do you have…?	Haben Sie…?	harb'n zee…?
expensive	teuer	toy-er
cheap	billig	bill-igg
bank	Bank	bunk
book shop	Buchladen	bookh-lard'n
chemist/pharmacy	Apotheke	App-o-tay-ker
hairdresser	Friseur/Frisör	freezz-er/freezz-er
market	Markt	markt
newsagent	Tabak Trafik	tab-ack tra-feek
travel agent	Reisebüro	rye-zer-boo-roe

Eating Out

Have you got a table for… people?	Haben Sie einen Tisch für… Personen?	harb'n zee ine'n tish foor… pair-sohn'n?
The bill please	Zahlen, bitte	tsarl'n bitt-er
I am a vegetarian	Ich bin Vegetarier	ish bin vegg-er-tah-ree-er
Waitress/waiter	Fräulein/Herr Ober	froy-line/hair oh-bare
menu	die Speisekarte	dee shpize-er-kart-er
wine list	Weinkarte	vine-kart-er
breakfast	Frühstück	froo-shtook
lunch	Mittagessen	mit-targ-ess'n
dinner	Abendessen	arb'nt-ess'n

Menu Decoder

Ei	eye	egg
Eis	ice	ice cream
Fisch	fish	fish
Fleisch	flysh	meat
Garnelen	gar-nayl'n	prawns
gebacken	g'buck'n	baked/fried
gebraten	g'brart'n	roast
gekocht	g'kokht	boiled
Gemüse	g'mooz-er	vegetables
vom Grill	fom grill	grilled
Hendl/Hahn/Huhn	hendl/harn/hoon	chicken
Kaffee	kaf-fay	coffee
Kartoffel/Erdäpfel	kar-toff'l/air-dupf'l	potatoes
Käse	kayz-er	cheese
Knödel	k'nerd'l	dumpling
Lamm	lumm	lamb
Meeresfrüchte	mair-erz-froosh-ter	seafood
Milch	milhk	milk
Mineralwasser	minn-er-arl-vuss-er	mineral water
Obst	ohbst	fresh fruit
Pfeffer	pfeff-er	pepper
Pommes frites	pomm-fritt	chips
Reis	rice	rice
Rind	rint	beef
Rostbraten	rohst-brart'n	steak
Rotwein	roht-vine	red wine
Salz	zults	salt
Schinken/Speck	shink'n/shpeck	ham
Schlag	shlahgg	cream
Schokolade	shock-o-lard-er	chocolate
Schwein	shvine	pork
Tee	tay	tea
Wasser	vuss-er	water
Weisswein	vyce-vine	white wine
Wurst	voorst	sausage (fresh)
Zucker	tsook-er	sugar